N. A. CHERNISS

The Information Machine

The Information Machine

THE UNITED STATES INFORMATION AGENCY AND AMERICAN FOREIGN POLICY

ROBERT E. ELDER

SYRACUSE UNIVERSITY PRESS

To Gene, my Wife

ABOUT THE AUTHOR

ROBERT E. ELDER, professor of political science at Colgate University, Hamilton, New York, is well known both to scholars in the field of international relations and to government officials concerned with the formulation and conduct of American foreign policy. *The Information Machine* is the second of his books to deal with a major foreign affairs agency of the U.S. government. The first was *The Policy Machine: The Department of State and American Foreign Policy* (Syracuse, 1960). He has also studied problems of personnel management in the foreign affairs agencies as a member of the Brookings Institution's special staff which prepared *The Formulation and Administration of United States Foreign Policy* (1960) for the Senate Foreign Relations Committee. He studied the foreign leader program of the Department of State as a member of the Brookings senior staff during the summer of 1960. He surveyed the overseas interests of domestic agencies of the U.S. government and related personnel problems as a consultant to the Herter Committee on Foreign Affairs Personnel during its preparation of *Personnel for the New Diplomacy* (1962).

A graduate of Indiana State University, Professor Elder holds the M.A. and Ph.D. degrees in international relations from the University of Chicago. In addition to his teaching duties at Colgate University, he is director of the Colgate Research Council and acting chairman of the University's January Program, and for twelve years he directed the University's spring semester study group in Washington. He is the immediate past president of the New York Political Science Association.

Preface

Americans distrust propaganda—especially government propaganda—yet they have allowed their government to fashion a powerful propaganda machine. This machine, which costs taxpayers about $170 million a year, is designed to convince people in the rest of the world that United States policies and actions are helpful to them, or at least not harmful to their basic interests. Congressional fear of the machine's propaganda talents' being turned inward to influence the American people is so great that only one among the United States Information Agency's hundreds of products can be obtained in America by regular subscription—*Problems of Communism*, a scholarly but hard-hitting anticommunist periodical, far less sophisticated in its approach to communism in the Soviet Union than many of the Agency's other publications. *The Information Machine* is intended neither as a justification of nor an attack on the concept of government overseas propaganda. Accepting such propaganda as a normal policy tool in today's world, it discards the emotionally laden term "propaganda" in favor of the more neutral term "information."

The exchange of information via private and public channels of communication is quite likely to be essential to the survival of mankind in an increasingly interdependent world. If competition for the minds of men is a basic requirement for the successful functioning of the domestic democratic political process, it is also a fundamental prerequisite to achieving greater cooperation among people and nations by helping to increase mutual understanding and by fostering an embryonic sense of world community. In a world of thermonuclear intercontinental missiles, the traditional nation-state is clearly obsolescent as the dominant political organizing device for resolving international problems and is far less able than in the past to meet positively the vital needs of its people for security, economic well-being, and broad cultural development. Mindless continuance of such atomized political organizations as the primary factor in world affairs (relatively functional from 1648 through 1948) only increases the probability of the personal atomization of a high percentage of the world's population at some indeterminate time in the future. Successful existence on this planet, let alone the exploration of others, may require the evolution of new or supplemental forms for the political organization of man—a process which can only take place if communication between people and nations is massively increased and men's perceptions of reality objectivized.

Viewed against the requirements of the emerging environment, the United States Information Agency (USIA) may be no more than a crude prototype of future information machines. Nonetheless, its organization and operations are important today. Its mode of operation and the functions it performs are not only meeting present needs; they may also contribute to the evolution or transformation of the nation-state system into a higher political form more relevant to continuing technological progress in the closing years of the twentieth century and in the twenty-first century. Today, USIA is a major supporting arm of American foreign policy. It is so necessary to the formulation and conduct of that policy that its director is the only representative of a government agency outside the Department of State's hierarchical organization (which includes the Agency for International Development and the Arms Control and Disarmament Agency) who regularly attends the secretary of state's morning staff meeting.

Some might argue that a study of USIA is relatively unimportant, because in many of the countries where it attempts to influence public opinion the mass public has very little to say about what government policy will be. However, USIA products are usually targeted at influential publics rather than at an inert political mass. The teaching of English by USIA personnel to members of a foreign country's parliamentary body (in the legislative chamber after adjournment at the close of the day) has a direct impact on members of a very important public. Others might feel that a study which describes the internal workings of the Agency in great detail is not useful, because it is obvious that the reorganizations so common in government (including USIA) will change patterns of organization sufficiently to outdate many factual details presented. It is true that "everything is always changing" in government, but it is also a fact that "much usually remains the same." Elements of USIA are reorganized, some of their functions even attached to other parts of the Agency; however, the remaining functions performed often remain about as they were, perhaps with a new emphasis. The function transferred may go on as before but report to a new chief. Many studies of government cover such broad problems that they do not really communicate how decisions are made, the processes and relationships between and within agencies, the differing perceptions of the participants, the nuts and bolts of the policy-making process—information which can make government real and comprehensible to students or other members of the general public who have never worked at a reasonably high level in the governmental bureaucracy. It is difficult even for experienced government personnel to evaluate recommendations made by a general study lacking detail because they cannot know the particular distillation of facts which have led to specific conclusions or suggestions.

It was for the purpose of learning how USIA presently functions, how it receives policy guidance or influences the formulation of foreign policy, how it translates foreign policy into information policy, and how it transforms policy into programs and products that the present study was undertaken. It is therefore a study of inter- and intra-agency contacts, of lateral and vertical relationships, with emphasis upon interactions affecting policy, program, or product. The time focus is on the period from 1963 to 1967, the Agency as it was led by Directors Edward R. Murrow, Carl Rowan, and Leonard Marks, though historical material is introduced as background. Today's USIA is an exciting, ever-changing, yet maturing organization. It is grappling with its problems more realistically and seriously than in times past. Although USIA is far from becoming a perfect information instrument, employee morale is generally good, and among its leadership there is a hope for a better, more effective future.

Communicating an understanding of USIA's purposes, products, organization, operations, and problems as they relate to American foreign policy is difficult. The Agency will not sit still for a "picture." Each major change sets off chain reactions and initiates new responses at points scattered throughout the "system." Each observer attempting to catch the essence of the Agency will view it from a different personal and time perspective.[1]

Although USIA is one of the five major foreign affairs agencies of the United States government, most members of the American public know little if anything about its policies, programs, or operations. Next to the covert Central Intelligence Agency (CIA), overt USIA is probably the least publicized domestically of the five; and with increasing public discussion of CIA in the wake of the abortive Cuban invasion in 1961, USIA may now have acquired a firm hold on last place. The Department of State, the Department of Defense, and even the Agency for International Development—often the target of Congressman Otto Passman's barbs—make newspaper headlines almost daily, in the American "provincial press" as well as in the *New York Times*. Occasionally USIA is mentioned. But, the fact that USIA program operations are directed outward and have their impact overseas, coupled with congressional fears of USIA's "propagandists" utilizing their skills on American voters, insures a small domestic public information program for USIA and relative anonymity within the continental United States.

Few Americans can give the headquarters address of the United States Information Agency: 1750 Pennsylvania Avenue, N.W., Washington, D.C. In woeful comparison with the Federal Bureau of Investigation, one of the most popular tourist attractions in Washington, the agency engaged in "Telling America's Story Around the World" draws annually only 20,000 Americans and foreigners combined to its Washington exhibit near the Voice of America studios in the Health, Education, and Welfare Building on Independence Avenue. While many Americans have heard of the Agency's Voice of America broadcasts, hardly any have listened to them. They may be aware of the magazine *America Illustrated*, released by USIA in the Soviet Union, but have not read it. Overseas, USIA's position on the "publicity" totem pole is often reversed. Many USIA materials are not specifically identified as such, but millions of average people as well as their leaders, in Africa, Asia, Europe, and Latin America, are aware of USIA operations. Serving abroad as members of the United States Information Service, Agency personnel take pride in the fact that taxi drivers or the local equivalent throughout the world generally know where to go if the instruction "take me to USIS" is given in the proper language. Most short-wave radio listeners overseas were familiar with VOA's "Columbia the Gem of the Ocean" theme and now recognize the older "Yankee Doodle" theme, reintroduced officially as VOA celebrated its twenty-fifth anniversary on February 24, 1967. USIS Information Centers, clearly marked, are often located near the heart of large cities overseas, for all to see and for many to visit and use (or abuse). USIA mobile motion-picture units may penetrate the back country to the end of the road, or occasionally a bit beyond, bringing an American message on the silver screen to thousands of rural dwellers at a single showing, many of whom have never visited their own country's capital city.

In spite of the lack of knowledge about USIA among the American mass public, what the Agency says or does, either in Washington or overseas, makes or could make a considerable difference in the effectiveness of American foreign policy. This is not to say that good information policy, programs, or operations can substitute for good foreign policy. USIA personnel are the first to admit that propaganda victories are the cheapest to achieve, and the most ephemeral. But, how American policies and programs are presented overseas and what information is provided about them may sometimes be the critical factor between acceptance, tolerance, or rejection.

At home, no USIA employee would argue that American overseas policies should be decided primarily on the basis of what the public opinion impact might be; but, almost to the man or woman, they would be likely to declare that policy makers should be aware of foreign public opinion and take it into account along with other pertinent factors as policy decisions are hammered out. Fortunately, though there is little knowledge about USIA among the American people generally, responsible leaders in the government have a somewhat better understanding of the Agency and its possible contribution to attaining the goals of American foreign policy. Unfortunately, in fact, they and their subordinates cannot always put this "understanding" into practice effectively, for the understanding required of them is much deeper than that which might suffice for the American public. Integrating the informational or psychological element into overseas policy is no easy task, and there is no real consensus automatically available to policy makers to determine what USIA's contribution to policy should be in each specific situation. The policy makers are sometimes too busy or too interested in the affairs of their own agencies to take the time to find out what USIA could do or to communicate to USIA what they are doing. But the fault is not all theirs, for USIA's personnel lack time and training to give adequate attention to such matters at all levels; and the Agency is still in the process of discovering its own role in the total overseas policy process, still attempting to determine what it "is" and where it is "going." For the behavioralist and relativist there can be no one theoretical or perfect way to achieve the meshing of broad policy directives with specific informational activities, irrespective of changing international actors or an unstable milieu. What was adequate yesterday, and barely so today, may fall short of (or overstep) the needs and opportunities of tomorrow.

This study of the United States Information Agency is a natural outgrowth of my own previous research and writing on other aspects of the foreign affairs mechanism. *The Policy Machine: The Department of State and American Foreign Policy* (Syracuse: Syracuse University Press, 1960) was made possible by a grant from the Ford Foundation's Fund for the Advancement of Education. *The Foreign Leader Program of the Department of State* (Washington: Brookings Institution, 1961) resulted from a study done for the Brookings Institution on contract to the Department of State. *Overseas Representation and Services for Federal Domestic Agencies* (New York: Carnegie Endowment for International Peace, 1965) was prepared while I was serving as a consultant to the Committee on Foreign Affairs Personnel, chaired by former Secretary of State Christian A. Herter, sponsored by the Carnegie Endowment, and supported by funds from the Ford and Rockefeller foundations. Research on *The Information Machine* was made possible by a series of grants from the Colgate University Research Council.

The Information Machine is primarily based upon material obtained in 200 interviews with USIA personnel in Washington, D.C.

Approximately 145 of the interviews with some 200 USIA employees were conducted from September through December, 1963, during a sabbatical semester. Updating interviews were held in September, 1964, January, 1965, January, 1966, and January, 1967. Interviews were for periods of from one to two and one-half hours. The more important Agency and other publications used to supplement the information obtained by interview are indicated by notes.

Although their substantive contributions to the book cannot be specifically identified, several individuals without whose assistance the book could never have been written deserve personal credit. In May, 1963, during my twelfth spring semester in Washington as director of the Colgate-Washington Study Group, I walked into USIA headquarters without forewarning and talked for an hour with Ben Posner (at that time the Agency's deputy director for administration and now its director for administration) about the possibility of studying the Agency. Through him the wheels were set in motion, and in July, 1963, I received a letter from Agency Director Edward R. Murrow granting me permission to do the research. When I reported to the Agency in September, 1963, to begin interviews, working out of the Agency's Research and Reference Service, it was a delight to discover that Frederic Bundy, a respected friend of eight years, had that very day taken over as deputy director of the Research and Reference Service and was to be my major point of contact in the Agency during the course of the study. It is difficult to single out the other Agency personnel who were most helpful to me throughout the study, but I must list at least six who were always ready to be of assistance: Reed Harris, former executive assistant to Murrow, then assistant agency director for the Information Center Service, now assistant director for policy and plans (Office of Research and Analysis); Oren Stephens, director of the Research and Reference Service during most of the period of the study, now heading the European Regional Research Office in Geneva, Switzerland; Edgar D. Brooke, presently inspector general of the Agency's foreign service; Wilson Dizard, one-time agency planning officer, formerly a special assistant to the deputy agency director and then to the agency director, and later assistant deputy director of the Office of Policy and Research for operational policy; Daniel Oleksiw, presently assistant agency director for East Asia and the Pacific; and Herbert McGushin, former deputy director of the Office of Public Information, who shortly before his untimely death, guided my manuscript through a gentle Agency review to assure that the study was factually correct. Of great help throughout the study were the objective observations of Louis T. Olom, staff director of the United States Advisory Commission on Information. I express my thanks to these men and to more than two hundred others who talked with me seriously about their own work and that of the Agency. They and thousands of others who serve with them are deserving of commendation for their continuing efforts to improve the Agency and its programs. USIA has come a long way since it was established as an independent agency on August 1, 1953, by authority of the President's Reorganization Plan No. 8, as approved by Congress. To indicate that major reliance in research was upon interviews with USIA personnel is not to blame those with whom I talked for whatever errors the careful and knowledgeable reader may find in the book. The inevitable mistakes and imprecisions are my own.

I acknowledge the assistance of my wife, Mary Gene Elder, for her help in preparing the index and for her willing acceptance of many extra family responsibilities during the four years it took to complete work on the manuscript.

Robert E. Elder
Hamilton, New York
November 6, 1967

CONTENTS

The Information Machine

I

Contemporary USIA:

Purposes, Programs, Organization, and Problems

"Raison d'être" and Mission

Why does the United States government require a special information agency to tell America's story to the world? Why not rely upon private commercial press services to carry American news and views of global interest? Every time President Lyndon B. Johnson or Secretary of State Dean Rusk publicly utter a single sentence on Vietnam, reporters representing major wire services and newspapers or television and radio networks, both foreign and domestic, listen and rush stories or pictures to their editors. American and foreign coverage is practically guaranteed free of cost to the taxpayer, except for the small cost of maintaining quarters for newsmen at the White House or Department of State. Why spend an additional $170 million a year to maintain the United States Information Agency, with its more than 3,250 American employees in the United States, plus 1,760 Americans and 6,950 foreign nationals serving at United States Information Service posts?[1] USIA personnel take great pains to explain that the Agency is not in competition with the commercial press, radio, or television. The United States government does in fact make use of the private communications services when it holds press conferences or arranges coverage of major policy speeches on television and radio. Policy statements by Johnson or Rusk are bold headlines in newspapers or staccato announcements by newscasters, but news services carry few complete texts of addresses; most reporters prepare reasonably objective summaries, but points of emphasis are determined by the views or interests of the newsmen or their editors. Even in America it is often only the *New York Times* that carries the full text word for word; such coverage is much less likely overseas. The press services cannot afford to send full texts to cities or countries where they are not of interest to mass publics. What begins in Washington as a reasonably careful defense of the foreign policy of the Johnson administration or a bold new idea for reso-

1

lution of an international problem may end up overseas, in Dar-es-Salaam or Karachi, as a sentence or so taken out of context in a vituperative editorial or newscast. Any follow-up statements issued by government officials in the United States to counter unobjective reporting overseas are likely to be handled in much the same fashion as the original speech. To enable American representatives overseas, diplomatic or otherwise (including American newsmen), to have rapid access to full texts of major American policy statements, USIA teletypes complete speeches to its posts at speeds up to one hundred words a minute. Local editors, reporters, and writers, more objective than others, can be given access to the documents, see the ideas as they were presented, and provide a fairer picture to their reading publics. USIS personnel and American diplomats can read the full text and, aware of the basic purposes of American foreign policy, develop talking points which can be used to counter any negative response in personal conversations, in stories released to the local press, and through commentary in USIS publications. The commercial press, whether American or foreign, is not interested—and should not be—in attaining the foreign policy objectives of the United States. This does not mean that such foreign policy objectives should not be pressed by United States government employees stationed overseas, backstopped by the U.S. Information Agency.

USIA exists as much to provide a view of the world to the United States as it does to give the world a view of America. The attitudes and actions of people throughout the world are of importance to American policy makers. While diplomatic contacts with foreign governments provide an understanding of official policy, there are few countries where there are not important segments of opinion which are pushing for change. For American officials to attempt to deal with their counterparts abroad without understanding the ideas competing with those presently motivating government action would be like sailing through the Bahama Islands by point-to-point navigation without charts marking reefs. The more the United States government can know what influential or potentially influential people overseas believe, the more effectively can American policy be adapted to their needs, along with those of the American people. Statements projected to foreign publics without an understanding of their culture, their domestic conditions, or their attitudes toward world affairs can rarely be expected to have the effect desired by the speaker. It is true that academic area specialists in the United States can supply some information of this type to American policy makers, but most students of foreign areas must rely upon reports from abroad. These reports, though they provide a broad base for understanding, may arrive somewhat slowly, and the area expert's emphasis is not upon the foreign policy of the United States government. Furthermore, most area experts are fully

involved in teaching or writing. Few of them are likely to have either the time
or the money to keep up with the day-to-day ebb and flow of discussion in the
foreign press. Their analyses, usually prepared for the academic press, are
often too late to be useful to the American policy maker, who must be able to
spot trends and counter problems before small fires become holocausts. For
the United States government to communicate effectively to influential men
and women overseas, it must know their problems and discussions day to
day. Otherwise, much of what America seeks to tell the world will be irre-
levant to foreign listeners. In *Facts to a Candid World,* Oren Stephens sums
up the reasons for existence of the USIA by noting that United States government leaders must take overseas public opinion factors into account in the
determination, enunciation, and execution of policy.[2]

Although a committee composed of USIA's top fifteen leaders drafted a
new official statement of mission for the Agency in 1967, the end result,
signed by Director Leonard Marks, differed only in emphasis from what had
been major elements in the Agency mission since 1963—but the alterations
are significant. USIA's cultural and informational role is given somewhat
more attention than four years earlier; mutuality of American goals and
concerns with those of other people are stressed, and support of U.S. foreign
policy rather than the achievement of its objective is called for. The single
official statement which best defined the USIA's mission from 1963 to 1967
was a memorandum of February 25, 1963, to the director of USIA (Murrow)
signed by President John F. Kennedy. Agency personnel seemed to view the
memorandum as "significantly" different from preceding directives when it
was announced in 1963, but a casual review of Agency history indicates that
the document, at least in its public version, was chiefly a restatement of what
have been primary elements in the Agency's mission since 1953—but there
were new words and a new emphasis, among the traditional ideas. The Kennedy memorandum assigned the Agency a twofold function:

> to help achieve United States foreign policy objectives by (a) influenc-
> ing public attitudes in other nations, and (b) advising the President,
> his representatives abroad, and the various departments and agencies
> on the implications of foreign opinion for present and contemplated
> United States policies, programs, and official statements.

Apparently no President had stated the Agency's advisory role in writing
before, though the advisory function was generally recognized in principle if
often ignored in practice by many other government agencies. Emphasis
upon the Agency's role in helping "achieve United States foreign policy
objectives" on the surface did not change older mandates for the Agency's
programs to support American foreign policy. In fact, this emphasis did give

oblique acquiescence to the transition from a somewhat cultural, long-term approach for USIA under George V. Allen to a more directly political, short-term approach developed after 1961 during Edward R. Murrow's tenure. The Agency's goal as stated in 1963 seemed no longer to be primarily "friendship through understanding," but appeared to seek concrete, visible, almost immediate results. Conveying a broad understanding of American culture and life was apparently somewhat subordinated to giving a specific understanding of and favorable responses to American foreign policy initiatives. The climate seemed significantly different than that of the Allen days. The new 1967 statement of mission takes a position somewhere between the Allen and Murrow positions, for the Agency in practice now seems to have adopted a moderate approach between the two extremes. The means of carrying out USIA's mission of influencing attitudes and actions set forth by the Kennedy memorandum were certainly not new: "personal contact, radio broadcasting, libraries, book publication and distribution, press, motion pictures, television, exhibits, English-language instruction, and others."

The Kennedy memorandum directs that: "Individual country programs should specifically and directly support country and regional objectives determined by the President and set forth in official policy pronouncements, both classified and unclassified." In addition, Agency programs should

> (a) encourage constructive public support abroad for the goal of a "peaceful world community of free and independent states, free to choose their own future and their own system as long as it does not threaten the freedom of others"; (b) identify the United States as a strong, democratic, dynamic nation qualified for its leadership of world efforts toward this goal, and (c) unmask and counter hostile attempts to distort or frustrate the objectives and policies of the United States.

Although the Department of State is the Agency's major source of policy guidance, it was not mentioned in the enjoinder to support American foreign policy objectives. Because other states are likely to emphasize ways in which United States policies appear harmful to other peoples and governments and to present those aspects of American life and culture which thoughtful American citizens do not approve, it is essential, as the memorandum suggested, for the Agency to emphasize the harmony of American policies with those of other nations and to present American life and culture in such a way as to "facilitate understanding of United States policies." Such a program did not necessarily call for untruths or distortion on the part of American information personnel; but it did require a presentation of ideas which would make it possible for foreign publics to retain or develop relatively objective views of the United States and its policies. It certainly did not preclude an exploration of American racial problems. Policies of counteraction, though negative in some respects, may sometimes be necessary for the creation, maintenance, or restoration of a "full and fair picture" of the United States abroad.

Dealing more directly with USIA's role in policy formulation, the Kennedy memorandum said:

> The advisory function is to be carried out at various levels in Washington, and within the Country Team at United States diplomatic missions abroad. While the Director of the United States Information Agency shall take the initiative in offering counsel when he deems it advisable, the various departments and agencies should seek such counsel when considering policies and programs which may substantially affect or be affected by foreign opinion.

Acceptance of an advisory function by information program experts in foreign policy matters has long been given lip service. Liaison between agencies at various levels assures that some such advice is given and considered, but both USIA and the other foreign affairs agencies lack sufficient personnel to make such an exchange of ideas as effective as true coordination might require. The memorandum did not necessarily limit itself to the foreign affairs agencies. It certainly did not exclude domestic affairs agencies when it suggested USIA counsel for "policies and programs which may substantially affect or be affected by foreign opinion." USIA has little liaison with the federal domestic affairs agencies, and is often in no position to know ahead of time when planned actions may affect foreign public opinion.

Finally, the Kennedy memorandum set what are still the limits of USIA responsibility abroad. Under the supervision of the chiefs of mission, Agency staffs "are responsible for the conduct of overt public information, public relations and cultural activities—i.e., those activities intended to inform or influence foreign public opinion—for agencies of the United States Government except for Commands of the Department of Defense." Thus, the top role of the ambassador is recognized. USIA is limited to the conduct of overt or "white" information activities—those which bear its name or which it would acknowledge if questioned; and the responsibility for public information on community-troop relations is preserved for the Department of Defense in areas where its Commands are involved, though in fact USIA may often be consulted. The 1967 statement, in its classified if not in its public portions, may well include some clarification of USIA's special role in Thailand and Vietnam. Assignment for the conduct of covert information programs, if such there be, was not made in the public portion of the 1967 Marks statement or in the Kennedy memorandum. History suggests that since there has been "black" propaganda in the past, like that produced by the Office of Strategic Services during World War II, such programs still exist somewhere within the United States government, especially in a "neither war nor peace" situation.

PRODUCTS AND ORGANIZATION

As an overt information agency, USIA can—and does—point with pride to the variety and number of activities it conducts from Washington and overseas to carry out its assigned mission "to help achieve United States foreign policy objectives." Most publicized—and possibly the most difficult to maintain policy control over—is the fast-moving Voice of America (VOA). By January, 1967, the Voice was broadcasting 824 hours weekly from its Washington studios, by short wave via relay transmitters in thirty-eight languages, using as many as twenty additional tongues for special programs of high international interest.[3] USIA estimates that between seventeen and twenty-six million people listen to the Voice on an average day; and about twice that number of different people listen during an average week. One-third of these listeners live behind the somewhat porous "Iron" or "Bamboo" curtains. The spread of the transistor radio is multiplying the number of listeners in less-developed areas. There are now more than 50 million radio sets in the Far East, over 31 million in Latin America, and about 4.3 million in Africa. A laborer in a rice paddy may be listening as he works, a transistor radio fastened to the top of a stake plunged into the mud. In addition to direct reception of broadcasts, VOA programs are often rebroadcast by local stations. In Latin America 260 stations in fifteen countries regularly repeat VOA broadcasts. USIA also distributes packaged radio programs in sixty-two languages to posts around the world for use by over five thousand local stations. With heightened American interest in Thailand, the USIS post there places over 640 hours of programming weekly on ninety radio stations, reaching three million receivers with multiple listeners. In Latin America, seven hundred stations broadcast eleven thousand hours weekly of taped VOA programs.[4]

Early in 1963, USIA doubled its short-wave broadcast strength when the world's most powerful long-range radio transmitter—boasting an output of 4.8 million watts and equal in power to the ninety-six strongest United States commercial stations—was placed in service at Greenville, North Carolina. By January, 1967, VOA broadcasts were beamed to foreign listeners by thirty-five transmitters located in the United States and overseas, with a total power of 15 million watts. In addition to the Greenville station, transmitters are located in Bethany, Ohio; Delano and Dixon, California; and Marathon, Florida. Overseas transmitters are near Colombo, Ceylon; Malolos and Poro, Phillipines; Monrovia, Liberia; Munich, Germany; Okinawa, Ryukyu Islands; Thessaloniki and Rhodes, Greece; and Wooferton, England. As these transmitters come into full operation in 1968, VOA will be able to reach any place in the world with reasonably strong signals.

In many respects as important as VOA's increase in power, jamming of its broadcasts by the Soviet Union was stopped on June 19, 1963. Except for a brief period in late 1959 and early 1960, the Russians had jammed VOA broadcasts since 1948. Now VOA short-wave signals can be heard clearly by audiences throughout most of "European" Russia. The abrupt change from "hit and run" broadcasting under jamming conditions to a type of programming credible and interesting to a much broader audience within the Soviet Union posed a critical challenge to VOA program planners. In November, 1966, with most of eastern Europe now able to listen to broadcasts under normal conditions, VOA Director John Chancellor[5] announced the "new sound" Voice broadcasts in English—the adoption of the "magazine format" of "Today" on television or "Monitor" on radio, a mixture of music, news, discussion, and humor with no more than several minutes devoted to a particular type of presentation. Regular news programs of thirty minutes continue, as do many of the more popular programs of the past; but Europe now gets the "new sound" five hours a day, and Latin America and Africa hear it two hours. The "new sound" is a far too long delayed move to adopt a lighter tone than the Voice had during the World War II days when Europe was occupied and people risked death to hear news broadcasts by VOA or the United Kingdom's BBC.[6] The "old sound," tolerable during the Cold War, is inappropriate in a more polycentric world.

Almost as dramatic in its operation as the Voice of America, and second only to VOA in the speed with which it reaches foreign audiences, is the Wireless File, approximately twelve thousand words radio-teletyped six or seven days a week to 111 monitoring posts abroad at speeds up to one hundred words a minute.[7] Adapted to provide items of interest to seven special areas of the world, its material is translated by the local USIS staff at receiving posts and then distributed to government officials and to press, television, and radio outlets. The Wireless File includes speeches or press conferences by American government leaders, commentaries on domestic and international political affairs, briefing and background information, and news and editorial summaries. It constitutes a form of policy guidance to the field posts. Analytical and interpretative material carried on the File was doubled during the first half of 1966. When the Agency covers special events, like a space shot, the Wireless File is much longer than its 12,000-word average. In May, 1963, its regular four-hour-a-day transmission was extended to eighteen during Astronaut Gordon Cooper's flight, as the Wireless File carried 24,000 words in seventy-seven special reports. In covering the flight, the German Press Agency (DNP) relied heavily on the File for its nationwide teletype service. USIS São Paulo reported placing 2,644 column inches of material in newspapers on the flight. USIS Hong Kong placed Wireless material in twenty-two newspapers.

In the press and periodical field, USIA publishes sixty-six magazines, newspapers, and other periodicals, totaling almost 30 million copies annually, in twenty-eight languages. All but six of these are produced at USIS posts overseas or in Regional Service Centers operated by the Agency in Manila, Beirut, and Mexico City. Typical post periodicals are *Span* in India, *American Miscellany* in Indonesia, and *Information and Documents* in Paris. *Free World*, published by the Regional Printing Center in Manila, appears in fifteen Far East countries after adaptation to individual post needs. Six magazines are edited in the United States: the Russian *America Illustrated* and Polish *America*, both *Life*-sized publications; plus *Al Hayat fi America* in Arabic, *Problems of Communism* in English and Spanish, and *Topic*, the new monthly African magazine, in English and French. Completing its twelfth year of continuous publication in 1968, *America Illustrated* is printed in Russian in the United States; many of its 64,100 copies are sold monthly on Soviet newsstands in eighty Russian cities.[8] Begun in 1959, the Polish edition of *America Illustrated*, called *America*, is also printed in the United States, with 33,000 copies a month sent to Poland. Under the agreement which makes this distribution possible, the same number of copies of similar periodicals published by the Soviet and Polish information services are placed on sale in the United States. *Al Hayat* is printed for Arabic-speaking nations at the Regional Printing Center in Beirut, with bimonthly runs of 50,000 copies. *Problems of Communism*, also a bimonthly publication but more "scholarly" in nature, is printed in 36,700 copies, 31,700 of which are in English and 5,000 Spanish. *Topic*, the African monthly magazine started in July, 1965, is done in 50,000 copies, 30,000 English and 20,000 French.

Numerous cartoon books have been printed by USIA, the total number of copies running into the millions. Over seven million copies were distributed in Latin America during the first six months of 1963 alone. Some were negative in tone, depicting the evils of communism; others were positive, indicating how less-developed countries could improve their living standards. Demands for *Toward a Better Life*, in the latter category, broke all previous records, with orders for more than 1.5 million copies. Until January, 1967, USIA also distributed five weekly or semi-weekly cartoon strips, but this program has been dropped; now political cartoons appearing in the domestic and foreign commercial press are reproduced and distributed to field posts by USIA after appropriate clearance with the original publishers. Most well known to Americans of the old cartoon strips was *Little Moe;* this humorously anticommunist cartoon, started in 1953, appeared regularly in five hundred newspapers in fifty-eight foreign countries. Although cartoon strips have disappeared, leaflet and pamphlet publication was increasing during 1966 and by 1967 they appeared at the rate of twenty million copies a year in forty-seven languages for use in 115 countries.

Television is a booming development within USIA, and motion pictures continue to be distributed at a high rate. During 1966, 2,082 television studios in ninety-four countries telecast USIA programs.[9] The number of sets rose sharply from some 12 million in 1950 to about 110 million by the end of 1966, and more than one hundred countries have television today. The Agency may now be reaching over 200 million people each year with one or more of its television productions, with many regular listeners. Thailand, a country of great interest to USIA in 1968, has an estimated 300,000 television receivers and five television stations. Fifteen viewers are said to make use of each receiving set. USIS placement of USIA materials on Thai television is averaging twenty-three hours a week. By 1967 in Latin America, the long-popular *Panorama Panamericano* and its replacement *Candilejas* (Candlelight) were off the air, and the new emphasis was on films produced in the field adapted to the needs of individual countries. USIA motion pictures were viewed by an estimated 700 million people in 120 countries during 1966. The high quality of USIA films was demonstrated by awards won in competition at film festivals in Berlin, Antwerp, Spain, and New York City. Films cited were "Beyond This Winter's Wheat," "My Friend, the Enemy," "Tomorrow in Their Hands," and "Night of the Dragon"—the last shown widely to create understanding of American policy in Vietnam. It was shipped in twenty-three language versions to 110 countries. In one Latin American capital, it ran for six days at the main theater, coupled with the heavily advertised *My Fair Lady*. In an African nation, the American ambassador used the film to supplement a speech on the American role in Vietnam before accepting questions from the floor. During 1966, USIS-Thailand alone produced twenty news magazines and twenty documentaries on development and security topics, a high rate for post-produced motion pictures.

If people abroad listen to the radio, read newspapers and periodicals, watch television, and attend movies, they also read books. During fiscal year 1966, USIA helped foreign publishers print 1,557 books in 10,668,349 copies[10] (comparable figures for fiscal year 1963 were 1,146 and 9,397,870). These books either illustrated important aspects of American life and culture or contributed "to the exposure of Communist theory and practice." In addition, that year the Agency assisted American publishers in printing 56 books in 1,599,016 copies (comparable 1963 figures 56 and 1,456,971). This enabled the publishers to bring out paperback reprints or to provide simplified editions of books in English for sale overseas at low retail prices. Many of these books find their way into USIA's 223 libraries and reading rooms, or 132 binational centers, 112 of which are in Latin America. In addition to providing reading materials, such information centers arrange lectures, seminars, concerts, and exhibits; they also teach English, with more than one million persons regularly attending classes in any given year. About 150 USIA exhibits were on tour during fiscal year 1966 (comparable figure for fiscal year 1963 was 300). The exhibits were mostly small, but a few were elaborate and of large size for maximum impact. All these media products are important to the carrying out of USIA's mission abroad, but also important are the personal contacts made by USIS personnel with national leaders, editors, parliamentarians, educators, community leaders, student or other groups, and local institutional officials. Through such contacts, ideas are obtained which help USIA "speak the language" which the people to be reached can understand, and friendships are made which help place USIA products on the air, in theaters, and in the press. Thoughts can be conveyed personally that could never be put on paper—spoken between friends and accepted in a manner never possible by cold contact with the printed word or picture. Such a summary of Agency products and activities ignores USIA leadership in sponsoring arrangements between private groups in the United States and abroad to engage in the exchange of ideas or mutual assistance, and it fails to mention USIS's major role in the selection of foreign leaders or students to come to the United States for travel or study or in maintaining friendly relations with these people after they have returned to their own countries.

Conducting this variety of activities requires both bureaucratic organization and relatively complex procedures—though Agency personnel like to think of USIA as small, tightly knit, and informal in its operations. With approximately 4,994 American employees, about one-third of whom serve abroad, and some 6,963 foreign local employees hired overseas, such a view of the Agency at first seems completely unreal. [11] Natural splits and divisions of interest do in fact separate the home office from the field, the Civil Service from the Foreign Service, the media from regional personnel, the technical people from the professional communicators, specialists in one media from those in another, specialists in one region from those in another, media or regional people from administrative personnel, and older senior-level employees from younger junior-level personnel. Yet, something about the nature of the Agency's work and its personnel does bind these groups together, build close friendships, and make personal relationships more important to Agency employees—both in the Civil Service and in the Foreign Service Career Reserve or Foreign Service—than might be anticipated. There are few who make a fetish of procedures; communication is often by word of mouth rather than by formal memoranda. Nonetheless, the Agency is far from an unorganized group of people meeting oncoming problems with hastily concocted *ad hoc* devices. A first overview of how USIA is organized, however formally or informally, to do its job will be useful later in understanding a more detailed analysis of its operations.

The director and deputy director of USIA stand at the top of the Agency's organizational hierarchy. The sixth and current director of the Agency is Leonard H. Marks, a Washington lawyer, long interested in educational television, who has been a law school instructor, an assistant to the General Counsel of the Federal Communications Commission, and a public member of the board of directors of the Communications Satellite Corporation. Serving as deputy director is Robert W. Akers, for many years editor-in-chief of both the Beaumont, Texas, *Enterprise* and *Journal*. These two men assumed direction of the Agency on September 1, 1965. Selected as executive assistant to Director Marks was Howard L. Chernoff, for a number of years general manager of the *San Diego Journal* and of stations KFMB-AM and KFMB-TV there. For two years before his appointment he was special advisor to the governor of American Samoa on communications, organization, and business administration. When Chernoff went on extended leave for medical treatment in late January, 1967, Thomas Lloyd Wright, a Texan who entered government service in 1961 with the Peace Corps and later served as director of USIA's Press and Publications Service, took over as executive assistant to the director.

Traditionally, the director of USIA has been "Mr. Outside," responsible for relations with the White House and the Department of State, and the deputy director "Mr. Inside," responsible for many of the Agency's internal administrative affairs. Under Director Marks, Chernoff and Wright have performed many of the administrative duties carried in the past by the deputy director, while Akers has functioned more in an editorial capacity, taking over guidance of media policy, upgrading a function performed between 1963 and late 1965 by an assistant deputy director of USIA for media content. Thus, Marks combined the "inside" and "outside" functions in his own office. Director Marks made a good first impression on Agency area and media directors by lengthening his weekly staff meeting with them so that some matters once discussed in a separate "think" session abandoned by Carl Rowan could again be raised. He also moved the staff meeting from Monday to the second working day of the week, thus eliminating the pressure of the weekend accumulation of Agency work which had often reduced the effectiveness of the weekly briefing session in the past. Although the Tuesday staff meeting is not yet considered an adequate substitute for the old Wednesday afternoon "think" session, area and media directors are less likely to feel that they would be better off if they could be clearing their own desks instead of attending the meeting. It is apparent to Agency personnel that Marks's lines to President Johnson and the White House are excellent. If Murrow's relationship with Kennedy depended upon his national image as a television personality, that of Marks with Johnson is personal and political. There is evidence that Marks's long interest in educational television, his experience as a member of the board of the Communications Satellite Corporation, and his close personal relations with the President are stimulating government action in support of expanded international information and educational activities via television, with the Agency playing a major role in developing new government policies and programs in this field.

In 1963, the number-three man in the Agency was the deputy director for policy and plans, heading the Office of Policy. This post was held during the Murrow-Kennedy period by Thomas Sorensen, a member of USIA's Foreign Service Career Reserve and an older brother of President Kennedy's special counsel, Theodore Sorensen. Taking over the number-three slot when Sorensen resigned to enter private industry was Burnett Anderson, a long-time Foreign Service Career Reserve (FSCR) officer who had served under Sorensen as assistant deputy director of USIA for policy and plans. Anderson's successor was Hewson Ryan, also an FSCR, who had served under Anderson as associate deputy director of policy and plans after previous experience as assistant director of USIA for Latin America. In 1967, Ryan's job as deputy director for policy and research should probably still be considered the number-three slot in the Agency, but since 1965 the executive assistant to the Director has taken over many of the daily administrative tasks formerly performed by the deputy director of USIA and is clearly in fourth or fifth place if not deserving of third ranking. Ryan and his associate deputy director, Barbara White—an FSCR—are leaders of the Agency's Office of Policy and Research, the chief policy arm of the director, deputy director, and executive assistant. They direct the formulation of basic Agency information policies, themes, and program emphases, and guide related research. Ryan has close supervision of the daily policy guidance to USIA's operating elements, assisted by a Policy Guidance and Media Reaction Staff created in October, 1967, formed by joining his old Policy Guidance staff and a small Media Reaction Unit which did special studies at the request of the White House or USIA leadership, often on short notice, formerly a part of the Research and Analysis Staff. Policy guidance maintains daily relations with the Department of State's regional bureaus and the Bureau of Public Affairs to obtain policy guidance and to pass on relevant information policy to USIA regional and media elements. Ryan and White are directly involved when critical day-to-day problems arise concerning the Voice of America, the Wireless File, or other media.

The other major functions of the Office of Policy and Research are divided between a Research and Analysis Staff, headed by an assistant director of policy and research (research and analysis) and a Policy and Plans Staff, headed by an assistant director of policy and research (policy and plans). The work of the Research and Analysis Staff is organized under eight divisions, five of which are concerned with attitudes of populations and communications systems in Africa, East Asia and the Pacific, Europe, Latin America, and the Near East and South Asia. A sixth division studies communist propaganda from any source and reaching any area in the world, as well as covering attitudes of people and communications systems in communist countries. Another division analyzes the effectiveness of USIA's media products overseas, cooperating closely with the Area offices and Media Services. A newly formed Editorial Division apparently assists in the review of Research and Analysis Staff products. The work of the Policy and Plans Staff traditionally has been performed by individuals. There are eight to ten special advisors, experts in such fields as armaments and arms control, the United Nations, student affairs overseas, labor and minorities problems, science, cultural affairs, or women's activities. Generally, they function as advisors to all parts of USIA on matters pertaining to their fields of expertise and maintain liaison with other agencies on problems related to their specialties. Several advisors serve as long-range planners, and another has the function of trying to stimulate Area Offices and Media Services personnel to apply research findings made by the Research and Analysis Staff. The responsibility for media content review, vested until September, 1965, in an assistant deputy director of USIA for media content, now rests primarily with Deputy Director of USIA Akers, assisted by two media content officers on the Policy and Plans Staff. For a brief period, early in 1967, the Policy and Plans Staff was organized into four units, one with five or six advisors primarily responsible for working with private groups outside the government, a second with four or five "advisors" renamed liaison officers responsible for maintaining relations with other agencies of government, a third assisting media content review, and a fourth performing planning and research applications functions. By October, 1967, the Policy and Plans Staff had returned to its more informal traditional form of organization. The Office of Policy and Research was created from the old Office of Policy in July, 1966, when USIA's Research and Reference Service was abandoned, its research functions attached to the new Office of Policy and Research and its reference elements incorporated in a new Information Resources Division in the Office of Administration.

Directly responsible for guiding the Agency's operations overseas in their assigned areas are six assistant directors of USIA, one each for Africa, Europe, East Asia and the Pacific, Latin America, the Near East and South Asia, and the Soviet Union and eastern Europe. Each is backstopped by a deputy assistant director. In matters concerning their regions the "area directors" have considerable discretion and power. Capable men with dynamic personalities, they are to USIA what the assistant secretaries of state are to the Department of State—what executive vice presidents are to the business world. Each assistant director is supported by a policy officer responsible for relating country programs and operations in the region to foreign and information policy, and a program coordinator who handles budget, personnel, and other administrative matters for the posts in the region and for the area office itself. Dealing more specifically with individual country programs and policies on a day-to-day basis are USIA's country desk officers, most of them responsible for at least two countries, many handling from three to five. USIA has programs in thirty-four countries in Africa; sixteen in western Europe; thirteen in the Far East; twenty-two in Latin America; eighteen in the Near East and South Asia; and seven in the Soviet Union and eastern Europe. The desk men are the drafters, expediters, and repositories of information, representing their countries to the Agency and the Agency to their countries. Their numbers are few and their tasks manifold. In each area office there are likely to be several regional or cultural officers to cover problems that cut across country lines at desk level. Area staffs are small, each assistant director and his deputy having no more than fourteen to twenty persons serving directly under him, mostly foreign service personnel. Each of the two top men in an area office is expected to spend 40 per cent of his time making inspections in the field; in Washington they bear heavy responsibilities within the Agency and maintain close liaison with their peers in other foreign affairs agencies. They are selected from among the senior officers in USIA's foreign service; usually, they have already been country public affairs officers at important USIS posts in the region they now direct.

Preparation of the media products to service the country and regional programs for which the assistant directors heading the area offices are largely responsible is done by USIA's media services, each headed by its own assistant director of USIA and a deputy assistant director. There is a Broadcasting Service, a Press and Publications Service, a Motion Picture and Television Service, and an Information Center Service. Staffed overwhelmingly by Civil Service personnel, the media services are far larger than the area offices. The Broadcasting Service, responsible for the Voice of America, has a domestic staff of 1,384, plus 164 Americans and 778 foreign local employees overseas. The other services range in size from the 251 employed by the Information Center Service to the Press and Publications Service's domestic staff of 420, plus 24 American and 326 foreign local employees abroad. [13] The media directors are assisted by program managers and sometimes by policy applications officers who have the job of maintaining policy liaison with the Office of Policy and Research and with appropriate regional policy officers, and of providing policy advice and guidance to media production personnel. Within each service, there is an administrative or executive officer and staff to handle administrative matters under the general guidance of the Agency's Office of Administration. In a manner typical of U.S. government organizations of some size, the media services are broken down into specialized divisions and the divisions into subordinate branches. The task of relating media production to foreign and information policy is a difficult and seemingly endless one, with many formal procedures and perhaps as many *ad hoc* informal ones to take care of unexpected or unusual problems. The media have been likened to feudal empires, resistant to outside policy direction, each pushing for greater use of its own products. The separateness is slowly giving way; liaison between leaders of the area offices and the media services is increasing; and the Office of Policy and Research, working under Deputy Director Akers, is making progress in relating forward planning of media production to Agency-approved themes and programs. To bring about a better understanding of field needs, more visits to the field are being made by responsible media services personnel. Also, more USIA foreign service officers are being assigned to duty in the media services when on Washington duty. This gives the Civil Service employees of the media a chance to rub elbows with Agency personnel who have used and will later use their products. Conversely, this experience helps the foreign service officers understand the problems faced by the media services in responding to requests of overseas missions.

Two USIA offices deal with important Agency publics, one public being the Congress. Working closely with the director of the Agency on congressional relations is the Office of the General Counsel, the general counsel himself playing a major role in congressional liaison—in addition to directing the Agency's legal staff. Because of congressional worry that American experts in overseas information might influence the American people unduly to obtain support for USIA programs, the Agency's domestic information program, conducted by its Office of Public Information, is unusually small. Its press releases are few and far between; it arranges for public appearances and speeches of Agency personnel, usually in response to requests; answers public mail; and prepares a semiannual report on Agency operations for the Congress—with only a small overprinting available for public distribution. Working with the public in a different way between 1963 and 1967 was the Office of Private Cooperation. It worked with American business, labor, and other groups to encourage private participation in achieving Agency objectives—getting nongovernmental assistance to meet special field needs or advising groups interested in programs of international understanding how to proceed. By October 1967, the Office of Private Cooperation was phased out, some of its functions taken over by the Office of Policy and Research and others by a new Private Resources Division in the Information Center Service.

Undergirding the performance of all Agency functions is the Office of Administration, headed by an assistant director of USIA and a deputy assistant director, which handles administrative services, budget, contract and procurement, finance, management, personnel, training, and foreign service problems. Controlling the Agency's security affairs, both physical and personnel, is an Office of Security. The importance of the Office of Administration to the successful conduct of Agency operations needs no defense. How efficiently it provides personnel, money, and materials to the Agency and organizes the bureaucratic structure, and how thoroughly it understands the Agency's mission and the nature of the world in which that mission is to be performed, will in the long run determine whether the Agency makes an effective and enlightened contribution to the changing national interest in an evolving world. A security check on the human element is well nigh a necessity. The McCarthy attacks early in the Agency's history emphasized the importance of careful security measures. The security function needs to be performed thoroughly but with intelligent restraint so as not to inhibit initative or new ideas. The Agency has developed a rational security program, apparently both humane and adequate to its needs.

However important the "home office" of USIA may be, the Agency's organization and activities in the field also demand attention, since the Agency's mission of information and influencing to support American foreign policy objectives is largely directed overseas. Abroad the USIA is known as the United States Information Service (USIS). It has about 104 headquarters posts at American embassies functioning as part of American overseas missions under the general direction of ambassadors. Each such USIS post is headed by a country public affairs officer (CPAO), often of FSCR-1 or FSCR-2 rank in USIA's foreign Service.[14] The CPAO has a dual obligation—to serve the ambassador who is head of the "country team," and to serve the U.S. Information Agency as head of its field post. Though the CPAO must support the ambassador, the country team, and clearly defined U.S. policy, he is legally entitled to direct communication with the Agency on any matter related to USIS program or personnel. He is expected to seek the ambassador's concurrence on most important matters; if there are differences which cannot be resolved in the field they can be taken up between USIA and the Department of State in Washington. In the meantime, the CPAO abides by the ambassador's decision.

A typical USIS post consists of a country staff of from five to nine Americans, with some fifteen foreign local employees.[15] In 1962, there were about twenty such medium-sized USIS posts, with twenty-nine larger and fifty-one smaller ones maintained overseas. The Americans at a medium-sized post might include in addition to the CPAO, a branch public affairs officer (BPAO)—serving in a major city other than the capital—a cultural affairs officer (CAO), an information officer (IO), a librarian, a binational center director (BNC), a public affairs assistant (PAA) or American secretary, and possibly a regional officer (this might be a research specialist). Foreign nationals serve under these officers as press assistants, radio-television-motion-picture assistants, librarians, translators, projectionists, student advisers, exhibits assistants, drivers, messengers, clerks, stenographers, and receptionists. The CPAO, CAO, IO, and probably a librarian, with a public affairs assistant, might be located in the capital city of the country. BPAO's, and often binational center directors and librarians, serve in cities other than the capital.

A USIS post has plenty to do. The CPAO must be a skilled juggler to keep all the balls in the air at once. He maintains liaison with the members of the country team who represent other agencies of the United States government, with information officers of other nations who are conducting competing programs in his country, with his own USIS personnel (both American and local) who may be performing a variety of tasks in a number of cities, with USIA from which he receives instructions and information and to which he must report on public opinion and actions taken or planned. He establishes as good relations as possible with members of the press, with radio and television personnel, with information officials and others in government, and with writers, educators, and leaders of business, labor, and cultural organizations. With more than thirty-five specialized media products placed at his disposal by USIA, he develops the contacts to assure local distribution of those materials suitable for the mass public or its leaders in his country. To build or maintain these contacts, he makes public appearances, entertains, helps when possible in community activities, and finds opportunities to hold serious discussions with influential individuals—while working to maintain the morale of his own staff. He is contact man, publisher, reporter, planner, and sometimes father confessor. Not only should he understand foreign policy, communications theory and techniques, the "workings" of a foreign society—and public opinion in that society—but also he needs to be a skilful administrator. The good CPAO, along with everything else, is an able communicator and a patient listener.

When the CPAO completes a busy tour of duty abroad and returns to the United States between assignments or for service in Washington, he is quite likely to be invited to the office of the director of USIA for a quiet, private discussion of public opinion conditions and the USIS program in "his" country. Unfortunately, during his tour he may have been too busy to take a penetrating look at the broader long-range developments in his country that will shape the operational environment of USIS there in the future. In his desire to have effective relations with public opinion leaders in his country in order to conduct successful information programs in the present, he may have wanted to be more responsive to current local attitudes than present or traditional American foreign or information policy toward the country would allow. In the midst of an overseas tour, he may hardly be conscious of earlier American information programs conducted there by his predecessors or of the relevance of USIA's history to the success of his programs in the present. His position on the country team under the ambassador reminds him daily of USIA's role as part of the government-wide foreign affairs machinery.

CURRENT PROBLEMS CONFRONTING AGENCY LEADERS

Questions being raised by Agency leaders and problems demanding their attention provide a way of finding out the directions in which United States Information Agency programs are moving, and an indication of what difficulties have not been resolved in the past. A quick review will demonstrate that USIA is looking ahead at the emerging world environment, is somewhat bound by past American foreign policy, has a growing awareness of the importance of its own history and that of its predecessor information programs, and responds to organizational changes imposed on the government-wide foreign affairs mechanism.

A major factor in the emerging world environment which must be taken into account by USIA and other foreign affairs agencies is the nation-building, modernizing, economic development surge of that large portion of mankind which with "rising expectations" is starting the change from traditional ways of life to modernity. USIA leaders are now aware of the Agency's potential role in nation-building, though USIA activities in the past were primarily limited to providing information support to the United States Agency for International Development missions overseas—except perhaps in Latin America where the Alliance for Progress necessitated broader information programs. Some top USIA policy officials now realize that motivation of change and even education to encourage acceptance of these modernizing activities which can usefully be undertaken at a particular stage in the development process are functions which USIA might fruitfully undertake in appropriate countries today—though they realize that USIA activities will vary in scale from country to country. Agency policy leaders have participated recently in conferences with the President's Advisory Committee on Foreign Assistance, chaired by James Perkins, president of Cornell University. In 1963, if USIA personnel had heard of Lucien Pye (by then considered a leading authority on communications and nation-building), [16] they did not mention him. By 1967, he served as consultant to USIA on questions concerning modernization. While liaison with the Agency for International Development is not closer at the working level in the Office of Policy and Research or at the country desk level in the area offices than it was in 1963, the Agency is concerned with the relative priority that should be assigned to education by electronic communications, as measured against the value of road-building or more traditional educational methods like communications devices to bring societies from tribalism to a sense of unity and nationhood. USIA representatives participated in government-wide consideration of new uses of television in international communication. Wilson Dizard, until 1967 an assistant deputy director of the Office of Policy and Research, is the author of a recent authoritative book on the present and potential worldwide uses of educational television. [17]

Historically, it has been characteristic of American foreign policy to attempt to isolate the United States from international disputes in which it has a vital interest. When finally driven by circumstances to take action, the American nation has often tended to over-involve itself, sometimes viewing its delayed actions in the national interest with self-righteousness as moral crusades. [18] In 1967, the United States was deeply involved in information activities reaching the people of Vietnam, and to a lesser extent those of Thailand; the depth of the involvement is indicated by the fact that 12 to 14 per cent of all USIA foreign service officers were serving in Vietnam. By decision of President Johnson in May, 1965, responsibility for all psychological action in Vietnam (except in direct support of military operations in the field) was delegated to the Director of USIA. [19] To implement the new responsibility, a Joint U.S. Public Affairs Office (JUSPAO) was established in Saigon; most of its 150 American personnel were regular USIA employees. JUSPAO's operations are carried out at both the national and provincial levels, addressed to the people. They are also directed to the Viet Cong, reached by radio, leaflet drops, airborne loudspeakers, and more indirectly by information provided to their relatives in government-held areas. JUSPAO also carries responsibility for reaching the North Vietnamese people, primarily by massive leaflet drops by the South Vietnamese and United States air forces. Voice of America Vietnamese-language broadcasts have been increased to six and a half hours daily. Television, motion pictures, periodicals, and newspapers supplement the other activities. In conducting massive psychological efforts to counter insurgency against the existing regime in South Vietnam, the Agency is performing a role which would normally be carried out by a government with its own people. Although attempts are being made by USIA personnel to train local government officials to take over this responsibility, they are not as yet very successful, for the population of Vietnam is not too nationally oriented and lacks motivation to learn to do what USIA is now doing for it. The growth of the American involvement can be indicated by changes in staffing in USIA required to backstop operations in Vietnam. From a one-man country desk in 1963, staffed by a FSCR-3 (middle level) USIA foreign service officer, present Agency backup of Vietnam activities is a five-man operation, headed by a deputy assistant director (of the East Asia and the Pacific Area Office) for Vietnam. In January, 1967, Agency officials just back from Vietnam or about to visit there considered the level of USIA operations in Vietnam and Thailand fascinating, but were ambivalent in their feelings as to whether USIA should be carrying out what would normally be the domestic information activities of foreign governments. In fact, USIA was drawn into its contemporary role because the job was not being done locally; and while the Agency is not really qualified to conduct such activist policies, it is in a better position than any other agency to do the required job, which supports the American military effort though directed at civilians. The fact that Agency personnel can question this involvement is significant, a sign that the old sense of American morality and righteous crusade has been replaced by a more mature attitude, a realization of the need for the United States to concern itself with realistic limits both on its commitments and goals in foreign areas. This new spirit is echoed by the feeling of concerned Agency leaders that the degree of stridency in present information policy directed toward mainland China needs to be carefully reviewed. It may be presumed that the Agency's China Policy will be reconsidered in the near future when the foreign affairs mechanism has done its research and paperwork and is ready to make a decision.

A government agency like USIA is in part a prisoner of its own past, never able to start over with a clean slate. It has set precedents and established patterns of behavior which limit perceptions of new possibilities. It has learned by doing, and earlier mistakes or successful experiences should not be forgotten. With many foreign service officers on the move, usually spending no more than two or three years at a post, there is need for a centralized Agency memory, both to know in detail the Agency's past and to store historical and present facts which may be needed at a moment's notice for use in policy making for the future. By 1967, USIA had a professional Agency historian actively at work on the history of United States information programs up to 1953 when the U.S. Information Agency was created. In 1963, personnel bemoaned the lack of an accurate and relatively complete Agency history which would serve as a review of past organization and policy. Any history then quickly available was based on the recollections of long-time Civil Service employees, many of whom are approaching retirement age, most with detailed knowledge of only a single segment of the Agency. The present one-man program to recapture the agency's past was finally established July 1, 1966, and the gathering of pertinent documents of both an official and unofficial nature is well begun. At the same time, the Agency also gained a small

Information Systems Staff which is engaged in developing procedures by which substantive information required for policy making or policy planning can be made available in Washington and at posts overseas for the use of rotating personnel. There is some current thought in the Agency that the rotation system borrowed from the diplomatically oriented Foreign Service of the United States is not really satisfactory to an Agency like USIA, which needs language expertise in esoteric languages, a thorough knowledge of local communications systems, and close friendly relations with local leaders overseas in order to carry out its tasks successfully. However, a system to make information rapidly available to policy makers would be necessary even if assignment periods at posts were lengthened. No human memory can adequately store and marshal the variety of information required. Furthermore, it is not likely that the rotation pattern will be significantly changed in the immediate future, so that processes for improving information retrieval will remain imperative for the foreseeable future. An Agency which has sought for over ten years to place most of its foreign service officers within the Foreign Service of the United States by lateral entry, and still would like to accomplish this purpose though it has made little progress to date, is not likely to set up a type of rotation plan which would serve to emphasize its differences from that Foreign Service—even though this should be no deterrent to unification. There was talk in USIA early as 1963 of computerized memory banks, and the Agency was even then cooperating in interagency programs to study such possibilities. The present effort is far more modest— perhaps more realistic for the time being. Many other things have greater priority than history and information retrieval in an Agency whose operational history indicates that it is fast-media conscious and day-to-day oriented. It will be some time before an information policy maker can punch out a situation, call upon the computer for pertinent information, feed the "facts" into a machine, and be provided with the "best" policy to meet the specific situation—taking into consideration relevant factors in American foreign relations throughout the world. Though man is imperfect, the machine will not soon be his master—or at least should not be.

A priority concern of the U.S. Information Agency in 1967 was the development of a Planning-Programming-Budgeting System (PPBS) in response to a presidential directive to twenty-two government agencies, including four out of five of the major foreign affairs agencies (Agency for International Development excluded) and most of the federal domestic agencies with substantial overseas interests, issued by the Bureau of the Budget on October 12, 1965.[20] When fully operational at USIS posts by 1970—if progress is made as planned—PPBS will make it possible for USIA leaders to study analyses of alternative objectives and alternative programs to meet objectives on a cost-benefit comparison basis from each of the Agency's 104 posts. The "new system" is related to the work done since 1963 by the Department of State on a Comprehensive Country Programming System, intended to increase the effectiveness of ambassadorial review of all American programs in his particular country, by providing him with information relating objectives, programs, and budgets of each agency functioning under his direction. The new system was in part responsible for the demise of the Research and Reference Service, which had been a major unit in USIA since the Agency gained independence, and the incorporation of those of its personnel studying program effectiveness into the Office of Policy—the newly joined segments becoming the Office of Policy and Research on July 1, 1966. By early 1967, USIA had experimentally introduced PPBS overseas, after drafting a "Program Memorandum"—incorporating objectives, programs, and budgets assessed against cost effectiveness—at the area office level in Washington for each of twelve USIS posts. Following a decision to move ahead rapidly with the PPBS program, planners in the Office of Policy and Research, working in consultation with the Office of Administration, drafted instructions on how to prepare a country "Program Memorandum" and forwarded the description of procedure to thirty-nine field posts. Headquarters personnel then attended regional public affairs officer conferences during the spring and summer of 1967 to explain further the Planning-Programming-Budgeting Systems and to discuss problems with field officers.

The purpose of PPBS is to collect information in a form which provides a better basis for making rational decisions concerning information policies and programs than was possible with the old Country Plan and the administrative budget—both still in use at most USIS posts. The administrative budget will have to be prepared even if or when PPBS has been installed at all USIS posts, because the submission of the Agency budget to Congress will still have to be done on an administrative unit rather than program basis. Congress has always believed, and still believes, that it can best prevent waste and promote efficiency by looking at administrative costs of things purchased or personnel hired to conduct programs. It is as yet unwilling to focus its primary attention on program cost-effectiveness. It has been suggested that the Congress would gain a better control of programs and budget if it would study a program budget for the upcoming year and an actual performance budget from the past year to check any waste or inefficiency. The Planning-Programming-Budgeting System is no cure-all either for the Congress or for solving USIA's problems of determining the effectiveness of Agency products. USIS personnel at posts will still have to judge whether they have persuaded people who count to change their minds or actions because of the use of a particular product. Though it is difficult to tell whether one million people seeing a movie has more or less impact than one million people seeing an exhibit, the relative costs of the two media per million exposures can probably be obtained. Unless the quality of the audience is significantly different, as it may sometimes be, ten million exposures are likely to be more valuable than one million, but not necessarily on a 10 to 1 ratio. By the study of who attends a movie or who reads a book, some gross presumptions are possible. PPBS will be dangerous if those using it believe it is accurate because they go through a special routinized process of marshaling information. PPBS is likely to be of more value as an emphasis, forcing USIS personnel to reassess programs, than as a mathematical means of projecting "accurate" results to be obtained by use of one or another among competing alternatives.

Issues other than those just cited as examples of problems related to the emerging world environment, to past American foreign policy behavior, to the history of information programs and the Agency's own past, or to the Agency's position as a foreign affairs agency within the government bureaucracy were also "worrying" USIA officials during 1967—all important in one way or another to improving Agency operations. Leaders were concerned with what new methods of information programming may be required in a more flexible and depolarized world; with how field inspections by assistant (Agency) directors for the area offices can be improved, consideration being given to visiting fewer posts but extending the period of time for each individual visit. There is still no adequate regular forum for the assistant directors of the area offices and media services to discuss broader Agency problems in a forward-looking way with top Agency leafers. There is a continuing tug and haul between how much of the Agency's programming should be prepared for use on a worldwide basis and how much focused on individual regions or countries—though the current trend is toward more individualization of product. There is renewed hope of getting a separate legislatively authorized foreign service for USIA (such a bill passed the Senate in the fall of 1967), but the concept of blanket entrance of present Foreign Service Career Reserve personnel into the O.S. Foreign Service has been given up (in the face of Senate opposition) as a means of providing an adequate foreign service system for USIA. Thus far the only complete step toward improvement of USIA's Foreign Service system is the annual induction of USIA's newly appointed foreign service officers into the Foreign Service of the United States, but it would take many years and much attrition among the senior members of USIA's present foreign service before all USIA officers overseas would become members of a common foreign service if no further steps are taken.

II

Limits on Information Policy:
Environmental Factors—Future, Past, and Present

The Brave New World and Historic Behavior

The United States Information Agency does not function in an environmental vacuum, its leaders able to reach policy decisions on the basis of theoretical considerations divorced from the brave new world of tomorrow, the old world of yesterday, or the transitional world of today. It is limited by, adjusts to, or finds opportunity in what it foresees, has seen, or currently sees —though its mechanisms for understanding the future, past, and present are as yet imperfectly developed. The Agency does look ahead, though few personnel are assigned a long-range planning function, for it must project its programs and budgets for a five-year period. It does look back, for it now has an Agency historian. It is well aware of day-to-day events, for a large portion of its personnel are engaged in meeting immediate problems. As early as 1957, the strident tone of Agency programs toward the Soviet Union was somewhat modified. As early as 1963, opportunities were seen for using a more reasoned approach toward certain influential elements in the Chinese Communist movement. Whether these shifts were made quickly enough, or whether they were sufficient fully to meet changing conditions and opportunities, may be relevant questions, but they are difficult to answer. The "new-sound" of the Voice of America in November, 1966, was a rather belated response to the end of jamming Voice broadcasts by the Soviet Union, to improved Soviet-American relations, a more prosperous Europe, declining bipolarity, and emergence of a pluralistic world. The signs of interest during 1966 and 1967 among leaders of USIA's Office of Policy and Research in the role of communications in nation-building, modernization, and development was a delayed response to the drive of the new developing nations for a better life. If the Agency has been slow to recognize the lessening of the Cold War and the rebirth of polycentrism or the true magnitude of the problem of creating modern nations from traditional societies, it may be in part because

25

neither the Agency nor the Department of State fully realized the scope of change taking place in the world nor the degree of effort which would be required to understand the emerging environment and adopt policies which would accept its limits and grasp its opportunities. Furthermore, much of the post-World War II foreign policy of the Department of State and information policy of the U.S. Information Agency and its predecessor organizations was limited by past patterns of American foreign policy behavior and the lack of experience of the United States as it assumed the role of a great power fully engaged in the world arena—no longer able to disengage itself from critical world problems. Policy makers and a nation's people are limited by their view of the nature of the evolving world environment and by habits of behavior which often persist beyond the time when they are functional.

An awareness of significant factors in the emerging world environment, which American policy makers need to take into consideration, and of some of the historic patterns of American behavior in the conduct of foreign relations will indicate the problem of developing forward-looking information policy and conducting effective information programs in a changing world. It is possible to single out five major trends or developments which are shaping a world different from the one we knew twenty years ago. These changes require modification of old habits of thought and action—both by policy makers and by ordinary citizens (American and otherwise). First, there is the impact of nuclear weapons systems, with their imperatives for limiting the resort to violence and for establishing new devices for world cooperation or integration.[1] Second, there is the social, economic, and political revolution de-stabilizing the less-developed areas, sometimes stimulating a sterile competition between ideologies, but requiring rational progress toward modernization assisted by the developed nations to make effective participation by the new nations in world affairs possible and future world stability probable.[2] Third, there is the changing internal nature of both communist and democratic societies, the former increasingly recognizing the importance of individual creativity to society; the latter, the importance of society to individual creativity. Whatever their stated ideologies, these developments downgrade the current differences in their philosophies or economic and political organization, inviting further depolarization and increased, though cautious, cooperation.[3] Fourth, the scientific and technological revolution, proceeding at breakneck pace, not only provides the means for more direct confrontation but also for satisfying human material needs, for increasing educational opportunities, and for exchanging views to develop mutual understanding. This revolution stimulates a dangerous population growth that must be halted if the benefits of science are going to improve individual opportunities and allow modernization of the new developing nations.[4] Fifth, there is the increasing importance of international or supranational organizations of a functional or regional nature which can assist in resolving problems that over-reach the capabilities of the traditional nation-state.[5] Policy makers in the United States have been about as tardy as their counterparts in other governments in adapting foreign and information policy to the requirements of the emerging world environment.

It would appear that the United States has not been realistic in assessing what might constitute a stable nuclear balance of power, first seeking counterforce capability and then maintaining a four-to-one ratio of missiles over the Soviet Union. Nor has it always been objective in fitting nuclear weapons into its defense policies. Who can forget the incredibility of "massive retaliation"? It is evident from a review of past American disarmament and arms control policy that the United States has not always taken positions which others could realistically accept—if agreement was in fact the goal of American foreign policy. Certainly American citizens and those of other nations have yet to be prepared psychologically for substantial arms reductions or controls which will make living tolerable in a nuclear environment. It is evident that the United States and the other developed nations have neither planned wisely enough nor sacrificed sufficiently to lead the developing nations toward take-off economically or toward as rapid a breakthrough to modernity as might be desirable either for world security or for increased world cooperation to lessen international tensions. There must now be a general awareness among scholars that the United States for far too long treated the Soviet Union[6] and the People's Republic of China[7] as unchanging monoliths, incapable of being influenced by policies pursued by other nations, of adopting new patterns of behavior, or of adapting their ideologies to meet world realities. Likewise, it seems possible that the United States has not foreseen all the consequences, the negative limits and positive opportunities for American policy in the world arena, of scientific and technological developments since World War II. Finally, any serious scholar of American participation in the United Nations must by now find it difficult to argue that the United States used its influence—when it was in a position of relative dominance in the United Nations—to strengthen that organization as a place for honest discussion and accommodation of conflicting interests. It seems all too obvious that the United Nations was not "the cornerstone" of American policy, but for many years served more as a useful policy tool in the Cold War. The nature of the world environment emerging after World War II necessitated changes in American foreign policy and in supporting information policy to assist in resolving problems or in seizing opportunities created by these five basic factors affecting world change. There has been a slowly growing recognition of this fact among government policy makers, and now the United States is moving almost grudgingly toward policies more compatible with developing trends. Identification of major emerging problems or environmental factors is relevant to foreign and information policy if it enables the governments concerned to reach decisions among reasonable alternatives and take responsible action—diplomatic, military, economic, and informational—alone or in concert, in international or supranational organizations, to help shape the future that can be created or to adapt to the future which cannot be held back.

A nation's past plays a major role in its present and can hardly help but influence its future. In many ways, the traditional responses of the American nation in world affairs are no more appropriate to a nuclear age than the ways of life in a traditional society are suited to nation-building, modernization, and development. Just as political leaders in developing nations find it difficult to find the proper mixture of respect for the past and steps toward the future, it was difficult for the policy makers of the Department of State who provided the general guidelines for information policy, formulated and implemented by USIA, to retool their policy-making machinery fast enough to meet new international responsibilities with maximum effectiveness. In an evolving world environment, yet dimly perceived, American policy makers had to act. Much of their behavior would have done credit to any great power in the past, but it was a different world. Just as actions taken by leaders in some developing nations place eventual attainment of modernization in jeopardy, the sum total of American actions since 1945 may have narrowed choices for the future, foreclosing alternatives which might have been far less costly. Instead of a prudent and persistent resistance to Soviet expansive pressures, the United States chose to wage a great ideological crusade—in which information programs were assigned an important part. The historic experience of the American nation shaped its foreign policy responses after World War II and in turn seriously affect what can be accomplished by USIA in many countries of the world in 1968, and perhaps for some years to come.

A summary review of historic American responses in international relations[8] will clarify American behavior patterns and their causes—and help explain lack of adaptation of American foreign and information policy to the world environment emerging after World War II. The United States as a young nation sought to isolate itself from the perils of great power politics.

Its geographic location and the opportunity to fulfil a continental destiny made such a policy feasible. Its lack of strength and limited experience in world affairs made such a policy practical. What was a boon to the internal development of the nation retarded maturation in matters of foreign policy, though it is possible that isolation helped preserve the nation's independence. Thus, the strength of the adolescent nation grew more rapidly than did its experience in dealing with the world outside its borders. Viewing European conflicts of the nineteenth century from across the broad Atlantic, Americans attributed their own noninvolvement to special virtues. They had little desire to enter into entangling agreements with the "evil" governments contesting in Europe and throughout the world for territory, trade, and power. Throughout the period of the nation's growth and democratic development —in spite of slavery before the Civil War and the race issue after—Americans viewed their social experiment as something unique and precious, to be preserved and developed as a model for other societies or in some fashion spread for the betterment of all mankind. This contributed to the feeling of moral superiority; during the long period of isolation, it built up a latent sense of mission that remained largely unfulfilled.

Growing naturally from the circumstances of the nation's development, there was a failure on the part of the American people and policy makers to grasp the realities of balance of power in an imperfect world, to understand the fortuitous circumstances which had allowed the United States to develop in relative peace and isolation. There was an over-idealization of the nature of man and a tendency to project the values which were suited to the American experience as those suitable for the entire world. As the nation became conscious of its power, toward the close of the nineteenth century, things that were "morally wrong" were viewed as in need of righting. When colonial peoples were mistreated as in Cuba, an American battleship sunk, the legal neutral rights of Americans disregarded on the high seas during wartime, religious groups mistreated in Nazi Germany, or war initiated by surprise attack, Americans had moral cause consistent with their sense of mission for which they could crusade. If Americans recognized by their entry into World War I or World War II the need to redress the balance of power in Europe somewhat belatedly, their motivations during the wars were still largely moral and their consciousness of postwar power politics somnambulant during the military struggles which were geared toward total victory and eradication of evil. American reaction to world events in the twentieth century was delayed by the fetish of isolationism until it became an over-reaction, with moral and idealistic overtones, hardly suited to rational or realistic peace settlements. The frustrations of dealing with men less idealistic, who sometimes were too "realistic," made moderate solutions of postwar problems difficult and reinforced the American desire for retreat from world responsibilities, which helped set in motion actions and reactions creating spirals of tension which threatened new cataclysms.

The historic patterns of American international behavior affected American foreign and information policy during and after World War II. After 1946, the over-reactions so typical of American policy were converted into harsher words and more strident propaganda toward the communist countries—a "Crusade for Freedom" directed from within the Department of State until creation of the independent United States Information Agency on August 1, 1953. After that time, with policy guidance provided daily by the Department of State to USIA, the Agency's products—including the Voice of America and the Wireless File—conveyed the fluctuating American policy line toward the Soviet Union, western Europe, or the Chinese Communists on a daily basis both to the areas directly concerned and to people almost everywhere in the world who were willing to listen. Although post-World War II American foreign and information policy was adversely colored by past experiences and traditional behavior patterns, there is legitimate hope that United States foreign and information policy have come of age in the 1960's, displaying a growing maturity that promises better performance in the future than in the past. Forced by nuclear realities, the United States has set itself and communicates more limited goals, has adopted policies—and stated them clearly to the world—aimed at achieving security which requires neither revolution in opposing states nor total victory. If there is an undeclared and slowly escalating war in Vietnam, Americans are no more eager to launch a crusade in Southeast Asia than they are willing to let the area fall to the North Vietnamese and their Viet Cong supporters—however much USIA broadcasts to India may raise fears of Chinese Communist aggression and allay them with a "strength image" of America.

For better or worse, there are many factors which make it difficult for USIA to forget the past completely and program only for the emerging, more cooperative world of the future. Many senior Civil Service employees in the Voice of America or in the Press and Publications Service have spent half of their productive years analyzing Soviet or Chinese Communist behavior with a critical eye. In some instances, these individuals are refugees from countries overrun or dominated by the Soviet Union or the mainland Chinese. As relations of the Soviet Union and the United States improved after 1962, there was a real and justified fear on the part of Agency personnel that people in many countries would come to believe there was no longer any reason to be cautious in future relations with the Soviet Union. There is still some leaning backward by Agency employees to offset hopes that may outrun realities. With its access to the flow of information available to the foreign affairs agencies, USIA is well aware that differences of interest between the Soviet Union and the United States continue in 1968, and the Soviet propaganda effort in many countries still distorts the American image. This requires counteraction, sometimes by reminding listeners of Soviet shortcomings by comparisons with the United States. The Soviet view of the struggle in Vietnam, if not the same as that of Communist China, is quite different from that of the United States government, and the Agency is engaged in a worldwide effort to explain and justify American policy in Southeast Asia. The Soviet Union is still competing with the United States before the eyes and through the ears of the people of the world in the scientific and technological development race, in protestations of peacefulness and willingness to disarm, in offers of technical or other forms of development assistance, in exchange programs giving opportunities for study or travel in the Soviet Union. For USIA to give up telling the American side of these same stories would be to turn over an "information victory" to the Soviet Union without a struggle. Furthermore, the Agency wants the Soviet people to continue their desire for more consumer goods, to recognize that their own government has not yet been able to resolve its agricultural problems. And, in any gentle way it can, the Agency hopes to encourage pluralism in eastern Europe—to offset the polycentrism so obviously developing in the Western alliance. If the Agency's approach is a "softer sell" in 1968 than in 1953, it is in part because such an approach is recognized as an effective means of influencing attitudes in a world trying to forget the Cold War. No one in USIA can be certain of the direction future relations with the communist powers may take. No doubt some conceive of a post-Maoist regime in Communist China that might reestablish a more tolerable level of Sino-Soviet relations—and are not certain what negative impact this might have on Soviet-American relations. Although the harshness of the propaganda line toward the Soviet Union is muted, the radio broadcasts, press and periodical activity, television shows, motion pictures, and books in information libraries continue to argue the cause of the United States versus the Soviet Union. If policy permits, as was the case on nuclear testing above ground or nuclear weapons in space, the Agency can call for cooperation between the Soviet and United States governments and their peoples. A harder line is taken throughout the world toward the Maoist regime and the current foreign policy of the Communist

Chinese, leaving open the hope for better Sino-American relations if time works changes in the nature of Chinese leadership.

There is such a residue of misinformation on or misunderstanding of the United States throughout the globe—probably only a fraction of it the fault of Soviet efforts in the past or Communist Chinese propaganda today—that there will long be a place for a positive information program to educate those willing to learn objective facts about the American polity, economy, and society as it now is and as it is becoming. Since nations and their leaders act on the basis of their perceptions, presentation of a "full and fair" picture of America and a careful gathering of information on the beliefs and attitudes of others by the U.S. Information Agency is essential if an adequate degree of cooperation to resolve the world's problems is to be achieved. "To see ourselves as others see us" is sometimes not a pretty picture. [9] Although interdependence is already forced upon nation-states, the informational prerequisites which will overcome historical misconceptions and educate their peoples to live secure, prosperous, and culturally cosmopolitan lives in a brave new world have not yet been created.

THE DEVELOPMENT OF AMERICAN OVERSEAS INFORMATION PROGRAMS

It is significant that United States efforts to win popular support for American policies overseas were conducted intermittently—primarily in time of war—until after World War II. At that time the wartime activities of the Office of War Information and the Office of Inter-American Affairs were transferred to the Department of State. Even then information programs were conducted in an atmosphere of Cold War, as yesterday's valiant ally became today's bitterest antagonist. When a nation is insecure—in war or its aftermath—its objectivity in analyzing itself and others is likely to deteriorate, especially if it lacks experience as a major participant in maintaining a balance of power in the world arena. Compounding this problem of formulating creative information policy in the immediate post-World War II years were the attacks on information programs and their administrators by Joseph R. McCarthy, the junior senator from Wisconsin, approaching the frightening height of his power just as the Department of State was transferring responsibility for information programs to the USIA in August, 1953. The McCarthy era's debilitating impact on United States information programs is best described by Martin Merson in *The Private Diary of a Public Servant,* specifically covering the period from February through July,

1953.[10] If information programs were initiated in times of national peril and continued in periods of international tension, the U.S. Information Agency was created when the very structure of American democracy was being sorely tested. This environment certainly colored the nature of information programs and purposes after August, 1953, as it had before that time, and made it more difficult to initiate adequate personnel programs for the new Agency.[11] It also drew the attention of members of Congress to criticisms of information programs and personnel, leaving a residue of distrust difficult to overcome, resulting in stricter congressional oversight of budgets and programs than might otherwise have been the case.

In such circumstances, it is not surprising that the real importance of USIA among the foreign affairs agencies of government was recognized only slowly. Many capable personnel had left the Agency, some driven from it; those with ability who remained found it difficult to replenish the losses—few ambitious young men or women were willing to risk their reputations by starting a government career in a new agency barely alive after the trial by fire. It is no wonder that Presidents did not provide USIA immediately with a prominent role in National Security Council affairs, that the Agency's loyalty to the United States had to be proved by a relatively harsh propaganda line toward the Soviet Union, and that the Agency would seek a personnel system adequate to its needs from 1953 through 1967 without congressional approval—whatever present hopes exist for a breakthrough in the future. That the Agency in 1968 does play a major role among the foreign affairs agencies of the United States government is evidence that USIA against great odds has overcome some of the limitations of the past. Emerging to a position of acceptance in the foreign affairs mechanism at a time when attempts are being made to synchronize the policies and programs of its parts, the Agency subjects itself to new limits imposed by the need to relate information policies ever more closely to the tasks of the Department of State, the Agency for International Development, and the Department of Defense.

From the time of the Revolutionary War onward, in periods crucial to the survival or progress of the United States, popular support for American policies has been sought overseas.[12] Benjamin Franklin, as he prevailed upon the French to intervene against the British in the war for independence, was an early if informal practitioner of the art of "propaganda." Abraham Lincoln, whose overtures to British workingmen to support the Union cause during the Civil War offended the British Foreign Office, also recognized the value of justifying United States government policies abroad. Such *ad hoc* ventures in reaching foreign publics, sporadic though they were, seemed natural to leaders of a young and democratic nation. Yet, it was more than 140 years after Franklin's visit to Paris that the American government formally created its first overseas information service. This step was taken by President Woodrow Wilson early in World War I, during April, 1917, with the appointment of George Creel to serve as chairman of a Committee on Public Information. The Creel Committee was authorized to seek domestic support for the war effort, but also had the task of operating overseas to counter the German propaganda effort. Creel himself considered "the fight for the minds of men" as of "almost equal significance" to victories or defeats in the muddy trenches of the Western Front. Congressional investigations and criticism, coupled with fear of official government propagandists influencing the American people, brought the Committee's work to an abrupt halt in March, 1919, shortly after the close of the war. There was not yet to be a permanent specialized government agency to tell the American story abroad.

It is true that within the Department of State a growing consciousness of the importance of public relations had led to regular use of the press conference by secretaries of state after 1913 to reach both domestic and foreign publics. In addition, materials were prepared in the Department during World War I and after for distribution through local channels abroad for publication in the foreign press. But, primarily, the Department worked through diplomatic channels, with only minor attention to foreign publics. During the 1920's and early 1930's, the American government was more interested in insulating its people from foreign propaganda than in competing with other powers in the world market place of ideas. If private international broadcasting had been initiated by American companies during the 1930's, there was not even an informal relationship of such efforts to American foreign policy until after 1939. By May, 1938, economic and propaganda penetration of Latin America by the Axis powers, Germany and Italy, led to the establishment of an Interdepartmental Committee for Scientific and Cultural Cooperation with the American Republics. This was followed in July, 1938, by a Division of Cultural Relations set up within the Department of State. These were small programs, reaching few people, more cultural than informational in impact, directed at Latin America.

As the war clouds thickened, with the fall of France and the beginning of the battle for Britain in August of 1940, the United States established the first of the "war agencies," the Office of the Coordinator of Commercial and Cultural Relations between the American Republics, headed by Nelson Rockefeller. This became the Office of the Coordinator of Inter-American Affairs (CIAA) on July 30, 1941. It was to have responsibility for the American information effort in Latin America throughout World War II. William

B. Donovan was named coordinator of information by President Franklin D. Roosevelt on July 11, 1941, and under him a Foreign Information Service headed by Robert E. Sherwood was created later in the summer. On February 24, 1942, Sherwood participated in the first broadcast by the Voice of America. When the Office of War Information (OWI) was set up under "Hoosier" Elmer Davis by Executive Order 9182 of June 13, 1942, the Foreign Information Service became the overseas branch of the OWI. Sherwood continued as director of OWI's overseas operations. CIAA and OWI are real progenitors of the United States Information Agency. Although they functioned in World War II and therefore engaged in "psychwar" activities "alien" to a "peacetime" USIA, they employed many of the same media to achieve their objectives. Television, of course, was not to appear until after the war. Both CIAA and OWI had difficulties in relating their work directly to specific government policies. In part, the problem was one of private individuals with communication knowledge drawn into government service temporarily fitting satisfactorily into the government bureaucracy. It was also a problem of the bureaucracy not allowing the "outsiders" a place high enough in the policy hierarchy to make the agencies privy to policy developments so that the agencies could effectively synchronize their efforts with new policies. Although much has been done in the ensuing years to improve the relationship of information policy and operations to American foreign policy, the early difficulties faced by CIAA and OWI, though greatly reduced, are not yet overcome.

Two years before the end of World War II, in 1943, CIAA's cultural operations were transferred to the Department of State. Then CIAA's duties were further modified and the agency renamed the Office of Inter-American Affairs (OIAA) by Executive Order 9532 of March 23, 1945. At the close of World War II, the transfer of all informational activities of OIAA and OWI to the Department of State was made by Executive Order 9608 of August 31, 1945. The transferred functions were integrated temporarily within an Interim International Information Service for a four-month period. Under William Benton as assistant secretary of state for public and cultural relations, large-scale wartime operations were phased out, informational needs surveyed, and a continuing program laid out. This interim body was succeeded at the beginning of 1946 by the Office of International Information and Cultural Affairs (CIC). CIC was still a transitional organization, fighting for its very existence, its budget and personnel reaching low ebb in 1947. Nonetheless, at the end of 1946, there were information staffs attached to seventy-six United States missions overseas, a daily 7,000-word wireless bulletin to forty missions for use of foreign publishers, a motion-picture service making films available in twenty-four languages, the Russian-language magazine *America* with a circulation of 50,000 sixty-seven information libraries and twenty-six cultural centers with forty-five branches, Voice of America broadcasts over thirty-six transmitters in twenty-five languages, as well as exhibitions and film strips for use of schools and other groups abroad. The 1946 budget of $31 million fell to $20 million in 1947. CIC was renamed the Office of International Information and Educational Exchange (USIE) in the fall of 1947 in a drastic reorganization. Legislative authorization for a worldwide information and cultural exchange program, in the works since 1946, was not achieved until Public Law 402 of the 80th Congress was signed by President Harry S Truman on January 27, 1948. William Benton, who had won the battle for legislative authorization, had already resigned as assistant secretary and had been replaced by George V. Allen. USIE was reorganized on January 28, 1948, being split in two. Now emerging were an Office of International Information (OII) and an Office of Educational Exchange (OEX). The so-called fast media were placed under the direction of OII, but libraries—later to be incorporated in USIA—were under the Office of Educational Exchange. In retrospect, the division of responsibility for informational and exchange activities within the Department of State in 1948 was an early step toward creation of a separate information agency in 1953.

Public Law 402 passed the Congress because "junketing" senators and representatives observed Soviet propaganda efforts in Europe firsthand during the fall of 1947 and were convinced that the people of other countries had to get a better understanding of the United States if they were to withstand the "aggressive psychological warfare" being conducted against America by the Communists. Public Law 402 enjoined the information service to tell the truth, explain United States motives, bolster morale of foreign populations, give a true picture of American life, counter misrepresentation, and support American foreign policy. The idea was to "sell" America. The new information service was intended to have a more direct and immediate impact than the cultural exchange program from which it was separated. The government service was viewed as supplementing or encouraging information efforts through private communications channels.

Although the information program had finally reached its nadir and now had the necessary recognition to attempt a comeback, it was still a long way from being out of the woods. Budgets began to increase, with $24 million in 1948, $33 million in 1949, and $47 million in 1950. Personnel rose from a low of about 2,500 to 4,370 in 1950. On the other hand, when the Department of State contracted out most of the overseas broadcasting to private firms, in keeping with the implications of Public Law 402 as to the government information program's supplemental role, congressmen objected to some of the scripts broadcast over the Voice of America and forced the Department to get back into full-scale broadcasting itself. The information output of the media divisions of OII, located far from where their products were being put to use, was often not tailored to specialized overseas needs. Establishment of a closer relationship of the media with the Department's country desk officers was an early attempt to meet this problem, but the relationship was a one-way street at best. Neither media personnel nor country desk men took advantage of this liaison to inject informational factors into foreign policy decisions. Well before the emergence of USIA as a separate agency in 1953, media operations in the United States were recognized as servants of the field. The introduction of individual country plans, prepared in consultation with field personnel, helped pinpoint specialized overseas needs.

In January, 1950, shortly after the first Soviet atomic explosion, in a speech before the American Society of Newspaper Editors, President Truman called for an expanded overseas information program, for a great "Campaign of Truth." The invasion of South Korea on June 25, 1950, and the American and United Nations response stimulated the Congress to appropriate ample funds for such a campaign. Including supplemental appropriations, more than $120 million were made available to the information service during 1951. If the Korean action brought increased appropriations, it also highlighted the need for greater coordination of the informational activities of the various agencies active in this field within the United States Government. Overseas information programs were being operated by military governments in occupied areas; by technical assistance, economic aid, and military assistance programs; and by the Department of State. Army broadcasts to its overseas personnel were picked up with relish by foreign audiences. America spoke abroad with many and sometimes conflicting voices. Military pressures upon President Truman resulted in the creation of an abortive Psychological Strategy Board (PSB) by Executive Order in 1951. Although the Board existed for about two years, it never quite found a role for itself and was dissolved in 1953; some of its functions were taken over by the Operations Coordinating Board established within the National Security Council structure. Critics point out that the PSB never had a chance, because psychological strategy is an integral part of the grand strategy of a nation, inseparable from political, economic, and military factors. The PSB apparently had little influence upon actions in the other fields, though its membership included the under secretary of state, the deputy secretary of defense, and the director of the Central Intelligence Agency. The Board's failure resulted not only from the problem of relating its works to the specialized needs of overseas operations but also from its inability to gain acceptance of PSB plans by the interested executive branch agencies.

In 1949, the Hoover Commission task force on foreign affairs felt that it would be desirable to separate the information and exchange programs from the Department of State, but as a practical matter recommended a lesser step. A general manager of the International Information and Educational Exchange Program was suggested, as a means of giving the programs more operating flexibility and relieving the assistant secretary of state of unnecessary detail. The suggestion was adopted by the Department. In a further move to give the information and exchange programs "independence" of action, they were given semiautonomous status within the Department by the creation of an International Information Administration (IIA) in January, 1952. The administrator of IIA reported directly to the secretary and under secretary of state and had greater administrative responsibility than had been given to the general manager. IIA was one further step toward establishment of a separate information agency.

Although these actions were helpful to the information program, the climate of opinion arising from warfare in Korea affected the tone of the information output, giving it a shrillness and rote anticommunism which cost the program any effective subtlety. *America* ceased publication under harassment from the Soviet Union. Credibility of the program's outpourings deteriorated abroad, even in "neutral" countries. Yet, there were those in the United States who thought the information program was not hitting hard enough against the Communists. The IIA program became an election issue in 1952, and was the subject of four simultaneous investigations at one point shortly after the Eisenhower administration took over in January, 1953. President Eisenhower had pledged during his campaign to make an attempt to increase the efficiency and effectiveness of government psychological activities. He kept his promise by appointing the President's Committee on Foreign Information Activities, with William H. Jackson as its chairman. The Senate Foreign Relations Committee, under the leadership of Senator Bourke Hickenlooper, had begun a careful bipartisan review of the information and exchange programs in the summer of 1952. The House of Representatives was conducting an investigation of program finances. More publicized than any of the first three, and psychologically damaging in its impact upon the information and exchange programs though it turned up little new information, was the witch-hunting expedition by a subcommittee of the Senate Government Operations Committee under Senator McCarthy's leadership, searching for Communists and sexual perversion. At the height of the congressional crossfire, Wilson Compton, administrator of IIA, resigned; he was followed as administrator by Robert L. Johnson, who also resigned shortly. Two competent university presidents up and two down. On top of these losses, appropriations were cut to $85 million, and a 25 per cent reduction in force was necessitated. Morale in IIA reached a new low; its programs ground almost to a halt; then the pressure eased late in the spring of 1953.

Although the Jackson Committee had not at first accepted the idea of a separate information agency, it finally approved a recommendation for separation by a committee studying reorganization of the executive branch headed by Nelson Rockefeller. John Foster Dulles, the new secretary of state, anxious to rid the Department of State of operational duties, also pushed for a separate information agency. As a result, Reorganization Plan No. 8, calling for a separate and independent information organ—the United States Information Agency—was presented to the Congress on June 1, 1953. When Congress took no negative action within the period allotted for its consideration of the plan, USIA came into existence on August 1, 1953. The new Agency was to continue to receive foreign policy guidance from the Department of State. The exchange of persons program was to remain in the Department, though USIA was to administer the exchange program overseas, because Senators J. William Fulbright and Karl Mundt—friends of the information and exchange programs—wanted to protect the educational exchange activities from too close an identification with "propaganda" activities in a separate agency. Theodore Streibert, a former New York radio executive, was appointed as the first director of USIA. It took the new agency almost a year to recover from surgery—the McCarthy attacks, its major reorganization and relocation, and the reduction in force carried through by the Eisenhower administration in the name of economy in government. By mid-1954, the Agency's administrative structure had been stabilized; reduction in force was a harsh memory; and the influence of Senator McCarthy was fast fading. USIA could now get on with its assigned tasks. There was much to be done.

Streibert, a tough, organizationally minded administrator was less interested in matters of information policy than in "getting more transmitters on the air" with money which had been appropriated several years before. Many policy matters were handled by Abbott Washburn, USIA's first deputy director, who was to serve with quiet distinction in the Agency until the appointment of Edward R. Murrow as director by President John F. Kennedy early in 1961. Washburn, a former manager of the Department of Public Services for General Mills, Inc., who had served as executive secretary of the Jackson Committee, was politically close to the White House during the Eisenhower administration. By the time Streibert resigned to return to private business in 1956, he was credited with having created a sound administrative framework for USIA and with restoring the morale of the Agency's personnel. He had taken the first steps toward improving the Agency's status in such interagency coordinating bodies as the National Security Council and the Operations Coordinating Board. Even before an Executive Order made USIA a member of the Operations Coordinating Board, Streibert had been invited first to luncheon meetings and then to all meetings of the Board. He was also invited to attend some National Security Council meetings. On such occasions, as USIA's representative, he "sat in the second row"—not "at the table" with the members—and participated only when called upon. Within the USIA, Streibert appointed roving area directors who spent half of their time in Washington and half in the field, thus bringing an awareness of the needs and problems of USIA's overseas missions more directly to bear on media products. He also began to modify the harsh, shrill propaganda line that had developed during the Korean affair and which endangered the Agency's effectiveness in many parts of the world. The Voice of America operations, at congressional suggestion, were brought to Washington from New York in 1954—a move which was to make the Voice somewhat more responsive to policy direction by the Agency. *America,* dropped during the Korean conflict, reappeared as *America Illustrated* in October, 1956, to enlighten Russian readers about American culture and life.

Arthur Larson, a distinguished labor-law expert, formerly a law professor at Cornell University, and then dean of the University of Pittsburgh Law School, became the Agency's second director on November 10, 1956. Larson was known politically for the excellent ideological advice contained in his book, *A Republican Looks at His Party,* and as a speech writer and idea man for President Eisenhower. Although his personal relationship with the President allowed him to sit "at the table" in National Security Council meetings after his appointment as director of USIA, his political background did not sit well with a Democratic Congress. During his brief tenure he gave consideration to tailoring media products to meet needs in individual countries and made a great effort to restore USIA's credibility with overseas listeners. In keeping with President Eisenhower's "People to People Program," he gave emphasis to expanding cooperation with private groups, initiating relationships between specific American cities with sister cities overseas. Lacking a real foreign relations background, Larson was still feeling his way and attempting to increase his understanding of the Agency when the Democrats attacked him roundly for what they considered to be inappropriate political remarks in a speech and followed this up by sharply reducing USIA appropriations. This led to his resignation as director and to the appointment in November, 1957, of George V. Allen, the career diplomat who had earlier taken over direction of the information and exchange program in 1948 after its appropriations had been slashed in 1947. Allen was to serve as director until August, 1960, when Washburn became acting director during an interim period until Murrow was appointed as the Agency's fourth director on January 21, 1961, with Donald M. Wilson as deputy director.

Although the Agency's daily handling of short-run problems did not diminish in importance during George Allen's period of leadership, Allen is remembered more for his efforts to concentrate on a positive, objective, and long-range approach, emphasizing the full and fair picture of American life and culture, and seeking to find areas of mutual interest shared by the United States and its people with other nations and peoples. He felt that more subtle information efforts in the long run would yield solid overseas support for United States foreign policy—or at least make it more tolerable or less objectionable. During his service as director, there was more teaching of English abroad, more publication of American books in translation, more worldwide English broadcasting over the Voice of America, greater participation in international trade fairs, and a larger number of American experts and professional men sent overseas to talk with foreign publics. He had a solid background of experience in foreign affairs and was quite capable of relating foreign policy to information policy and operations. He kept somewhat aloof from daily operations, however, because of his greater interest in the long-term approach. The close relationship of the Agency to the President was continued during his tenure, and he was a full participant in National Security Council affairs. Abbott Washburn, who worked with him as deputy director, was largely responsible for administrative matters, as he had been during Larson's period as director. A man of balanced interests and capabilities, with Agency experience both in policy and administration, Washburn was well fitted to serve as acting director during the period between Allen's resignation and the takeover by Murrow and Wilson.

In spite of real progress by USIA after 1953 under Streibert, Larson, Allen, and Washburn, a number of recalcitrant problems remained for the Agency to cope with under Democratic administrations in the 1960's.

Expansion of facilities and operations had been slow during the Agency's first eight years of existence. Budgets fluctuated through fat and lean years, from $84 million in 1954 to $102 million in 1959, with a low of $77 million in 1955 and a high of $113 million in 1957. Although USIA sought a legislatively authorized career service from the Streibert period on, Congress always turned a deaf ear to its pleas. A career service established administratively by USIA, patterned after the Foreign Service of the United States, became operational in 1960, but it only partially met the Agency's real needs. Directors sought in a variety of ways to find an efficient means of evaluating the results of Agency programs, but they found it difficult to create a satisfactory organizational device or to utilize any really precise methods of measurement. When the separate information program was established in 1953, the Department of State kept responsibility for the cultural and educational exchange programs. This left USIA employees administering exchange programs overseas for the Department of State, a questionable practice to many observers but one to which no easy solution has yet been found. Most significant of all was the Agency's struggle through the years to gain recognition of the information factor in foreign policy discussions well before decisions were finalized. In spite of some improvement, adequate coordination of political, military, economic, and psychological or informational factors in policy formulation and execution remained a serious problem for the U.S. government in 1961.

Edward R. Murrow's prestige as a nationally known and respected television personality rubbed off on USIA, and employee morale was high during his period of leadership. Murrow had twenty-five years of experience with the Columbia Broadcasting Service, serving as vice president, director of public affairs, and member of the Board of Directors before accepting his USIA assignment. Deputy director of the Agency under Murrow was Donald M. Wilson, who had worked eleven years with *Life* magazine and then as a member of President Kennedy's press staff during the 1960 campaign. Although the deputy director could have served as alter ego to the director and had Agency interests across the board, the two men divided their responsibilities, until Murrow's health failed when Wilson increasingly assumed a broader role. For the most part, Murrow tended to be Mr. Outside and Wilson, Mr. Inside. This is another way of saying that the director was more involved in interagency affairs, in congressional and public relations, or in consideration of broad long-range policy. The deputy director concerned himself more with intra-Agency affairs, with administrative matters, and day-to-day operations. In fact, the director was drawn into many short-term operations, and the deputy director often thought in long-range terms: the director was interested in some Agency administrative problems, and the deputy director attended many interagency policy conferences. The working relationship was flexible, with adjustments made according to workload, special interests, and in time Mr. Murrow's illness. If Murrow's modesty prevented him from consciously bringing the full weight of his personal power to bear upon President Kennedy, he was accepted nonetheless as a close adviser to the President on international affairs when psychological factors were invloved. The Agency's White House relations had never been better. Wilson's direction of the Agency's day-to-day working relationship was considered exceptionally good. He actually ran the Agency for a period of about six months when Murrow was in poor health before Carl T. Rowan was appointed by President Lyndon B. Johnson as Agency director. The Murrow period will be remembered for its emphasis upon relating media programs and products to foreign policy. If cultural programs of a less policy-directed nature were not actually downgraded, many in the Agency felt that at the very least the balance between the short-range impact activities and longer-range cultural matters had been seriously disturbed.

When Rowan assumed direction of the Agency on February 28, 1964, he attempted to carry forward the new policy emphasis. Rowan as director tended to delegate more responsibility within the Agency, discontinued a Wednesday afternoon discussion and "think session" with area and media directors that had been valued by its participants, and perhaps found the task of influencing the White House more difficult in the Johnson administration than it had been for Murrow with Kennedy as President. Rowan came to USIA with experience as a newspaper reporter, as an author, as deputy assistant secretary of state for public affairs, and as ambassador to Finland. One of his most important actions during his tenure as director was his joint signature with Secretary of State Dean Rusk in September, 1964, of an interagency agreement providing for the lateral entry of USIA Foreign Service Career Reserves into the Foreign Service of the United States. Unfortunately, this action was not to get support from the Senate Committee on Foreign Relations. Rowan offered his resignation as director of the Agency to President Johnson in July, 1965, and returned to the newspaper field as a nationally syndicated columnist. Wilson, who had remained as deputy director during the Rowan period, playing a major role in Agency affairs, offered his resignation in August, 1965, to become general manager of Time-Life International. Leonard Marks and Robert Akers became director and deputy director of USIA on September 1, 1965. Much had been accomplished by

USIA and its directors since 1953, but there was more to be achieved if USIA was to fulfil its actual potential to serve the national and world interest in an enlightened way. On October 12, 1965, scarcely a month after Marks and Akers officially assumed their new duties, President Johnson's directive calling for development of a Planning-Programming-Budgeting System by some twenty-two agencies of the government was issued. This was just one reminder that USIA functions within a wider government structure.

USIA AND FOREIGN POLICY: THE GOVERNMENT-WIDE SETTING

The United States Information Agency is only one among many agencies of government involved in the formulation and implementation of American foreign policy; its products are directed outward to influence publics in other nations rather than inward to educate the domestic public. As American involvement in world affairs has grown in scale, and as the American commitment to sustained participation has been institutionalized, the processes of making and carrying out government overseas policy have become more complex. Some knowledge of post-World War II developments in the government-wide policy machinery are necessary in order to understand the role of the external "information machine" within the U.S. government foreign policy mechanism. [13]

By tradition, though the primary responsibility for the conduct of foreign affairs rests with the President, the Department of State and its secretary have been the President's "strong right arm" in initiating and executing foreign policy. Even though this relationship still exists today in large measure, there is now broader participation in the consideration of foreign policy matters by other government agencies. The competition with the secretary of state for the ear of the President poses problems for all concerned, but the potential effectiveness of American participation in world affairs may be increased as a result of better coordination of policy initiatives or reactions to overseas problems.

American pre-World War II interests abroad had been limited in nature, somewhat passive or responsive, calling for occasional negotiations, but consisting largely of political and economic reporting or the performance of consular functions. The so-called Foreign Service generalists who carried out most of the overseas tasks were in fact rather narrow specialists, hardly expert in military, economic, or informational matters. They were suited by selection and training to the tasks they performed. The secretary of state, dependent upon such a staff, also became a diplomatic and political specialist, his vision narrowed by the type of staff work done for him and the relative inactivity of the United States in world affairs. American participation in World War I had been tardy, followed by a quick return to isolation and insulation; the experiences of 1917-18 did relatively little to broaden Department of State concerns or to elevate the interests of other government agencies in overseas problems.

The impact of World War II was a different matter. Not only was the involvement more prolonged and the cost greater, but the United States emerged at the close of the war as one of the super powers, no longer able to escape worldwide responsibilities without irreparable consequences to its security and way of life. During the course of the war, diplomatic, military, economic, and informational policies had to be formulated and implemented—with a degree of internal and external coordination never before attempted, and not always successfully achieved. The experience of collaboration with other states during the war helped swing the American role overseas from its historic isolation and passivity to broad involvement and continued participation. An effective assumption of this new role required the creation of new peacetime foreign affairs agencies (for example, the Economic Cooperation Administration in 1949 and USIA in 1953) the upgrading of overseas interests of the old-line domestic departments, and coordination of their disparate but potentially related activities. As the interrelationship of political, military, economic, and information policy was being recognized, the boundary line between foreign and domestic policy was fading away. International actions, it was discovered, influenced the domestic posture; domestic actions affected the international posture. To complicate matters further, American diplomats and propagandists were no longer reserves to be called up in time of international emergency. They were on the front line of a Cold War. Therefore, the new and complex machinery of policy formulation and implementation had to be geared for instantaneous operational reaction to onrushing world events, without losing sight of long-range goals relevant to the developing world environment. Since the policy machinery is really a mixture of people and procedures, molded by both habit and past knowledge or needs, it is not surprising that even with an awareness of new problems the adaptation of the governmental mechanism to meet its world affairs responsibilities has been less than perfect—though substantial improvement has occurred. The very size of the complex machine, too large for any one man to understand fully, is a problem. The variety of resources, skills, perspectives, and information which lie within it cannot easily be drawn upon to serve the President, as chief policy maker, in the national interest. How well the machine is staffed and organized to enable the President to make rational policy decisions and to help him gain acceptance of them at home and abroad may be the critical determinant of future national progress, survival, decline, or demise.

Still occupying a central role in the initiation and execution of foreign policy after World War II was the Department of State. The Department's regional bureaus were in touch daily with American embassies around the world, and the information the department received was widely disseminated throughout the government. In the years since the war, its officers have chaired (many if not) most intergovernmental committees dealing with foreign affairs matters, unless the concern was clearly at a technical level rather than of a broad foreign policy nature. Although the Foreign Service of the United States serves the interests of a number of other government agencies as well as the Department of State, most Foreign Service officers have been interested primarily in the concerns of the Department and preferred to serve in its regional bureaus when on Washington assignment rather than with other agencies. After its founding by Department of State order on May 8, 1947, the Department's Policy Planning Staff under George Kennan's direction gave the Department of State a clear edge over other government departments and agencies in influencing postwar overseas policies. The creation of the National Security Council by Public Law 253 of the 80th Congress on July 26, 1947, was eventually to downgrade for a period the role of the staff and the Department as the more ponderous National Security Council structure developed during the Eisenhower administration. The shift was less apparent because of President Eisenhower's high personal regard for Secretary Dulles, but the committee work—in which USIA representatives participated—to prepare for National Security Council (NSC) sessions or for agreed implementation of NSC policies approved by the President reduced Department of State officials to the position of committee members, though often they were committee chairmen.

The coming of the Kennedy administration in 1961 brought changes which both strengthened and weakened the Department's position in foreign affairs. The President himself played an active role, often overruling Department positions. Although President Eisenhower wanted the various interested departments and agencies to reach agreement, if possible, within the National Security Council framework and only "splits" were brought to him for decision, President Kennedy wanted to know the basic disagreements before they had been covered over by diplomatic generalizations. He made decisions which were clearly on one side or the other of an issue rather than based on a compromise between department or agency positions. The old National Security Council structure was simplified, and the role of the Policy

Planning Staff—renamed the Policy Planning Council—elevated. Members of the Council played a major role in the preparation of new Policy Guideline Papers and later National Policy Papers to replace those ground out over a fourteen-year period by the National Security Council procedures. The Department of State was given the primary role in developing policy. While State officials were to consult other interested parties in government (for example, USIA), the recommendation to the President was to be that which State considered best. Such recommendations could be appealed, and were. The use of National Security Council meetings for discussion purposes was sharply reduced by President Kennedy and cut even more by President Johnson— who preferred to meet for luncheon discussions with the secretary of state, the secretary of defense, and his adviser for International Security Affairs (Dean Rusk, Robert McNamara, and McGeorge Bundy or W. W. Rostow), a development that tended to relegate USIA and some other NSC participants to the sidelines. Formal meetings of the NSC fell to perhaps three in six months under President Johnson and were primarily held to underscore the importance of particular decisions by the President. On the other hand, during the Kennedy administration, the primary responsibility of the Department of Commerce for promoting American exports, of the Department of the Treasury for certain international economic matters related to balance of trade, and of USIA for overseas information programs tended to delimit State's scope of activity and concern, increasing the problem of coordinating overseas policies by dispersion of responsibility to an increasing number of agencies. President Johnson continued this practice.

Recalling the U.S. Information Agency's advisory role to foreign affairs or federal domestic agencies with policies which may have a psychological impact overseas, the number of departments and agencies with interests abroad and the variety of their interests which may affect foreign policy poses a real control problem—not only for USIA but also for the President himself. Among the major foreign affairs agencies, in addition to the Department of State and USIA, are the Department of Defense, with its obvious interest in weapons systems, manpower, and military policy; the Agency for International Development, with its politico-economic interests in economic development and modernization; and the covert Central Intelligence Agency, which collects information not obtainable through normal diplomatic sources and conducts operations which cannot be acknowledged by overt agencies of government. Among the lesser foreign affairs agencies are the Export-Import Bank, which makes hard loans repayable in dollars, usually for purchasing goods (including arms) from American sources of supply, and the Development Loan Fund, which makes soft loans repayable in the currency of the borrowing country for economic development projects, often in situations with heavy political overtones. More highly publicized is the Peace Corps, created by the Kennedy administration to render a host of "nonpolitical" technical assistance services to less-developed countries upon request. Working in a difficult but important field is the United States Arms Control and Disarmament Agency, responsible for research on arms control, for international negotiation on arms reductions or controls, and for directing American participation in any arms control system arranged by treaty. Also conducting programs overseas relevant to the successful conduct of American foreign and information policy are five federal domestic agencies: Agriculture, Treasury, Commerce, Labor, and Health, Education, and Welfare. The Department of Agriculture maintains overseas agriculture attachés who are the chief suppliers to the U.S. government of world agricultural "economic intelligence," reporting on marketing opportunities abroad and on foreign production that might compete with American commodities. The Treasury Department maintains representatives abroad who observe and report on financial and monetary developments related to a country's balance of payments, reserve, and exchange rate situation—and on the fiscal implications for the United States. Department of Commerce overseas interests are mostly met by commercial specialists within the Foreign Service of the United States who report on the needs of foreign importers and on resources for export that are of interest to American businessmen and manufacturers. These specialists now provide commercial services overseas, conduct trade promotion operations, and do market research. Department of Labor overseas interests are serviced by labor attachés who are members of the Foreign Service. These attachés gather and appraise information on foreign labor movements and developments, and attempt to promote an understanding of the United States, its foreign policies and methods of labor organization in labor circles. Health, Education and Welfare is engaged in activities calculated to encourage relationships between foreign and American educators, and its role will be substantially upgraded if and when the International Education Act of 1966 is funded by the Congress.

Other domestic agencies with significant overseas interests affecting American foreign relations include the Atomic Energy Commission, the Federal Aviation Agency, the Department of Justice, the National Aeronautics and Space Administration, and the Department of Interior. To mention all of these agencies still neglects the Civil Service Commission, responsible for personnel requirements under which many of the domestic affairs agencies must function overseas, or the Bureau of the Budget, which must assist the President in blending the budgets of this variety of agencies into a program mix which will be in the national interest, not only in individual countries but in its total worldwide impact.

Such a summary of the interests of some of the major government agencies whose activities in Washington or overseas affect the effectiveness of American foreign and information policy begins to suggest the problems faced by the President of the United States in coordinating policy and action in the contemporary world—and indicates some of the organizational and policy limits within which USIA must function. The task of forging consensus on goals, and an effective degree of consistency in implementing policies designed to achieve them, among powerful departments and agencies was and is a formidable challenge to the concept of presidential leadership of the executive branch and to the primacy of the Department of State in foreign affairs.

As dispersive forces threatened the effectiveness of policy making and its implementation at home and abroad, a major organizational device designed to strengthen or maintain presidential control over foreign affairs was the National Security Council, functioning under the National Security Act of 1947, as amended. Serving as a coordinating forum, located in the Executive Office of the President, it is the highest committee in the executive branch of the federal government for the resolution of national security and foreign policy questions. Its statutory members are the President, vice president, secretary of state, secretary of defense, and the director of the Office of Emergency Planning.[14] Government leaders such as the secretary of the treasury, the director of the Bureau of the Budget, and the director of the U.S. Information Agency have standing invitations to participate in NSC discussions. The chairman of the Joint Chiefs of Staff and the director of the Central Intelligence Agency are always present in an advisory capacity. Other government leaders are invited if formalized items of interest to their agencies are to be discussed. The National Security Council's interdepartmental nature and the formalized multiple working levels that hammered out papers destined for its consideration or that prepared papers to guide detailed implementation of those NSC papers approved by the President resulted in many compromises and weakened action taken during the Eisenhower administration. To strengthen the hand of the Department of State, in an effort to give policy decisions a sharper cutting edge, President Kennedy, on February 18, 1961, had revoked the executive order which had created the Operations Coordinating Board. The Board, through its subordinate interagency working groups had since 1953 discussed and agreed on what programs each participating government agency would conduct in support of policies approved by the President after discussion in the National Security Council. Kennedy also abolished the NSC Planning Board, which had attempted to achieve some degree of interagency agreement before discussions were held with the President at the National Security Council level. After February, 1961, though the Department of State was required to consult other agencies, it did not have to accept their views. Thus, the Department of State could make decisions, escaping the compromise problems of the Eisenhower administration. In fact, a good bit of the formal organizational underbrush which had been cut back quickly re-emerged informally—if it ever actually disappeared, because State found it necessary to reach some degree of consensus at the working level or risk having other agencies take their cases against State's position to the President. With no government-wide system to provide interagency oversight of the more informal system, the charge was soon made that there was too little coordination. Several informal or *ad hoc* committees might be working on aspects of the same problem without knowing what the others were doing. A presidential adviser might call a group together on a special problem without realizing that there was an overlap with an existing committee.

In March of 1966, with the National Security Council serving more as a psychological platform from which President Johnson could announce policy than as a forum for interagency discussion, a new two-level interagency coordination system was announced by the President. Now established was a Senior Interdepartmental Group (SIG) to be chaired by Under Secretary of State George Ball, and Interdepartmental Regional Groups, to be chaired by the appropriate assistant secretaries of state. Serving on SIG, with the under secretary of state, were to be the under secretary of defense, the assistant secretary of defense for international security affairs, a representative of the chief of staff of the military services, the director of the Central Intelligence Agency, the administrator of the Agency for International Development, and the director of USIA. SIG met weekly until Under Secretary of State Ball's resignation in September, 1966. Although the new under secretary of state, Nicholas deB. Katzenbach, expressed interest in SIG, he called no meetings of the group until the fall of 1967. The Interdepartmental Regional Groups (IRG's) have representation from the same organizational elements as SIG, but at the regional level—i.e., the assistant secretary of state responsible for a regional bureau or the assistant director of an area office in USIA. IRG's have met regularly since March 1966, some weekly, others more or less often. In both new organs, the state representative is executive chairman, empowered to make decisions after consultation

—formalizing Kennedy's assignment of leadership to state in 1961. State also outranks other participants in interagency meetings at the country level since March 1966, when its country desk level was overlayed by "country directors" of higher rank.

SIG has been active since the fall of 1967, sometimes meeting twice a week on questions related to foreign assistance legislation, balance of payments, or Cyprus. SIG has also begun review of resource allocations of the foreign affairs agencies, aided by the cost-effectiveness analyses of the new Planning-Programming-Budgeting System (PPBS). The IRG's display a similar interest in PPBS analyses at the regional level. PPBS, which increases the effectiveness of program review in Washington, has largely replaced state's experimental Comprehensive Country Programming System—intended to increase the effectiveness of ambassadorial review and control of all American programs in a particular country. It is said that the timing of PPBS submissions from the field with different deadlines by the agencies in Washington makes it more difficult for the ambassador to judge the internal balance among agency programs in his country. Thus, Washington control of program review by SIG and the IRG's under strong department of state leadership is upgraded.

Even with new balances of power among the foreign affairs agencies and between Washington and the field, informal advice to the President, on information policy or on the psychological impact of other government policies overseas, will often be provided by the director of the USIA. The relationship of the USIA Director with the President can be impersonal but influential because of national reputation, as was the case with Murrow and Kennedy. It can be personal and influential, because of past friendship and successful cooperation, as in the case of Marks and President Johnson. In providing the President with sound advice, the Agency Director will depend primarily upon his own small staff in the Office of the Director and upon the Office of Policy and Research, supplemented by information gathered from almost any Agency element or USIS post overseas.

III

A View from the Top:
The Office of the Director

In Search of Purpose and Effectiveness

In its early years, under Theodore Streibert, USIA was a rather strident propaganda machine, still conducting a "Crusade for Freedom" and emphasizing anticommunist themes; its products were relatively hard hitting and far from subtle, a mechanism of bipolarity in the tense post-World War II confrontation of East and West. Streibert was more interested in getting the machinery to operate and making USIA business-like than in any real change in the policy line. In the face of developing pluralism in both East and West after 1956, post-Hungary and post-Suez, Arthur Larson sought to modify the harshness of approach, to increase the Agency's overseas reputation for credibility, to adapt Agency products to individual countries, and to encourage the cooperation of American private groups with their counterparts overseas. In 1957, George Allen further downgraded the negative short-term thrusts and emphasized the "full and fair picture" of America, cultural understanding, and products less directed to the achievement of immediate political advantage. Such a thumbnail analysis of the period from 1953 to 1961 may be an oversimplification, but it is a gross indicator of Agency trends during the Eisenhower administration.

The new Kennedy administration which took over in 1961 was dedicated to breaking the stalemate between East and West, to getting "America on the move." It was too sophisticated a regime to return to the bombast of the early Eisenhower period, yet dissatisfied with the almost immeasurable long-term results likely to accrue from the more cultural approach of USIA under Director Allen. After Edward R. Murrow assumed direction of the Agency in March, 1961, there was a dramatic change in purpose and programming which heightened the importance of USIA's policy relationships with the White House, the Department of State, and other foreign affairs agencies. From tending "to tell America's story around the world" to everyone every-

52

where—or to anyone anywhere who would listen—the Agency rather abruptly made a greater attempt to "target" its products to selected audiences, choosing the "best" techniques available to reach them with specialized messages. From building good will and friendship or a general understanding of American life and culture, the Agency shifted its emphasis "to achieve maximum influence leading to political action." The themes of all the media were to be synchronized, their messages, hopefully, made mutually supporting. When "freedom of choice" by the people of Berlin concerning their political future became a key element in American information policy, USIA's media and field posts were to carry the message, carefully related (if possible) to local problems, to influential foreign audiences capable of acting to support American policy—either domestically or in the international arena. In retrospect, the political action "now" emphasis under Director Murrow—responding to President Kennedy's pressures to sharpen Agency purposes and programs—was an over-reaction to Director Allen's approach. Events of the time, including the Cuban missile crisis and Soviet policy on Berlin, made the politicization of information policy appear realistic to many observers and Agency personnel—if not to USIS field officers. Although Carl Rowan assumed Agency leadership in February, 1964, to serve as director in the new Johnson administration, he continued the tone and emphasis initiated by Murrow—slightly amended after the Soviet Union ceased to jam Voice of America broadcasts in 1963 as Soviet-American relations thawed.

Director Leonard Marks, after September, 1965, slowly embarked on a new course, without noisy fanfare. In 1968, the political action emphasis may remain, but it is balanced by a renewed interest in and respect for cultural affairs. The worldwide emphasis on themes of the Murrow period is gone, replaced by a recognition of the need to use only those themes suited to individual field posts—with many media products produced in the field. Marks showed an unusual appreciation of the relationship of Agency structure and process to the information policy-making and program-producing processes, and a willingness to listen and weigh proposals for organizational or procedural improvements. Taking advantage of Deputy Director Akers' interests and experience, Marks raised the level of review of media products designed for worldwide distribution and placed guidance on a daily routine basis. He made it clear that the Agency's number-two man had authority over the media services and removed the worrisome quarterly confrontation of individual media directors with top Agency leaders and representative assistant Agency directors of area officers on projected worldwide media programs. In a second organizational change affecting Agency policy,

Marks moved in July, 1966, to improve the relationship of his Office of Policy to the Agency's research efforts, conducted before that time by a separate Research and Reference Service, establishing a combined Office of Policy and Research. The steps taken represent a continuation and improvement of structures created during Murrow's tenure as agency director—now applied to increasing the effectiveness of better-balanced Agency programs. To provide creative leadership to a young but maturing agency like USIA, with its wide area coverage and variety of media, is not an easy task for the director, his executive assistant, and his deputy director. Judgment of USIA's performance under their direction is often made in an excessively short-range time perspective. Does the Agency they lead gain acceptance abroad for current American foreign policies? An effective USIA supporting "poor" foreign policies can compound national error. USIA's responsibility for the nature of American froeign policy is limited to advising on the psychological or public opinion implications of such policy—too often on the day after it is announced or in the week following. In assessing the U.S. Information Agency's developing role as a responsive "instrument" of American foreign policy and in the policy-making process, more attention deserves to be given to longer-range considerations. How can American foreign and information policies help guide the United States and other nations of the world through the re-ordering necessary to adapt the international system to new conditions of interdependence? At a time when mankind's struggle for progress takes place under a mushroom cloud, shortcomings or failures in USIA's organization and procedures—or in its leaders—can contribute to international conflagration and national disaster. Excellence and a planned relationship of present policy to future requirements may lead toward a more rational cooperative world.

GENERAL FUNCTIONS OF THE AGENCY LEADERS

The director, his executive assistant, and the deputy director of USIA are responsible to the President of the United States for USIA policy, programs, and operations, and they serve as personal advisers to the President on the psychological impact of American foreign policies overseas. They preside over USIA itself and are the Agency's top representatives in interagency discussions. Aware of the daily pulse of foreign affairs, they are compelled to keep their eyes on the far horizon. They are the Agency's chief public relations men to the domestic public, often called upon to give speeches on the

Agency and its work. Yet, they are concerned with foreign policy decisions of the secretary of state or the President, with stones thrown at an American Information Center in Latin America, with the appointment of a new country public affairs officer to USIS Bangkok, with budget-pruning efforts of Congressman John Rooney of New York—chairman of the House of Representatives subcommittee responsible for USIA's appropriations. Whether the background of their experience be radio, television, labor or communications law, diplomacy, or newspaper work, their interests must encompass all of these plus motion pictures; English teaching; book, pamphlet, and periodical publication; and exhibits. Experts in public information, they must become knowledgeable on foreign policy matters. Practitioners of communications, they must wed their art to politics. Writers or speakers, they must deal with broad and "niggling" problems of administration. They make policy, but they must also review media products, inspect field operations, and evaluate the efficiency of the Agency they head. The breadth of their responsibility is both a help and a hindrance. What they lack in detailed knowledge is compensated for by the broad perspective they bring to bear on Agency problems.

The director, his executive assistant, and the deputy director are likely to be drawn into problems which threaten to make political headlines, when subordinates cannot reach agreement with other government departments, when a major change in policy, program, or operational technique is considered. Although there is some routine in their schedules, the impact of events can make even a routine meeting a moment of important decision, or provide the informal discussion for an informed decision in time to be effective. They must act themselves; they must also inspire others to act and must provide broad guidelines for such actions. In an agency just beginning to assert its strength in the hurly-burly of Washington affairs, the nature of the leadership provided to Agency personnel by the director, the executive assistant, and the deputy director is important to morale and Agency effectiveness. In a world of unforeseen events, they must react quickly and responsibly and envision the results of alternative American responses on the minds of men around the globe. They must have the unusual strength of body and mind required of all top-level government leaders; a capability for selecting the relevant from a mass of information; a precision of expression to communicate clearly to all of those whose cooperation makes a major agency of government function. No man is big enough for these jobs when he is appointed; fortunately, many men grow when thrust into the mainstream of events, challenged by the tasks set before them. The success of the director, his executive assistant, and the deputy director—no matter how able—in fulfilling their functions to a reasonable degree depends upon the organization and procedures set up to expedite their labors.

PERSONAL STAFFING

The Office of the Director is one of the smallest of USIA's twenty-two elements, with a staff of thirteen, even counting the top Agency leaders themselves. If the staff serves as a screen to control the workload of the Office's leadership trio, it is too small to be a roadblock to initiatives or ideas generated in area, media, or administrative offices. Area office directors or their deputies have easy access to the director, his executive assistant, or the deputy director, depending on which is exercising primary responsibility over the matter to be raised, but do not abuse the privilege. The Agency runs at a semi-hectic pace, and few waste time with personal appointments unless the matter is urgent. The phone is often quicker, with secretaries listening and recording decisions taken or assignments given. Both the director and the deputy director keep two secretaries working overtime. Each also has a special assistant, usually a Foreign Service Career Reserve officer of senior ·rank, who serves as his "man Friday"—sometimes seven days a week. The normal role of the special assistant is to see that major problems reach "the boss," and that when they do that the paperwork or information necessary for decision is ready before a final discussion is held. The assistants also search the Agency for problems of which the director and deputy director should be aware or which should be discussed in staff meetings. They serve as sounding boards for ideas before decisions are finally made. They write speeches for Agency leaders; this involves gathering material from the appropriate USIA elements and preparing a rough draft for submission to the Agency director or deputy director for comment, then rewriting, rechecking, and getting a final clearance from the relevant Agency units. The special assistants work closely with each other so that the Agency leaders can know at all times what the others are doing.

The role of the executive assistant to the director was clearly elevated by Director Marks when he assigned to Howard Chernoff day-to-day operating responsibilities carried under Directors Murrow and Rowan by Deputy Director Donald Wilson. Marks combined in the functioning of his own office many of the duties formerly carried out by the director and the deputy director. While Deputy Director Akers is acting agency director when Marks is traveling overseas, his primary assignment is direction of media content in products designed for worldwide use. This represents Agency recognition of the importance of a task formerly performed by an assistant deputy director of USIA for media content. The executive assistant no longer serves just as an anonymous alter ego for the director, as Reed Harris did for Edward R. Murrow and as Lester Edmond did for Carl Rowan. Until illness required Chernoff to take medical leave in late January, 1967, he served on the firing line of daily administrative operations, often working on tasks distinct from those drawing the attention of the agency director. Lloyd Wright, the present executive assistant, has greater responsibility in his own name than did Executive Assistants Harris and Edmond, though he may be no more influential in shaping Agency affairs than were Harris and Edmond behind the scenes. The assignment of some of the duties formerly performed by the deputy director has probably raised today's executive assistant to a rank among the Agency's top four or five officials, but *The Agency in Brief* for 1966 overlooks the "promotion," ascribing to the position the same degree of anonymity assigned it under Murrow and Rowan.

Murrow's executive assistant, Reed Harris, had earlier been a deputy and later acting administrator of the International Information Administration —one of the IIA leaders attacked by Senator McCarthy in 1953, an able man and a symbol to Murrow of resistance to McCarthyism. Returning to government service after a stint of operating his own public relations firm, Harris was an anonymous extension of the director's eyes, ears, and voice. In case of emergency or illness, he could be detailed temporarily by Murrow to head any Agency element. Once a broad precedent had been laid down by Murrow, Harris made decisions on problems related to the original decision, relieving the director of detail. As a member of the Agency's Program Review Committee, USIA's major all-Agency device to review budgeting and spending, Harris represented Murrow and served as an observer in his behalf. Similarly, he was a member of what was then called the Senior Field Officers Assignment Board, which met weekly to handle placement of all FSCR 1's and 2's in USIA's foreign service. The executive assistant sometimes accepted speaking engagements when the director's calendar was overcrowded. He decided which speech requests Murrow would accept— and turned down as many as twenty in a single day. In the evening he often rode home with Murrow in the director's government limousine, discussing the day's problems and decisions. He was one of those who urged upon Murrow additional appearances before USIA employees. Although it was difficult for Murrow—a modest and shy man—to understand why anyone wanted to listen to him, his meetings with personnel obviously increased Agency morale. During Murrow's illness and absence from the Agency, to be followed by his resignation, Agency leadership shifted to Deputy Director Wilson, who became acting agency director. The staffing load normally carried by the executive assistant fell for a time upon Wilson's special assistant William Green. Carl Rowan, as director of USIA, became similarly dependent upon Lester Edmond, his executive assistant. Wright, the present executive assistant, is chairman of the Agency's Program Review Committee, a responsibility of the deputy director before Marks became director. The executive assistant still serves on the Personnel Assignment Board, known as the Senior Field Officers Assignment Board in the Murrow era.

THE DEPUTY DIRECTOR'S NEW ROLE

Though Deputy Director Akers serves primarily as "deputy" to Director Marks, an important part of his role today is orchestrating media policy to insure that the content of media worldwide products is consistent with American foreign policy in general and not in conflict with specialized American policies in different regions of the world. This task arose from a need to establish more efficient and acceptable policy control over the Agency's media services, largely Civil Service staffed, with little overseas experience, occasionally insensitive to what would be abrasive to people overseas, sometimes more interested in their craft as writers, broadcasters, or motion-picture makers than in conveying American policy ideas to foreign audiences. Relating media content to policy was not a particularly serious problem under USIA's first director, Theodore Streibert, for the assistant directors of the Agency's area offices were regarded primarily as supporting the media services. Under Director George Allen, though the fast media received firm policy guidance, the concept of presenting a full and fair picture of American life and culture without close attention to "the policy line" tended to give the directors of the Agency's media services growing autonomy in the planning of their "slow media" programs and products. After Director Edward R. Murrow had a careful look at Agency operations, in keeping with the Kennedy administration's view of USIA as a more direct policy tool, he sought an increasingly "integrated total operation" by USIA, with area and media elements to be more effectively coordinated. This required additional intercommunication, development of a broader consensus, and firmer policy direction to the media to insure that the Agency's mission "to achieve U.S. foreign policy objectives" was carried out. He created in the Office of Policy an assistant deputy director of USIA for media content and appointed Edgar D. Brooke, now the Agency's inspector general, to the new post.

The media perform two functions, direct support to the areas and field posts in achieving the objectives of individual Country Plans and more general support for United States worldwide objectives, as set forth in the Agency's policy themes or emphases. To meet the Agency's tactical needs country by country, the area offices budget for media products which their field posts will require and negotiate with the media for the services required to support Country Plans. With budget control, the area offices can insist on media conformity to policy needs. To meet the Agency's strategic worldwide objectives, the media services budget for multi-area products which they will develop and offer to the area offices to be used at field posts. Field posts tend to base their media product recommendations on "local" needs, trying not to offend sensibilities, inevitably moved by what presently seems "tolerable and practical." Murrow, as director, recognized a need for headquarters support through worldwide media products for general American foreign policy objectives—regardless of whether they were currently acceptable or popular locally. The local view stresses compatibility, but the worldwide approach seeks to change or modify views. Many African countries have little interest in the recurring tension between the Soviet Union and the United States over the status of West Berlin or in supporting the current American involvement in Vietnam. Although an individual USIA Country Plan from an African post would be unlikely to emphasize U.S. policy either on Vietnam or on Berlin, the United States may some day require diplomatic support in the United Nations on such issues. Lack of knowledge may lead both popular and government opinion in the less-developed areas to criticize the United States for its stance in Vietnam or Berlin, as a result of acceptance of ideas generated elsewhere or because the implications of United States unilateral withdrawal of support to South Vietnam or West Berlin—as viewed by American policy makers—are not understood. Such negative views of U.S. policy can have spin-off effects, creating suspicion of other American policies. By presenting the Vietnam or Berlin situations as challenges to "self-determination," USIA worldwide media products attempt to relate the local interest of the new nation-state in Africa to American foreign policy and possibly influence public opinion to be more favorable or at least less unfavorable to American efforts.

It is true that the expertise for identifying the Agency's overseas information problems resides in the area offices, while the creative responsibility for producing programs and materials for distribution overseas rests largely with the media services—though in the Marks era more media materials are being produced overseas—either at individual USIS posts or at Regional

Service Centers. Media personnel in Washington tend to lack an understanding of the psychology of foreign audiences or not to possess it in the same degree as area office personnel. This is because most media employees are Civil Service personnel with limited overseas experiences; most area assignments are held by foreign service personnel with a number of tours of duty overseas behind them. In upgrading the strategic worldwide approach in media operations, Murrow sought a better focusing of Agency efforts to support American policy interests which transcended local or regional considerations.

It was the job of the assistant deputy director (media content) to insure the orchestration of media products—both content and timing—in support of multi-area strategic objectives. The task was not easy at first, for the post originally had little line authority, and its occupant relied heavily upon persuasion. He did play a prominent role in Agency planning meetings, chairing Tuesday afternoon gatherings with area office and media service policy officers sponsored by the Office of Policy and attending Murrow's Wednesday afternoon "think" sessions to participate in discussions with the heads of USIA's major elements. He was recognized as having a review responsibility over important media products, and lived from beginning to end with such documentary films as "Journey Across Berlin" or "Anatomy of Aggression." Television programs, often produced on contract in New York, received a quick review by the assistant deputy director (media content) before being rushed overseas.

Strengthening central control by the assistant deputy director (media content) in behalf of the Agency director over multi-area plannable media products was the initiation in mid-1963 of a Director's Quarterly Media Projects Meeting, the first of which was held on July 1 of that year, with others following in October, January, and April. The assistant deputy director (media content) was responsible for seeing that each media service prepared a three-month projection of its major worldwide projects. For example, the Information Center Service prepared and forwarded a document entitled "ICS Projects Proposed for the 1st (2nd, 3rd, or 4th) Quarter." The media were encouraged to discuss their proposals with area offices or with other media services before the director's meeting. The reports were descriptive capsules, with dollar tags attached, though the discussions were largely program and policy oriented. Attending the quarterly meetings were the assistant director for administration, the assistant directors of the area offices and directors of the media services, the deputy and associate deputy directors (policy and plans), the deputy director and director of USIA, with their special assistants, and the assistant deputy director (media content). Of the quarterly reports and meetings, media personnel indicated in 1963: "This device has the most teeth in it of anything the director has to influence the media." A round of discussions between media services and area offices, from the desk through the element head level, preceded the meetings. The assistant deputy director (media content) kept the meeting record and reported the results. Projects were approved, disapproved, approved in principle with a request for more detail, approved in principle with suggested modifications, or approved for use in a limited area.

Started in January, 1962, to help Agency integration of media activities, a monthly report was made by each media to the director, with copies to other media and to the Office of Policy, of projects likely to be of interest to other media. These monthly reports are brief, seldom more than one or two pages, but are a device for cross-fertilization and coordination. With the media thus informed, material which will be of use to several media can be gathered or tapes made on location. This decreases the chance that media will work individually to develop aspects of a project which could be better done by collaborative effort. An older coordinating device is a monthly progress report by each media, distributed widely within USIA and to the field, to indicate products in the planning stage and the status of major media products already underway. The assistant director (media content) was often drawn into formal or informal discussions of media products while the media were preparing their reports or during the production of a particular film or pamphlet.

In appointing the Agency's second assistant deputy director for media content on February 15, 1965, Carl Rowan—in a memorandum to heads of all USIA elements—wrote:

> He will speak for me in determining how we use our production resources. I expect him to participate in the planning of all major media products and all Area projects involving any substantial media output. I am delegating to him authority to approve or disapprove such products and projects, and his determinations will be as binding and have the same weight as if they came from me. There has been a good deal of discussion over the years where policy leaves off and operations begin—where control of content becomes control of creation. I suggest that we do away with these artificial divisions. When I see a script, a pamphlet, a TV film documentary, I want it to meet my standards on all counts and to come to me with the full endorsement of the Assistant Deputy Director or not at all . . . It goes without saying that any decisions can be appealed, in the first instance to the

Deputy Director for Policy and Plans, in the second to the Deputy Director, and, of course, finally to me.

Although the Director went on to say that by assigning this authority and review hierarchy he did not want to "discourage discourse between myself and all of you," the memorandum still had that effect and immeasurably strengthened the hand of the assistant deputy director (media content).

The most trying experience for the media services in the pattern of policy control which developed under Murrow and Rowan was the agency director's Quarterly Media Projects Meeting. In a single afternoon, projects long planned could be rejected, causing great disappointment. Though the system was intended to bring a quick review of projected media services programs and products by the Agency's top leaders, the exigencies of daily operations, travel for inspection overseas, or unexpected crises sometimes resulted in actual review by deputies or lower-level assistants who attended sessions in behalf of their superiors. To lower the tension which built up before the Quarterly Meetings, where all was won or lost in a single cast of the dice, Director Marks utilized Deputy Director Akers' interests and abilities creatively, elevating the level of review and escaping the pressures of the quarterly confrontation. Akers now reviews programs as they are developed, can make suggestions for change and then take a look at the revision—perhaps approving the program or product after minor revision and without significant delay. The area directors and others who participated in the quarterly meetings have not been denied a voice in decisions. Akers is quite likely to touch base with all of the principals involved, but he serves as an intermediary between the area offices and the media services. In his position as deputy director he is in a position of authority to moderate their differences of view.

THE EXECUTIVE SECRETARIAT AND THE OPERATIONS CENTER

Sharing the duties of "paper shuffler" in the Office of the Director for the top three Agency officials with USIA's Operations Center and performing administrative services for the Office of the Director is a tiny Executive Secretariat of four or five persons. For a twelve-year period after the Agency achieved its independence, the Executive Secretariat performed review functions of considerable importance, though much of its work was seemingly routine. Under the direction of an experienced Civil Service information employee who had been with the information program even before USIA became an independent Agency in 1953, the Executive Secretariat was responsible for checking every telegram or letter being sent overseas from the

Agency to see if it were in the proper format; written correctly, with necessary clearances; understandable, meeting security regulations; and consistent with other messages that had gone out on the same subject. Most Agency messages went overseas in the name of the director, and the Executive Secretariat gave approval in his behalf. Even official informal letters written and signed by Agency personnel passed through the Secretariat for information and review. In November, 1965, the review function for field messages was transferred to the Communications and Records Branch in the Agency's Office of Administration.

Also responsibilities of the Executive Secretariat were a screening function, determining what information or documents should be seen by which of the top Agency leaders, and operation of the Agency's duty officer system, which functions nights, weekends, and holidays. Late in 1965, a USIA Operations Center was set up to perform the function of determining what telegraphic information from abroad coming into the Agency was of sufficient importance to be seen by the agency director or deputy director—or by other Agency officials. The new Operations Center was also to conduct watch duty operations on a twenty-four-hour basis and assume control of the duty officer system, formerly under the aegis of the Executive Secretariat. Although the Operations Center was established in fact as a unit separate from the Executive Secretariat in late 1965, its independence did not become official until February, 1966.

All incoming telegrams to USIA and about 65 per cent of the Department of State's telegraph and airgram traffic is automatically routed to the Operations Center by USIA's Communications and Records Branch to be screened for possible reading by the director, executive assistant, or deputy director. Also monitored by the Operations Center in behalf of the Agency leaders are the United Press International and Associated Press tickers, the Foreign Broadcast Information Service's reports on foreign broadcasts, and USINFO's—USIA's own news releases which are being sent overseas. The USIA communications flow is rather small for the size of the Agency, with 2,250 telegraph messages a month (some 335,000 words) received from overseas and 1,400 (220,000 words) dispatched to the field. [1] Air pouch messages received monthly total about 900, with 400 single address pouch messages and 200 circular pouch messages (those sent to more than one addressee) a month sent abroad. USIA receives monthly a total of about 10,000 Department of State telegrams in and out, and another 6,000 a month total of State's airgram flow. Relevant Department of Defense and Agency for International Development messages are also received. In fact, there is a comprehensive exchange of messages among all the foreign affairs agencies in which USIA participates. All telegrams coming into USIA go to the Operations Center, but letters addressed to the director, the executive assistant, or deputy director are delivered to the Executive Secretariat, which determines who will prepare an answer and the form of the reply—unless the letter is from a member of Congress. Congressional mail is the responsibility of the General Counsel's Office.

In a fast-moving world, USIA must be prepared to react to global events on a twenty-four-hour basis, seven days a week. Until late 1965, responsibility for screening messages for rapid action by top Agency officials had rested with the Executive Secretariat during the regular working days and had been carried by specially assigned duty officers nights and weekends. With the establishment of the Operations Center to monitor telegraphic traffic, five members of USIA's Foreign Service Career Reserve are detailed for periods of six months to a year to serve as watch officers, working on overlapping shifts round the clock (from 7:30 A.M. to 5 P.M., from 3:45 P.M. to 1 A.M., and from 11:45 P.M. to 9 A.M.). They serve under a chief of the Operations Center who is helped by two staff assistants. The Operations Center also took over direction of the Agency's duty officer system, which insures that regular USIA officers are available for consultation by the operations watch officer at any time, day or night. Although the Agency's top officials are in their offices long after the Agency's official closing time of 5:30 P.M., and some may be on hand before its 8:45 A.M. opening, an Agency duty officer is on tap every weekday evening and night from 6 P.M. to 8:45 A.M. He is physically present in the Agency from 6 to 9 P.M. on week nights and all day on Saturday and Sunday and is subject to call at his home anytime. The Operations Center maintains a roster of fifteen senior Agency employees, mostly from the area offices or media services and with overseas experience, each of whom stands night duty for a week at a time in rotation. If a "Flash" or "Immediate" (the old "Niact") message is received over USIA's communication system, the Agency duty officer may be wakened from his sleep at home, praying that the message is unclassified. If it is classified, he must dress and come in to 1750 Pennsylvania Avenue, N.W.—often from the Maryland or Virginia suburbs—to be apprised of its contents. A standby officer for each Agency element is always on call to be consulted if the duty officer needs to take immediate action. A "Home Directory of Key Personnel" maintained by the Operations Center enables the Agency duty officer to roust out almost any senior USIA employee on short notice. Through arrangements with the Operations Center at the Department of State, any fast-breaking event reported in State's communications series is communicated immediately to USIA, with the Agency duty officer on the receiving end during the night hours.

MORNING BRIEFINGS

Morning briefing sessions are less hectic in USIA under Director Marks and in the Johnson administration than they were under Director Murrow in the Kennedy administration. In the Murrow period, the director attended the secretary of state's morning briefing—held on three days a week (Monday, Wednesday, and Friday)—and the deputy director attended an informal White House briefing held for the Special Assistant to the President for National Security Affairs and appropriate members of the White House staff—also attended by representatives of State, CIA, and Defense. Currently, neither the executive assistant to the director nor the deputy director attend White House briefings, though Director Marks attends the Monday, Wednesday, and Friday 9:15 A.M. briefings for the secretary of state. Marks's own weekly staff meeting normally starts at 8:30 A.M. on Tuesdays and sometimes runs until 10 A.M. Neither Defense nor the Central Intelligence Agency is represented at State's morning briefings. Marks is the only head of an independent agency present.

During the Murrow period, there was a daily flurry of listening to morning newscasts before attendance at the State or White House briefings, a hurried exchange of ideas between the director and his executive assistant and between the deputy director and his special assistant before they rushed off to the briefings. There is no such excitement in today's USIA. The rush of the day's events is left to Deputy Agency Director for Policy and Research Hewson Ryan and those of his assistants responsible for the fast guidance of Agency elements. The agency director may be in touch with Ryan during the day if a significant problem develops, but their regular exchange of information takes place late in the afternoon, usually between five and six. The deputy director, working on longer-range media materials, is less interested in the day-to-day surge of world events. In the Murrow period, the director and deputy director returned to the Agency from their morning briefings and met Monday, Wednesday, and Friday at shortly after 10 A.M. with the executive assistant and the deputy director for policy and plans (now called the deputy director for policy and research) to discuss the briefings' potpourri of events and resulting problems for USIA. After a time, Murrow had even invited the director of the Broadcasting Service to attend this session, because of the special problem of policy guidance to a fast media like the Voice of America. It was not until 10:15 to 10:30 on these days that the interchange of ideas had been completed and the regular day's work could begin. Today's exchange of ideas is less regular, more informal, depending upon special need.

STAFF MEETINGS

Director Marks holds a weekly staff meeting for twenty to twenty-five of his most important advisers at 8:30 A.M. on the second working day of the week, usually on Tuesdays unless there is a Monday holiday for government workers.[2] Murrow's weekly staff meetings, held at 10:30 A.M. on Mondays usually brought together about thirty-two top Agency officials, and sometimes the number ballooned to almost double this figure. The weekly meeting is intended particularly to give participants a chance to raise problems, though some of those present report on activities of their elements, occasionally making the meeting something of a "bragging" session. Essentially what Marks wants is problems identified and solutions suggested. The discussion may be on the Soviet Union's new magazine *Sputnik*—a *Reader's Digest*-type periodical introduced in the American market —or on problems of briefing foreign correspondents on a presidential trip overseas, since the President's staff is more concerned with what will be reported back home in America while USIA is particularly interested in the proper handling of representatives of the foreign press. A Marks staff meeting is of an operational nature, considered by participants to be more of a briefing session than a place for real discussion. When Marks first took over direction of the Agency, many of those who attended the briefings hoped they would encompass some of the free discussion and looking ahead that Murrow had encouraged at his Wednesday afternoon "think" sessions, later dropped by Director Rowan. Participants in these discussions had enjoyed the give and take, and the opportunity to lift their sights from day-to-day problems; most felt something had been lost when they were stopped. Marks holds his weekly staff meetings in the conference room adjoining the offices of the director and deputy director on the seventh floor of USIA's headquarters building. There does not seem to be too much substantive difference between a Murrow staff meeting in 1963 and a Marks briefing session. Perhaps it is true that the Murrow staff meetings were more for morale purposes and to keep people energized, though Murrow did pass on the high spots of the day or past week for his office and pinpoint upcoming problems. The Marks meetings are more clearly for identifying problems which can then be followed up with leaders of individual elements later in the day or week in an attempt to work out satisfactory resolutions of difficulties.

There is no longer anything like Murrow's second major staff meeting of the week, the "think" session held on Wednesdays between 5 and 6 P.M. No other device has yet been found within the Agency to replace it as a freewheeling, forward-looking discussion of upcoming problems. Smaller than Murrow's weekly staff meetings, it included the Agency's top four or five officials and the heads of all the major elements. No record of proceedings was ever distributed. The meetings's purpose was to look ahead, from a few months to several years, to explore emerging problems. The assistants to the director and deputy director searched the Agency for problems demanding immediate top-level attention, recommending topics for the meeting agenda. At times no agenda was provided, and participants raised problems as the spirit moved them, Quaker-meeting style. After the presentation, whether formal or informal, there was an all-out, no-holds-barred discussion. The purpose of the exchange of views, sometimes heated, was for exploration rather than immediate decision. Internal problems which hinged on area-media relations were likely to provoke greater controversy than presentations by outsiders involving USIA relations with other agencies. Although the look into the future was limited by the practicality of the participants, who were for the most part directly involved in daily operations, men faced with operational responsibilities are sometimes the first to feel the pinch of developing problems.

Although Director Marks has been more successful than Murrow in controlling the size of his weekly staff meeting, it is still difficult for the director to keep the meeting small enough to preserve informality. Chiefs of larger divisions, media and area policy officers, and even desk officers would like to attend. These important but lower-ranking Agency officers must be satisfied with irregularly scheduled special meetings every month or so to keep them in personal touch with Agency leaders. On one occasion, the United States ambassador to Belgium spoke to Agency personnel through the desk level, with the director introducing the visitor and participating in the questioning —to the delight of those present. At another time, fifteen foreign local employees of USIA visiting in the United States for the second time under Agency auspices were interviewed by this same broad group of Agency personnel, with the director becoming a key questioner. The importance of giving policy-level employees an opportunity to hear informal remarks by the director and deputy director, not only to get a sense of the leadership's way of thinking but also to appreciate that their own contribution to USIA is valued, can hardly be overestimated. There is a need for the director and deputy director to communicate to personnel at all levels within the Agency. The annual honor awards ceremony for outstanding service to the Agency, normally scheduled in August, is open to all Agency personnel. The director customarily talks "off the cuff," with from one-third to one-half of all the Agency's domestic personnel present in the Department of State's west auditorium. The director may help open the Agency's United Givers Fund drive, making a statement on the general purposes of USIA, relating the Agency and the drive to the American way of doing things. A special day may be set aside to honor an Agency element. The Voice of America was singled out on its twentieth anniversary in 1962. President Kennedy, Secretary of State Dean Rusk, Agency Director Murrow, and Henry Loomis, then director of the Broadcasting Service, spoke to Voice personnel assembled in the Health, Education, and Welfare Department's auditorium, with one hundred representatives present from other parts of USIA. The Voice's twenty-fifth anniversary was celebrated on February 24, 1967; the cast was different but the purpose the same. Government workers are far from being blasé about the "big brass"; they are pleased at being recognized by their leaders as necessary cogs in the complex machinery of government.

AGENCY COMMITTEES

Although the weekly staff meeting is primarily the responsibility of the director, traditionally it has been the deputy director who presides over the Agency's two most important operating committees which make recommendations to the director for decision. In the new division of labor under Director Marks, however, it is the executive assistant who chairs the Program Review Committee and the Personnel Assignment Board, successor to the Senior Field Officers Assignment Board of the Murrow period. Deputy Director Donald Wilson chaired the two committees under both Murrow and Rowan, but Howard Chernoff and Lloyd Wright, his replacement, have guided the committees in more recent years. Although the executive assistant was not a formal member of the committees during the Murrow period, he attended sessions in behalf of the director, to keep the director aware of what was being done and to make the director's views known to the committees. Carl Rowan's special assistant was actually a member of the Program Review Committee. With such representation, directors rarely, if ever, overrode committee recommendations. The Program Review Committee operates during all stages of the budget cycle, reviewing programs and costs proposed by each Agency element for the upcoming fiscal year and advance projections of programs and costs for a five-year period, allocating funds and determining priorities among programs after congressional appropriations for the new year have been made, and considering program changes during the year which involve transfers of funds of more than $30,000. Members of the committee, serving under the executive assistant, are the deputy agency director (policy and research), the assistant director (administration), one assistant director of an area office, one assistant director of a media service, the general counsel, a special assistant to the director, and the Agency budget officer, who serves as executive secretary to the committee. The area office and media service representatives serve two-and-a-half-month concurrent terms and are then replaced by other area office and media service assistant directors. The Program Review Committee is a hard-working group, meeting four or five hours a day for fifteen to twenty-five days a year to inquire of the element heads who appear before it if "programs are feasible, correctly priced, and effectively support Agency and government policies." [3] Since money or its absence makes programs possible or impossible, helps or hinders them, the Program Review Committee plays a major role in determining "how" policies will be translated into "what" programs.

The Personnel Assignment Board recommends to the director all appointments, assignments, and transfers of senior members of the Agency's foreign service, the FSCR 1's and 2's—of whom there are some 175 in a foreign service of nearly 1,700, including limited and staff appointments. Country public affairs officers, since they head country programs overseas, also fall under the board's jurisdiction, even though they may sometimes not yet be senior officers. After a review of all possible candidates for a position, the area office assistant director recommends an individual he believes can do the job and presents his justification to the board. There is free discussion; then the executive assistant can accept the proposal, reject it, or defer judgment. Most of the senior officers are well known to the members of the board, and usually the assignment is obviously correct—the best that can be made in the circumstances. The board meets once every three weeks for about an hour and may consider four senior-level personnel assignments at a single session. Serving under the executive assistant as board members are the deputy director (policy and research), a special assistant to the director, the six area office assistant directors, the assistant director (administrative), the assistant director (personnel and training), and any element head of the Agency who is a member of the foreign service. Since the proper placement of available senior personnel has a significant impact on how well Agency operations implement programs and policies, an effective Personnel Assignment Board is of great assistance to USIA in the fulfilment of its mission.

INTRA-GOVERNMENT RELATIONS

During the Kennedy administration, the director and the deputy director of USIA were consulted by the President and drawn into formal and informal National Security Council discussions as never before. Murrow had accepted his appointment by Kennedy as Agency director with the understanding that he would be in on policy takeoffs as well as the crash landings. He had ready access to the President. When the United States delayed resumption of nuclear testing in 1961 for eight months after the Russians had resumed testing with massive explosions, it was Murrow who had prevailed upon the President and others in the National Security Council to let the full impact of the Soviet action strike home to people everywhere and to give the USIA time to explain carefully why the United States had to resume limited testing. When America finally resumed testing, there was little criticism from the world audience. When Murrow was ill during the Cuban missile confrontation of 1962, Deputy Director Wilson stepped into the breach. USIA distributed fifty thousand photographs of the Soviet missile sites which were published throughout the world. In an attempt to break through Soviet jamming to reach the people of the U.S.S.R. and eastern Europe with information on the Cuban crisis, the Voice of America massed fifty-two transmitters around the Soviet Union, broadcast on eighty frequencies in ten languages, using power equal to that of eighty-six United States radio stations, nearly 4.5 million watts. The message penetrated the noisy curtain. These examples are indicative of the Agency's increasing role in national security affairs in the 1960's. From attendance on invitation at National Security Council meetings during the Streibert period, to regular participation under Larson and Allen, Murrow and Wilson were not only accepted as participants in full-scale NSC meetings but singled out to be members of the Council's smaller executive or *ad hoc* subcommittees on Cuba, nuclear affairs, and counterinsurgency. Although USIA was never a legislatively authorized member of the National Security Council, there was no longer any doubt about USIA's influence in Council deliberations or with the President during the Kennedy administration. During the Eisenhower administration the National Security Council normally met weekly on Thursday mornings; the streamlining of procedures by Kennedy reduced the meetings to about once every two weeks, except in time of crisis when meetings were sometimes held twice a day. The National Security Council meeting as a formal group for discussions has been used even more sparingly during the Johnson administration. President Johnson has preferred to meet more informally with the secretary of defense, the secretary of state, and his National Security Council adviser. Formal meetings of the Council were sharply reduced, held essentially for psychological rather than policy-making purposes. Although USIA was not quite in the inner sanctum (participating in Johnson's luncheon meetings with McNamara, Dulles, and Bundy or Rostow), in time of crisis (for example, during the intervention of

American troops in the Dominican Republic and the period of making arrangements for Organization of American States forces to replace the United States soldiers) Carl Rowan served as a close adviser to the President. Because of Director Marks's personal relationship with President Johnson, USIA's role in security affairs remains high. The assignment of responsibility for all United States psychological action in Vietnam to the director of USIA in May, 1965, is indicative of the Agency's current involvement in important foreign affairs actions. Marks accompanied President Johnson on his trip to the Manila Conference in late October, 1966, and was with the President during the Asian tour which followed. Foreign media reaction reports prepared by USIA before and during the Conference and throughout the trip were of particular interest to President Johnson. Today the National Security Council meets irregularly, the counterinsurgency group of the NSC—of which Director Marks was a member—met rather regularly. The Senior Inter-Departmental Group met weekly while Ball was under secretary of state, and now has resumed operations under Katzenbach. An experienced liaison officer of USIA's Office of Policy and Research oversees preparation by relevant Agency elements of papers required for participation by the director, the executive assistant, or the deputy director in either formal or informal interagency meetings bearing on national security affairs.

Probably as demanding in time as relations with the White House and interagency coordination, and in many ways as important to Agency operations, are the relations of the top Agency leadership with members and committees of Congress. Several play a role in congressional relations, though Director Marks spends more time on congressional matters than the others. USIA is not a "typical" department of government, performing long-approved tasks, or servicing the interests of farm, business, labor, or educational groups. It is a relatively new agency with an overseas mission— to which Americans are just beginning to become accustomed—which rarely serves the immediate special interests of any domestic interest group. It has no built-in domestic support for its policies and programs. To the contrary, portraying American life and culture or supporting American foreign policy abroad brings congressional criticism of USIA no matter what is done. The Congress is composed of reasonably diverse elements, individual congressmen taking a wide range of views about what should be said (or not said) about the United States or its policies overseas. Many of its southern members feel required to "resist" integration—an American domestic policy which helps American foreign policy when reported overseas. A few congressmen still object to USIA as "too soft on Communism," forgetting that the most effective psychological approach is hardly likely to be that of continuously "tarring and feathering" the competition. There are other members of Congress who are opposed to the very programs USIA is responsible for publicizing overseas—Agency for International Development (AID) activities, for example. President Johnson's budget for fiscal year 1968 proposed that 85 per cent of American development aid be given through multilateral agencies. For USIA, this was a new and interesting figure to tell the peoples of the world. In the past, there was much criticism overseas of American unilateral giving and fear of "strings" attached to United States aid. Some members of Congress approved increased multilateralism; others opposed it vigorously—and criticized USIA broadcasts. These factors, coupled with the residue of mistrust in the information program stemming from the transitional period after World War II and the McCarthy era, force the director, the executive assistant, and the deputy director to take their congressional liaison duties seriously.

Contacts with the members of Congress are largely of five types: speeches to informal congressional clubs; briefings for new members; appearances with members on radio or television shows prepared by them for showing in their home states or districts; luncheon or office meetings; and performances before (or inquisitions by) congressional subcommittees. Chance conversations at social affairs are also important, but more random and informal.

It is not unusual for one of the three to be "on the Hill" by 8 A.M.—perhaps accompanied by the Agency's general counsel—for a breakfast discussion with fifteen to twenty early-rising congressmen, members of one of the "chowder and marching" or "session" clubs which abound there. They may speak before the Senate secretaries; also to the Democrat or Republican administrative assistants in the House (the Burros Club or the Bull Elephants), separately, of course. Questions are asked good naturedly; informal replies, given. Ed Murrow was a natural for appearances with members of the House for their district radio or television shows. A veteran performer in either medium—though not as much at ease as he looked—and a figure of national prominence, he helped attract listeners that the congressman might not normally get. While rendering a useful service to the member, he was able to talk about USIA. Luncheon with individual members of the House or Senate Appropriations Committees to explain USIA operations or programs is more effective in modifying opinions (and less terrifying) than the group confrontation in the committee room. If Agency business is too pressing, office meetings with committee members are a necessary substitute for the luncheons, which are time consuming. Appearing before any congressional committee requires careful briefing. The director, the executive assistant, and the deputy director must not only know the facts but also have answers for "needling" questions, political or otherwise. [4] The members of Senate and House committees "pick at" the USIA director. They may give lower-ranking Agency personnel an even harder time. During the Agency's early years, Agency directors made it a practice to appear at the opening committee session on the Agency budget and then turned over defense of the budget to administrative personnel and experts. Murrow once went so far as to sit through the Agency's entire budget hearings, kicking off with an opening statement and entering the discussion to backstop his experts when the questioning grew political or broader than their specializations. Marks has gone Murrow one better. He carries the main burden of testimony himself, accompanied by the assistant director of USIA for administration, the Agency budget officer, and the executive assistant. The effectiveness of such appearances depends as much upon careful preparation as it does upon the personality of the director. For appearances like that before the Senate Foreign Relations Committee, preparation is backstopped by the general counsel; for defending the budget, by the assistant director (administration). Deputy Director Akers may respond on short notice to an invitation to attend a briefing for new congressmen being held at the Department of State.

To mention participation by the Agency's leaders in National Security Council affairs and congressional matters is not to forget discussions with the director of the bureau of the budget during the budget cycle, conversations with the secretary or under secretary of commerce if trade-fair plans or operations require a high-level resolution of USIA and Commerce Department differences, or dealings with the director of AID in the process of conducting that Agency's overseas information program. There are meetings with the President, often in crisis conditions; some at other times, on more routine business; others, for purely ceremonial purposes. Luncheon meetings, appointments, phone calls with the leaders of other agencies, and attendance at Cabinet meetings if a matter concerning USIA is on the agenda, are all part of the day's work. Agency personnel weigh carefully the wisdom of involving the director, the executive assistant, or the deputy director in problems where intra-agency differences at lower levels are preventing a solution, but the phone call, letter, or personal contact by one of the Agency's leaders is always an arrow in USIA's sling—perhaps more often used by USIA than some other government agencies because of the fast-moving nature of the communications media.

If much of the time of USIA's leaders seems to be devoted to the day-to-day, the short range, it is only fair to say that they are rarely looking back—except occasionally to evaluate performance (even inspection reports are geared to how a better job can be done in the future). They are almost always concerned with looking ahead, even though it only be the next twenty-four hours. The director and the deputy director may engage in relatively long-range planning by calling in the heads of the Broadcasting Service and the Motion Picture and Television Service for a discussion of their future needs and methods for improving their cooperation. The executive assistant is directly involved in the five-year projection of spending and programs during the budget review, and the deputy director is well aware of upcoming media production. But much of their time is spent in quenching fires started elsewhere, meeting the critical short-term problems that thrust themselves upon the Agency daily. It may be a phone call or visit to an irate congressman. Assistant directors of the area offices and media services are daily on their appointment calendars, often with operational problems to be resolved. They may even be called to review a motion picture before it is released for distribution overseas. They are in regular contact with the deputy director (policy and research) or his assistants, who have both short- and long-range interests. They may also discuss any current administrative problem or longer-range issue with the assistant director (administration). Occasionally, they go overseas to inspect several USIS posts in a given area. For the most part, they are provided reports of inspection visits to the areas by area office assistant directors, or by the foreign service inspectors designated by the Agency's inspector general. They may talk briefly with returning country public affairs officers.

THE INSPECTOR GENERAL

An Agency Inspection Corps attached to the Office of the Director, operating with a six-man staff, functioned from the fall of 1958 to August 31, 1962, when it was disbanded on short notice by Director Murrow. A new type Inspection Corps was re-established by Director Carl Rowan on July 1, 1965. By fiscal year 1967 the inspection system was operating at a level which would make inspection possible at each USIS post about once every three years. Seventeen posts were inspected by thirty-three inspectors between July and December of 1966. Seventeen additional inspections by forty-four inspectors were projected for January through June of 1967. Criticisms of the old Inspection Corps abandoned in 1962 were its cost—approximately $250,000 per year—disagreement of the area office directors with its recommendations and a resultant failure to act on Inspection Corps suggestions, and a feeling that the inspections were too detailed and got lost among "the nuts and bolts," lacking creative operational ideas. From the fall of 1962 until July 1, 1965, responsibility for inspection of overseas operations of USIS missions was given to the assistant directors of the area offices. The area office directors were generally quite satisfied with the arrangement. They were in a position to implement changes in field operations rapidly, for they naturally did not disagree with their own recommendations. Across the board, they were a vigorous, lively group, stronger men than would likely be designated for service with an Inspection Corps (sometimes an assignment near the close of career for senior personnel). The area office directors had a vital interest in the inspections, their own future careers depended on a job well done. But they were of course subject to reassessment to the field after their terms of service as assistant or deputy assistant directors of area offices ended, and they were well aware that later they might be serving with some of the people whose operations they were second-guessing. More seriously, they were also so involved in program direction that they were called upon to deal with many operational details. The assignment of field personnel, traditionally a most important element in field inspections, had to be dropped for want of time. This had served as a valuable cross-check on post ratings of personnel—often based on the judgment of a single post supervisor over a six-year period. Although the area office directors and their deputies attempted to be objective in behalf of the Agency director, outsiders found it hard to believe that they could view operations for which they were responsible with dispassion. While the Agency found drawbacks in the old Inspection Corps system, there were also shortcomings in dependence upon the reports of area office directors.

It has been said that a swimmer may drown, but people swim. Aware of the problems of re-creating an Inspection Corps, as of February 15, 1965, Director Rowan appointed Edgar D. Brooke as inspector general to serve in the Office of the Director with the task of creating and managing a new system of inspection of USIS missions, including efficiency reports for all personnel except public affairs officers—traditionally rated by area office directors. In large measure, the new inspection system stemmed from a stipulation in the interagency agreement approved by Secretary of State Dean Rusk and Agency Director Rowan for the lateral entry of USIA Foreign Service Career Reserves into the Foreign Service of the United States—the requirement for an independent rating of USIS personnel by Agency inspectors. Plans were drawn up by the inspector general and approved by Rowan, which called for inspection of twenty-one posts during the period from July 1, 1965, through December 31 of that year.

It did not appear to the inspector general as he set up the inspection system that USIA would be willing to free six of its outstanding officers for a two-year assignment as inspectors. On the other hand, he believed only the best officers should make inspections. As a result, the system established makes use of *ad hoc* inspectors, available for periods of two to four weeks from their regular assignments. This means that headquarters personnel, perhaps the assistant director (administration) or a special assistant to the deputy director (policy and research), can temporarily focus their insights on post inspection and, at the same time, gain knowledge useful in the performance of their regular tasks. Under the current ground rules, no foreign service inspector will inspect a post at which he has served as PAO or, in recent years, in another high-level job. At least one member of a two- or three-man team, and preferably all, should have had active duty in the area of the post being inspected. All inspectors should be currently serving in another geographic area. Under this system, a good officer now serving in Africa may "escape" to a European post for several weeks, or an officer from Europe inspect an African post, where he may gain insights into the problems of African students studying in Europe. Although the inspectors are less experienced, they are likely to be energetic and interested, near the peak of their careers or talented "comers." USIA inspectors are viewing USIS activities at the same overseas posts covered by the Department of State's Inspection Corps, are often present at a post at the same time, can exchange ideas, and are sometimes able to correct the misconceptions of State's inspectors about USIS operations.

The inspectors do not assess the validity of the psychological objectives and supporting projects of the Country Plan or the new Country Plan Program Memorandum. This remains the joint responsibility of the area office directors and the public affairs officers concerned. They do assess post performance under the accepted Country Plan or Program Memorandum, assess post organization and operations, and write efficiency reports on American foreign service personnel. To speed the task and to allow the post to make improvements in operations before the inspectors arrive, a post checklist is forwarded well before the scheduled inspection. The checklist contains some four hundred questions, most to be answered by a simple "yes" or "no." These indicate the desired types of activities and operational climate, covering the areas of program planning and direction, post management, use of media services, special activities (English teaching, educational exchange, American studies, cultural presentations, trade fair exhibitions), and special target audiences, as well as administrative or personnel problems. The inspectors carry with them a shorter checklist of seventy-five questions as a guide and reminder, covering the same areas of interest. While post reports by the old Inspection Corps were detailed and ran up to 140 pages in length, reports under the present system range in length from 5 to 7 pages and deal with matters that require high-level attention. Only matters that are going exceptionally well or very poorly are included in the report. A copy of the report will be shown to the ambassador, but it is returned to the inspector general without amendment. Before being finalized, it is reviewed with the area office director concerned and his judgments incorporated. In addition to the post report, there is the efficiency report on all post personnel, describing each employee's appearance, his family and representational qualifications; his manner, attitudes, and interests; his performance and job effectiveness; his experience and training in terms of Agency needs and possible long-range career goals; and his readiness for promotion. The emphasis throughout the inspection is not on finding fault but on helping the post and its personnel improve the USIS operation, both short- and long-range. Many informal suggestions are quickly accepted and implemented by the post; those which may require additional funds or headquarters support are discussed with the area office director by the inspector general. It is too early to make a rational assessment of quality or impact of the new inspection system, but it represents an imaginative effort to improve the old Inspection Corps and appears far better than the self-inspection system which existed from 1962 to 1965. One of the advantages of the new system is its relatively low cost. The inspection experience probably benefits the inspector more than his absence from his regular job harms USIA or USIS operations, providing a net benefit to the Agency. The Agency director once more has an independent and objective inspection system to assist him in the management of USIS operations overseas. Although the director, the executive assistant, and the deputy director do make a few brief inspections of USIS posts, they have real need of staff assistance to maximize the potential usefulness of the inspection process.

Role in Planning for the Future

A major problem for the Agency's leaders is finding time for introspection. Thinking is most often geared to seeking a solution to a single problem—usually involving acceptance or rejection of a plan staffed-out within the Agency. The breadth of their interests and the insistence of daily operations—the tough decisions that must be made on the seventh floor—preclude sustained involvement in planning ahead. They can assign a problem called to their attention to someone else to look into. They can be drawn into a discussion after a forward-looking idea has been developed and is ready for critical review. By their attitudes, they can encourage those serving under them to think courageously about the future. By their actions, they can set up procedures to make sure that the Agency continues to look far enough ahead to insure that it meets oncoming problems—with the proper personnel, technical facilities, and policies.

If their role in maintaining the Agency's external relations seems to reduce the time of the director, executive assistant, and deputy director for internal matters, it is well to remember that they are the Agency's most influential spokesmen to get its ideas accepted by other elements in government. The pace of the jobs at the top—with many extra-Agency contacts competing with intramural duties—insures that most of the Agency's operational policy decisions, long-range planning, and research papers originate elsewhere in USIA. The Agency element assuming major responsibility for policy and research in behalf of the Agency leaders is the Office of Policy and Research—the Agency's policy cockpit, headed by Deputy Director of USIA for Policy and Research Hewson Ryan, the Agency's third-ranking leader.

IV

The Policy Cockpit:
Office of Policy and Research

The deputy director of USIA (policy and research) controls USIA's policy nerve center. His Office of Policy and Research (IOP)—with its three major operating elements: the Policy Guidance and Media Reaction Staff, the Policy and Plans Staff, and the Research and Analysis Staff—responds to daily stimuli, studying the effectiveness of Agency operations and directing the Agency's policy reaction to current events. It senses environmental change of a longer-range nature and assists in adapting Agency programs and products to emerging requirements. It transforms foreign policy into information policy and arouses concern for public opinion and psychological impact in interagency groups making foreign policy or conducting overseas operations. Said another way, the head of the Office of Policy and Research supervises preparation of daily policy guidance for USIA's operating elements; directs the formulation of basic Agency information policies, themes, program emphases, Country Plans, and the Country Plan Program Memoranda; oversees the Agency's research program which analyzes the appropriateness of Agency objectives, determines target audiences, and analyzes program cost-effectiveness on a regional and media basis; insures that significant findings in research studies are related to policy operations; represents the Agency on interdepartmental groups concerned with foreign affairs, maintaining liaison with the White House, the Department of State, and Defense Department and other agencies; and advises the director, the executive assistant, and the deputy director of USIA and representatives of other government agencies on overseas public opinion factors relevant to the formulation of foreign or information policy and to program execution overseas.

The director and deputy director of USIA hold Executive Level 2 and 4 posts and are presidential appointees. After 1964, the deputy director (policy and plans) and his chief assistant, the associate director (policy and plans), held Executive Level 5 posts. They were not presidential appointees. Now known as the deputy and associate directors (policy and research), they were probably by 1967 the Agency's third- and fourth- or fifth-ranking leaders. Today both are members of USIA's Foreign Service Career Reserve. Thomas Sorensen as deputy director of USIA (policy and plans) under Murrow, and until December 31, 1964, under Rowan, had been a Kennedy appointee. He was taken from a middle-level Foreign Service Career Reserve rank after ten years in USIA's foreign service and assigned to what was at that time a GS-18 position. Sorensen was an experienced operator to whom the other political appointees (the director and deputy director) could turn for expertise on program operations. Sorensen's associate deputy director was Burnett Anderson, an even more experienced "nonpolitical type" Foreign Service Career Reserve officer, who carried heavy operational responsibilities during the Sorensen period. Anderson became deputy director when Sorensen resigned to become Vice president of the International Technical Assistance and Development Company, a division of Aerojet-General Corporation. Sorensen, as a presidential appointee, tackled thorny problems that threatened political repercussions and was responsible for effecting the close policy-product relationship introduced in the Kennedy administration by Murrow—understandably receiving little applause from Agency personnel in carrying out either of these tasks. The deputy director of USIA for policy and research (until July 1, 1966, policy and plans) still serves as the Agency's bridge between political concern and operational or research expertise, though the politicization of policy is now likely to be carried more directly by the director, the executive assistant, or the deputy director of USIA. As chief formulator of operational Agency information policies, the deputy director of USIA (policy and research) must sometimes be—as Sorensen was—forced by the tempo of events to direct rather than consult Agency elements on what should be done, for he is a conduit from the director to the Agency as well as the Agency's top representative to the director. Ryan as deputy director (policy and research) has much less time than did Marks, Rowan, or Murrow to serve as an Agency spokesman to the domestic public or to the Congress, as an Agency leader to generate personnel morale, or as an Agency committee chairman to bring diverse elements together for discussion and recommendations on common problems. He does attend a brief meeting with representatives of the policy guidance staff, which assists in providing fast policy guidance to the Agency, every weekday morning at 9 a.m. On Tuesdays, he is likely to be found at the director's weekly staff meeting by 8:30 a.m. Every Tuesday he meets with his chief assistants in the Office of Policy and Research for a weekly staff meeting at 3 p.m. On Wednesday noon, he lunches—nose-bag style—with the area office assistant directors (plus the assistant directors of USIA for administration and for personnel and training) and may have placed an item on their discussion agenda. Each Thursday at 3:30 p.m. he meets with IOP's special advisors and liaison officers serving on the Policy and Plans Staff. Every other Friday at 2:30 P.M., he takes part in a broad discussion with policy officers from the area offices. Late each weekday, between 5 and 6 P.M., the deputy director (policy and research) confers with Director Marks, reporting the grist of the day's events in an exchange of views. During crisis periods, he is on the phone several times a day talking with the assistant director of USIA for the Broadcasting Service (director of the Voice of America). Although conflicts between IOP and the Voice of America have occurred in the past, Ryan's relationships with VOA are cooperative and affable. In addition to these relations within USIA the deputy director (policy and research) works informally with the Policy Planning Council in the Department of State and with the assistant secretary of state for public affairs. In the Department of Defense, he consults with International Security Affairs, with the Joint Chiefs of Staff on psychological operations, and with elements responsible for the armed forces radio and television operations. Under his direction, IOP is responsible for preparing the director, the executive assistant, or the deputy director for participation in any interagency meetings—for example, backstopping the director's role in the Senior Inter-Departmental Group or in subcommittees of the National Security Council.

In spite of the number and variety of his duties, Ryan maintains a calm and analytical approach, perhaps because of his early academic experience as a language instructor at Yale University. Before his appointment as deputy director (policy and research), his scholarly attitude and administrative ability had been responsible for his success as assistant director of USIA for Latin America—a post particularly important to USIA because of the Alliance for Progress. Although Ryan's duties are in considerable measure operational and may border on the political, his university background stands him in good stead, for the Office of Policy and Research is involved in advance planning, in the application of communications research to operations, taking into account broad considerations of long-range interest to the Agency and to the United States. He is assisted by the associate director (policy and research) who typically has directed most of the daily policy guidance, dealing with problems affecting the fast media or with area office guidance to country public affairs officers in the field on current events.

The maturation of USIA and its growing acceptance as a major foreign affairs agency, coupled with the activist role of the Kennedy and Johnson administrations in foreign policy and their interest in information programs as a policy tool, have helped to upgrade the importance of the role performed by the deputy director (policy and research) and the Office of Policy and Research. Also affecting USIA's status and interagency relationships was dominance over foreign affairs by the President and his White House advisers during much of the Kennedy administration. Perhaps in overstatement, but typical of reactions by personnel in many agencies during 1963, when the Department of State's leadership in the formulation of foreign policy was being challenged, a close adviser to Deputy Director (policy and plans) Sorensen said: "Now the White House makes the big foreign policy. State supervises its coordination. You must get foreign policy guidance from the White House to know what policy really is. It's the only safe place to get it. The White House doesn't always check with State if it doesn't like what has been done." The feeling is shared by many in USIA that

> Kennedy expected more from the propaganda weapon than Eisenhower did. Ike felt he had to have an information program. Kennedy saw it as a sensitive, responsive tool, its utility to be considered whenever U.S. power was to be brought to bear. He and his staff were highly political and ran international affairs as they did domestic, with full use of public opinion. They expected action and results out of the propaganda arm.

With such moods abroad in Washington, USIA policy makers in IOP were encouraged to submit speech drafts to the White House, in addition to commenting to State on its draft, if they did not like a State draft they reviewed. On more than one occasion, when material was to reach foreign publics, President Kennedy called direct and asked IOP staff members their opinions, discarding a State draft for a USIA draft read to him by phone. By 1966, there was a tendency by most USIA personnel to discount the number of times such events occurred or to downgrade the importance of the policies affected, but such contacts did take place and were indicative of a trend. Compounding State's slow loss of expertise in the overseas information field during the period after 1953 when USIA became an independent agency, they must have some adverse impact on State-USIA guidance relations —though these are still considered satisfactory by both agencies. In part USIA's growing influence in the White House from 1961 to 1963 stemmed from the fact that President Kennedy admired and respected Ed Murrow for his demonstrated ability in the television field, that Don Wilson had been an efficient press aide to Kennedy during the 1960 campaign, and that "Tom" Sorensen was the older brother of "Ted" Sorensen, the President's Counsel and close adviser. Nonetheless, Carl Rowan was relied upon by President

Johnson, personally reviewing for Johnson the Agency output during the Dominican crisis after the public announcement on April 29, 1965, that American marines had been landed. Leonard Marks has an even closer personal relationship with the President, so that Agency relations with the White House can hardly be said to have diminished, though their nature may have changed. USIA was not alone among Washington agencies in feeling closer to the White House on matters pertaining to its overseas interests during the Kennedy years, viewing the President as an arbiter who could and would override the Department of State. Part of this sense stemmed from the President's vitality and interest in detail; where Eisenhower sought careful staffwork with differences worked out by agencies concerned and wanted only the most recalcitrant problems brought to him for decision, Kennedy was more willing to intervene before differences were buried in compromise language. Part was the result of the President's assigning primary responsibility for certain functions or missions with foreign policy implications to individual departments other than State, though leaving to State the responsibility for over-all policy direction. The delegation of primary responsibility for JUSPAO in Vietnam to the director of USIA by President Johnson in May of 1965 in one sense continues the dispersion of control of overseas programs set in motion during the Kennedy administration. Whether this trend has been offset by Johnson's downgrading of the National Security Council as a broad vehicle for discussion of national policies while placing greater reliance upon McNamara, Rusk, and Bundy or Rostow, is not entirely clear. The creation of the Senior Inter-Departmental Group and the Inter-Departmental Regional Groups in the spring of 1966 will help in strengthening State's over-all leadership in policy making, if properly implemented.

SOURCES OF GENERAL POLICY GUIDANCE TO USIA

During the Eisenhower administration, elaborate interdepartmental procedures within the National Security Council structure produced policy papers which, when approved by the President, became the policies of the United States government. Papers dealt with fundamental concepts, with policy for a single country or geographic region, or with a functional problem not related to a specific geographic area. After 1953 the Operations Coordinating Board (OCB) generated agreed operational policies to guide departments or agencies with overseas activities in their implementations of the

broader National Security Council statements. Department of State personnel, often at the country desk level in the regional bureaus, played major roles
in drafting many NSC and OCB country or regional papers, though functional papers were likely to be drafted elsewhere in the department or in
another more appropriate agency. USIA and other foreign affairs agencies
were important participants in the drafting process and in discussions—
contributing to, reviewing, and commenting on drafts—often forcing compromises since no agency could be forced to implement the elements of an
OCB paper relating to its responsibilities unless it approved. State had no
final say, though its representatives chaired many of the OCB working group
meetings. Critics have declared the NSC-OCB structure produced bland
products, lacking drive or thrust, comfortable to all but exciting no one, too
often subjected to parochial interpretation by individual agencies in the
process of implementation. Thus, the process is said to have reduced individual agency initiative without achieving efficient coordination. Some
alleged that NSC-OCB operations stalled policy on dead center—the least
common denominator acceptable to all participating agencies. The processes were time consuming. More serious is the charge that the mountain of
paperwork produced by the structure during the Eisenhower years tended to
build up an internal consistency in American policy which made it difficult
for middle-level policy officers to make bold recommendations for changes
in direction as emerging world conditions called for fresh policy assessments
in the areas with which they were concerned. There was little mood for
change at the top.

To cut through the entangling web of the NSC-OCB policies and to reas-
sert White House policy leadership over the executive agencies, President
Kennedy abolished the Operations Coordinating Board on February 18,
1961. He also eliminated some of the formal procedures used to develop policy papers for the consideration of the National Security Council and the
President. For example, the Policy Planning Board became officially
extinct, but survived informally, for interagency contacts continued at that
level. And if the OCB working groups with regular meeting times disappeared, there were still interdepartmental meetings at this level scheduled on
an *ad hoc* basis. Under the Kennedy administration, working groups or task
forces were created as emergencies arose or as problems were foreseen which
required the working out of new United States policies. Task forces often
utilized the new Operations Center in the Department of State as their headquarters. It was said that groups came into existence dealing with aspects of
the same general problem which had little contact or were unaware of the
other's existence. Some feared coordination had been succeeded by chaos. In

retrospect, this appears not to have been so. The strengthening of the Department of State's Policy Planning Staff, reborn as the Policy Planning Council under Walt Rostow's leadership, provided a strong integrating policy planning unit located in the Department of State, maintaining close relations with the staff of the President's National Security Adviser, McGeorge Bundy (until March 1, 1966, when he was replaced by Rostow). New Policy Guidelines Papers[1] replaced the old National Security Council and Operations Coordinating Board country or functional papers. The new papers, like those before, were worked out under Department of State leadership, in consultation with the interested agencies. They included both statements of general policy and more specific guides for operations. During the preparation of the Guidelines Paper, the President and his advisers intervened at earlier stages in the policy-making process than during the Eisenhower administration to make decisions between clear-cut alternatives rather than allowing the departments to compromise many of their differences at lower levels as they had in the past.

By 1963 the Policy Planning Council at State had assumed the leadership in producing a more formal type of guidance, the National Policy Paper, for those countries in which the United States had a sharp concern. The Guidelines Papers remained in use elsewhere, updated by interagency discussions at the desk level and signed off in USIA by the appropriate area office and the Office of Policy. The National Policy Paper represented an attempt at greater uniformity and better coordination of all foreign affairs agency activities. National Policy Papers (NPP) are discussed with the field, but the major contributions to the NPPs and use of them is at the Washington level. If the Guidelines Paper and the newer National Policy Paper lay down broad overall directives for American action in a particular country, they still lack sufficient detail to guide USIA's monthly and daily operations. There remains the task of assessing the general situation in the country and the statement of United States aims and proposed actions from an informational-psychological perspective, to spell out more specific objectives and supporting activities to be achieved or conducted by USIS personnel. This analysis, known for many years as the USIS Country Plan, will be replaced by the new Country Plan Program Memorandum over a two- or three-year period—probably by 1970. Both the Country Plan and the Country Plan Program Memorandum are the responsibility of the country public affairs officer, USIA's top representative in the country concerned. The Country Plan, as well as the Country Plan Program Memorandum, introduced in thirty-nine USIS posts during the spring of 1967, is prepared by the CPAO in consultation with the members of his USIS staff and with the representatives of other United States agencies. The CPAO's drafts are subjected to careful review in USIA, particularly at the country desk, policy officer, program coordinator, and area office director levels, and must be approved by USIA's deputy director for policy and research. The Country Plan and the Country Plan Program Memorandum must also be approved by the United States ambassador who heads the country team of which the CPAO is a member. Revision or updating of such plans is to be completed annually by July 1, and in practice may occur oftener, i.e., when a new CPAO is assigned in a country or should a new development require revision of a Guidelines Paper or a National Policy Paper. Approved Country Plans or Country Plan Program Memoranda serve as guides to action overseas and in Washington, a measuring stick against which the CPAO and USIA headquarters officials can measure progress of individual USIA country programs during the year.

The Country Plan is a significantly shorter document than the Country Plan Program Memorandum, ten pages or less compared to fifty or sixty pages. Assessment Reports and Statistical Reports required of USIS posts in addition to the Country Plan will no longer be required with the Country Plan Program Memorandum. This will constitute an annual saving of some eighty to ninety pages in post reporting, according to an experienced program coordinator. The old USIA Country Plan is prepared in five parts, Part I being the Objectives section of the Guidelines or National Policy Paper. Part II of the Country Plan is an analysis of the objectives and includes a discussion of operations and actions of an overt or unattributed information nature which USIA can undertake in support of the objectives and in fulfilment of its assigned mission. Part III states as clearly as possible the specific objectives of information programs in the country. One such objective might be that the country adopt an educational philosophy or system patterned after that of the United States. Part IV is a spelling out of the target groups to be reached be priority in attempting to achieve each objective. Special groups within government, among public opinion molders, in the educational field, or student, business, and cultural groups may be singled out as requiring attention. Part V of the Country Plan details the projects and programs related to each objective down to specific media products, a film on teaching social studies or a pamphlet on higher education in the United States. Country Plans may be broken down by quarters so that the CPAO and those backstopping country programs in Washington can plan activities and emphases more specifically throughout the year.

The newer Country Plan Program Memorandum is a six-section document. Part I states the objectives of the United States government in the country. Part II states as clearly as possible USIA's information objectives in the country. Part III identifies the target audiences to be reached. Part IV lists the major themes to be emphasized in USIA programs and products. Part V presents the current activities being conducted by the USIS post. Part VI is a pro and con discussion of possible alternative activities, asking what else could be done. Part VII is a discussion of why present activities are conducted, of what should be continued and what added. Part VIII is the USIS post's recommended program for the upcoming year. The analysis in Parts VII and VIII is done on the basis of the cost-benefit or cost-effectiveness of each program considered—assessing expense against the number and quality of exposures; against the interest, awareness, and understanding audiences will have of the program or product; against the attitudinal change which may be expected; and against the behavioral change which may follow. Two major differences emerge between the Country Plan and the Country Plan Program Memorandum. The latter adds a special country themes section in Part IV, making possible selection from among broad Agency themes those appropriate to an individual country. It also adds in Part VII a cost-effectiveness analysis, directed at the program to be recommended, complete with figures and evaluation in one document—instead of forcing headquarters personnel reviewing USIS Country Plans to consult a Country Plan, Assessment Reports, and Statistical Reports separately and then collate them in their minds in order to make a judgment of the post's suggested plan. Thus, the post is required to coordinate these materials in the process of doing its planning, which should result in improved recommendations and make evaluation simpler at headquarters.

If the Guidelines Papers, National Policy Papers, Country Plans, and Country Plan Program Memoranda are usually country-centered, two other sources of general policy guidance to USIA, given special attention in both area offices and media services and always on the minds of Office of Policy and Research personnel, are worldwide in nature, spelling out policy and operational emphases that know no national boundaries. The most basic of these, already discussed, is the Agency's statement of mission as defined in President Kennedy's memorandum of February 25, 1963, to the director of USIA—replaced early in 1967 by a new statement of mission signed off by Director Marks. Especially relevant in the Kennedy statement of mission is the paragraph which says:

> Agency activities should (a) encourage constructive public support abroad for the goal of a "peaceful world community of free and independent states, free to choose their own future and their own system so long as it does not threaten the freedom of others";(b) identify

the United States as a strong democratic, dynamic nation qualified for its leadership of world efforts toward this goal, and (c) unmask and counter hostile attempts to distort or frustrate the objectives and policies of the United States. These activities should emphasize the ways in which United States policies harmonize with those of other peoples and governments, and those aspects of American life and culture which facilitate sympathetic understanding of United States policies.

Providing more specific guidance, consistent with these general admonitions but more adapted to the ebb and flow of world events, are five worldwide policy themes, which change from time to time through agreement between State, USIA, and the White House, though they are generated from within IOP. USIA media must show cause when they produce materials for multi-area use with an emphasis or purpose outside the agreed worldwide themes. Country desk officers in the area offices in the past were even expected to review individual Country Plans for compatibility with the worldwide themes. Responsive to local pressures, the CPAO's in the field were and are often less enthusiastic about pushing worldwide themes than Agency officials in Washington. The new Country Plan Program Memorandum now makes it possible for themes to be emphasized selectively country by country. At one point during 1963, the Agency's five worldwide themes included: (1) pinning the tag of peacebreaker upon the Soviet Union in the Berlin Wall episode, when the tenuous balance of power in Berlin was threatened; (2) emphasizing the interest of the United States in genuine and responsible disarmament, as opposed to the Soviet Union's unrealistic call for complete disarmament without feasible timetables or sufficient inspection; (3) identifying Soviet action in support of the "troika" principle in the United Nations as against the best interests of the United Nations, and emphasizing that a strong United Nations was important to protect the interests of small nations; (4) supporting the principle of self-determination of nations, posing American support for free choice and pluralism against the Communist stress on acceptance of an ideology which is antagonistic to national freedom; and (5) stressing the need for modernization of less-developed nations and the importance of United States economic assistance as a means of achieving independence and continued political viability. The first three emphases were considered by Agency personnel to be points that could be made and possibly "won" quickly. The latter two themes were thought likely to remain on the list for an indefinite period. An emphasis then emerging was that of developing the strength image of the United States, to encourage nations or governments that want to remain free of outside control to feel that they can rely upon American power and assistance if they resist threats to their independence or neutrality. Such a theme may require general statements like that once made by President Johnson, that the United States possesses military strength more powerful than that of all the rest of the world combined—as well as pointing out by word and action that such power can be brought to bear in a limited way to resolve problems short of nuclear attack or general war. A foresighted stress on American strength may possibly have diminished the psychological impact upon less-developed peoples when the Chinese Communists announced their first successful nuclear explosion.

By late 1965, the five themes had become (1) the pursuit of peace, (2) strength and reliability, (3) free choice, (4) rule of law, and (5) the United Nations.[2] In comparing the 1963 and 1965 themes, "strength and reliability" was officially added to the list. Berlin, troika, and disarmament were no longer mentioned. "Free choice" and the "United Nations" were the only clear carryovers. In 1965 five additional emphases calling attention to social, economic, and scientific progress within the United States provided additional guidance. These concerned "Racial and Ethnic Progress," "Economic Strength," "Economic Democracy," "Scientific and Educational Strength," and "Cultural Development, Diversity, and Distribution." These "twin fives" provided general guidance to personnel in the media services and area offices in Washington and to the CPAO's and their assistants in the field, and were also consciously and unconsciously applied by those responsible for fast policy guidance on a daily basis—one of the most dramatic of USIA's Washington operations.

THE FAST GUIDANCE MECHANISM: STATE AND USIA

Daily policy guidance between the Department of State and the United States Information Agency is said to be a "two-way" street. Focal points in this interagency exchange are policy guidance personnel on the Policy Guidance and Media Reaction Staff of the Office of Policy and Research and State's Office of Policy Guidance in the Bureau of Public Affairs. As fast-breaking events around the world require reaction by the United States government, the Department of State has the primary responsibility for reporting and justifying American policy to the domestic public. The Agency has a similar responsibility to convey and explain the reasons for American policy to overseas publics. Responsibility for the formulation to over-all American foreign policy is centered in the Department of State, but USIA has a responsibility to advise the Department of State on the overseas informational and psychological impact of such policy. Since it is likely that what the Department of State says for home consumption will also be reported abroad, and since in the formulation of policy the Department of State must take into consideration the informational-psychological factor along with other integers in the policy equation, a close relationship between State and USIA is a necessity for an effective American response to world events. Because of the American government's deep involvement and role of leadership in world affairs, its policy reactions should be swift and sure, with a minimum of error or omission in formulating foreign policy or translating it into information policy for domestic and overseas publics.

If the Voice of America is to have listeners or USIA's press service is to have readers, USIA must carry news while it is still "hot"—or lose both interest and credibility. If it is to support American policy, it must make its own limited policy contribution and learn what over-all policy is then approved in a reasonably short time span or its commentary may come too late to be politically effective. USIA cannot afford to be an "uncertain trumpet."[3] Its fast media must report without hesitation. If they are to fulfil USIA's assigned mission, they must also effectively convey a message. Relationships between State and USIA take place at a variety of levels, in regular staff meetings and informally by telephone, and are of both a formal and informal nature. Speedy and coherent response by State and USIA to the daily quota of crises can only be assured by carefully planned and intricate procedures performed regularly by capable and experienced personnel. A closer look at the organization, functions, procedures, and relationships of USIA policy guidance personnel should help to clarify one important aspect of State-USIA relations as well as Office of Policy and Research relationships to other elements of USIA requiring fast policy guidance.

Policy guidance personnel on USIA's Policy Guidance and Media Reaction Staff consists of a chief and deputy chief, plus five area officers, one each for Africa, Europe, East Asia and the Pacific, Latin America, and Near East and South Asia. All but the chief are in direct personal contact daily with personnel in the Department of State, the deputy chief working closely in State with the director of the Office of News, the director of the Office of Policy Guidance, and the senior deputy assistant secretary of state for public affairs who is responsible for the Department of State's news releases. The area officers deal primarily with the public affairs advisers in State's regional bureaus, each covering his assigned region. Their essential functions are to help identify issues of the day to which USIA must react, to discover what policy alternatives are open to the Department of State on each issue, to advise on the likely informational-psychological impact of the alternatives upon their areas, to discover what the policy decision is to be, to consult on the manner in which the news will be released to the domestic public, and then to prepare appropriate guidances for USIA media and area offices on how the policy should be announced overseas. Backstopping this liaison by the policy guidance area officers with public affairs staffs in State's regional bureaus in some instances may be contacts by USIA country desk officers with desk officers in State's regional bureaus.

Early duty is assigned to at least one of the policy guidance area officers daily. The duty officer must report in by 7 A.M. to read summaries of overnight news breaks and FBIS reports on foreign broadcasts. Quickly he must identify the information problems most likely to plague USIA's top policy makers and fast media during the day. By 7:30 A.M., when the deputy chief of policy guidance comes in, the duty officer is ready to brief his "boss." Most policy officers in USIA as well as policy guidance personnel are "glued" to morning radio broadcasts from 8:00 to 8:15 A.M. After these, there may be a flurry of telephone calls between the media services or area offices and the Office of Policy and Research. By 8:30 A.M., the deputy chief has collated and relayed USIA's questions by phone to State's Office of Policy Guidance in the Bureau of Public Affairs. USIA's questions, along with those posed by State's Office of News, are raised and discussed at an 8:45 A.M. staff meeting of the assistant secretary of state for public affairs. Three days a week— Monday, Wednesday, and Friday—the assistant secretary proceeds from his staff meeting to that of the secretary of state at 9:15 A.M. Here he can ask for guidance and discussion on the release of information on current policy matters. Immediately after the 8:45 meeting, the Office of News in State has prepared a budget of the day's news issues, a list of specifics on which the department is likely to be questioned by newsmen during the day. Questions appropriate to regional or functional bureaus of the department are forwarded to the public affairs advisors in the bureaus concerned. The public affairs advisors are requested to prepare and staff-out answers with proper clearances.

Back in USIA, Deputy Director (policy and research) Hewson Ryan has a fifteen-minute daily staff meeting starting at 9 A.M. with the chief, the deputy chief, and others from policy guidance as appropriate to apprise himself of the day's events, to raise possible information problems, and to suggest solutions. At this meeting, the deputy director can pinpoint the issues which must go higher for decision before USIA reacts. Many matters he can decide on the basis of past guidances and his own experience. By 10 A.M., the deputy chief of policy guidance and his area officers are fanned out in State. At 10:15

A.M. in State, once a week, the deputy chief of policy guidance hears a report on the secretary of state's morning meetings given by the director of the Office of News or by the senior deputy assistant secretary of state for public affairs. The deputy chief can raise problems and make suggestions on how the news should be handled. By 11:30 A.M., the public affairs advisers from State's regional bureaus meet with director of State's Office of Policy Guidance, and representative from the Office of News, to answer items on the joint USIA and Office of News daily "budgets," which had been forwarded to them some two hours earlier. Papers prepared in response to the questions are turned over to USIA's deputy chief of policy guidance. In the meantime, the deputy chief's area officers have returned to USIA about 11 A.M. and have begun to compare notes. State's regional areas may hold different positions on a particular problem. When the deputy chief returns about 12:15 P.M., he may bring with him an agreed position reached in State and announced at the 11:30 meeting. By 12:30 P.M., policy guidance personnel have prepared policy reports with suggestions on how to handle the day's news for distribution at a briefing held primarily for policy officers of the area offices and policy application officers of the media services, but attended by most USIA elements except those essentially concerned with administration. Among the twenty-five persons usually present are five from USIA's Press and Publications Service, writers from the Policy and Columns Staff who produce commentary for the Agency's daily Wireless File.

The deputy chief of policy guidance, using informal notes, ticks off relevant information which he has acquired during the morning at State, perhaps a comment based on a point made at State's morning meetings or concerning specifics lying behind what State's Office of News director is telling newsmen at his "noon" press briefing. The deputy chief's remarks may include classified information of a background nature drawn from intelligence reports related to information in the public domain. An upcoming visit by a foreign dignitary to Washington may be discussed, with some assessment of what the purpose of the trip is, what the visitor may request and what the likely American response will be, along with suggestions for possible television, press, and radio coverage. Armed with this type of information, USIA policy makers at all levels are better able to evaluate a news development and judge what weight to give it in area or media guidances. There may be some reaction to the verbal report, some specialized information contributed from one of the policy officers present, perhaps a brief discussion. The policy officers also receive reports drafted by the policy guidance area officers on the basis of their morning contacts in State. These are scanned and queries directed to the deputy chief or to the appropriate area officer. Carrying a security classification, the "IOP Meeting Notes" indicate rather generally how each of the important news events of the day is to be played by USIA media in support of American foreign policy. The policy officers return to their offices at the close of the thirty- to forty-minute briefing and distribute copies of the IOP area officers' reports as they are or make distribution after adapting them to the needs of their particular media or area. Telephone calls or personal discussions with appropriate individuals can speed the process if the time factor is critical.

There is currently little criticism of the fast guidance mechanism or of general State-USIA policy guidance relationships either in State or USIA. There is some sadness among "old-time" public affairs officers at State who note the department's loss of overseas information expertise since USIA became independent in 1953, who recognize that the review of USIA's budget by State's regional bureaus has become quite perfunctory, who watch the slowly diminishing cooperation between the assistant secretary of state for public affairs and the director of USIA since it has been established that the director outranks the assistant secretary, who wonder about the long-range impact of USIA's closer relations to the White House since 1961, and who wish USIA would be more receptive to State's recommendations on changes in USIA field operations than the Agency in fact is. Part of this feeling is a nostalgia for things past that may never be again; part is rooted in pragmatic concern for a proper coordination of foreign policy and information operations. USIA as an information agency may sometimes be anxious for policy guidance on an issue on which policy for good reasons has not yet been decided, but it recognizes that many matters today involve the interest of a number of departments. If serious differences arise, it is not the secretary of state but the President who may finally have to make the decision. In the meantime, there may be little policy guidance that State's Office of Policy Guidance can provide to USIA. There are some general regrets, but there is mutual respect among the participants in the fast guidance process. Although there is no current move to make any major adjustments in the fast guidance mechanism, an upgrading in level of personnel assigned policy guidance area responsibility is sometimes suggested.

POLICY GUIDANCE: NOTES, GUIDES, AND THE WIRELESS FILE

The 12:30 P.M. daily briefing of USIA policy officers by the deputy chief of policy guidance and the IOP area officers is only one among several important guidance activities performed by policy guidance personnel. On an *ad hoc* basis, IOP News Policy Notes (NPN) are issued in a numbered series whenever a written guidance for the use of the media is required to sharpen or adapt the Agency's policy line for an impending event. The NPN's may be addressed to one or more Agency elements and are normally drafted by a policy guidance area officer, cleared with the appropriate policy officers in the area offices, possibly with desk officers, with the media services, and by the Department of State, and then issued by the chief of policy guidance. For example, when the tenth anniversary of the Hungarian Revolution approached in 1966, a News Policy Note indicated the general information policy line to be taken in eastern Europe, in Hungary itself, in the Soviet Union, and in the rest of the world. So far as USIA media are concerned, the News Policy Note takes precedence over any cables from an American ambassador, any call from a State country desk, or the recommendation of one of USIA's area directors. While the media concerned might call the divergent views it received to the attention of the Office of Policy and Research, it would normally be for the Office of Policy and Research to consider the conflicting views and either accept some change or reject them in toto. If a media service director feels strongly enough about the NPN in its draft form, he can go directly to the deputy or associate deputy director of USIA (policy and research). If no agreement is reached at this level, he is then free to take his case to the agency director or deputy director. Usually accord is achieved before the matter goes clear to the top. Often the problem is simply how best to make application of a broader guidance already approved by the deputy director of USIA (policy and research) or associate director (policy and research) to a specific problem which had not been foreseen when the general statement was formulated. Subordinates are less likely than their superiors to want to make exceptions, and the matter must then be taken to the IOP leadership. A guidance drawn up to cover an event in world terms often requires a new look when media specialists attempt to apply it to some particular country or area. A balance must sometimes be found between the over-all tone and recognition of diversity. IOP attempts to give guidance which will be acceptable both to the media and area elements concerned, but theoretically it could make a decision acceptable to neither which could only be overturned by an appeal to the director or deputy director of the Agency. In practice, accommodation is likely at the IOP level. In essence, the News Policy Note is a headquarters document addressed to USIA's media services. Copies of an NPN may be forwarded to appropriate USIS posts overseas.

Another vehicle for policy guidance is the Information Guide, specifically prepared for field use. If the IOP policy guidance man for the European area receives material from the public affairs advisor in the Bureau of European Affairs in the Department of State which he feels should be communicated to European USIS posts, he drafts an Information Guide, consulting with officers at several levels in the office of the assistant director of USIA for Europe. The document is generally classified and sent air pouch or by telegram. An area office policy officer may initiate an Information Guide himself if he convinces State and USIA's IOP that it is needed and submits his draft for review.

Flashed overseas on occasion by the Wireless File of the Press and Publications Service is an assessment of events of worldwide significance drafted by the chief of policy guidance which constitutes guidance to PAO's in the field on the items covered. Perhaps on the issue of racial integration, the President of the United States comments on a statement by a southern govenor. The chief's explanation of why the President took such action is cleared with policy officers in the area offices and with State, and adapted to individual regions if necessary. Regional policy guidance is also provided by the Wireless File.

Although much of the guidance system is formalized, the men who participate in the policy guidance routine develop a policy consciousness and awareness of specifics which allow them to make occasional informal suggestions to remedy "boners" which pass unrecognized by others who concentrate less on policy matters. A young foreign service officer assigned to policy guidance for Africa noted that the Voice of America was referring to "rebels" in Angola during African broadcasts, a term used by *Agence France Presse*. Reuters and *Agence France Presse* are excellent news sources on African affairs, but unconsciously or not they use terms that are "slanted" because of the historic colonial relationship of England and France to African areas. The young officer spoke up, the Voice changed its usage, and Africans now hear about "nationalist" uprisings in Angola—a small change but perhaps a significant one.

THE POLICY AND PLANS STAFF

When Thomas Sorensen was deputy director of USIA (policy and plans) heading the Office of Policy in 1963, aside from the Policy Guidance Staff, IOP was essentially staffed by individuals performing discrete functions with little mutual exchange of ideas—though most of them were sometimes present in a single discussion session along with personnel from other Agency elements. There were eight to ten advisors, each serving as an expert on certain types of substantive problems or dealing with a particular type of organizational groups. There was a single Agency planning officer, and a separate research applications officer. And, of course, there was the assistant deputy director (media content), with an assistant who performed a media review function somewhat similar to that now performed by USIA's Assistant Deputy Director Robert Akers. For a time in early 1967, personnel performing or assisting in the performance of these functions were reorganized into four groups—advisors, liaison officers, planning officers, and media content officers—under IOP Assistant Director (Operational Policy) Wilson Dizard. There were some four advisors, two liaison officers, three planning officers, and two media content officers. The operation in January, 1967, was approximately the same size as in 1963. There were advisors for cultural affairs, labor and equal opportunity, science, and women's activities. There were liaison officers for policy liaison and military liaison. By July, 1967, the Operational Policy Staff had become the Policy and Plans Staff, and its leader was Assistant Director (policy and plans) Reed Harris. By October, 1967 it had added a defense affairs and a business advisor as well as a business and intelligence liaison officer. The business advisor and the business liaison officer was an obvious remain of USIA's Office of Private Cooperation which had existed from 1963 to 1967. By late 1967, there were two planning officers and a research applications officer. Two media content officers continued to serve primarily as a backstop to USIA's deputy director in his role as reviewer of Agency media adaptation of policy to product—working closely with the planning officers. The Operational Policy Staff and the Policy and Plans Staff under Dizard and Harris played a major role during the latter half of 1966 and during 1967 in retooling the Agency's machinery for relating research findings of the Research and Analysis Staff to policy and in achieving more efficient and more flexible country planning by USIS posts.

The advisors and liaison officers,[4] with their interests in definite subject-matter fields, consulting with private organizations or maintaining liaison with other government agencies, are usually civil service employees, serving at the GS-14 or -15 level. Their diverse functions include giving advice to the director, his executive assistant, and the deputy director of USIA and to the top leaders of the Office of Policy and Research. They may be requested to advise on a particular problem or they may forward suggestions up the ladder on their own initiative. In turn, speaking for their superiors, they advise the area offices on policy matters and the media services on programs and products to be used overseas. They face up and down within the Agency; and they also face outward, giving and receiving. They must keep abreast of technical developments and policies in the agencies of government or private organizations with which their subject-matter specialty is most closely related, and exchange views at their level on problems in which USIA, other agencies, and private organizations have a shared interest. In addition, advisors and liaison officers must be aware of general developments or emerging problems in their fields both in the United States and abroad. Thus, the labor and equal opportunity advisor must understand problems of integration and private organizations concerned with it in the United States and follow daily events related to this issue, giving advice on how USIA should handle integration news overseas. He must also understand labor conditions in a variety of countries abroad and how best to communicate American domestic policy on labor matters and American foreign policy to overseas unions and laborers.

While the advisors and liaison officers are generally supposed to limit their advice to matters which have global impact, they are also drawn into consideration of more detailed area problems because of their expertise in their functional fields. Although they have assisted in drafting the five themes or areas of emphasis which provide worldwide policy guidance and which have sometimes remained constant for a year or more, much of their time is taken up in meeting the surge of crisis on a day-to-day basis via telephone to the fast media or the area offices. Whether Negro children die in the Sunday bombing of a church in Birmingham in 1963 or whites throw bricks and bottles at Negroes participating in a voter registration protest march in Grenada, Mississippi, in 1966, an advisor suggests how such news is to be conveyed overseas by the Voice of America, both in tone and order of presentation. The advisors and liaison officers also review products of the slower media, checking pamphlets or films going overseas. They may on occasion be drawn into the daily morning meeting of the deputy director (policy and research) when their expertise is relevant to USIA's handling of the day's events. They do papers or provide oral briefings which prepare their superiors for participation in high-level interagency meetings, but it is not unusual for them to represent USIA at middle-level interagency gatherings. They sometimes draft statements in behalf of USIA for those parts of policy papers prepared by State or the White House staff which may bear on USIA interests or functions. On the whole, the relations of the advisors and liaison officers appear to be closer to Agency personnel dealing in day-to-day matters rather than those with long-range policy concerns. In spite of this, they are aware of their need for depth and concern with matters developing more slowly but persisting over time. They are intelligent and articulate, both orally and on paper. Although they are journalists and men or women of action, they are relatively scholarly and thoughtful as well, sometimes withdrawing from consideration of minutia to concentrate attention on broader problems. Essentially policy minded, the advisors and liaison officers are interested in developments or events primarily in terms of what the information response should be to support American foreign policy goals and current operations. If they assist in the coordination of USIA policy both internally and within the government-wide spectrum, they still work mostly as individuals and rarely as collegial bodies. Their relations are primarily with others rather than among themselves.

The advisors and liaison officers and other IOP personnel have an opportunity for some group interchange of ideas at the weekly IOP staff meeting, chaired by the deputy director of USIA (policy and research), held on Wednesdays at 3 P.M. Here the deputy director (policy and research) may give a brief sketch of upcoming problems and events. Items of special relevance to IOP are then discussed informally. Advisors or liaison officers may raise problems themselves for general consideration. Occasionally, a member of the staff reports on a point he has previously been assigned to follow up. The focus is primarily short-term at the Wednesday IOP staff meeting, but more general discussion and a longer look ahead is taken at a meeting of the advisors and liaison officers with the deputy director of USIA (policy and research) on Thursday afternoons at three o'clock. The associate director (policy and research) may also participate in the discussions. Unless there is a world crises, the time forcus is likely to be three months to a year ahead, though by 1967 it was conceivable that talk might range five to ten years into the future. Advisors and liaison officers are asked to raise problems they forsee which may affect USIA information policies or media products. They are in a position to know of developments through their relations with private organizations or other government agencies. Problems discussed at these sessions are sometimes put on the agenda for the next USIA director's staff meeting and discussed by the heads of all Agency elements.

Planning officers on a Policy and Plans Staff are not likely to be ivory-tower scholars removed from practical problems, but neither are they tied to daily operations as is the desk officer in an area office. They may assist in the implementation of new administrative programs. For example, in 1967 they drafted a "Handbook on the Country Plan Program Memorandum" for field use, intended to make a more technical guide prepared by budget officers in the Office of Administration understandable to field offices, during the process of Agency adoption of the new Planning-Programming-Budgeting System. They may assist in determining Agency policy for a specific upcoming event—for example, the Agency response to the fiftieth anniversary of the Bolshevik Revolution in 1967. They had an interest in the recent new statement of Agency mission, considered by the Agency director and the heads of major USIA elements. They were aware that it would be less rhetorical than the 1963 Kennedy mission statement, and would probably lack any directive to the Agency to "sell" democracy or free private enterprise. The planning officers assist in the policy review of the old Country Plans and the newer Country Plans Program Memoranda submitted from the field posts, which not only treat Agency field operations in some detail for the upcoming year but also project Agency activities for five years country by country. Later, it is possible that they will assist in drawing up worldwide or regional Planning-Programming-Budgeting papers similar to those now being prepared by a number of field posts for single countries. Through the assistant director (policy and plans), they may sometimes be drawn into broader considerations, such as the usefulness of educational television in modernization or nation-building in the newer developing countries overseas. They work closely with the media content officers on the Policy and Plans Staff to insure the Agency policy will be adequately supported by effective media products. They review research studies of the Research and Analysis Staff to determine what the implications of research findings may be for the area offices, media services, and field posts—drafting Program Action Memoranda (PAM) under the direction of Assistant Director (policy and plans) Harris. The Program Action Memoranda were introduced after the incorporation of the research function in the Office of Policy and Research in July, 1966. The new PAM's replace the older Research Applications Memoranda initiated in July, 1963---then done by Wilson Dizard as the Office of Policy's research applications officer.

The planning function in USIA had a varied history. Never assigned more than two or three personnel, the position of Agency planning officer sometimes stood vacant for periods several months between 1963 and 1967, or was filled by an officer working almost full time on a special study without time for attention to a broad range of problems which might require a look ahead. From 1953 to 1961, the planning function was closely tied to the preparation and revision of Agency position papers for meetings of the National Security Council, the Operations Coordinating Board, or their subsidiary subcommittees or working groups. Following the simplification of the National Security Council machinery and the demise of the Operations Coordinating Board in February, 1961, Agency Director Murrow and Deputy Director of USIA (policy and plans) Sorensen moved to relate planning more closely to Agency operations, at first through a small working group and later by naming an Agency planning officer. After a six-month interim with no Agency planning officer, John P. McKnight, an FSCR-1, was assigned to the post in March, 1963, and the function assumed some degree of importance, only to fall vacant again in 1965 when McKnight was reassigned to overseas duty. At the same time, Dizard—the research applications officer who had worked closely with him—was assigned as a special assistant to the Agency deputy director. By January, 1966, Dizard had been appointed Agency planning officer and was working on a special project related to his personal research interests—the rapidly expanding potential of international television broadcasting via communications satellites—for the new Agency director, Leonard Marks. He did participate in the Office of Policy's weekly sessions with Agency policy officers, attended the Agency director's weekly staff meetings, and was tied to the program coordinators in the area offices and to the Office of Administration by his general policy oversight of five-year budget projections. He did not receive USIA's operating messages, but did see long-range planning documents from State and major studies produced by the Agency's Research and Reference Service. From time to time, he was drawn into discussions with members of the staffs serving the National Security Council or White House, and he sometimes served on interagency working groups.

A small working group had been appointed by Murrow on a "one-shot" special study basis in 1961 to re-evaluate and take a forward look at what USIA's European program should accomplish through the 1960's. The four-member team, under Lewis Schmidt, then assistant director of USIA for administration, first received briefings and read materials gathered from Walt Rostow and State's Policy Planning Council, from top State Department personnel working on European affairs, from the Central Intelligence Agency, and from USIA's own European Area Office and Research and Reference Service. After spending five weeks at headquarters, it moved to the field for a second five-week period, visiting USIS posts in all major western European countries—including West Germany, France, Italy, Austria, Belgium, Spain, and the United Kingdom. In addition, the study group talked with staff members of European regional organizations such as NATO and the Organization for European Economic Cooperation. In its studies, the committee was attempting to spell out what informational relations with Europe would be consistent with Guidelines Papers accepted as national policy within the procedures of the National Security Council mechanism. There were tremendous cross currents within Europe during the early 1960's, little understanding within Congress of the need for an information program in Europe, and a resultant need for solid knowledge to justify and give direction to USIA's European activities. The report of the study group became a guide to Agency policy. One of the group's members became the Agency's assistant director for Europe to lead the area office in the implementation of the study's recommendations.

Some time after the working group had completed its operations, McKnight was appointed as Agency planning officer to "roam the entire Agency reservation" and conduct planning activities on a more permanent basis. He was a former Associated Press overseas reporter who had served with the information program for almost a decade after 1951, as a public affairs officer in Korea and Argentina, then for three years as the Agency's assistant director for Latin America, and finally for a year as federal executive fellow at the Brookings Institution in Washington. Interested in communications theory, McKnight was an experienced information operator both overseas and in Washington—who read a book like Terence Qualter's *Propaganda and Psychological Warfare* as part of his job and was writing a book of his own after hours. One of his functions was to project Agency planning into the future, from five to ten to possibly fifteen years ahead, asking where does USIA want to be then and how does USIA get there? He was to fulfil this responsibility in part by his oversight of the Agency's five-year projection of its programs and needs for the Bureau of the Budget during the annual budget cycle. The five-year projection was at that time a relatively new device; and the planning officer, the budget officer, and the representatives of Agency elements had to "feel their way" toward meeting this obligation. Working with Agency personnel at a variety of levels, McKnight tried to lay out basic assumptions concerning the conditions under which USIA would be operating during the next five years and then tried to set forth some realistic objectives for this period. From this point of departure, he tried to get the area offices and media services to translate assumptions and objectives into specific area and media programs. Finally, a dollar tag was put on the projected programs.

McKnight's second major function as Agency planning officer was to identify problems and try to get mechanisms set up to work toward solutions. When he took over the planning post, McKnight first proceeded to identify some forty to fifty long- or shorter-range problems facing the Agency, either concerning substantive information policy or administrative practices. Then he found out which were already being resolved by Agency working groups, shortening his own list to thirty problems. Of these, he concluded that eighteen had no solution or could be lived with. The remaining twelve he detailed in a memorandum to Murrow, then director. After some discussion among the Agency's top three leaders—Murrow, Deputy Director Wilson, and Deputy Director (policy and plans) Sorensen—five priority problems were selected for special attention. One of these was classified. The other four were the unfavorable attitude of many foreign intellectuals toward the United States, the failure of the Agency to bring past experience to bear in making present decisions, multiple-year planning of the Agency's research program to provide necessary information on appropriate areas or target groups at the right time, and the limited nature of the Agency's personnel training program in view of apparent training needs.

In keeping with McKnight's thesis that planning should not get involved too deeply in the problems it identifies, the Agency planning officer's involvement in the handling of the problem concerning the attitudes of foreign intellectuals toward the United States was important but limited. In a brief memorandum to Agency personnel with some field experience in working with foreign intellectuals, he posed several questions and invited the experts to participate in two or three informal discussions. On the basis of these meetings, he assigned an FSCR on detail to the Agency to research additional material available, drafted assumptive guidelines pertaining to the problem for the areas and media, and then requested the Research and Reference Service to test out the assumptions. At this point, for the time being and except for keeping a general watch over further developments, the planning role was considered completed. On the problem of bringing past experience to bear on present decisions, planning's participation was even more minimal. The problem having been assigned priority by the Agency director, it was turned over to a special group in the Office of Administration. This particular problem was recognized as involving all the major foreign affairs agencies of the government, and one of the special assistants to the assistant director of USIA for administration was assigned to represent the Agency in meetings with those from other departments or agencies working on the same problem. By the July, 1966, reorganization, which placed the Library of the Research and Reference Service in a new Information Services Division in the Office of Administration and created an Agency historian, the task of information retrieval was assigned to a small Information Systems Staff attached to the Information Services Division. Essentially, McKnight was able to turn the problem of multi-year planning for Agency research over to the Research and Reference Service to spell out. Responsibility for working on recommendations to improve the Agency's in-service training programs was assigned to the Training Division, then in the office of Administration.

Relations among senior personnel of USIA, highly informal, are often based on past associations and personal friendship. McKnight as Agency planning officer profited from this, as he had access to all key personnel and in turn was accessible to both his "bosses" and element heads. He was used as a sounding board by the Agency director or the head of the Office of Policy; he had a close relationship with the assistant deputy director for media content and with the assistant deputy director for policy and plans, who attended meetings of the State Department's Policy Planning Council. McKnight was USIA's deputy representative at Policy Planning Council meetings. Early in his identification of Agency problems, after he took over as planning officer, McKnight noted that studies of the Research and Reference Service did not seem to get ground into the operations of the area offices and media services or the overseas missions. In a memorandum to the deputy director (policy and plans), then Sorensen, he pointed out that this would not be done unless someone were more specifically responsible for seeing that it was done. In response, Sorensen appointed Wilson Dizard to the Office of Policy as research applications officer in July, 1963. Dizard was returning to the Agency after a year attached to the staff of the Center for International Studies at Massachusetts Institute of Technology. His assigned task was to stimulate the application of research findings of the Research and Reference Service to policies and programs of USIA's area officers. It was actually December of that year before he could settle down to relating research to policy—through no fault of his own. The thinker as distinct from the operator in government has no nagging, daily tasks. In a sense, he is a new phenomenon, his role not fully understood in government nor his work pattern rigidly defined. For years, the thinker has been "done without." To many, he has yet to prove his real value. In an understaffed government agency, the new thinking breed, with "little to do," is a natural personnel reserve to take on special assignments—regardless of whether they are relevant to the thinker's function. McKnight, as Agency planning officer, was drawn off into personnel recruiting trips to college campuses. Dizard had scarcely settled into his office when he was assigned in August, 1963, to the staff of then Vice President Johnson to assist and take part in two vice presidential visits to Europe. Talent is scarce and, in an operationally oriented system, the thinker is all too likely to be drawn into the maelstrom of current events. In such cases, he becomes the victim of the very disease which he is supposed to be treating.

At the time of Dizard's appointment as research applications officer, public opinion studies were being conducted overseas regularly in a number of countries under the direction of USIA's Research and Reference Service, to determine what target audiences thought and why. While the instincts and insights of USIS officers at overseas missions were helpful, they were not in fact precise or accurate enough to serve by themselves as guides to effective operations. This meant that studies sponsored by the Research and Reference Service needed to be read and studied by USIA policy officers in the area offices at headquarters and the research findings applied to operations in individual countries and to relations with specific influence groups in these societies. In the rat race of daily area operations—with messages to and from the field, with review of media products, and with increasing interagency relationships in Washington—the men on the area office "firing line" had little time to read, reflect, and relate research to policy. The Research and Reference Service did its best, sending them copies of what were considered particularly relevant studies, complete with covering summary and an appended full report. Research and Reference was not encouraged to suggest policy implications directly; its job was limited to objective study without prejudice or preference for any particular policy or operational device. Such a separation of research and policy was intended to avoid problems of emotional involvement by researchers in support of particular Agency policies, which might have colored their studies or reports and made them less accurate, more subjective. If researchers got their information "on the air" to the area offices, there were few listeners, for area personnel were tuned to channels communicating less analytical and more operational material. It was to alleviate this lack of real communication that Dizard was appointed to the IOP staff as research applications officer.

Dizard was to help relate research reports to area needs. He became a regular and thorough reader of Research and Reference Service products. He worked closely with the areas in developing suggestions for applications of the knowledge derived from research to programs. The device for informing the area and for stimulating thinking in the area about the usefulness of a particular piece of research was the Research Applications Memorandum. It was drafted by Dizard in consultation with the appropriate area office and signed by Agency Deputy Director (policy and plans) Sorensen. When Dizard discovered a study of substantial interest to a particular area office, he was likely to talk with the office director and other area personnel and to brief himself generally on present policies and programs. He then did a rough draft of the memorandum which was reviewed by Sorensen, sent to the office director for comment and suggestions, rewritten to accommodate area views, and resubmitted for further area comment. If the draft now seemed acceptable to the area, it was returned to Sorensen for his approval. If it passed this hurdle, it was finally forwarded as an "instruction" to the office director. The drafting process demanded area attention, necessitated an exchange of views, and resulted in a guidance for action.

Two early research studies singled out for consideration by the research applications officer indicate the type of problems dealt with. One was a seven-nation survey of opinion in Latin America on the Alliance for Progress. Another was a study of the opinions of African students attending educational institutions in Paris. Both surveys were of significance to information policy in more than a single country. One concerned a large-scale modernization program in a transitional and developing area; the other, an age and occupation group often "opposed" to the United States and yet important for future American relations with many countries. From the Latin American survey, it was learned that most people lacked knowledge about the Alliance for Progress; most had not seen any Alliance projects, and their opinions where based only on hearsay. Their expectations about the program were limited and realistic. On the basis of this and other information, Dizard was able to indicate the implications of these facts for information programs supporting the Alliance for Progress in Latin America. The implications for Latin America, it should be pointed out, were not applicable willy-nilly to other areas with different conditions and attitudes. For example, Latin Americans tend to distrust government intervention in their affairs; in Pakistan, on the other hand, where the British built a record of accomplishing things through government action, the Pakistanis are now likely to expect government programming from their indigenous leadership as well. In the same way, attitudes of African students in Paris could not be applied to all African students in Europe. Those who study in Paris speak the French language, come from former French territories, and were trained in French schools in Africa. They have different beliefs from those who may be studying in Great Britain, who speak English, come from what were once British territories, and were trained in British-type schools. Similar United States information programs could not be directed toward them during their study in Britain and France and be expected to achieve the same results. The complexity of the problem of relating research to policy was clear; there were no easy conclusions; the interrelationship of many factors had to be weighed and the instruction which was the end result structured to be effective within the context of the situation to which it was to be applied. In large measure, the role of the research applications officer was considered experimental. In fact, with Dizard's assignment as a special assistant to the deputy director of the Agency, the function was allowed to become dormant. Some have pointed out that selecting a single piece of research and trying to get agreed policy implications was too simple a process, that this procedure alone did not resolve the problem of making research useful to Agency operators. To say this was not to deny the importance of the gap between research and policy, between daily operations and more basic aims. It was only to say that the task of finding useful relationships between research and policy was more complex than that originally envisioned.

The renewal of USIA's interest in policy planning and its relationship to research in 1966 was born of a necessity for greater precision and measurement of effectiveness in the new Planning-Programming-Budgeting System, becoming operative 1967-70. It is also the result of the interest of Agency Director Marks in directing the Agency's research efforts to specifically identified Agency problems, rather than continuing regular reports of a broader nature calculated to furnish a wide spectrum of knowledge—from which operators (assisted by Research Applications Memoranda) might find some useful ideas which could be related to the performance of their daily tasks. The end of the organizational separation of the Research and Reference Service from the Office of Policy and reincarnation of the research elements of the Service as a Research and Analysis Staff within an enlarged Office of Policy and Research was a symbolic gesture as well as a pragmatic act to change the nature of research studies. The Program Action Memoranda, based on the policy-oriented research, are likely to be more relevant to policy officers. By January, 1967, when the new system had been operational for a little over a third of a year (though officially reorganized as of July 1, 1966), approximately fifteen studies had been prepared by the Research and Analysis Staff, for twelve of which Program Action Memoranda had been prepared. When a study only confirms what is already Agency policy, no PAM is prepared. The new PAM's are prepared after consultation by planning officers on the Policy and Plans Staff with the area offices and media services concerned, but are not subject to clearance. The resulting PAM is forwarded to the leaders of the Office of the Director, the Office of Policy and Research, the area offices, the media services, and field posts. East African media studies done in 1966 were the basis of one PAM. Although several policy implications may be suggested in a single PAM, they may only be binding in one country or region. The readers of the PAM's must involve themselves in considering the suggestions, for they must respond to the suggestions with appropriate action. Within two months of issuance, a check is made as diplomatically as possible to see what programs and products have been changed, dropped, or added as a result of the PAM directive.

The planning officers of the Policy and Plans Staff also are responsible for the preparation of Policy Program Directives (PPD) spelling out Agency policy for situations not specifically foreseen in Agency budgeting. These can be drawn up at any time, as one was before the fiftieth anniversary of the Bolshevik Revolution in 1967. The PPD stated the situation and the problem it posed for the Agency. Then Agency objectives in connection with the event were stated. At this point, the PPD was turned over to the media content officers of the Policy and Plans Staff. They indicated to the media services what the policy was to be. Hypothetically, it might have been: "For credibility go along, but don't build it up." They then asked what material the media services had that would further the policy. In return, the media services presented a list of what was then available, and if this appeared to be insufficient, also indicated what they might prepare especially for the occasion. The media content officers, in consultation with the media services and the planning officers, then told the media services what special programs or products were desired. Theoretically (and for a brief time at least), under the Policy Program Directive system, the assistant deputy director (operational policy) could direct the transfer of funds from one media to another to meet a specifically determined need. Prior to the initiation of the PPD's, only the Agency's Program Review Committee could make transfers of $30,000 or more, and such transfers were only made during the last two quarters of a fiscal year. Although the media content officers are involved in the process of issuing the PPD's, their major role is "bird-dogging" what is said and how it is said in which worldwide media products of USIA, and assuring that this conforms to Agency policy. In performing this role, they backstop the Agency deputy director, who actually has the final responsibility for control over worldwide media products in most instances. The media content officers share with Agency Deputy Director Akers tasks formerly performed by the assistant deputy director (media content) under Directors Murrow and Rowan. IOP lost an assistant deputy director when Akers took over direction of the media content function, but it gained an assistant director of USIA (research and analysis) on July 1, 1966, when research elements of the Research and Reference Service (which ceased to exist) became the Research and Analysis Staff of IOP, and the Office of Policy became the Office of Policy and Research.

THE RESEARCH AND ANALYSIS STAFF

Establishment of a Research and Analysis Staff as an integral part of the Office of Policy and Research is part of a serious effort by Director Marks to make better use of Agency research in guiding the formulation of information policy and the conduct of information programs. There has been a tendency since 1963 for the research effort increasingly to service the "front office," though the continuing needs of the area offices and media services were recognized in the establishment of the research applications officer and the use of the Research Applications Memoranda. The newer Program Action Memoranda are intended to help the area offices and the media services make better use of research studies, and to give the Agency director a better device for insuring that they do in fact utilize research findings. These steps, coupled with Director Marks's injunction to the Research and Analysis Staff to do more special policy-oriented research and fewer recurring general studies, indicate a high Agency interest in improving the policy-research relationship. Whether or not the integration of the Research and

Analysis Staff with IOP is the final answer to the problem, Agency aware-ness of the problem and willingness to try to do something about it is com-mendable. USIA, like many other government agencies, is essentially staffed by "operators." USIA's leaders and their assistants confront a series of psychological or informational crises overseas, and too often in the past they have responded intuitively on the basis of general knowledge and experi-ence—possibly on occasion manning the same old pumps when the well had run dry or grabbing the nozzle of the hose on the gas pump in haste and spreading gasoline on the fire. The director, executive assistant, the deputy director of USIA are on the political front line, not far from the President, the secretary of state, and the secretary of defense. The deputy director (policy and research) is besieged daily by a series of pressing policy problems he cannot postpone resolving. The area office directors and their staffs are run-ning on a speeding treadmill, with more problems to be "solved" than they can deal with carefully, and a mass of paper to keep up with that must be scanned rather than read—even though USIA is notoriously "word of mouth" as compared with the Department of State. The media service direc-tors are tenaciously trying to find out what policy is on a day-to-day basis, and seeking to get it translated into products to be fired at targets which most of their personnel have never seen. In the Alice in Wonderland world of government, which "believes" Parkinson's Law, it is highly unlikely that sufficient personnel would ever be assigned in the Office of the Director, the Office of Policy and Research, or the area offices to allow work to proceed at a more leisurely, scholarly pace. Such circumstances are nonexistent even on American college campuses in the late 1960's. Without time to do research or give really thorough consideration to problems, Agency leaders require research assistance to enable them to make realistic decisions.

The gap between the researchers and the operators in USIA was pain-fully clear in 1963. In what may have been an overly harsh judgment, but containing the seed of truth, an able regional division chief in the Research and Reference Service could then still ruefully declare:

> Operators don't know what research is for, don't know what ques-tions to ask, and when they get the answers they don't know what to do with them. They are suspicious that the researchers are trying to usurp their policy-making jobs. Research only clarifies the real alter-natives, within assigned terms of reference. The researcher realizes that other factors may have to be taken into consideration in policy formulation. He only wants the policy-makers to realize the conse-quences of their decisions.

The problem of relating research to policy is not a unique problem, plaguing only USIA. The Department of State has toiled patiently through the years to bring its regional bureaus—its "money-changers in the temple"—into a realistic and fruitful relationship with the Bureau of Intelligence and Research—its "scholars in an ivory tower." The regional bureaus in State used to and still may ask the "wrong" questions, find the "wrong" services useful—though Roger Hilsman as director of intelligence and research introduced policy-oriented studies there some years ago. Area offices of USIA have also tended to ask the wrong questions, though what they ask is useful to them. They are interested in summaries of newspapers or foreign broadcasts, because they are too busy to read them in detail. They may still be interested in knowing Nikita S. Khrushchev's middle name, though the researcher may wonder for what purpose. Ph. D.'s in area studies or survey research from America's great universities are likely to find it difficult to be satisfied for long doing routine summaries or reference work. They want to do more than save time for the area offices. By 1967, they had largely escaped reference duties, had been allowed to cut back the number of regular routine, repetitive studies, and could concentrate on fewer assignments more directly relevant to Agency policy.

This is not to say that the old Research and Reference Service (IRS) did not offer a wide variety of factual and analytical services for USIA elements in the past—many of which were welcomed and put to good use. To overstress problems and underplay successful working relationships perhaps downgrades the usefulness of the functions the Research and Reference Service did perform in support of USIA objectives. Old IRS did provide operational research and analysis needed in forming Agency plans and programs, did design and direct original research on foreign attitudes and opinions, communications systems and habits, and media effectiveness. From 1959 to 1966 the Research and Reference Service was headed by Oren Stephens—author in 1955 of an excellent book on America's overseas information program, *Facts to a Candid World*[5]—who knew USIA well from the policy-making side. From 1954 to 1957, Stephens had been deputy assistant director of the Office of Policy and Programs---the forerunner of today's Office of Policy and Research—at a time when small area staffs were attached directly to IOP; the area and deputy area directors were then viewed as personal arms of the Agency director, staffless, spending most of their time traveling in the field. (Thus, the policy guidance area officers are a vestigial organ and field inspections by the directors and deputy directors of area offices a vestigial function—each now adapted to a changed situation.) When reorganization moved the area staffs from IOP and placed them under the area directors, Stephens became planning director, Office of Plans (IOP), until becoming director of the Research and Reference Service in early 1959. After several years of experience in the Research and Reference Service, Stephens moved in 1963 to reorganize the Service. Until that time a Soviet Bloc Division and an Area Analysis Division, with area branches handling the other areas of the world, functioned alongside a Survey Research Division which operated worldwide. The area branches were staffed with well-trained social scientists who based their research conclusions on reports or policy messages from field posts, on material obtained from broadcasts emanating from foreign countries, and on intelligence documents from other agencies of government. The Survey Research Division was staffed by skilled professionals highly trained in survey research, whose studies were based on overseas surveys, usually conducted by contract research groups. Both the area branches and the Survey Research Division maintained working relations with the area offices, but not with each other. Their findings, based on different sources of information, did not always appear to "jibe." Any coordination of their reports had to be done at the level of the director and deputy director of IRS, placing a heavy load on what was then the IRS Planning and Review Staff. In the 1963 reorganization, the Survey Research Division was abandoned, its members dispersed and placed in individual regional divisions—where the findings of survey and general social science research were joined to produce a better balanced product than either the old area branches or the Survey Research Division could produce separately. Differences in assessments were discovered earlier and checked out, before reports were prepared. The IRS assistant director (research), now the deputy assistant director (research development), preserved the morale and expertise of the scattered survey researchers, and helped the regional divisions take a second look at field and intelligence reports, often based on observation and intuition rather than "scientific inquiry." After the reorganization in 1963, the Research and Reference Service was mainly composed of six regional divisions, matching the Agency's area offices, and a Media and Technical Resources Division. The chiefs of the regional divisions were concerned with discovering and reporting the basic values and aspirations of the Agency's audiences in their regions; with understanding their views toward the "Cold War" (assessing the political climate); with analyzing other propaganda reaching them; and with initiating specific studies of individual target groups within their regions—students, labor, newspaper editors, etc. The chief of the Media and Technical Resources Division was responsible for studies done on communications channels and listening habits or on the impact of specific media products or programs on a worldwide basis, even in a single area if the study was coordinated with the appropriate regional division. Old IRS also maintained the Agency Library—of books, periodicals, and government documents—under an Agency librarian.[6] The IRS executive officer conducted the administrative business of IRS and maintained relations in behalf of USIA with the intelligence community—of which USIA is not a member, but from which it receives the relevant products of the participating agencies. The 142 members of IRS staff was composed almost completely of Civil Service personnel.

In principle, there was close contact between IRS and the area offices or media services. In fact, it was difficult for many reasons to establish and maintain close relations with the area offices. The area offices felt that too many research products were aimed primarily at the Agency director or the Office of Policy—reaction reports and summaries of Communist propaganda. At one time, longer-range research reports ran 150 to 200 pages, and personnel in area offices were too busy to read them. But IRS cut these down to between 10 to 25 typed pages, with a table of contents and a summary page preceding the report, so that the busy reader in the area office could give it the three-minute look and know the findings in general without reading the main section of the report. Area office country desk officers may have read these reports in full during a lull between international storms; in times of crisis—unless directly pertinent—reports received little attention. After all, the area office desk officer read much of the same information flow as the IRS regional division analyst. He just didn't have the time to think about it or put his thoughts to paper. IRS was hopeful that the appointment of planning and research applications officers in the Office of Policy would be helpful in getting research applied to operations. Although this type of work dramatized the usefulness of some research products and indicated an interest in research application by Agency leaders, the area offices remained overburdened. It was true that a particular dramatic survey result communicated to an area director might stimulate an abrupt reorientation of programming in a particular country. Whether less startling findings were plowed regularly into information operations at the country desk level in the area offices was less certain.

Although these shortcomings were widely recognized within the Agency, the July 1, 1966, reorganization—which transformed the Research and Reference Service and the Office of Policy into the present Research and Analysis Staff and the Office of Policy and Research—was more an outgrowth of Agency adaptation to the new Planning-Programming-Budgeting System. With PPBS, operators required more detailed quantitative knowledge, information which could be provided by emphasizing operational and policy-oriented research at the expense of longer-range and more basic studies. Integration of the research program within the new Office of Policy and Research allowed for a closer relationship between the Agency's top policy officers and researchers both in the planning stage of research projects and in the assessment of the relationship of their findings to policy and programs. A higher percentage of research studies are now directed at problems made explicit by PPBS, and the research findings can now be stated clearly and communicated to the operators by the new Program Action Memoranda—which must be plowed into operations.

By January 16, 1967, after a period of reorganizational turmoil during its first six and one-half months in the Office of Policy and Research, the Research and Analysis Staff was headed by an assistant director of USIA (research and analysis), the key operational figure in the over-all organization of the staff being a deputy assistant director (operations), who presided over a coordinator for domestic operations and a coordinator for overseas operations. Attached directly to the office of the deputy assistant director (operations) was a five-man Media Reaction Unit, responsible for preparation on Monday, Wednesday, and Friday each week of a Foreign Media Reaction Report based on events around the world of interest to USIA leaders—and to the President of the United States.[7] The coordinator for operations (overseas) was responsible for direction of seven regional research officers (down from a high of twenty some years ago) stationed overseas, each assigned to a single USIS post but expected to move about from post to post in his region as required, assisting USIS officers to set up research studies related to problems that arise in the field. The coordinator for operations (domestic) carried a heavier administrative load, providing direction to six area divisions, plus a Media Analysis Division and a Special Studies Division. Area divisions, with three to six people on their staffs (somewhat reduced in size from IRS days), represented Africa, Latin America, East Asia and the Pacific, the Near East and South Asia, and Europe. A Communist Propaganda Division with a staff of nine covered communist propaganda as it emanated from communist countries or as it surfaced anywhere in the world. A Media Analysis Division with sixteen employees was the successor to the old Media and Technical Resources Division. A Special Studies Division of the same size was responsible for studies required to service the Bureau of the Budget or the White House staff. The area divisions were particularly interested in attitude studies in their areas to determine if the

Agency had the right objectives, was addressing the correct audience, and was stressing appropriate themes. The Communist Propaganda Division, in addition to special reports, prepared a major paper monthly on trends in communist propaganda themes, undoubtedly differentiating between sources originating propaganda as well as between what themes reach what audiences in what countries. The Special Studies Division produced broad studies not related to USIA media products; for example, on the Agency's future language requirements, special problems of wives of foreign service officers, on future facilities requirements of the Voice of America, on what type of material should be carried on the Wireless File, or what should be the emphases of Agency research programs. The Media Analysis Division's major function was that of assessing the effectiveness of particular media products. It might cooperate with the Area Division for Latin America in an attitude-product study in Argentina—possibly using the survey research technique. It was also engaged in what are called "country priority studies," attempting to provide a more scientific rationale for setting country budgets. In these it attempted to find out what media products are needed, what opportunities are open that have not been utilized, the uses already being made of other USIA media products, and the relative importance of the country to America within its region. Some twenty to thirty factors were considered before assigning a country a top, medium, or low priority. Proposed publications or products of the media services were "dummied up" and sent to the field for test reactions. In the past, the Broadcasting Service was most interested among the Media Services in the type of studies done by the Media Analysis Division. More recently, there has been a growing pressure for similar assessment of products by the Press and Publications Service, the Motion Picture and Television Service, and the Information Center Service.

By October, 1967, the Special Studies Division and the Media Analysis Division had apparently been combined in a Program Analysis Division, and an Editorial Division had been established—possibly to perform the role played by the Planning and Review Staff of the old Research and Reference Service, and the Media Reaction Unit had been joined with the old Policy Guidance Staff to become the Policy Guidance and Media Reaction Staff. Also missing were the coordinator for operations (domestic) and the coordinator for operations (overseas). Operational leadership of the Research and Analysis Staff was apparently provided by the assistant director (research and analysis) and the deputy assistant director.

Outside the operational structure of the Research and Analysis Staff, but performing an important liaison function and providing a reservoir of expertise on survey research methods, is the deputy assistant director (research development). His major responsibility is to improve USIA's utilization of "external research," that done by private scholars or organizations and that prepared by other government agencies. He maintains relations with the Department of State on foreign area research and holds a monthly seminar meeting with academic personnel interested in communications theory and research. He is aware that the Agency needs regular reporting by Foreign Service Career Reserve officers from field posts, but many have had little if any training in survey research or experience in doing empirical studies. The role of the 89-member Research and Analysis staff is to develop additional mechanisms to provide advance guidance for policy decisions and operational guidance subsequent to policy decisions.

The shift to shorter-range policy-oriented studies related to the Planning-Programming-Budgeting System is made clear in a memorandum on research priorities issued by the assistant director of USIA (research and analysis) on September 26, 1966. Research priorities in order of their importances as of that date were:

> A. Studies of effectiveness of Agency programs, tied to the PPBS program. B. Attitude studies designed to test Agency objectives, audiences and themes—also in large measure tied to the PPBS program. C. Studies of communication principles, techniques and environment. D. Media reaction reports. E. Studies of Communist and other propaganda activities. F. Servicing of requests from Areas, Media, other elements, other Government agencies and the private sector that do not fall in the above categories.

Contrast this to the five major emphases of Research and Reference Service research in 1963: (1) to study basic values and aspirations of people in less developed areas and elsewhere; (2) to study the climate of opinion on international issues and the general image of America; (3) to study the reaction of individual target groups to specific events; (4) to study the avenues of communications to people overseas by both mass and personal communications techniques; and (5) to study the impact or effectiveness of United States and Soviet information and products and programs overseas. In 1967, approximately half of all research studies are concentrated on the impact and effectiveness of Agency programs—as a result of the introduction of the PPBS program. [8]

Through the years the Agency has found it difficult to measure its effectiveness in a scientific manner. Without sufficient empirical evidence, there is a tendency for USIA to rely on the enthusiastic comments of the operators, themselves caught up in a program or an event; to seek evidence from isolated letters; to accept courtesy-biased responses as hard fact. By drawing implications from faulty and unsystematic techniques, the Agency can produce faulty programs and make unsystematic mistakes. Field reports often measure the effectiveness of particular activities. A program is considered effective because so many column inches of material have been placed in newspapers, so many hours of broadcasting have been done. This by itself may tell the Agency very little if anything about what people were reached and what attitudes were changed or reinforced. Survey research conducted through multi-purpose polls by neutral contract organizations can escape the courtesy bias. Pepsodent would learn little if it sent out its employees to say: "I'm from Pepsodent. What is your favorite toothpaste?" Reliance primarily upon reports from field operators, in a way, would place the Research and Analysis staff and USIA in this position. To counter this weakness in the regular reporting system, the Research and Analysis staff still sponsors surveys. The Research and Reference Service had sponsored several "World Opinion Surveys," beginning in 1963. The first was run in twenty countries; the second, in thirty. These serviced the needs not only of USIA but also of the Agency for International Development, the Department of Defense, and the Arms Control and Disarmament Agency. The surveys covered questions from basic values to specific reactions to programs or activities. The number of questions varied in the forty-five-minute survey research interviews, but certain basic questions were repeated in each study, and "issue questions" changed in response to world developments. Interviewing was done by indigenous personnel, sometimes by locally run public opinion organizations, but usually administered with outside professional guidance. Although survey research is a useful tool, there are limits to its usefulness. Country public affairs officers and the Department of State are all too well aware of the sensitivities of national leaders abroad to the conduct of such polls in their countries. Distrust has followed the "surfacing" of American polls or studies in several countries. The survey research technique must therefore be used with caution. USIA does not have the money to do many polls. Its coverage of the world by polls is far from complete. So if it cannot do a survey in one country, it may be possible to do one elsewhere. The situation changes from year to year on where use of the survey research techniques will be allowed. When interviews are not possible, USIA must rely on talks or interviews with travelers who have recently come from restricted areas. Sometimes it is possible to project attitudes discovered in one country to a neighboring state with some degree of accuracy. As surveys declined in popularity overseas, Director Leonard Marks stopped the "World Opinion Surveys," preferring to keep more targeted studies to meet special problems. Between 1963 and 1966, results of USIA polls were made public after two years, with the Research and Reference Service publishing a monthly list of studies as they became available for scholarly research or for the use of newspaper reporters. Much newspaper publicity attended the release of the first polls when the policy of making results public was first introduced in 1963. Reporters then seemed to become "inoculated" and paid little or no attention to them for several years. Dropping publication of the studies in 1966 is regrettable from a private research point of view, but their release two years after completion was, so far as national politics is concerned, a delayed time bomb that might go off at any time—possibly in an election year. It is possible that publication by chance at the wrong time might impede negotiations or harm relations with a foreign state. There is always congressional fear that polls paid for by public funds will be published and encourage American citizens to clamor for programs that are unpopular on Capital Hill. And there is an abiding concern on the Hill that USIA as a propaganda agency must never be allowed to turn its skills inward toward the American people.

CHANGE 1963-67: AN ASSESSMENT

Viewed as a whole, the Office of Policy and Research in 1967 appeared to be a more efficient instrument than the Office of Policy in 1963. The struggle of the Office of Policy to assert its policy leadership over the media services during 1963 had given way to what seemed to be more general acceptance of leadership by the Office of Policy and Research in 1967. In part. this stemmed from the new role of the deputy Agency director in guiding media content. In some measure, it represented the working of time. The sharp turn toward direct support of American foreign policy by USIA under Director Murrow in 1961 put tremendous pressures on the media services and created resistance among Civil Service personnel there hitherto more interested in their craft than in relating their message to foreign policy. Blending artistry effectively with the twists and turns of policy required new relationships with the policy makers and the overcoming of old prejudices. The push during the Murrow period toward worldwide themes posed the policy problem in its most difficult form. To enforce worldwide policy themes in individual countries was to arouse resistance in the area offices, for what was an effective theme in one area might be anathema to people in another—and lose friends faster than the country public affairs officer could make them. The fact that Murrow was stressing preparation and use of more worldwide products at the same time forced the media services into policy collisions with the area offices when both were particularly sensitive—the media services because they were being asked to subvert their art to policy considerations, the area offices because they were asked to use themes and products less than accepta- ble to their overseas clientele in some instances. By 1967, media services personnel had almost six years of experience in integrating policy and prod- uct. Agency themes were more carefully tailored to individual countries and areas, and the emphasis on worldwide products had been reduced—with increased media production in the field adapted to the needs of individual countries.

The internal organization of the Office of Policy and Research was much neater in 1967 than was that of the Office of Policy in 1963, though neatness is not necessarily a virtue. The new tripartite organization into three Staffs— Policy Guidance and Media Reaction, Policy and Plans, and Research and Analysis—reduced substantially the number of individuals reporting directly to the deputy director of USIA (policy and research) from the num- ber who were directly responsible to the deputy director of USIA (policy and plans). In 1963, the advisors and what are now the liaison officers all required direct oversight by the deputy agency director (policy and plans), as did the planning officer, the policy applications officer, and the assistant deputy director (media content). There were many more personnel in the Office of Policy and Research in 1967—almost entirely because of the addition of the Research and Analysis Staff—but the task of directing the Office of Policy and Research was less frenetic than that of directing the Office of Policy in 1963 and allowed more time for thoughtful forward planning by the deputy agency director (policy and research). The Policy Guidance Staff, already effectively organized in 1963, has had no need for substantial change; it has served as an organizational tie as the media reaction function was upgraded. Lack of direct leadership of the advisors and others now joined in the Policy and Plans Staff resulted in a fragmentation of knowledge and effort in 1963 which has since been remedied. The placement of the Research and Analysis Staff in the Office of Policy and Research, whatever the immediate cost to basic long-range research—with emphasis on servicing the Planning-Pro- gramming-Budgeting System and the stress on Program Action Memo- randa—will upgrade the use of research findings in the area offices and media services and reduce the time required by area office and media service person- nel to read studies not relevant to their daily needs. Budget examiners in the

Bureau of the Budget believe that product-oriented USIA is adapting more rapidly and successfully to the PPBS than state—whose output is largely words, which are difficult to measure in terms of relative cost-effectiveness.

To say these things is not to conlude that USIA's policy-program problems have been resolved or that the present organization of the Office of Policy and Research necessarily will long endure. The installation of the Planning-Programming-Budgeting System was still in progress during 1967. Refinement of the new techniques required by the PPBS program will take much effort. Too quick a dependence upon the new methods of marshaling information on objectives, audiences, communications systems, and media products can lead to an easy acceptance of conclusions based on "facts" ground through the mechanism—before the degree of their accuracy or dependability has been thoroughly cross-checked. Hopefully, the relatively short-range focus of the Research and Analysis Staff in 1967 was caused by the process of installing the Planning-Programming-Budgeting System, geared to the annual budget cycle with at most a five-year look ahead. The new precision—when in fact it becomes precise in measuring effectiveness—will be helpful. The assignment of the deputy assistant director (research development) to full-time "external research" duties can lead USIA toward a greater awareness of new insights provided by communications theory and research. The fact that area offices were not able to absorb and use more basic long-range studies in the past does not mean that the Agency does not need to take the long hard look into the future. An Agency responsible for the psychological impact of policy overseas on leadership groups and the masses has almost endless research requirements ahead if it is to develop sophistication in determining with precision the point on the coercion-persuasion continuum most effective in furthering the real security of American citizens over time in a nuclear world—a large portion of which is struggling from traditional ways of life through an unstable transition period toward modernity.

To believe that any form of organization of the Office of Policy and Research is sacrosanct or likely to persist unchanged is utter folly. The Research and Analysis Staff went through two or more reorganizations within a matter of weeks in late 1966 and early 1967. What has happened at least twice since the disappearance of the Research and Reference Service could quite possibly happen again—particularly if the Agency sets itself to meeting its long-range research requirements. There was talk in early 1967 that the Media Reaction Unit might be removed from Research and Analysis and attached directly to the deputy director of USIA (policy and research). By mid-year it was joined to the old policy guidance staff. When

Deputy Director Akers decides to leave USIA, or there is a politically imposed change of leadership, it is quite possible that leadership of the media content guidance function will be relocated, possibly requiring a build-up of that part of the Policy and Plans Staff which now serves as his secretariat. Change has taken place since 1963, and it will take place after 1968. Organization backstops the relationships of people doing a job, and new personnel with different personalities may require a readjustment of the formal administrative structure if only to allow their informal patterns of organization to function effectively.

V

At the Critical Crossroads:
The Area Offices

Important and influential as the leaders and their staffs in the Office of the Director and the Office of Policy and Research are, it is the personnel in the six area offices—each headed by an assistant director of the Agency—who labor at the critical crossroads of policy making, research application, media direction, and field operations. Their perception of the implications of research on overseas attitudes or of values and semantics for program and product effectiveness, plus their working relations with the field, the media, and other agencies of government—as well as with the Office of the Director or Office of Policy and Research—determine in large measure how effective USIA will be. Area office personnel have many jobs. They are usually quite busy—meeting field requests, monitoring media products, reading operational and policy-related messages, drafting memoranda, maintaining interagency contacts, attending staff meetings, participating in working groups, conducting inspections of the field, and generally projecting a sense of policy and operational guidance to the media and field. The workload of a country desk may vary over time; i.e., Indonesia required much attention in 1963 but little by 1967. Vietnam requirements went up sharply between 1963 and 1967.

Geographically oriented toward assigned areas—Africa, Europe, East Asia and the Pacific, Latin America, the Near East and South Asia, and the Soviet Union and eastern Europe—the area offices are internally structured in a five-function, three-layer hierarchy. At the top the area director and his deputy serve as alter egos. One step down, a policy officer and a program coordinator—relatively equal to each other in rank and degree of influence (though one or the other may be recognized as senior in a particular area office), divide area policy and administrative responsibilities. At the bottom, there are desk officers, each covering from one to five countries in the area, and area functional officers, with concern for cultural, economic, or other area-wide matters. A single individual often serves both as a country desk officer and an area functional officer. A single area director guides a domestic staff numbering from fourteen to twenty—which helps him serve and direct an overseas USIS area operation employing 22 to 293 Americans and 65 to 1,600 locals; deal with four USIA media elements ranging in size from one with 247 domestic employees, one American, and three local employees overseas to another with 1,384 domestic employees, plus 164 American and 778 local employees overseas. [1]

The major elements in USIA's policy-operations hierarchy can be conceived of as a pyramid, the top portions more concerned with policy making and the lower sections enmeshed in operations—though all layers are concerned with both policy and operations, since the two are entwined. At the top are the Office of the Director with a staff of 13, the Office of Policy and Research with 132, and the six area offices with 108. The four media services, with 2,373 domestic staff members, as well as 189 Americans and 1,107 locals overseas, have a personnel total of 3,669. The overseas USIS staffs include 1,628 Americans and 6,963 locals, a total of 8,591. [2] Viewed in this perspective, and in terms of the responsibilities, the "pyramid" appears very narrow at the top (down through the area offices) and more broad at the base —even though production of media materials and conduct of field operations require substantial personnel support.

Prior to 1960, USIA had only four area offices: Europe, Near East and Africa, Latin America, and the Far East. With the rush of African states to nationhood, a separate area office for Africa was created in 1960— the year African specialists like to call "Africa's Year" of recognition. As of July 1, 1962, a separate area office for the Soviet Union and eastern Europe came into being, based on the area's importance and lessening East-West tensions in the European theater. Overseas staffing in Africa is similar to that in other overseas areas, but the new Soviet-eastern European area is unique. The assistant director for Africa works through an overseas USIS staff dealing with Africa composed of 153 Americans and 544 locals stationed in thirty-six countries (two of which are not in Africa: France and Israel). The assistant director for the Soviet Union and eastern Europe has no USIS missions in his countries, and has only seven American employees in Poland and five in the U.S.S.R. Elsewhere in the area, there is one in Hungary, one in Bulgaria, one in Czechoslovakia, and three in Rumania. USIS programs in Iron Curtain countries were terminated in 1950, and for years the cultural section of the embassy carried on information-related activities. Relations have yet to be normalized to the point of re-creating USIS missions. Four of the USIS American personnel and thirty-four locals overseas controlled by the Soviet Union and Eastern European Area Office are stationed in Vienna —well outside the area with which they deal. Radio in the American Sector (RIAS) of Berlin (8 Americans and 506 locals) and USIS's program in Yugoslavia (16 Americans and 99 locals) operate under USIA's area office for western Europe.[3]

"Old hands" in the overseas information business recall that when the activities of the Office of War Information and the Office of Inter-American Affairs were first transferred to the Department of State in 1945 the typical "area set-up" employed thirty to thirty-five people to conduct a smaller program than USIA runs today. In response to a feeling that the areas did too much and that the media did not have enough authority, the media were expanded (developing some area specialization) and the areas were cut back. By 1953, shortly before the creation of USIA, the area offices had become much smaller and were attached to the public affairs advisers' staffs in the State Department's regional bureaus. In the new Agency, small area staffs were attached to the Office of Policy and Programs (a predecessor of the Office of Policy and Research) until 1957. The new USIA area directors served as eyes and ears of the Agency director through travel to the field. Operations were thought of as being conducted by the media services.

In 1957, the small area staffs were placed under the control of the area directors. The new area offices were largely staffed by members of USIA's Foreign Service Career Reserve. The much larger media services remained staffed primarily by Civil Service employees. The FSCR's served long assignments overseas and returned for brief Washington tours, where they struggled to learn the intricacies of the bureaucratic jungle at headquarters and then escaped with a sense of relief to the field. The entrenched Civil Service employees of the media services, wise in Washington's ways, developed expertise in their individual fields which could not be matched by generalist FSCR's and operated program empires which even the Agency's top leaders (let alone the area offices) were hard pressed to influence or control. This situation was tolerable when George Allen served as director of USIA and the emphasis was upon long-range programs or the presentation of "the full and fair picture of America."

It became less so when the Agency moved to sharpen the relationship between USIA operations and American foreign policy under Murrow. An overly optimistic Agency memorandum describing the new look after 1961 declared:

The diffusion of effort and output that characterized USIA during the first years of its existence is ended. No longer is the Agency's mission "to tell America's story abroad"; no longer does USIA scatter its fire indiscriminately to all segments of all populations. "Targetting," always an ideal, is now a reality. Audiences are carefully selected—together with the techniques of reaching them and the contents of the message—to achieve maximum influence leading to political action. All USIA media function in synchronization: if the theme is Free Choice, and the peg Berlin, each medium devises a message best communicated through its instrument. The messages are carefully related each to the other and each supports the other. This results in a multiplied opinion impact.

Steps were taken within the Agency to adopt the "new" coordinated approach—including the appointment and later strengthening of the role of an assistant deputy director (media content), the initiation of a director's Quarterly Media Projects Meeting, and a new emphasis upon policy applications in media programming; but the staffs of the area offices were not and have not since been materially strengthened to monitor products or give policy guidance. The new emphasis on targeting required deeper understanding by area office personnel of communications theory and more detailed knowledge about attitudes of special groups in each country. Although an Agency research applications officer was assigned to the Office of Policy to identify some relationships of research to policy, area office staffs did not have time to use research reports effectively in daily operations. With the establishment of the Policy and Plans Staff and the Research Analysis Staff in the Office of Policy and Research, plus the new Program Action Memorandum system, basic research-policy-program relationships are identified for area office personnel, though fewer general and regular research reports are being generated and circulated. It may still be too soon to judge what useful information has been lost to the area offices under the new arrangement (information which had for the most part been made available and not used) or what has been gained and actually put to use. Will the Reference Branch of the Agency Library pick up all the reference services relinquished by the Research Analysis Staff, or will the area office staffs have to do more work for themselves and thus require additional personnel? With the Research and Reference Service gone, where will area office personnel get operational information? Whether the new integration of information demanded of the field in its Country Plan Program Memoranda under the new Planning-Programming-Budgeting System will lighten the load of the area offices—as some hopefully foresee—is also unclear. The attempt to increase precision in planning, programming, and budgeting seems likely to keep work loads high, though a better job may be done when the new system is fully operational. The area offices were definitely too small in 1963, and still were too small in 1967. An increase in the size and stature of the area office staffs would have been a natural response to the 1963 statement of Agency mission because of its special admonition to USIA to provide advice to other agencies in Washington on the overseas psychological impact of diplomatic, military, or economic policies during the policy formulation process. Before 1961, the Operations Coordinating Board mechanism gave USIA a chance to comment on policy even after broad policy had been decided within the National Security Council structure. USIA personnel could offer psychological advice in the interagency working groups dealing with policy implementation. With OCB abandoned and the new USIA mission assigned, Agency area officers at all levels were encouraged after 1963 to maintain interagency contacts and intervene with psychological advice as policies formulated in other agencies worked up the decision-making ladder, before policy making or policy implementing was finalized. The area office staffs were never fully able to carry out their assigned advisory function, particularly at the desk officer level. There is no clear evidence that they do so today. To eliminate the function in a new statement of mission would provide no solution. All Washington agencies should be aware of the psychological impact overseas of their proposed actions, even when this is not an overriding factor in a particular decision. USIA should act to staff its area offices so that they can continue to meet old responsibilities and evolve to meet new requirements of greater precision in Agency programming and better advising to other agencies of government.

AREA DIRECTION— THE ASSISTANT AND DEPUTY ASSISTANT DIRECTORS

The area directors and their deputies are powerful men, who carry weight in Agency affairs—in Washington and with the country public affairs officers overseas—by virtue of strong personality, long experience, broad knowledge, bureaucratic finesse, hard work, and hierarchical position. Since an area director and his deputy area director spend approximately 40 per cent of their time abroad inspecting USIS posts in their regions, it is unlikely that they will both be physically present in Washington at the same time for more than three months of any given year. Less distant (when present in the Agency) from those he rules than is an assistant secretary of state, the area director is viewed with respect rather than awe by his subordinates; but he is no less the "boss" of the area. Relations are informal, but the pecking order is clear. Because of his personal involvement in area problems, whether they be of a policy, personnel, or budget nature, the area director—or the deputy director as acting area director in his absence—is in daily touch with the members of his small staff. Everyone in the area office has access on short notice to the area director, or may be phoned or visited by the area director without warning. Much of the communication within an area office is oral rather than written, face-to-face rather than indirect. The area "hive" does now in fact have a single entrance, but its occupants were "always" on the same floor and normally housed within fifty feet of the area director and deputy area director.

Formal staff meetings supplement informal contacts. Patterns vary, but normally the area staff meets alone with the area director or acting area director several times a week at 9 or 9:30 A.M. and is joined once a week (often on Friday) or once a month for a larger session by representatives with an area interest from other USIA elements or other agencies. Representatives of the appropriate regional bureau and the Bureau of Educational and Cultural Affairs may attend from State. The smaller meetings run from thirty minutes to an hour; the larger, for an hour or more. In the narrow area family discussions, operational problems are raised in cross-reporting by the participants, and some decisions are taken on the spot by the area director or acting area director. More difficult problems may be assigned to one or more members of the staff for further study. The area director may want to consult with the deputy agency director (policy and research) or the executive assistant to the director before making up his mind. The larger sessions are more for briefing than for decisions, for getting reactions from media representatives and informing them of upcoming events. An officer just returned from a visit to the field may report on his observations, indicating trends and highlighting problems, perhaps throwing in a personal aside about field personnel well known by all present. A representative of the relevant area of the Research and Analysis Staff may lead off with information from a recent research or intelligence report. There sometimes is light sparring between the area director and media representatives, or those present from other support staffs; but it is the area director's meeting, and he outranks the visitors. Real discussion is usually reserved for later private conferences.

The area directors tended to view Murrow's Monday 10:30 A.M. staff meeting as little more than a "tribal rite," but their own broad staff meetings are sometimes similarly judged by participants. Those with close access to the leadership have already received most of the information which will be discussed or given their advice on what should be done. If the spreading of "the word" is necessary, to them it is somewhat repetitious. Agency decisions are rarely made in large meetings. Although Director Marks' weekly meeting, attended by the area office directors, has only twenty to twenty-five participants, that of Director Murrow normally included thirty to thirty-five and sometimes grew to fifty or sixty. The area directors took Murrow's Wednesday afternoon "think" session more seriously than they ever have the weekly briefing sessions.

The area directors meet as a group with the deputy director of USIA (policy and research), the assistant director (administration), and the assistant director (personnel and training) every Wednesday for a nose bag luncheon. The agenda may include several items, each raised by the individual interested in the particular problem. In one single session they discussed regional research officers, relations of USIA with the Department of Health, Education, and Welfare and with the Bureau of Educational and Cultural Affairs in the Department of State, reimbursement by the Bureau of Educational and Cultural Affairs for exchange activities conducted overseas by USIA, and when Agency film screenings could be more conveniently scheduled for review purposes. In the Murrow period, the area directors held a late-morning discussion among themselves and then picked up Director Murrow for luncheon at a nearby restaurant every Wednesday. During the hour-and-a-half discussion at lunch, Murrow would throw out a question or problem for consideration. It was after such a discussion that Director Murrow finally decided to retire the USIA film *Circarama*, shown for a number of years at USIS exhibits overseas. The film, though it drew hundreds of thousands of visitors to envelop themselves in scenes depicting many aspects of American geography and life, had carried no clearly defined policy message. Marks has continued the idea of a luncheon meeting, drawing in both the area directors and the directors of the media services; it is now held once monthly at the Department of State. The area directors consider the monthly discussion less useful than weekly predecessor, partly because they must share the director with their media service counterparts. It is a more formal session; held less often, it plays less of a role in airing problems requiring discussion. The larger the meeting and the more varied its participants, the less frank discussions are likely to be.

The area directors are not dependent upon staff meetings or luncheons to reach the Agency director, executive assistant to the director, or deputy director with questions or problems. They can consult the deputy agency director (policy and research), and do if it suits their purposes; but they often bypass him and go directly to the Agency director or deputy director. Direct access to any of the Agency's responsible officials is no more than a telephone call, a stairway, or several floors by elevator away. Close and continued contact is necessary, since the area directors are the voice of the Agency director. They must understand his philosophy, and they must follow lines of argumentation that reflect the policies he has approved. If a problem affects basic Agency policies, more than one area, personnel appointments at a high level, or a sensitive issue like Cuba, the area director is likely to touch base with the director before "sounding off." He goes to the director if he cannot resolve an inter-agency dispute at his own level and seeks to get support via the director to the head of the other agency and thence to the recalcitrant negotiator. In an emergency bearing on his area, if the director, executive assistant to the director, or the deputy director cannot be reached, the area director acts in the director's behalf either within the Agency or in dealings with another government agency—and hopes that his decision is right. Policy problems are usually taken to the director; personnel or administrative problems, to the executive assistant. Lesser questions of policy might be discussed with the deputy agency director (policy and research) or his associate director. Each of the men near the top "knows" what the others think on most issues.

The busy area director or deputy area director has many interagency contacts—including attendance at staff meetings held by an assistant secretary of state, an active role in interagency working groups serving to funnel policy papers to the President or to the National Security Council, and follow-up business luncheons with individual fellow participants on points of mutual interest raised in staff meetings or working groups. These relationships and the related paper flow help him know what diplomatic, military, or economic initiatives are in the planning stage, allow him to inject psychological perspectives before policies are jelled into inflexibility. The area director may attend an assistant secretary of state's staff meeting once a week, along with representatives of the Agency for International Development, Defense, Treasury, Commerce, and the ubiquitous Central Intelligence Agency. Each participant raises matters of importance to his agency. The USIA area director often has a direct interest in one or more of these reports, and informal luncheon engagements—whether with the assistant secretary of state or the area director's counterpart in the Agency for International Development—facilitate further bilateral discussion.

Some working groups bring together personnel with line functions from government agencies and presidential advisers with staff functions to recommend courses of action on aspects of problems or programs of major interest to the President. For example, Daniel Oleksiw as director of USIA's Area

Office for East Asia and the Pacific sits with one of President Johnson's special assistants and State's deputy assistant secretary for Vietnam among others on a Vietnam Interdepartmental Committee which meets about once a month on call. When Hewson Ryan, now deputy director of USIA (policy and research) was area director for Latin America during the Kennedy administration, he met almost weekly with a Latin American Policy Group chaired by an assistant secretary of state and attended by the coordinator of the Alliance for Progress, two special assistants to the President—Arthur Schlesinger and Ralph A. Dungan, the deputy assistant secretary of defense for international security affairs, and the secretary of the joint chiefs of staff. In addition, he sat on an interagency Cuban task force, chaired by the deputy assistant secretary of state for Latin America, which included members from the Departments of Justice, Defense, and Health, Education, and Welfare, plus CIA. In 1967, Oleksiw attends Interdepartmental Regional Group meetings about every two weeks, chaired by the assistant secretary of state for Latin America. His deputy for Vietnam attends a weekly meeting of a Vietnam Public Affairs Working Group chaired by the deputy assistant secretary of state for public affairs who specializes on Vietnam problems.

As might be expected, there are different perspectives in State and USIA over the most suitable location of State's Bureau of Educational and Cultural Affairs (CU). Area directors believe CU should become a part of USIA. Generally, they look more favorably upon the results of their greater collaboration with regional bureaus in State than upon their fewer dealings with CU, though they are pleased that in recent years a U.S. Information Agency FSCR has served as deputy assistant secretary of state for educational and cultural affairs. Similar interagency placement of high-level USIA personnel is considered desirable in the Agency for International Development and in the Department of Defense. It is difficult for area directors to understand why if USIS officers in the field perform services for the exchange program, its Washington headquarters should be a part of the Department of State instead of USIA. They understand Senator William Fulbright's point that the conduct of propaganda activities should be separated from the operation of educational exchange programs, but they believe a relatively antiseptic organizational arrangement could be established within the framework of USIA. They argue that cultural and exchange affairs would not play second fiddle to propaganda and information affairs if removed from State—as it does to political affairs in State, pointing out that three of USIA's area directors during the Kennedy administration had cultural affairs and three information affairs backgrounds. This certainty of equal recognition of cultural and informational expertise in USIA is not always echoed by USIA desk officers with cultural affairs backgrounds.

In spite of receptivity to research, indicated by approval when a research applications officer was first established in the Office of Policy and interest in the reorganization which created the Research and Analysis Staff, area directors tend to have more philosophical interest than actual time to apply research findings to operations. Although they were interested in the planning officer in the Office of Policy and accept the new Program Action Memorandum system involving, by May, 1967, a new research applications officer on the Policy and Plans Staff—successor to a short-lived Operational Policy Staff as a major element in the Office of Policy and Research—their outlook is operational and often intuitional. They realize that no one else in Washington can do their regional planning for them. Events come so rapidly, changed political situations so unexpectedly, that while they do plan ahead in a number of ways, they are dubious of getting net favorable results from formal forward-planning. Research often moves too slowly to resolve the short-range problems which consume most of an area director's time. The area director often draws conclusions from cable information and acts on that basis long before a relevant research paper is started, let alone completed and called to his attention. As area directors view onrushing events, they are forced to make responses to unpredictable political events that do not allow them to plan and follow through on projected policies and programs. As one area director said, "Preparing five-year budgets for the Bureau of the Budget can be ridiculous."

Area directors have less respect for overseas opinion polls than most Americans have for Gallup polls at home. They realize the inexperience of even reputable polling organizations in overseas situations. They are aware that indigenous personnel conducting surveys overseas have on occasion found it easier to fill out the questionnaires themselves than to do the required interviews. Area directors have an understandable willingness to depend upon reports from personnel at field posts who have the same operational interests and background as their own. Reports from and personal visits to the field give them a sense of effectiveness of USIA programs in their areas which sometimes seem more useful to them than more dispassionate arrays of figures marshalled by researchers who may not have made on-site inspections of conditions, who must rely on data gathered by unknown contract or specially hired local personnel. Their schedule of staff meetings allows them opportunities for oral briefings and exchanges of views which often have greater impact on them than more formally presented materials. They are much more likely to be influenced by reports produced by working groups of which they are members than by studies generated by researchers. Men who joke that nine-tenths of their time is taken up by budget matters and the other nine-tenths by personnel problems do not feel that they have much time for planning, research, or evaluation—or for digesting studies which attempt to do this type of thinking for them. For men so busy, the new PAM's should be helpful.

Area directors were not unwilling to make use of Research and Reference studies, nor were they in other ways uncooperative. They played an important role in the drafting of the old Research Applications Memoranda. They are willing to consult during the preparation of the Policy and Plans Staff's PAM's. Nonetheless, it was possible early in 1967 for an area director to say that he had not yet felt any impact from the replacement of the Research and Reference Service by the Research and Analysis Staff—though he was enthusiastic about the new Planning-Programming-Budgeting System which the new Staff's policy-oriented research is geared to support. The nature of the job shapes their information-gathering procedures, and the personalities of the area directors determine what kinds of information they find most useful in performing their jobs. Area directors tend to think research is useful when it backs policies they favor or supports staffing needs they have recognized. Much of the research performed by the old Research and Reference Service was not meaningful or functional for them. They hoped to initiate more studies which would be useful, but never got around to doing it. They wondered if the researchers—many of whom are civil service personnel—had sufficient overseas experience or knew the total information operation well enough to ask the right questions or to make practical but imaginative analyses of foreign situations. The need for cost-effectiveness figures in the PPBS documents which can only be obtained through the use of research studies is likely to make research more relevant to area directors. They were always cooperative. They worked with the Research and Reference Service in setting up the regional research officer program overseas. Traveling from post to post as requested, the regional officer is able to help regularly assigned personnel conduct research projects related to post needs, i.e., determining the effectiveness of a monthly film newsreel or of a tabloid-type monthly newspaper. The few regional research officers now abroad are called on for more assistance and guidance than they have the stamina to provide. Area directors were aware in 1963 and are aware today that it is possible to relate foreign policy and psychological policy, goals and specific objectives, content and sophistication of message to the audience for which it is intended; to identify which media have access to particular target audiences, and to determine the capability of individual media to convey the message that needs to be communicated. They know evidence can be gathered concerning the influence of USIA programs on individuals and mass publics, but they believe the real payoff is how influential the person (or group) influenced is in his (or its) political environment—on which it may be more difficult to obtain empirical evidence. Although area directors are willing to cooperate in making overseas research more effective and in implementing the Program Action Memoranda suggestions, they also want to bring to bear practical knowledge from other resources at their disposal in formulating policies and programs for their areas.

Important as relationships of area directors are to USIA's media services, patterns for dealing with media personnel vary area by area and from media to media, making generalization difficult. The area directors have the responsibility of making certain that the media adapt their products to meet the policy needs of each area, of individual countries, and even of specific target groups. The area directors helped work out the new Country Plan Program Memorandum system under the PPBS program which has broken down the old Agency lockstep on worldwide themes and made it possible to adjust the use of themes to individual country needs. Area directors vary in their degree of involvement in media-related matters, some intervening only when basic questions arise and dealing only with media directors, and others entering into a variety of relationships and involvements that bring them into almost daily contact with media personnel at every conceivable level. Normally, the area policy officer carries the brunt of policy surveillance of the media, assisted by his country desk officers or regional cultural officers. But when there is disagreement at these levels, or during the annual area review of media projects proposed for the ensuing year, the area director is called into the discussions. Apparently there is less expertise on eastern Europe and Africa in the media services than on some other areas; and as expected the area directors for these regions work closely with the media, either personally or through their own subordinates.

Scars of past battles between the area offices and media services remain, but most of the wounds are healed and new injuries are less likely to be fatal. The area and media directors meet regularly in staff meetings or working groups, know each other well, and have ample opportunity to learn how the other "breed" thinks. An increasing number of media directors or deputy media directors are being drawn from USIA's foreign service. Although their jobs are media oriented, their past experiences are similar to those of the area directors. This was less true before 1963. Media directors, like their subordinates, were and sometimes still are civil servants, specialists in their particular media, less interested in policy content than in the "art form" their media represents. Also like their subordinates, they may know what makes a good motion picture, an interesting television show, or a fine exhibit much better than they understand the policy impact of what they produce on a foreign audience. The area directors have learned, by and large, to limit their suggestions to matters of content, to the implications of how a particular scene or statement will affect a particular regional or national audience. They search as hard as the media directors do for the elusive fence between content and form, but sometimes wonder if media personnel are not still more intent on producing a good film than in producing the desired policy impact on Country X.

Area directors read scripts for articles or radio shows from time to time and often attend screenings of motion pictures or television films, though the bulk of this review is done at the policy officer or desk officer level. Most Voice of America broadcast material is audited after the fact rather than before. The introduction and continued use of policy applications officers with a foreign service background in the media services (whatever their job title) makes it possible to work out more problems at the policy officer level and to reduce the involvement of the area and media directors. Increased use of foreign service officers in media service posts will help in improving area-media relations—as will the increasing assignment of media service personnel to overseas tours as more media production is done abroad—but the "problem" of the civil servant media specialist cannot easily be overcome. Control of the budget for media products prepared for regional needs assures the area directors of a necessary degree of policy control, sometimes at great pain to media personnel who like a particular project proposal which does not have the policy punch to make it acceptable to the area office. Preparation of useful media products requires communication by area personnel to media people of what is needed. A large portion of media production is done by contractors outside government working for the media. Contractors, one step removed from direct contact with the area offices, are much less sensitive to changing policy than are media directors and their policy applications officers. Fortunately, the system of policy control for most media products insures review at several points and levels in the production process and a particularly close look at the final product before acceptance by area directors or even higher-ranking Agency officials. Differences which cannot be settled between area and media directors are likely to be carried at least to the Agency's deputy director for policy and research.

Area and deputy directors play an active role in the budget process, though detailed responsibility for preparation of the budget rests with the program coordinator working in conjunction with a budget officer, the latter attached to the Agency's Office of Administration. Justification statements for the budget are reviewed by the area directors, though drawn up under the direction of the policy officer on the basis of drafts submitted by the country desk officers. Area directors get into the budget process early, helping spell out the guidelines and points of emphasis which are sent to the field before the posts submit their budget recommendations. The field requests are reviewed when they arrive in Washington by the program coordinator and appropriate desk officers. The area director goes over the recommended projects and monetary levels with the program coordinator, perhaps consulting with the desk officers in the process, making whatever modifications he feels are needed.

One of the most interesting procedures during budget preparation, and sometimes the most excruciating for media office budget personnel, is the discussion by the program coordinator—quite often with the area director in attendance—with representatives from each media service concerning what media products will be budgeted by the area next year to meet individual post media needs under what is called "direct media support." The media representatives have seen the post's submissions of requests for such media products or services before the sessions. Too often they are not aware of the area office's final thinking on new emphases and program levels. They come to the meetings with their own ideas and make a strong pitch for expanded use of their wares. What may be a windfall of projects and funds for one media is likely to mean severe cuts and economic drought for another. Whoever has observed unhappy and dejected media personnel emerge from a disastrous budget session of this sort, having argued for maintenance of one or more projects at the old level but now facing the moment of truth and reduction, can never forget the sight. How surprised the media personnel actually are on such occasions, or how much of their behavior is showmanship in preparation for a stronger stand next year, is difficult to determine. Area directors claim that the media are aware ahead of time of major changes in program emphasis, but they admit that the amount of prior communication to the media on such matters is not always sufficient. The cost-effectiveness analyses provided in the new Country Plan Program Memoranda may go a long way toward preparing the media service representatives so that in the future they will approach the budget sessions with more realistic expectations. For example, exhibits have generally received low PPBS ratings and may be expected to decline still further than they already have between 1963 and 1967.

When the individual country projects and funds have finally been approved by the area director—including those media support items which have survived or been enlarged—the policy officer prepares a justification of the proposed area budget, noting accomplishments to date, the situation or conditions in the area and individual countries, and the need for the funds and projects proposed for the next year. The policy officer's draft is then discussed with the area director and, after approval, is forwarded to the program coordinator for consolidation in the over-all area budget presentation. Again, the area director approves the final consolidated budget statement. Then the area budget is forwarded to the Office of Administration to be included in the over-all Agency budget proposal for the upcoming year. Before the budget is finalized and forwarded to the Bureau of the Budget, the area director must defend his area budget before the members of the Agency's Program Review Committee, traditionally chaired by USIA's deputy director but more recently by the executive assistant to the director. At this point, the area director can consider himself fortunate to have been involved in the budget process from beginning to end, though it may take a month of his time during a year. The questions asked are critical and pointed. A failure to give a satisfactory answer can cost his area programs and personnel.

However carefully prepared the budget may be, it is unlikely that the money finally appropriated will be spent exactly as budgeted. Any time during the fiscal year, after the budget has been approved and the area is operating on it, program changes initiated by area offices involving costs of $30,000 or more must be presented to and defended before the Program Review Committee by the area director. Most area directors also inform the Program Review Committee of any transfers of funds over $10,000, though the actual transfer requires no formal appearance or justification. Media services budgets for worldwide products were also subject (for a time at least) in 1967 to transfer between media during a year, as developing events created special needs not foreseen earlier. This was to be done through the Operational Policy Staff of the Office of Policy and Research. Change in emphasis involving sizable transfer is not just a matter of whim, for conditions in countries overseas alter rapidly, new needs emerge, old programs lose their reason for being. The time from the first call for a new budget until the final spending of it may be well over two years. A lot can happen in that time.

People carry out budgeted programs and make policy decisions. Personnel and staffing problems weigh heavily upon the area directors and their deputies. No other single responsibility takes more of their time or is in their thoughts more often. They are very much aware of the need for good personnel in Washington and in their areas overseas, and are constantly struggling in a competitive situation for the best men they can obtain. To a degree, the individual areas become inbred; everyone knows everybody from past service together and looks ahead to future assignments with old friends. An area director knows personally most of the personnel serving in his area in the field—and all of those working with him in the area office in Washington. Area specialization is more likely in USIA than in the Department of State, because USIA officers work more directly with people and less through a foreign office and must know the language and culture of an area thoroughly. The area director has normally served as a country public affairs officer at several posts in his area and expects to return to the areas as a CPAO on his next overseas assignment. He is sensitive to the problems of the personnel serving under him because he knows he is dependent upon them for meeting his present responsibilities and because he has gone through what they are going through and will soon be back in their shoes again. During his tenure as area director, he plays a major role in the promotion and assignment of all personnel serving in his area overseas or in his area office. His authority to accept or reject personnel proposed for service under him is almost absolute, giving him greater control over personnel assignments than an assistant secretary of state has for his area of responsibility. The assistant secretary can raise an objection but finally has to accept an individual assigned by State's personnel office if after review the personnel offices find this in the interests of the department and Foreign Service.

The area director's greater authority does not necessarily assure him of getting the kind of personnel he wants. The area director for a less-developed area, where the illness and medical evacuation rate is relatively high, finds that personnel from his area get offers to serve in salubrious climates or stimulating capital cities in other areas. Belgium looks better than the Congo to a man with a family. But if European assignments are sought after, the area director for Europe still has worries. His representatives must have considerable sophistication and high ability. Personality and intelligence are at a premium. Personal contact is important in Europe. Less is gained there by distribution of give-away materials. The area director for Africa may have an excellent man who has served well in the area and is exceptionally well trained, but educational facilities for his children may be inadequate, his wife may not be in the best of health, or he worries about too many tours in an environment which places an emotional strain upon his family because of its distinctive non-Western culture. These are the reasons Agency tours are for two years in Africa and three in Europe.

The problem of finding adequate replacements as men finish their tours is symbolized by the large Staff Control Chart on the wall in one area director's office, which can be read clear across the room from his desk. All area posts are represented, and every major American-staffed position listed. A colored disk beside each position indicates the present situation with regard to finding a replacement for the incumbent. Five different colors indicate whether a man is due out in six months with no replacement yet selected, in six months with a replacement selected, in a year with no replacement yet selected, in a year with a replacement selected, or whether there is a critical replacement problem with no clue to replacement. The same area director, whose area contains a high percentage of hardship posts, also maintains a Relief and Rehabilitation Chart, indicating when his officers are entitled to rehabilitation leave. At most African posts, officers and their families are entitled to such leave every six months for a visit to a European vacation area.

In Washington, there are also staffing problems for the area director. As officers are rotated at posts overseas an attempt is made to have several weeks of overlap so that the new man is given orientation on his new assignment by the experienced officer who is leaving. This is not the case when officers come in for Washington assignments. The man to be replaced has normally already departed. In USIA—as in State where the same condition often prevails—it is considered more necessary that the field be continuously staffed than the home office. Even area directors often come into their posts without a chance to talk with their predecessors, though some are returning to the United States for the first time during their service with the Agency to work in the tangled bureaucratic web of Washington. The deputy area director is available to brief the new area director—if he is not off making an inspection tour overseas. As one area director put it, "You just start running and eventually you get in step." The same problem exists at the desk level, and the area director is often dependent upon a desk officer who is carrying an extra two or three countries after the departure of another desk officer who had covered them; it is this same overburdened desk officer who will be responsible for orienting the new desk man when he finally arrives—perhaps after eight to twelve years in the field—on the nature of his job. The staffing pattern in the area offices is probably the most skimpy in the Agency.

The U.S. Information Agency is a "maturing" organization, relatively stable in structure, but facing many personnel problems which an old line organization like the Department of State has already confronted and partially resolved. State's regional bureaus worried ten years ago about loss of their personnel to training programs, with the personnel involved fearing that training might sidetrack rather than advance their careers. Now USIA's area offices react in much the same way. Certainly area directors hate to see their best men leave for full-time training, but promotion of men to high-level posts in the Agency after such training—as has occurred in several instances —will encourage young officers to accept training opportunities in the future. Area directors are involved in the careers of those working under them, bringing people they know in from the field to staff the area offices and by their recommendations for good performances insuring advancement for such officers. State's career counseling operation was getting off the ground ten years ago. USIA now has a relatively new foreign service career counseling program; but the area directors still informally advise and assist young officers. Careers are still "made" by contacts and by a push up the ladder by a satisfied boss, as has often been the case in the Department of State. This will continue no matter how effective career development offices become in either agency.

The Agency still has the high degree of civil service and foreign service separation characteristic of the Department of State before Wristonization during the 1954 to 1958 period. Area directors are likely to feel that "something must be done" about this.[4] Many civil servants are relatively specialized and would not profit by regular service abroad. Many posts in the Agency are too specialized (or require continuity of relationships in the United States) for foreign service personnel to fill. The Agency might still benefit from having all its personnel in a single system, even though some individuals went overseas only for brief training or inspection visits, others served overseas for perhaps one tour during a lifetime, others divided their time possibly half-and-half between the field and Washington, while still others spent most of their time at posts overseas and occasionally did a tour at headquarters. The problem of two systems in a single agency, with which State has yet to come fully to grips, is still bothersome in USIA. Foreign service officers are being assigned to some positions in the media, and some progress has been made between 1963 and 1968 in freeing civil servants for overseas experiences. Area directors are aware that more of this needs to be done and of tenure problems which also plague USIA. Many foreign service officers have a right to foreign service staff tenure if their Foreign Service Career Reserve ratings are terminated; and the Civil Service is protective of individual rights—making an area director wonder if it is worth trying to fire an inefficient individual. An area director feels that there is no easy way for him to rid himself and the Agency of "deadwood," some of which accumulated in the Agency's early days before it had the experience and status to draw the type of personnel it can now hope to attract.

Area directors and their deputies probably have less direct relationships with members of the Congress, with the general American public, or with staff members of foreign embassies in Washington than do the assistant secretaries of state. Although an area director may know some senators or representatives, he would rarely conduct official business with them directly or alone. In some instances, an area director might accompany USIA's general counsel to the Hill for a discussion with a member of Congress—but this is an exception. His contact with the Congress in 1963 normally came during the annual budget hearings before committees of the House and Senate, when he had to stand ready to appear any time his area's budget came up for consideration. Inspection trips overseas by area directors or their deputies were often held up while the area leaders waited to be called across town to give testimony on their area budgets for the ensuing year. This was not the case by 1967, because Agency Director Marks and the assistant director of USIA for administration had taken over "all" of the defense of the Agency budget before the Congress. Congressional letters to USIA, dealing specifically with a particular area policy or program, are funneled from the general counsel's office to the area concerned. Replies, though drafted at the desk level, are approved by the area director or his deputy. Direct telephone calls are received from members of Congress or their staffs. The area director or the deputy area director answers questions asked and then informs the general counsel of the gist of the discussion. Congressional letters received directly are also checked out with the general counsel before a reply is sent, for the general counsel has most of the congressional liaison responsibility for the Agency, including legislation but not the budget presentation. Congress is less interested in the operations of an area office than it is in a particular Voice of America broadcast or issue of *America Illustrated*. The area office does not consult with members of the Congress or even with the general counsel in the formulation of area information policy. Ordinary citizens seldom seek interviews with area directors or their deputies. Occasionally the area director takes a telephone call, and he reviews and approves letters drafted by desk officers in reply to letters from "John Q. Citizen." Area directors seem to avoid the embassy "cocktail circuit," making no apparent effort to maintain regular liaison with foreign information officers stationed in Washington.

Although area directors or their deputies seem overburdened by meetings, responsibilities, and relationships in Washington, USIA programs are actually conducted overseas. Area directors, who are responsible for USIS policies and programs in their areas, personally supervise and inspect USIS posts and programs in these areas. They cannot escape reading a portion of the numerous reports or special inquiries from the field received in the area offices in Washington, nor can they avoid consulting with staff members at headquarters before approving instructions sent to the field. Top-level guidance and leadership to the field is one of the most important of their tasks. In addition to direction from afar, area directors and their deputies spend between 33 and 50 per cent of their time in the field giving advice and inspecting installations. Field relations are time consuming. The area director and his deputy each make from three to six inspection trips abroad in a single year. Individual trips last from one month to six weeks. Area leaders visit every post once or twice a year, staying from one day up to a week at each location, depending on the size and importance of the post. There is no doubt of the value of such inspections which further personal relationships between area directors and field personnel. Public affairs officers in a given area gather together once a year at a city in the area for an exchange of views with USIA leaders (always the Agency's director or deputy director), including the area director, present at the conference. USIS personnel in Ouaga-dougou, Usumbura, Douala, and Yaoundé know Washington has not forgotten them or their wives, whatever the living conditions or climate. The negative impact of absence from Washington on continuity of direction of the area offices and on maintenance of close contacts on policy matters with personnel in other foreign affairs agencies in Washington is the other side of the coin. It was thought that the re-establishment of an inspection system under the inspector general might lighten the overseas inspection load of the area directors and their deputies, but this has not proved true. As one area director explained in early 1967:

> Inspection once every three years is no substitute for visits by an area director, just as two- to three-day visits by the area director are not a substitute for longer formal inspections by the Inspection Corps. Though country public affairs officers are supposed to run USIS posts, actually a large contribution is made by the area director. Post direction is the result of the combined efforts of the area office director or his deputy and the CPAO.

The degree of preparation for trips may vary by area, but careful plans are generally made. Before departure, an area director or deputy area director is likely to review relevant materials from the State Department, Department of Defense, and Central Intelligence Agency. He will read recent monthly reports from the posts he intends to visit. In the African area, this entails reading sixteen reports of from two to twelve pages for a single trip. The area director also meets with the assistant or deputy assistant secretary of state and with Defense personnel responsible for foreign or military policy in his area, solicits questions or problems to be explored with overseas personnel from the desk officers in his own office, makes sure that he is aware of any problems the media services are having with the posts to be inspected, and consults the Office of Administration on any special budgetary or personnel matters he should look into. His schedule is worked out in advance, day by day—with time of arrival and departure, air carrier, and flight number—well before he leaves Washington's Friendship or Dulles airport. At each post, he is likely to start his inspection by talking with the ambassador or chargé d'affaires, asking how USIS is supporting the mission, in what ways the mission leader is working with USIS personnel, what special problems are emerging on the horizon, what USIA policies or programs may need to be altered, and how USIA might respond to test the post's ideas of what needs to be done. A second discussion will be held with the deputy chief of mission, usually much closer to mission operations, a third with the chief administrative officer, and possibly a fourth with CIA's station chief. With this round of meetings concluded, the area director talks with as many members of the USIS staff as possible, including their wives, to get to know them better, to discuss Agency operations and plans, and to understand their problems, hopes, and personal plans. The inspection task is made easier by the fact that the area director is usually a former country public affairs officer, with experience at several posts in the area he is inspecting; his job is possibly more difficult at the same time, however, because he knows as friends (or competitors) many of the men and women with whom he talks.

Discussions at one post completed, he moves on, writing reports as he travels along the inspection trail. Reports are succinct, six to eight pages in length, in the form of recommendations on policy, program operations, and general philosophy which the area director expects to be carried out in the future. The area director gets results from his inspections faster than the members of the USIA Inspection Corps did from theirs from the fall of 1958 to August 31, 1962. Areas tended to disagree with the reports of the old inspectors, to drag their heels in response to suggestions, partly because the Inspection Corps was an independent administrative body attached to the Office of the Director and possessing no line authority. The field officers accept policy suggestions from the area director; they often questioned Inspection Corps reports, which sometimes criticized post objectives as being unrealistic in view of particular political, economic, or social situations. The three general responsibilities of the Inspection Corps were (1) to evaluate the content and effectiveness of USIA programs in relation to the situation existing in any particular country; (2) to check the efficiency and economy of such operations; and (3) to evaluate personnel in terms of their attitudes and potential as well as their general performance. Under normal circumstances, each post was inspected every three years. At least two weeks were spent at small posts and three to four months at the largest posts. Two inspectors usually went to larger countries. Inspections were often scheduled to overlap with those of the State Department Inspection Corps, permitting common problems to be assessed on the spot. Although inspectors were sometimes accused of being overly critical, a former inspector general of the corps emphasized that they tried to be as constructive as possible. With only six inspectors, annual visits to posts were impossible. The corps must sometimes have felt frustrated, because as one area director said: "Nothing the inspectors recommended was done. Inspectors often didn't know the particular area or its special programs, so the area officers didn't pay attention to them, but fought their recommendations." Some area directors believe the Inspection Corps should not have questioned the post's objectives (which had already been looked at "carefully" by the USIS mission, the ambassador, the area director, and USIA's Office of Policy) and should have confined themselves to making judgments about how well the post was implementing them. On the other hand, how "carefully" each review was made might be questioned. Personnel in a review hierarchy sometimes are hypnotized by prior signatures of approval, and members of a "team" may find it easier to approve of each other's judgments than to disapprove. Disagreement with post judgments does not prove that the old Inspection Corps was wrong—nor does it indicate that the Inspection Corps was right. It is difficult to build a full-time Inspection Corps capable of broad evaluation, with its eyes on the things that "really" count rather than on the picayune, and staffed by imaginative inspectors rather than "inspection types."

The Agency's present *ad hoc* inspection system has probably resolved this problem and some others. For example, the current system of inspection under the inspector general does not make any assessment of the validity of the psychological objectives or supporting projects in a post's Country Plan or Country Plan Program Memorandum. Some problems remain. The assumption of inspection responsibilities by area and deputy area directors in 1962 without any increase in area staffing, at the same time that the Agency was being encouraged to play a more important role in blending psychological perspectives into the policies of other foreign affairs or domestic agencies, was unwise. This is not to say there is no need for field visits by area directors and their deputies, but they should never have been the sole inspectors in behalf of the Agency. There is no easy solution to meeting the problem of stepped-up policy liaison duties of the area directors with officials of equivalent rank in other agencies. It would be helpful if the area director himself could spend more time in Washington, but he is likely to feel a need to get overseas about as often as he is at present. It might be helpful for each area director to have two deputy directors, one of whom would spend less time in the field and assume primary responsibility for interagency advisory functions in Washington. This would enable the Agency better to play its advisory role, and at the same time make some additional time available for area inspection overseas, allowing area inspectors to spend more than two or three days at a post, possibly improving their contribution to post operations without sacrificing the number of posts covered.

POLICY DIRECTION — THE AREA POLICY OFFICERS

At the right hand of an area director or his deputy area director on policy matters is the area policy officer. Often considered the third-ranking man in an area office, policy officers eat, talk, and sleep foreign and information policy—particularly in an area dimension but also in individual country terms. It is their business to be aware of general directives relevant to their areas, such as President Kennedy's statement of the Agency's mission or its 1967 replacement, as well as more specific Policy Guidelines or National Policy Papers, Country Plans or Country Plan Program Memoranda—even the latest speech by Arthur Goldberg at the United Nations, if it has bearing on their particular area. They develop some capacity to relate long-range directives or statements to daily policy problems and attempt to provide policy guidance to the area and deputy area directors, the media, and the field as requested or needed. Broader policy papers are an integral part of their thinking; they must also be alert for each nuance of the Department of State's developing policy line, and this alertness calls for a close relationship with public affairs advisors in State's regional bureaus, and with USIA's policy guidance man for their area (whom policy officers outrank) or one of the top men in the Office of Policy and Research. Policy officers keep abreast of political reporting from the field. They receive daily policy briefings from the deputy chief of policy guidance, and in turn pass on pertinent information from the briefings to personnel in their areas—both the Washington and overseas staff—using this information to monitor fast media operations. Within their own area office, they work closely with the area director and area deputy director, with the area program coordinator whose specialty is budget, personnel, and administrative problems, and with the country desk officers. Policy applications officers or program managers are their usual points of contact in the media services, though they may deal there with specialists at a variety of levels. Area policy officers are consulted on the applicability of worldwide media products to their areas. They write policy guidances to the field and coordinate or help draft the written narrative which accompanies the area budget presentation, relating personnel and materials to policies, objectives, and programs. They are interested in the optimum scale of operations, the methods of maintaining credibility, the appropriate target audiences, the best means of reaching those to be influenced, and the proper balance between political and more cultural activities for maximum policy effectiveness. Policy officers have usually had extensive field experience; they have at their disposal many facts and statistics on their areas. Nonetheless, they often feel many things "by the seat of their pants," whether from a kick for past error or just long occupancy of the chair of a policy officer. They show considerable interest in research products of State's Bureau of Intelligence and Research and in policy-oriented research by the new Research and Analysis Staff, but they were also great users of studies by the Research and Reference Service. Policy officers are verbal and relatively introspective men, and they generally view ideas in shades of gray rather than as absolutes.

Much of the policy officer's sense of "what is" policy comes in one way or another from the Office of Policy and Research. Policy officers tend to consider the relationship with IOP personnel as lateral rather than as hierarchical, yet they receive considerable policy direction from members of the IOP staff. Policy officers may give direction on policy for their area to IOP in time of crisis—like that in the Dominican Republic during the spring of 1965. Some policy officers, unsure of their relationship with IOP, are somewhat uncomfortable about the area-IOP working arrangement. Guidance to the policy officers may come from the Office of Policy and Research by means of the daily 12:30 P.M. policy guidance briefing, the weekly session with the deputy director (policy and research), an informal exchange of views with one of the advisors or liaison officers in IOP, or consultation during the preparation of Country Plans or the new Country Plan Program Memoranda which are reviewed in IOP. The daily briefing by the deputy chief of policy guidance is more directly and immediately useful to the fast media representatives—those from the Voice of America or the Press and Publications Service—than to the slower media or the policy officers from the area offices. Policy officers attend, or send one of their desk officers when they are busy, as much to monitor the guidance being given to the media or to volunteer any specialized area knowledge that may be useful as to gain information. Since they sometimes substitute for the policy guidance area man who covers the regional bureau dealing with their area in the Department of State, they attend the daily sessions to keep up to date on developments so that they can fill in if illness or absence for other cause necessitates their making the regular morning visit to State to gather information for the noon briefing. Most of the sessions seem routine to the policy officers, but from the information gained they prepare a daily summary for distribution within their own area office, discuss the IOP summary with individual country desk officers as appropriate, or relay copies of the IOP summary to area office personnel. Immediately after the Nuclear Test Ban Treaty was signed and the United States was urging other states to ratify the agreement, there developed a belief in many nations that a detente had been achieved between the United States and the Soviet Union. During this period, the noon meeting briefing officer often stressed to the policy officers present the need to avoid stressing relaxation of tensions and the importance of keeping policy statements on an even keel in order to prevent overreaction to this limited step in improving Soviet-American relations. The noon briefing normally does not generate any policy debate from the policy officers of the area offices or the representatives of the media. Generally, they understand what is said, and little or no discussion is required. Nonetheless, the daily briefing may contain a number of items relevant to a single policy officer; for example, on a single day guidances may be presented concerning problems in the Philippines, Malaysia, Indonesia, Japan, and Communist China—all of direct relevance to the policy officer for USIA's area office covering East Asia and the Pacific.

Although the noon briefings are considered routine, the discussion meeting chaired by Deputy Agency Director (policy and research) Hewson Ryan every other Friday at 2:30 P.M. is another matter. Ryan may kick off the discussion himself or may provide a guest speaker to raise problems for discussion. Present are policy officers from the area offices and policy applications officers from the media services, plus the top three Office of Policy and Research leaders and possibly some of IOP's special advisors or liaison officers. About twenty people attend these sessions. The area policy officers meet informally at luncheon each Tuesday from 12:30 to 2 P.M., usually discussing area office policy relations with IOP and achieving consensus on points which they may wish to use later at the Friday meeting or elsewhere. The deputy agency director usually invites the policy officers present, from either area offices or media services, to raise any problems they have which they believe are of importance. He may also report some new policy emphasis or mention a research finding that can be applied by the policy officers. The meeting almost always turns into an open discussion; final decisions are not sought, but emerging problems are identified. Unless there is a particular world crisis situation demanding immediate attention, the sessions are likely to be related to long-range media needs of the Agency. Since the area offices use media products at their overseas posts, the area policy officers have a real stake in these discussions.

The IOP advisors or liaison officers, with their functional specializations which cut across area lines, work closely with individual area policy officers.

For example, in emphasizing a "strength image" for America, the IOP policy liaison officer might stimulate the policy officer in the East Asia and Pacific Area Office to find out whether an American "show of force" would be likely to help or perhaps be counterproductive with people in Southeast Asia. This would require the policy officer to seek information from the Research and Analysis Staff or from State's Bureau of Intelligence and Research which, in the long run, would be used by the policy officer as he helped formulate area policy. The area policy officers are anchor men in the area offices for drafting precepts and giving area approval for individual Country Plans or Country Plan Program Memoranda. In turn, all Country Plans or Country Plan Program Memoranda must finally be approved by planning officers on the Policy and Plans Staff of IOP. This means that area policy officers are in frequent contact with the planning officers on policy matters concerning individual countries. If the relationship with IOP at times seems to be lateral and at other times hierarchical, it is really both. In dealing with IOP, the area office is working with just another office of USIA. Policy officers certainly do not consider themselves clearly subordinate. But the head of that office is the number-three officer in the Agency, thus outranking the area directors. However, the area directors have direct access to the director and deputy director of USIA, the Agency's number-one and -two officers, and can run around end if they disagree with a decision made by the deputy agency director for policy and research. IOP works cooperatively as an equal most of the time with area offices, though perhaps it is a little more equal.

Relationships of policy officers with the area and deputy area directors, the program coordinator, the desk officers, or the cultural affairs officers (one type of area functional officer) in the area offices may differ, depending on the personality and experience of the individuals involved. Policy officers are usually members of USIA's foreign service. They are often former desk officers. They are quite likely at some future time to be tapped to become deputy area directors. But they sometimes are junior in years and experience to the program coordinator, who may in such a case have more influence and impact on policy by control of personnel and budget matters than the policy officer does. Area directors also vary in their degree of concern with policy. One works directly with his country desk officers on policy matters. Another works through his policy officer, with the policy officer giving most of the guidance to the desk level. Some area directors write their own guidances or newsletters to the field. Others allow policy officers to draft the materials and sign them with little change. In some instances, the policy officer serves as acting director of the area office when the area director and his deputy are both absent at the same time. The policy officer on rare occasions may attend Inter-Departmental Regional Group meetings to consider general strategy in his area or to help develop Policy Guidelines or National Policy Papers. The policy officer normally chairs and is responsible for area office review panels on Country Plans or Country Plan Program Memoranda, attended by his two superiors in the area as well as by the program coordinator and the desk officer for the particular country being discussed. The Department of State also has an opportunity to review either of these documents, and the policy officer is likely to maintain a close relationship with appropriate area and country personnel in State.

Although the relationship between the policy officer and the program coordinator in an area office would be expected to be exceptionally close, a degree of separation can be sensed. Their offices are likely to flank that of the area director, being set apart physically rather than adjoining, psychologically separated though in relatively close proximity. While the policy officer is almost always a member of the foreign service, the program coordinator is more likely to be a civil servant. The program coordinator rather than the policy officer is likely to provide the thread of continuity and knowledge of the past in the area office, though there are exceptions. While policy officers must be aware of cost and personnel factors, and program coordinators should be aware of the policy implications of personnel training or budget reductions, the lines of communication between policy officers and program coordinators in area offices appear to be more tenuous in some instances than those of a policy officer with either the Office of Policy and Research or the media services. In some cases, policy officers and program coordinators apparently have closer relations with the area director and the desk officers than with each other, though the policy officer does cooperate in the preparation of the narrative material in the budget presentation. Policy officers also give advice to the program coordinator on budget priorities, and even on personnel assignments. One program coordinator stressed the interrelationship of his duties and those of the policy officer and spoke of constant intercommunication. On the other hand, a policy officer may have only limited participation in negotiations with the media services on direct support items, though the details agreed to by the program coordinator have considerable influence on how policy will be conducted in the field. Program coordinators indicate that policy officers say "cut down this program" because of a policy change but that the policy officers do not know "how much" to cut it in terms of funds or personnel. A program coordinator might cut it down enough to get funds for another program slated for expansion rather than with the impact of the cut on the old policy and program in mind. As one program coordinator said of the relationship, "It doesn't work perfectly, but the decisions are not irrevocable." It is possible that the relationship between the policy officer and the program coordinator in most area offices is "close" in fact, but not as "close" as it ought to be in theory. Taking time factors and human limitations into consideration, possible improvements in interrelationship are probably somewhat limited—though some feel the use of the new Country Plan Program Memoranda will aid in developing closer coordination and better understanding. While individual contacts between policy officers and program coordinators are not as numerous as they might be, they are both likely to be present if weekly "brainstorming" sessions are held by their area director, or they may exchange views with each other and their other area colleagues at a weekly noon "picnic"—when all area officer personnel bring their lunches and discuss area problems as they eat.

A policy officer may be given primary responsibility by his area director for policy relations with the desk officers, but this is not done in all area offices; when the responsibility is delegated, the policy officer may hold one or more meetings of all desk officers in the area each week, discussing substantive policy problems. This can lead to a thorough exploration of a particular question. For example, information needs growing from the Trade Expansion Act of 1962 were discussed by the policy officer and his desk officers in the European Area Office. They consulted IOP's advisor on aid-economic affairs, checked out intelligence reports from the Central Intelligence Agency, and talked with the director of the Foreign Agricultural Service and others in the Department of Agriculture. (Policy officer relations with other agencies of government, except State, tend to be of this special *ad hoc* nature, with few regularized or continuous contacts.) After this spade work had been done, USIA media personnel were called in, and finally the idea evolved that presenting the human aspects of the American farmer, helping western Europeans understand the relationship of the farmer to the consumer, might help develop larger United States agricultural markets in Europe and decrease the likelihood of future "chicken wars." From this cooperative exploration came a film, "The Farmer and I," produced by the Department of Agriculture for $45,000 from its own budget, to be shown in western Europe. Top USIA officials, including the director, the assistant deputy director for media content, and the area director for Europe, not to mention the policy officer who had generated the idea for the film from discussions with his desk officers, reviewed the film before it was sent overseas for showing. In addition to such group projects, the policy officer works individually with the desk officers, giving advice, reviewing drafts of instructions to the field and helping them resolve the problems of their countries within a broader regional and worldwide context.

Much if not most of a policy officer's time is taken up with insuring that area-targeted media products conform to area policy guidelines. This includes the Broadcasting Service's (IBS) "Voice of America" programs, the Motion Picture and Television Service's (IMV) products, and the Press and Publications Service's (IPS) cartoon books, pamphlets, or periodicals. In addition, the policy officer will help review materials to be made available by the Information Center Service (ICS) in its libraries and information centers overseas. Voice of America broadcasts are normally monitored after the fact, both by policy officers and desk officers, and offending scripts are called to the attention of the IBS policy applications officer or discussed directly with the area officers in IBS responsible for checking broadcast scripts. For many years, the area policy officer for Latin America and appropriate desk officers reviewed IMV's "Panorama Pan Americano" television show, checking the script regularly. There is now more emphasis on public affairs specials dealing with economic integration in Latin America and problems of development, with timely commentary—also subject to review by the policy officer and desk officers. If the policy officer has objections to an item, it may be thrown out or the treatment of it may be modified. Although differences can be carried to the area director and to the director of the Motion Picture and Television Service, they rarely are. The problems of working out a new show or series, though more complicated, appear to give the policy officer excellent policy control. If the area office wants to introduce a new series or have a movie on a particular topic produced, possibly after suggestions from the field, the policy officer drafts a general guidance paper to suggest to the media concerned what the area wants. After discussion between the policy officer and media personnel, IMV may turn the guidance paper over to a private contractor to do a "treatment," or synopsis, of the proposed series or show. Then, the policy officer, perhaps seeking the guidance of his area director and desk officers, reviews the synopsis, possibly giving blanket approval or sometimes indicating radical changes. The type of policy problem encountered in working through IMV with contractors to produce a television "soap opera" series is demonstrated by one contractor's first treatment or story synopsis in 1963. The proposed soap opera was to involve: the mayor of a town, who it turned out had three illegitimate daughters, one of whom was psychotic; plus three communist saboteurs; and one alcoholic. It was apparently quite difficult for contractors who prepared scripts for American audiences, which have a great thirst for violence and melodrama, to channel their talent into producing the message USIA wanted to convey—more likely, in this case, how the mayor of a small town encouraged people to work together to plan and bring about improvements in their local community. Although the use of "soap operas" has been sharply reduced since 1963, the policy-review process remains much the same in 1968. After the story is toned down or otherwise altered by policy review, details are worked out by IMV with the producer and the contractor writes a full script for the show. Again the draft is reviewed by the policy officer. The contractor may then go ahead and produce the show, and the completed product will be screened for minor alterations by the area director, policy officer, and appropriate desk officers—probably also the deputy agency director. Quite often, the policy officer and the others involved in screening media products actually see the show at an earlier stage, in "rough-cut production," where the picture is shown without sound track and with someone reading the script. After this review, the picture moves into final production. Early in the whole process, test shots of sets and the voices of the actors may be reviewed to assure that the sets will appear authentic and the actors' language suitable for the area. The policy officer has the same type of close review control if a production is done "in house" by IMV. He also attends screenings of media products intended for worldwide use to comment on their applicability to his area. The need for intervention by the policy officer to assure that policy guidelines are met has been lessened since 1961 by the introduction of policy applications officers in the media services. These men may lack specialized knowledge of the area for which the product is done, though they are foreign service officers and have had overseas experience in some area and sometimes have junior officers assisting them who have had experience in all major areas of the world. Review of a program in a regular television series is done in a single day. Time elapsed during the series of reviews of a motion picture may be more than a year. Cartoon books, produced by contractors for the Press and Publication Service and distributed unattributed to USIA, reach millions of readers overseas, can be targeted for particular areas, and are reviewed carefully by policy officers. Policy control problems may be similar to those of television series and motion pictures. In its first review of a "comic book" on cooperatives addressed to laboring groups in Latin America, the policy officer discovered that the book's cover dramatically pictured attempted sabotage on the "Co-op" by the local hidden Communist, with the hero arriving just in time to prevent the arsonist from achieving his goal. Actually, the guidance to the contractor had called for a straight presentation. But the contractor, who had previously done cartoon books on communism in Latin America for USIA, carried over the negative approach—which USIA sometimes uses—inappropriately in this instance.

Opportunities for the policy officer to look at all types of products at different stages seems to provide ample time for policy review, but does not necessarily assure that the product will have the desired policy impact. Actually, some television shows or motion pictures are pretested at the posts before public showings, perhaps screened by nationals employed by USIA. There is not always agreement even within the area offices on what is good or bad about a product. The area director, the policy officer, and the desk officer may disagree. Busy as they all are, they may not attend every review screening, and the producer occasionally gets somewhat different advice from the desk officer who sees it at midpoint, the policy officer who saw it earlier, and the area director who comes in for a screening of the final production. Backstopping the collective balance of these individual judgments are research surveys or polls conducted abroad on contract for the Research and Analysis Staff—or before 1967 for the Research and Reference Service. The polls are considered accurate, quite sophisticated, and useful in Latin America and adequate even in India. Area offices, however, show some reserve in accepting results from areas where polling organizations are only beginning to build up staff and area knowledge. As such research material is further developed, policy officers are likely to make selective use of it to determine people's aspirations and what they believe can or should be done to help them achieve their goals.

Perhaps one policy officer overemphasized the breadth of his relationship to the field when he claimed to represent and service public affairs officers collectively in his area in the same way that desk officers concerned themselves with one or several countries. In fact, the policy officer and the program coordinator combined may stand in such a comparative relationship with their public affairs officers. The policy officer in an area office plays a key role in the annual review of Country Plans or Country Plan Program Memoranda submitted by the country public affairs officers from the overseas posts in his area. While Country Plans or CPPM's must finally be approved in the Office of Policy and Research, if there are political changes within a country during the year covered by the plan, the policy officer assumes leadership in revision of the plan to meet the new situation and official approval of the Office of Policy and Research is not required. Although the Country Plan or Country Plan Program Memorandum review constitutes a relatively long-range policy relationship with the field for the policy officer, he is more concerned on a daily basis with reading reports from the field and in reviewing instructions to the field. Because the policy officer is concerned with policy primarily, he reads any Assessment Reports sent in from the posts which spell out their operations and contacts, their successes and failures; but these are considered to be of more direct interest to the program coordinator. The policy officer is more interested in communicating to the field the latest turn in policy, though he also may informally pass on to the posts gimmicks that have worked in another country or area—because posts have few interrelationships among themselves and they must learn from Washington what USIS officers in other countries are doing. One formal means for communicating area policy direction by the policy officer is a regional policy guidance statement prepared for the Wireless File. Just as an over-all or general guidance may be included in the Wireless File from the Office of Policy and Research, so a regional guidance may be drafted by the policy officer in each area office. Another formal means of policy communication to the field is the Information Guide, issued as the occasion demands from the Office of Policy and Research on the basis of Information Guides prepared in the Department of State and forwarded to USIA. Policy officers are consulted to see if the particular guidance is pertinent to their area, and it goes or does not go to area posts depending on their recommendations. Reversing the initiation process, a policy officer may become convinced that an Information Guide to his field posts is necessary. If he can persuade the Department of State and the Office of Policy and Research that he is right, such a special guidance will be prepared by IOP and sent, after review by the policy officer.

The policy officer's informal means of channeling policy direction and useful ideas to the posts is through the "Area Newsletter," usually drafted by the policy officer on the basis of material submitted by country desk officers, but often signed and approved by the area director. Sent out regularly on a biweekly or monthly basis, or *ad hoc*, the *Newsletter* is a multipurpose publication. Material from a News Policy Note, drafted by an IOP area man (but reviewed by the appropriate policy officer) as a guidance to one of the media services in Washington, is sometimes included in a *Newsletter*. The *Newsletter* may also be used to clarify and summarize guidances which have gone out over the Wireless File. It also chats about personnel shifts, personal events, and other matters of interest within the Agency at headquarters and passes on similar information about people and happenings at area field posts. From a program point of view, it communicates the bright ideas that have been used at one post and found successful so that another post may try them if they seem appropriate. For example, in Ecuador a member of the USIS staff conceived of sending out USIA exhibits and motion pictures together via railroad to reach areas difficult to get to by automobile. From the railroad company, he obtained two freight cars "free" which he painted up, placing large signs on the outside and installing electric generators and display walls within. A freight train would then drop the two cars at a siding in the hinterland; a local employee of the post was along to operate the exhibit and to show the movie at night to a captive audience, not used to having such exciting things occur. This operation, supplementing the post's mobile motion-picture units at low cost, had the advantage of being able to travel in all weather —even when roads were axle deep in mud during rainy periods. As important as the policy officer's varied contributions are to the functioning of the area office and of field posts in the area, he is matched in importance by the program coordinator, his hierarchical counterpart in the area office.

OPERATION AND ADMINISTRATION — THE PROGRAM COORDINATOR

As a program officer, the program coordinator much more than the policy officer—though in a different way—is the translator of policy into programs to accomplish Agency objectives. The policy officer in an area office learns what the public response of the Department of State will be on matters of foreign policy, helps adapt this policy line for his area, reviews media products for conformity to area policy, and communicates the policy line to USIS personnel in his area overseas. The program coordinator, as he reads the policy officer's sharps and flats, grace notes and arpeggios, must play the program keys in a manner to produce information music which will be listened to and appreciated, perhaps responded to, by overseas audiences. Although the program coordinator is responsible for area administrative matters, like budget, personnel, and management, he also may, as a program officer, be an originator of programs and program ideas as well as a developer of those suggested by the posts. The role of the program coordinator, in the broadest sense, is to see that within his area the most effective use is made of material and human resources, taking into account the changing area situation and the policies of the United States government. He can marshal resource factors, spot needs, and figure out how to strengthen USIA's program impact overseas. This requires that he keep abreast of all current projects to understand their changing degree of effectiveness in achieving policy objectives so that he can shift resources from those of lessening use to the new priority needs of the field programs. It is his job to coordinate the activities and products of the media services in balance and timing so USIA's objectives are achieved in his area of responsibility to the extent possible. This means that current and projected budgets as well as immediate and future personnel capabilities need to be developed to provide realistic support for present and advanced program planning. In a changing and sometimes unpredictable world, continuous adjustments in use and projected use of resources are inescapable. The program coordinator is as much a re-programmer as a programmer. To simplify by eliminating the time and personnel factors, looking only at media products and funds that the program coordinator must allocate after receiving budget suggestions from the field, one experienced program coordinator diagrammed his area programming procedure in the following manner:

AREA PROGRAMMING

SEVENTEEN MAJOR ITEMS OF DIRECT MEDIA SUPPORT

(Assorted Products)

Program coordinator utilizes available funds on the
basis of the following priority recommendations:

1. Policy priorities in the area
2. Country priorities in the area
3. Media effectiveness in the area

Twenty-two Principal Posts in the Area, Each Receiving a
Planned Mix of the Media Service Products

These are the responsibilities of the program coordinator, but the authority for his decisions rests with the area director, subject to approval by the Program Review Committee within the Agency and the Bureau of the Budget without, and requiring the ultimate sanction of the Congress and the signature of the President of the United States. It should be made clear that the program coordinators are making budget decisions on office space, houses, vehicles, record players, mobile units, air conditioners, and even pencils, as well as "great decisions" on programs. Along with budget matters, they are worrying about the training needs of area personnel and how to find time to make individuals available for such study, advising their area directors on staffing needs and possible replacements and attempting to obtain from the Management Division of the Office of Administration approval for another secretary or an additional desk officer in the area office. There are many "nuts and bolts" that demand attention in the job, and the program coordinator must constantly lift up his eyes from tightening the single screws which endlessly seem to be coming loose and listen to the sound of the complex motor he is operating to make sure it is running efficiently. Of necessity a practical man, he ought also to be sensitive and foresighted.

Luncheon with other program coordinators on Tuesdays helps broaden his outlook. In routine times, such sessions are not very exciting. Matters of mutual interest which the group can support to bring about changes in administrative policy common to all areas are discussed. If there is consensus, the collective views will later be presented to appropriate representatives in the Office of Administration. Program coordinators do not always agree among themselves. After listening to their arguments for and against placing the low-priced book program in the budget of the Information Center Service rather than leaving it in the individual area budgets, Administration can decide whether to put the program in the Information Center Service budget. At the luncheon, program coordinators exchange ideas and may learn about a film done for another area which might with minor adaptations be useful in their own. The period from late 1966 through 1967 was not a routine one for the program coordinators. Much of their time at the weekly luncheons was devoted to problems of installing the new Planning-Programming-Budgeting System at field posts. Five posts in Latin America, for example, were trying the new system for the first time on an experimental basis. The program coordinator of the Area Office for Latin America was organizing an Agency team—including research and budget specialists—to go to Brazil to learn the problems of adjustment to PPBS at firsthand while helping the USIS mission there prepare its first documents under the new system. Among the problems faced is the multiplicity of detail that must be reduced to numbers, placed in statistical form. Not the least problem of the change-over is that plans for the future start about six months earlier than under the old budget system—in January instead of July or August. This means that some spending projected will be completed thirty months later, which is a long time with the world in flux.

Area staff meetings give the program coordinator additional perspective. Whether his area director holds a 9 A.M. staff meeting or not, the program coordinator is likely to start his day at about 8:45, reviewing telegrams that have come in from the posts overnight, returning telephone inquiries of the previous day, and placing several calls on questions requiring answers from outside the area. If there is no staff meeting, he may informally make contact with the area director or area deputy director, the policy officer, and several of the desk officers before he settles down to what he has selected as his one or two most pressing problems of the day. If there is a staff meeting, the area director will go over the major communications from the field and assign action within the area, go around the circle of the area staff present to hear reports of current problems, to listen to questions, and to stimulate some brief exchange of ideas.

Out of the meeting by 9:45 A.M., the program coordinator tries to rid himself of telephone calls and telegrams by ten o'clock and then turns to his "problem of the day." To check it out and make a decision, draft a telegram to the field, and get concurrences from top Agency officials should take him two hours; it will take all day because of a host of necessary interruptions, questions from desk officers or the area deputy director, a short meeting with several media representatives, or reading and approving drafts of desk officers' telegrams to the field. One program coordinator's "problem of the day" in 1963 was whether to continue the English-teaching program in Senegal—an item of direct media support, carried in the area budgets. English teaching was not "popular" in the Agency at the time because it was not "policy oriented" enough for the Murrow period. His area had taught English in twenty-four of its thirty-three countries. The potential for a good program seemed to be present but was not being realized in Senegal. He felt the program was too diverse because it reached too many students who were not presently influential and who apparently did not possess the potential to become so. The ambassador wanted the teaching program continued. The program coordinator decided to cancel the program, getting concurrence from the Agency director's office, to shock the post into directing its efforts more effectively. In his telegram, the post was urged to single out the few students who mattered most and to use the tutorial system to continue teaching them; since the English teacher's contract was not renewed, reliance was to be upon the post officers and their wives. The ambassador was told by informal letter why the action was taken. By the end of the day, the messages had been cleared and sent; an annual cost of $25,000 had been "saved." After making this decision, the program coordinator returned to cleaning up correspondence in his in-box. The day might have been spent in deciding whether the area should allocate money to have fifteen out-of-stock books reprinted, at a cost of $1,200 each. With a tight budget, no funds allocated for reprinting, and no reserve available, the reprinting would mean knocking out other titles scheduled for printing or perhaps postponing replacement of furniture at the posts. Before making up his mind, he would consult the Information Center Service personnel dealing with the book program, and possibly the area director. In the long run, it would primarily be the program coordinator's decision. Although these decisions may appear to be made off the cuff, the program coordinator from continuous immersion in the subject matter of his field feels that he knows the posts' real needs, his area director's philosophy, and current policy emphases.

Not all decisions are negative or of such limited scope. When there are major foreign policy shifts and an area is given higher priority than it has had for several decades, the program coordinator's role becomes one of taking advantage of increased resources effectively. This was true of the program coordinator for Latin America in 1963. His program lacked short-wave language broadcasts in the days of neglect before the Alliance for Progress. He now can push for an increased use of radio in the area and increased production of specially packaged radio programs to be placed by the posts locally. He can encourage the establishment of a Regional Service Center that will print as well as do the editorial work on pamphlets dealing with current labor and student affairs topics. He can stimulate the establishment of a feature news service operating from the Regional Center and encourage USIA labor information officers and student affairs officers at posts in his area to work closely with the center in the preparation of a variety of materials to be distributed in the area. If he believes that information and mental persuasion are not enough, he may attempt to put funds into media products that motivate action, that emphasize self-help and teach people how to help themselves escape from paternalism and a static society to embark on cooperative change. He can make use of motion pictures and cartoon books for this purpose; or he may push for the use of cartoon motion pictures. He can augment the daily Wireless File to his area, establish branch posts at key interior cities, open new reading rooms, binational centers, and information centers. As television spreads in the major cities, he can increase packaged shows and put funds into weekly productions which millions of people will see. And he can increase the number of American positions in the area, local employees abroad, and even increase the staff in the area office in Washington. Since USIA funds overall did not quickly increase after 1961, this probably meant cutting back binational and information centers or English-teaching programs in areas other than Latin America. One program coordinator's opportunity may well call for ingenious retrenchment by one or more of his area counterparts.

Nothing in the program coordinator's job is more important than his role in the budgeting process. Here is where his expertise can be brought to bear in a way which influences program impact in his area; for example, the binational center problem of the Kennedy administration. Binational centers are normally headed by a USIS officer with a joint board of directors composed of Americans in residence in the country and citizens of the country who have an interest in the United States. Programs include English teaching, lectures, musical performances, art exhibits, folk dancing, and whatever brings people together to learn about the United States or to enjoy its cultural products or folkways. As the Kennedy administration upgraded the direct relationship of USIA activities to influencing political action by foreign governments, the programming at binational centers, to oversimplify, developed a plethora of lectures speaking favorably of American foreign or domestic policies and a relative famine of cultural activities, such as folk dancing. Popular interest in the centers diminished in some cities; a few local members of boards of directors resigned in others. These losses were countered by putting additional funds into binational centers in critical areas and "sweetening" the program changes by helping support better lecturers than had hitherto been obtained, thus hopefully cutting attendance losses, regaining participation up to the old level, or even attracting larger crowds—while still operating with the new policy emphasis. By 1967, under Director Marks, a more moderate pattern between cultural and political extremes had been established and binational center programs were flourishing—in Latin America and elsewhere. Funds had been obtained for assisting the centers in making capital improvements. It was found that new buildings attracted more students to take courses, which brought in additional funds from the tuition charged, making some of the centers self-supporting. The objective now is to help many of the binational centers reach the take-off point of supporting their own programs in the future.

Basic to the budget process is the Country Plan or the new Country Plan Program Memorandum. On the basis of precepts worked out earlier and sent to the field, thus well aware of new emphases which have been evolved by the Office of Policy and Research in consultation with the White House and the Department of State, the field posts submit their annual Country Plans or new Country Plan Program Memoranda. In working with the Country Plan, the program coordinator has available Assessment Reports from the posts and some statistical reports which enable him to evaluate the new plan against past programs. The Assessment Report is judgmental rather than statistical. If a writer or columnist in a foreign country, whom USIA has been seeking to influence, changes his position to one more in line with Agency objectives, this will be reported. If those opposed to American policies are obviously trying to increase their efforts to counter American policies, this is taken as evidence of the success of American efforts (though this kind of response does not seem to be of real advantage to the Agency). If there is increasing use of press packets sent out to newspapers, or if there is favorable editorial comment on American policy accompanying the appearance of such material, the country public affairs officer will note that reaction to such materials has been excellent. He may also report on the attitudes of some of his personal acquaintances. While this does not actually allow the program coordinator to measure progress toward objectives, it can convey some sense of present difficulties and serve as the basis for a rough estimate of the relative usefulness of the different media. Statistical reports backstop this by giving figures on visitors to libraries, the number of books withdrawn, and attendance at lectures or exhibits. Program coordinators use statistical reports more as evidence to support the budget than as an evaluation tool for their own decisions.

Country budgets are sent in from each post in an area, and will continue to be even with the Planning-Programming-Budgeting System because the Congress requires an administrative budget on which to base appropriations. Country budgets, running from fifty to one hundred pages, cite costs, give descriptions, and include justifications of programs. The program coordinator reviews the budgets country by country, in company with the appropriate desk officer and the area budget officer from the Budget Division of the Office of Administration—with whom he works closely at every stage on all budget matters. Program coordinators feel that the posts generally ask for the same amount for items each year. Perhaps the PPBS program will make this less true in the future than in the past. The individual budgets indicate what the posts desire in the way of USIS American staff, local employees, travel, *per diem*, local printing costs, plus radio, television, lecture, press, or exhibit activities—these latter being items of direct media support. The media services have received copies of the post submissions; thus they know which and how much of their products the posts are requesting. The media services review these requests and then come up with their own recommendations to the area offices. During late September or early October, the program coordinator is likely to meet daily or every other day with different media representatives to negotiate what his area will purchase in the way of media products in the upcoming budget. Policy officers may put in a token appearance at these sessions. Some area directors involve themselves more than others, but primarily it is the program coordinator's show. Individual post budgets are not discussed in these negotiations; the program coordinator works in terms of area level for a particular product in terms of last year's programs, with a general knowledge of what the posts as a whole plan to do next year and what the new policy emphases in his area are. To protect himself against unexpected needs which the posts have not foreseen, the program coordinator sets aside a flexible reserve in his area budget which he does not commit to any specific media product ahead of time. In the past, the media have often been sorrowfully surprised by a program coordinator's low level of requests for their services. The chance that this will occur in the future will be substantially reduced as the media services are provided with Country Plan Program Memoranda at the same time as the area offices under the Planning-Programming-Budgeting System.

If the area director has not involved himself on a day-to-day basis with the budget up to the area-media negotiations, he now turns to a final review of the budget with the program coordinator and prepares himself for defending the area budget before the Agency's Program Review Committee. While the program coordinator is not the man on the firing line before the Committee, he will be present, held in reserve to answer questions on details or otherwise backstop the area director. Essentially, the Program Reveiw Committee is interested in any increases proposed. These must be carefully justified. Typical of the budget procedure at all levels and in all agencies, continuing programs without changes in level receive less scrutiny. If the area plans to place more emphasis on stimulating American studies by students or teachers in its area, it will have to indicate the opportunity and need for this type of program, and the coordinator must explain why this is done instead of expanding some other media program. For arguments to support their conclusions, the area director and the program coordinator refer to their approved Country Plans or Country Plan Program Memoranda and to a variety of special reports. The Program Review Committee can view the budget proposal in a time perspective because of the five-year projection of area budget requirements, which the program coordinator has worked out on the basis of a projection of world conditions developed by Agency planning officers. The Agency budget review ordeal is over for the area director and the program coordinator in a single day, normally in one long, hard afternoon. Following this, there is still a six-hour defense of the budget by the area director and the program coordinator against shrewd questioning by one or more of the Bureau of the Budget's examiners with responsibility for USIA. Although the Bureau of the Budget examiners sometimes seem to be poking in the dark, their quality is generally excellent, and they press hard to discover whether careful thought has gone into preparation of the budget. They have an almost uncanny ability to find the soft spots and to shatter illogical budget arguments. After Bureau approval of the over-all USIA budget proposal, the area director and the program coordinator may brief the Agency director and the assistant director (administration) who now defend the Agency's budget before the subcommittees of the Appropriations Committees of House and Senate which recommend to Congress what USIA appropriations should be. Before Marks assumed this responsibility, the area directors and program coordinators had been on the front line themselves. Although

Senate subcommittee hearings are often conducted as educational or infor-mation-gathering sessions for the senators, House subcommittee hearings tend to be more sharply critical, sometimes involving ridicule of programs and of those giving testimony. Speaking metaphorically, the House often tends to shoot the Agency down and pick the bones, while the Senate usually studies the living organism and attempts to sustain it or provide new vitality. USIA has felt in the past that it suffered when appearing before the House or Senate subcommittees because it lacked sufficient tangible evidence of its accomplishments. Perhaps the new quantitative approach of the PPBS pro-gram will be of some help in the future. As is the case for all agencies of the government when appearing before Congress, the investigators tend to place USIA on the defensive by raising specific evidences of error or asking gener-ally why political conditions and relations with the United States have deteri-orated in a country where USIA has a sizable program—implying that the Agency is at fault. Program coordinators realize that errors can be made, that programs may fail to accomplish their purposes for a variety of reasons, and that USIA is only one competing influence among many in any given country. They would prefer to concentrate in congressional hearings on posi-tive suggestions of how to improve programming. Once the Congress makes the appropriation, the Agency is in business for another year, subject to Bureau of the Budget oversight. As conditions fluctuate or as one type of media production is held up and another makes greater progress than expected, the program coordinator finds it necessary to re-program area funds during the year, working with the concurrence of the area director in shifting smaller amounts and preparing the area director to appear before the Program Review Committee to gain approval for changes of $30,000 or more.

Program coordinators are less talkative about their personnel and management problems, though their responsibilities cover these fields as well as budget. On occasion, they are sent out from the Agency on recruiting tours to college campuses to meet with students interested in taking the test to serve USIA as members of the Foreign Service of the United States. Pro-gram coordinators assist junior officer trainees just entering the Foreign Service when the trainees are assigned to the area during their training period in the Agency before going to overseas assignments. They believe there is much less counseling of personnel throughout career in USIA than in the Department of State, and note that most middle-level USIA Foreign Service Career Reserve Officers talk over career problems with their area directors rather than with USIA's Personnel Division. While program coordinators note that some young officers might think twice before turning down a head-quarters assignment for training, they believe most look forward to training assignments; and some of the Agency's best young officers have been placed in very responsible positions in the Agency after such assignments. They believe that the Training Division, because of limited ceilings for instructors, must rely too heavily on lecturers assigned regular jobs in the Agency who do not therefore do as good a job as if they were on a full-time teaching assignment. The program coordinator is involved in working out staff ceilings for the area office and for his area posts overseas. He often shares with the policy officer the task of preparing annual personnel ratings on area office employees at desk officer and secretarial levels. He also collaborates with an area man in the Agency's Personnel Division and sometimes with area desk officers to help the area director and the area deputy director make assignments and replacements in Washington and at posts abroad. He is aware of special problems of health and language which make it difficult to get personnel to serve in his area overseas. For Washington assignments, most program coordinators believe that foreign service officers should be assigned posts either in the area offices or media services, that area-media relations will be improved if an increasing number of foreign service officers are assigned media duty when they are in Washington—though they realize that many media assignments are not attractive to foreign service personnel. Program coordinators work with the Agency's Management Division in determining if the amount of reporting from the field can be reduced, to improve Agency forms, and to offer suggestions on administrative regulations. From time to time, the Management Division of the Office of Administration will send a representative to the area office to conduct an organizational or procedural survey. It is apparent from this review of the duties of the program coordinators in USIA that their tasks resemble those of the executive directors of regional bureaus in the Department of State. It is not surprising that from time to time they work together with the executive directors on interagency committees or occasionally deal directly concerning personnel, budget, or management problems,   since State Department Foreign Service Officers perform many administrative tasks at embassies overseas to backstop USIS operations.

No Common Mold — the Country Desk Officers

It may be meaningful to speak of the "country desk officer type" when writing about the desk level in the Department of State, where the career regimen and the sheer size of the Foreign Service of the United States provide personnel for country desks with relatively common ways of thinking about problems and even—in many instances—striking personality similarities. Desk officers in the area offices of USIA are not cast from a single die. Because the Agency has not had a legislatively authorized foreign service since its establishment in 1953, and because only recently has it been allowed to bring young people from college campuses into the foreign service shortly after graduation, many of USIA's present desk officers have entered the Foreign Service Career Reserve after some years of experience at other types of work. Backgrounds range from former college professors with Ph. D.'s and an interest in cultural affairs to former public relations men for the Jam Handy audio-visual organization. Differences are further encouraged by the split in USIS duties overseas between cultural and informational affairs, which would insure a minimum of two types of country desk officers for USIA. The fact that rotation from the field to Washington has been less regular by the Agency than by the Department of State also leads to an individuality among desk personnel now missing at State. Country desk officers at State have looked forward to this type of assignment since entry into the Foreign Service. One may serve as a junior desk officer before returning later in career, for example, as officer in charge of Malaysian affairs. Many of the country desk officers in USIA are serving their first headquarters tour after eight to twelve years in the field. Probably half of them do not consider the desk as a stepping stone to further preferment but as unpleasant headquarters duty to be tolerated until their return to the field. State's foreign service officers have often been policy oriented from entry; USIA's personnel at lower field levels tend to be primarily operations oriented. The Washington experience in a job with heavy policy responsibilities is considered a challenge and a choice assignment by some of the young USIA officers; certainly most of them do not seek out media assignments unless it be as policy applications officers. But they do not see policy as the focus of their careers as many of State's Foreign Service officers do. The number of headquarters policy posts seems too small to make such career planning realistic to them, and careers at USIA are not yet so carefully planned that a young officer can know that he has been tabbed for a political specialization as is the case at State. Nor does it seem likely that he will serve very many tours in Washington during his career. Even if the country public affairs officer, the peak assignment on the field career ladder, has to be policy oriented, he is as likely to be measured by the success of the operations he directs as by his policy suggestions. Thus, while USIA may have some very effective country desk officers, and their role is as important in many ways to USIA as the State desk officer's is to the Department of State, there is an observable difference in their status within their respective agencies and in their attitudes toward their jobs. Part of this is because the State desk appears to be less under-staffed, more likely to deal with a single country or usually two at most (sometimes with several officers assigned to one country), and the policy portion of the job seems to outweigh subordinate functions. USIA desks, which in most instances seem overworked, are normally responsible for coverage of two or three up to five countries, with the policy element in the job balanced with an operational servicing, expediting function for field posts. To say all this is not to look down on operations as compared to policy; quite to the contrary, in USIA there can be no pure policy specialist; there must be a policy-operation synthesis if the work is to get done and the Agency's objectives to be accomplished. The creation of the new country director level in State results in an age and experience differential that will further distinguish State and USIA personnel responsible for individual country affairs.

USIA desk officers have general responsibilities for policy advising and planning, but as one desk officer declared, "My basic function as a desk officer in an Area Office is to support USIS posts in their support of United States policies in my five countries." This may be policy guidance or it may be servicing a field request. Examples of expediting field requests are abundant. A post in Southeast Asia requests one of USIA's media services to forward special microphones which can be hung around the neck. They are to be used by calypso-type performers, popular in the area, whose songs can and often do include potent political propaganda. It is necessary that the performers move around as they sing and dance, and that their hands be free to play their instruments. Since these details are not included in the request, the media service concerned questions sending eight such microphones to a single post; one standard microphone appears to be enough. The desk officer has a copy of the order and receives a copy of the rejection notice to the post. Knowing the area and understanding the request in its full political, cultural, and technical context, he contacts the media employee responsible and in strong terms defends the post request. The microphones are sent. In another vein, an airgram arrives from the USIS post in Burundi, with the action copy going to the desk officer covering Nigeria, Liberia, Ghana, Ruwanda, and Burundi. An ambassador from the young state to the United States will arrive in Washington later in the week, and the field requests picture coverage of his arrival and of the credential ceremony when he meets the President. Copies of the airgram have gone to the Press and Publications Service responsible for still pictures and to the Motion Picture and Television Service. The desk officer checks with the protocal office at the Department of State to find out when the ambassador is scheduled to arrive and when he will present his credentials. He then informs the media services involved of the time and place so they can take the pictures requested. The desk officer is the field's friend, but he is also its critic. If a field post's requests are out of line, he serves as buffer between the media and the field, backing up the media service's refusal to respond to the request. If the field overemphasizes English-language teaching—as we have noted that it was thought to have done in 1963—he takes the initiative in cutting the operation back to preserve balance in the country program.

The country desk officers also have policy responsibilities, contributing in many ways to the policy guidance given to the field and to the media. The desk officer for China, Hong Kong, and Taiwan affairs is the Agency's specialist on China policy and is expected to maintain his expertise on the complex set of factors involving Taiwan, China, the Soviet Union, and communist ideology in the Far East and to follow the shifting nuances in their interrelationships. In performing this responsibility, he advises the Agency in Washington and also field posts in Taiwan and Hong Kong. USIA, of course, has no posts in Mainland China. His primary media relationship on Chinese affairs, therefore, is the Voice of America which beams broadcasts to China from transmitters in the Philippines. In addition to working within the Agency, desk officers are expected to coordinate their efforts at the desk level in other agencies, serving on working groups or maintaining contact by phone. They may deal with State, the National Aeronautics and Space Agency, the Department of Defense, and to a lesser extent with the Agency for International Development or even the Peace Corps. This interagency assignment has long been in effect, but was upgraded in the response to the Kennedy memorandum spelling out USIA's responsibility to give advice on psychological and informational aspects of policies or programs conducted by other government agencies. There is still much to be done to make this policy guidance function effective at the desk level. To perform his policy functions, the desk officer must be a repository of knowledge, aware of past events and policies and up to date on current happenings and projected events. He is also a drafter of policy statements—many of which are incorporated in documents covering broader topics drafted elsewhere and signed by much higher-ranking officials. The desk officer is likely to perform the policy aspects of his job well if he is an omnivorous reader with a retentive memory (plus a good filing system), possessing practical, political common sense and a persuasive personality. Hopefully, his years of experience in the field in his area will make him aware of what can be done in a particular political climate and what cannot be done, when to present only the facts explaining why the United States has acted as it did, when to ask for verbal support or acquiescence, and when to call for more direct involvement and action.

The country desk officer (though usually an FSCR 3 or 4—at midpoint or above on the career ladder) is near the bottom of the policy-making totem pole at headquarters. If he runs into difficulties in intra-agency dealings or in relations with other agencies on policy matters, he can push the matter to higher levels, certainly to his area director, and, if he finds support there, sometimes to the deputy agency director for policy and research, even occasionally to the Agency director himself. Desk officers are not likely to fight the battle to the top very often on internal Agency policy and are even less likely to insist on interagency confrontation if they disagree with a policy statement drafted in another agency. They are more apt to make their argument, and then if their point of view is not accepted give their clearance signature while noting that they do not concur with the judgment. The good Agency desk officer is well aware that his vision from the country desk level is often limited, that it is good politics not to fight too long against those with whom you must continue to work, that in three months if he is right his position may be more acceptable and he can raise it again with some hope of success. He has no way of knowing at any given time for sure if a decision is colored by a national defense interest of which he has not been apprised. At certain times, policy matters may be escalated—during periods of tension in his area—so that only the assistant secretary of state for the area and top Defense Department representatives know what is actually happening. The United States Information Agency, when it is informed about developments in such a situation, receives the information through the Agency director, his deputy, or the deputy director for policy and research. They may not be free to pass the information down the line. When the going gets the toughest, the desk officer is very likely to be on the sidelines while decisions are made in the White House with only the special assistant to the President for national security affairs, the secretary of state, and the secretary of defense present with the President. Even the assistant secretary of state by this time may have been sent to the showers, or is "on call" rather than "on duty." Even in such a period of relative blackout of information, the country desk officer is likely to be receiving "99 and 44/100 per cent" of the relevant flow of information within the government on the country involved in the crisis.

If the desk is near the base of the policy hierarchy, perhaps one policy notch above the policy applications officers in the media services—though normally of lower rank in the Foreign Service Career Reserve—the desk officers have a serious review responsibility for Country Plans or Country Plan Program Memoranda and Country Budgets submitted from the field by the country public affairs officers in their countries. It is not impossible for a new desk man to report into the Agency, find his predecessor already departed for the field, and the Country Budgets on his desk for review. This would be less serious if the rotation from the field to Washington were a regular and recurring experience—as perhaps it should be for certain carefully selected individuals, so that the desk man had gone through this process on a previous headquarters assignment as a junior assistant to a desk officer. It would be less serious if after he arrived there were an orderly system of orientation on the Agency and his duties, but with the desk often vacant and its responsibilities being carried by another desk officer already burdened by his own set of countries, the normal process is to pitch the new desk man into the fray immediately upon his arrival. He learns by doing, which can sometimes be a costly process. The odds are that he will survive the first few bureaucratic grenades hurled from ambush and become in time an effective desk man. He is one of the better Foreign Service Career Reserve Officers or he would not have been selected to be a country desk officer. The area offices are small, informal supervision can be close, and others are present to offer him advice if he asks for it—and he can hardly avoid doing that.

His area director may call the country desk officer in for consultation on matters concerning his countries, probing his thoughts and commenting on his ideas, accepting some, rejecting others. The daily or weekly area staff meeting, chaired by the area director,provides another forty-five-minute exchange of views and updating on important developments in the area. Here the desk officer presents events and problems developing in his own countries, hears other desk officers make similar presentations, learns about broader problems of a policy or program nature from the policy officer and the program coordinator, and may receive instructions from the area director to gather information within the Agency and prepare an action message for signature. A more informal weekly luncheon or office meeting with the area office staff and representatives from the media services and possibly from the corresponding regional bureau in State allows the desk officer to see the over-all area view, to see individual media responses to comments by the area director or other members of the area office staff. Sometimes such meetings start with an intelligence briefing by a representative from the Research and Analysis Staff on area developments—what groups in opposition to governments are doing, what information lines the Soviet Union and Communist China are pumping into the area. His policy officer may hold meetings with him and other desk officers on special policy questions. The desk man will discuss with the policy officer his views on the Country Plans or new CPPM's submitted from the countries he covers; pass on to the policy officer what he wishes communicated before the noon policy briefing to the policy guidance area man in the Office of Policy and Research, though he may sometimes call directly, letting his policy officer know what he has said. He works closely with the program coordinator on Country Budgets; the desk man better than anyone else may know what is considered vital by one of his posts. He views his policy officer as someone helping provide guidance to the media on "what USIA should say," and his program coordinator as someone providing guidance to the media on "what USIA should spend." He is consulted when the saying or spending in question affects one of his countries. Drawn into questions of policy and budget, he is in a good position to interrelate the two, and to make an effective review of Country Plans and Country Budgets; increasingly he will be reviewing CPPM's.

The desk officer has many relationships within the Agency that reach beyond the area office. If China is in the news, the diplomatic situation "hot," the desk man in charge of China affairs may have daily contacts with the deputy Agency director and associate deputy Agency director for policy and research, with the deputy Agency director on media content questions, and with the policy guidance area man in the Office of Policy and Research. He may be asked to prepare material to be incorporated in the weekly report to the President signed by the Agency director and drafted by the associate deputy Agency director for policy and research. On military questions affecting his country, the desk may be in touch with the policy liaison officer on the Policy and Plans Staff in the Office of Policy and Research—with either initiating the contact. If the Office of Policy and Research produces policy statements, many of them are drafted by desk officers. Portions of the daily fast guidance to the field by the Office of Policy and Research are often drafted by appropriate country desk officers. On policy guidances by the Office of Policy and Research via Wireless File, the drafting can be done either in the Office of Policy and Research or perhaps even by a policy man in the Press and Publications Service, but the product would be reviewed by the appropriate desk officer. Where the original draft was done would probably depend upon the area or country or media emphasis of the message, possibly on who had the time to do the job.

The country desk officer also has many working relationships with the media services. If a matter concerns more than one of the media, he may call the area man in the Office of Policy and Research and have the message relayed through him. If it related to a single media, he would be more likely to contact the policy applications officer (whose status in the media service is akin to that of the policy officer in the area office) or one of the policy applications officer's area men (somewhat junior in rank and experience to country desk officers), who are responsible for entire geographic regions: for example, East Asia and the Pacific, Europe, or Latin America. Voice of America scripts which have been broadcast to the country desk officer's countries are forwarded routinely to the desk for review. If something is objectionable— whether the desk officer discovers it from his own reading or gets it from a field message after the broadcast—the desk man calls the Voice desk covering policy for his area in the Broadcasting Service. If the Voice area man has doubts ahead of time, or if script writers have questions, they may query the country desk officer on a policy point. The problem of policy guidance to the fast media, the Voice of America and the Wireless File particularly, is primarily that the speed of reaction required sometimes necessitates post- rather than pre-audit of messages. Honest mistakes are made under pressure. Desk men feel that in the past—and even to a certain extent in the present—Voice personnel considered VOA to be semi-autonomous, operat- ing a separate kingdom; for example, there is an Indian desk officer, respon- sible for the same area coverage on VOA matters as is the area country desk officer for India. Legitimate differences of interpretation of general policy guidance, always possible, may not be apparent to the policy man in the Voice or the Press and Publications Service until after his position is ques- tioned by the country desk officer. Part of the desk officer's task is to main- tain good relations with media personnel so that they will call him with their small questions. Questions with political overtones and those which indicate real differences between the country desk and the Voice are quickly elevated to the Office of Policy and Research, possibly to the deputy Agency director (policy and research). Although it is the policy officer who has the main re- sponsibility for review of Motion Picture and Television Service films, it is the country desk officer who has the country knowledge and will be drawn into review of a picture if his country is involved. The country desk officer covering Nigeria is interested in a particular show in a television series to be shown in his country. Nigerians are generally aware of European educa- tional systems but may know little concerning the informality of student life in America or about the United States educational system. One show may focus on a Nigerian athlete attending Harvard University, featuring his achievements and—more broadly—satisfying the Nigerian curiosity about the nature of American education. The desk man may work with the writers in the Motion Picture and Television Service, or with a contractor, sit in on the screening until he feels the product is "right" for the people in his country. The desk officer may also review exhibits (prepared by a division of the Infor- mation Center Service if three dimensional or in the Press and Publications Service if of the "flat" poster variety) which are to be displayed in his coun- tries, deciding which of the IPS exhibits should be shown and which not shown. Similarly, articles included in Press and Publications Service publi- cations are often read by country desk officers. None of these pose the prob- lems of swift reaction by USIA that the Voice and Wireless File do. Nonethe- less, review of the slower media products is a difficult and important func- tion. Because the time element is not so pressing, "errors" are less easily forgiven. The task still requires a high sensitivity to area sentiments and level of understanding or appreciation, but even with less haste it remains more art than science. The role of the country desk officer is essential in this review because most contract personnel have little area knowledge and many of the media personnel, including a few of the policy applications officers, are Civil Service employees who have had limited field experience.

A great effort was taken to make Research and Reference studies more useful to the area offices and to the area country desk officers. The impact of the old research applications officer in the Office of Policy and Research and the regional research officers at some posts overseas was never fully felt at the desk level. The desk man might have reviewed a proposed Research Applications Memorandum before it was approved by the area director and by the deputy Agency director for policy and plans to make certain it was valid for his particular countries. The desk did become involved in the surveys to be conducted at its posts under the general direction of regional research officers, who did work overseas under the country public affairs officers to help them formulate and conduct research studies. The desk did help the Research and Reference Service at headquarters draw up the questions to be used in his countries, after querying the field to make sure the ambassador was willing to have the study conducted. The desk also took part in the evaluation of the studies made in his countries. By involvement of desk level personnel in the planning and evaluation of such studies, it was hoped that desk officers would increasingly be able to suggest studies that would be useful to them or to the area offices, and be willing and able to make effective use of the findings. In part, they were prevented from improving the relationship with the Research and Reference Service by their own overload and frenetic work pace, by the demands of meeting daily problems that would not wait for research studies, and by the separation—whether psychological or real—of the desk man, a Foreign Service Career Officer who is in essence a field operator serving briefly at headquarters, from the largely Civil Service personnel of the Research and Reference Service, who were Washington centered and visited the field on rare occasions at best. It was heartening when an area country desk officer declared in 1963, "IRS studies of overseas conditions are important. When media products need to be targeted to specific audiences, the studies help in the evaluation of what is being done and also suggest new program ideas to me." The step up in policy-oriented research studies by the Research and Analysis Staff and the preparation of a number of Program Action Memoranda by the Policy and Plans Staff should enable more country desk officers to make better use of Agency research in 1968 than was the case in 1963.

Outside USIA in Washington, the country desk officer's most important working relationship is with the Department of State—sometimes with State's country desk officers, perhaps more often with personnel in the public affairs advisor's office in the appropriate regional bureau, or with the country or regional level personnel in the Bureau of Educational and Cultural Affairs. At the desk level, there are apparently no regular interagency meetings, though from time to time interagency working groups are created which meet intermittently led by one of State's country directors. The desk officer may go to State for meetings of this type once a month; more rarely, twice a week. USIA desk officers are likely to deal directly with State country desks in regional bureaus during the early stages of American involvement in a problem area like Vietnam. Working groups set up at the office director level, in fact, often function with desk representation. As the crisis grows, the working group tends to wither on the vine while decisions are made at higher levels. Later, operational working groups may be established to help coordinate expanded programs. On smaller problems, which call for a single quick meeting, State tends to cut the USIA desk level into the situation late in the game, if at all, often through the regional public affairs advisor's office rather than the State country desk. USIA desks grouse a bit about meetings called at an hour's notice, and even more about not being invited when a policy is being considered that will have overseas public opinion impact. At the desk level, more than the office director level in USIA, there is a feeling that implementation of the Kennedy memorandum on psychological advice by USIA during the formulation of government policy with possible overseas effects "has a long way to go." As one desk officer put it, "The new mission is one thing on paper; another, to put in practice." USIA desk officers feel that policy papers too often come over "out of the blue" from State's regional bureaus for clearance that have far-reaching opinion implications abroad. USIA has not been consulted during the time the policy was being formulated. Desk officers at USIA find "it hard to enter at this late date on things with psychological or press implications." Apparently the regional bureaus in State sometimes believe that it is sufficient for them to consult State's own Bureau of Public Affairs, and forward papers to USIA almost as an afterthought. USIA desk officers point out that "State's 'P Area' is largely domestic news oriented." USIA's regular daily relationship with the regional bureaus, of course, is through the policy guidance area man in the Office of Policy and Research, not a country specialist, who deals with personnel in the regional bureau's public affairs advisor's office who are neither country specialists nor policy experts. Bedeviled by overwork as most USIA desk officers are, it is almost impossible for them to keep their ears to the ground, take the initiative, and call State to get their "two cents' worth in" before the policy is finalized for clearance. A few desk officers find the time and take the trouble to do this. Working relationships between some USIA desks and State are good. USIA desks, providing they have time to read the "paper flow," are well informed on both USIA and State communications to and from overseas posts. The formal channel of communication between a USIA desk and a State country desk is considered to be through the regional bureau's public affairs adviser's office. USIA desk officers feel that a desk-to-desk relationship is better and often use the shorter circuit. To an outside observer, desk officers in USIA and State appear to have more in common in their jobs than with the public affairs officers in State's regional bureaus. Some USIA officers do serve in regional public affairs advisers offices, and once in a while a Foreign Service Officer who normally might be assigned in State serves as country desk officer in USIA. Personal friendships with personnel in the other agency help strengthen interagency liaison in these instances. A further exchange of assignments should in the long run broaden mutual agency understanding and lead to better cooperation at lower levels. The USIA desks also have many relations with the Bureau of Educational and Cultural Affairs (CU) in State. This is normal, because USIS officers in the field perform the cultural and educational functions of embassies in most instances, taking the initiative in selection of personnel for visits to the United States and in handling the appearances of American musicians or actors overseas. Many USIA Foreign Service Career Reserve personnel serve their Washington tours in the Bureau of Educational and Cultural Affairs. Those with this experience behind them follow educational and cultural affairs closely and sometimes have considerable influence in CU even after they have returned to USIA duty. The USIA desk may check with CU to determine when the chairman of the Council of Ministers of Nepal will arrive so that he can arrange coverage of the visit by the Voice of America, the Motion Picture and Television Service, or the Press and Publications Service. He may call with suggestions on the arrangements for three Indian economic journalists who are arriving to tour the United States on "foreign leader grants." If CU is dragging its heels on a cultural presentation which the USIA desk man believes would be of value in his countries, he may try to get State moving. If higher USIA officials are recalcitrant on a particular project, he may seek to get the action taken by CU or attempt to get CU to support his position. Typical of USIA personnel, the desk officer is likely to think that the Bureau of Educational and Cultural Affairs should really be a discrete element in USIA rather than an adjunct of State. In another type of relationship possible with State, USIA desk officers make no contributions to studies done by State's Bureau of Intelligence Research, but they do consult such studies along with those prepared by their own Research and Analysis Staff. Desk officers may lecture on USIA and on its programs in their countries to groups in training at State's Foreign Service Institute.

The Department of State is normally the hub of the USIA desk officer's relation with other executive branch agencies. Compared with USIA's direct relations with State, dealings with other government agencies at the desk level are quite limited. While USIA officers talk at the desk level with a wide variety of agencies, including International Security Affairs in the Department of Defense, the Agency for International Development, the National Aeronautics and Space Agency, the Central Intelligence Agency, and the Peace Corps, these are usually faceless relations by telephone. Desk officers recall from their field service that relations are much closer with other agencies there than in Washington. Situations vary, of course, and if military affairs loom large in relations with a particular country, the contacts with the Department of Defense are likely to increase in number. Surprisingly enough, though much of the work of the Agency for International Development must depend for its success on a climate of opinion conducive to development in the countries with which it is working, at the desk as well as other levels in USIA the contacts with AID seem to be minimal. The desk officer's relationship with the legislative branch of government is also somewhat limited. He is unlikely to testify or pay a call to a congressional office on the Hill. Answers that he may draft to congressional mail, at the request of his area director, are forwarded through USIA's congressional relations personnel in the Office of the Counsel of USIA to be signed by the Agency director. Desk drafts often progress through this review ladder without alteration.

In dealing with foreign embassies in Washington, the State Department may initiate a particular project, quite properly, and then USIA may deal directly from the desk level if necessary. For example, the desk officer for Nigeria worked with the Nigerian Embassy, as well as with the National Aeronautics and Space Agency, on the overseas public opinion aspects of the negotiations for sites in Nigeria for "Syn-Com," the stationary communications satellite project. The desk officer also participates in informal relationships at embassy social affairs, particularly with cultural and press attachés, and he may issue them invitations to his own home. Such contacts, considered valuable by the field-oriented desk officers, are less numerous in Washington than overseas, partially because of the absence of entertainment allowances at headquarters. Desk officers feel that informal relations established in a social atmosphere save much time later in routine business contacts.

The relations which the area country desk officer maintains with others continue over time—picked up by a successor when the desk man is rotated back to the field; the size of the bureaucracy with which he works is large—individual contacts by phone or in person take a great deal of time; the problems with which he wrestles are persistent and recurrent. Maintenance of a written record is important. Much of the information he gathers or the thinking he does must be set down on paper, either to communicate instructions, queries, or proposals for action to those with whom he works or to make possible retention of information for future use. If the country desk officer seems to be less drafting officer than is the desk officer in a regional bureau at State, the difference is in degree. He gathers as much information as the State desk man before doing his drafting. A large portion of his time not consumed in reviewing media products, in attending working-group sessions or staff meetings, in servicing the field, or in drafting is spent in reading to keep abreast of emerging developments in his countries, both the short-term triumphs and catastrophes and the long-range trends toward progress or chaos.

USIA desk officers either scan or read carefully from fifty to two hundred "pieces of paper" a day which cross their desks for action or information. These may vary in size from a one-line telegram to a ten-page report. Arriving in two batches, morning and afternoon, they must be moved from the in-box to the out-box during the day or the next morning's take will overflow the desk. Everything from the posts in his countries comes to the desk officer, whether field messages on substantive matters or operations memoranda requesting equipment, whether addressed to the area office or to a media service. Interdepartmental memoranda circulating between government agencies in Washington are also routed to him when they bear on his countries. Of State's telegraph traffic, 65 per cent reaches USIA; anything relevant is forwarded to the desks, including embassy operations memoranda. By the time the desk man receives State's "weeka," which summarizes each event of interest to the United States which occurred in the country reported on during the past week, he is likely to have already read much of the material elsewhere. The "weeka" is prepared in the field under the direction of the embassy first secretary. A USIS officer often will have contributed the psychological section and be listed as one of the drafters. Desk officers get reports from CIA, but feel that they get only a small part of the total flow. "Of course" they read reports on their countries from State's Bureau of Intelligence and Research and from USIA's Research and Analysis Staff, though research specialists are less certain that their studies are read. Research materials or reports from other government agencies dealing with his countries also reach the desk. FBIS reports, items of interest picked up from government radio stations and other sources, reach the desk every day. The desk man even reads personnel evaluation reports from the field, being forwarded to the area director, since the desk sometimes advises the area director on personnel matters. Whether the desk officer emphasizes political, economic, or cultural affairs in his reading, along with his coverage of informational and psychological events, depends upon the interests of the individual officer and upon the situation in the countries he covers. The Vietnam desk officer is likely to pay more attention in recent years to military and political affairs, to scan economic and cultural materials more quickly. Positive economic and cultural activities are difficult to emphasize in a country when military and political problems agitate the entire countryside—though they may hold the key to the future.

In addition to the official government flow of information, the desk men do considerable collateral reading. The Brazilian desk officer reads several magazines published weekly in Brazil—*Vision* (Visao), *The Cross* (o Cruzeiro), and *Headline* (Manchete). He also reads the Brazilian Embassy *Bulletin*, distributed to Brazilians and those Americans interested in Brazil. In the evening at home, he checks over *Diario las Americas*, a regional paper printed in Miami, finding it less valuable than Brazilian publications. He reads the *New York Times* on Sunday and the *Washington Post* daily. From time to time, he buys the *Baltimore Sun* off the newsstand because it has good coverage of Latin American affairs. In addition, he receives copies of studies prepared for Congress, for the Brazilian government, for the United Nations, and even studies prepared on Brazil by private research organizations. The USIA Library, now part of the Information Resources Division in the Office of Administration, regularly forwards to him listings of current material appearing on Brazil, so that if he has time he can read relevant books or periodical articles. In 1963, USIA's desk officer for Vietnam and Laos summed it up this way: "I read the equivalent of a novel a day, seldom leave the desk before 7:30 P.M., and more often than not will be in the office part of the day on Saturday and Sunday." Although not all desks are dealing with a crisis area and hence are not this heavily burdened, most if not all desk men do more than what would be a full week's work for an average American professional man.

There is little government material on their countries to which desk officers do not have access for information or action, and there is little material concerning their countries prepared in the Agency or the field that they do not help draft or review. The desk officer will be involved in anything from drafting an instruction to the field on a minor action to contributing material which will wind up as part of a National Security Council Action Memorandum or National Policy Paper, from a note commenting on media policy conformity on one television show to drafting a segment of a memorandum which will reach the President, from a brief answer to a congressman requesting information on behalf of a constituent to the revision of a post's Country Plan or CPPM. He will draft portions of (or review) country guidances to be carried by the Wireless File, and will prepare country briefing books on the information and psychological situation and on USIA programs in his countries for the use of FSCR's leaving for field assignments or members of Congress planning overseas study tours to his countries. He may draft the information and psychological sections of briefing books maintained by the Department of State on his countries. He will draft a message of instruction to a field post on some aspect of the country program and follow it up with an "official informal" letter which provides background information and advice to an officer at the post, a copy going to the country public affairs officer as well as to the particular addressee. He never goes behind the CPAO's back to deal with official business matters in personal letters to friends serving under the CPAO. He drafts the narratives which support his nation's Country Budgets which will be reviewed and collated by the area policy officer, and he even answers letters on USIA programs in his countries from members of the general public for USIA's Office of Public Information. He is in on almost everything, large or small. If he is a good drafter and earns the respect of those above him on the policy ladder, he exerts considerable influence upon policy and operations; a successful desk officer can say, probably quite truthfully, "About 95 percent of what I recommend is accepted by my superiors." Although not part of the job description, reports written by desk officers after visits to field posts—which supplement the field inspections by the area directors and deputy area directors—may be followed up by directives to the field drafted by the desk and signed off by the area director. For the young FSCR, in his late thirties or early forties, the country desk officer experience is one that should benefit his future career in many ways, from the breadth of view it gives him of USIA and government-wide operations, from the personal contacts and friendships he makes with headquarters personnel at his own level and above him in the hierarchy, from the knowledge he must master and the practice he gains in making policy assessments, from the skill he develops in drafting statements of policy and in working out agreements with others, and from the opportunity to gain an understanding of the Agency's research tools and evaluation methods which can sharpen the impact of his later field operations. The desk is indeed a choice assignment for the young man who aspires to become a country public affairs officer in the field or an area director in Washington.

Variants of the country desk officers, who cover one or more individual countries, are the regional affairs and cultural affairs desk officers also found in several of the area offices. These desk men sometimes are responsible for one or more country desks, as well as for handling regional or cultural matters. The regional affairs officers are primarily interested in attitudes toward international organizations to which countries in their regions belong. They also follow developments related to international conferences held in their regions. For example, the United Nations Conference on Trade and Development held in Geneva during the summer of 1964 was closely observed by the regional affairs officer in the area office for Europe. Working relations are likely to be maintained with State's Bureau of International Organization Affairs. A regional officer may actually service special USIS posts overseas assigned not to a regular United States country mission but to one or more international organizations; i.e., in Paris, USIS/USRO, which is USIA's mission to regional organizations such as the Organization for Economic Cooperation and Development, and the Council of Europe; in Brussels, USIS/USEC, USIA's mission to the European Economic Community; and in Geneva, USIS/USIO, USIA's mission to the cluster of international agencies with headquarters there. Personnel at these regional missions do research and prepare publications, but their products are distributed through regular USIS country posts. Along with his regional duties, the regional affairs officer for Europe is also the desk man for Switzerland. The regional affairs officer keeps track of and attempts to influence public opinion in all countries in his region on questions affecting international organizations and conferences, including the United Nations and conferences held under its aegis. The regional affairs officer in the Area Office for East Asia and the Pacific is especially interested in the Southeast Asia Treaty Organization. This particular regional affairs officer is also a cultural affairs officer. Agency cultural affairs officers maintain relations with the area offices in the Bureau of Educational and Cultural Affairs in the Department of State to help bridge the gap between the Bureau's responsibility for educational and cultural exchange in Washington with USIS's responsibility for operations in the field. Cultural affairs officers are function oriented rather than country centered. In the Area Office for Latin America, the cultural affairs officer is concerned with programs related to youth and labor groups. Cultural officers also attempt to coordinate USIA programs and exchange activities with work already being done in the area by the Rockefeller Foundation, the Ford Foundation, or other private foundations. When regional affairs or cultural affairs officers have no responsibility for a country desk, they tend to have more time for program or policy matters and for research considerations than do typical country desk officers. The policies envolved by regional and cultural affairs officers and the operations derived from them are fitted into the individual Country Plans or CPPM's in their areas and carried out by USIS country posts. Both types of officer represent an administrative attempt to focus on problems in geographic areas that cut across national lines. In essence, they are regional or cultural affairs desk officers and derive benefits from serving in an area office similar to those accruing to the country desk officers.

VI

Credibility, Creativity, and Policy:
The Media Services

Trends in Policy Control

A major problem of USIA and its predecessor information organizations has been policy guidance and control of programs (broadcasts, publications, motion pictures, exhibits, etc.) produced by the media services—the Broadcasting Service, the Press and Publications Service, the Motion Picture and Television Service, and the Information Center Service. Much personnel time in the Office of the Director, in the Office of Policy and Research, and in the area offices is directed toward these ends. The media services have been likened in the past to "feudal empires," resisting guidance and willfully pursuing their own policy paths. This is less true today, but the problem of adjusting media programs to policy remains. Resulting tensions between the area offices and the media services are not likely ever to be completely eliminated.

Under Murrow, USIA took steps to make the media services more responsive to policy direction as its emphasis was shifted from "telling the truth about America" (correcting distorted views of America held abroad) to persuading influential people overseas to act in support of American foreign policy, to accept or tolerate American policy, or to oppose policy less vigorously because they understand the reason for it. The media services before 1961 generated many products with considerable freedom which, taken as a whole, provided overseas publics materials that made a relatively objective view of American life and culture possible. In most instances, such culturally oriented products actually forwarded USIA's broad, basic purposes. Steps were taken by the Kennedy administration in 1961 to make the media services more directly subject to policy direction and to reduce the emphasis on purely cultural activities. None were more important than the strengthening of the Office of Policy by appointing an assistant deputy director for media content, the creation of policy applications officers in the media to serve as a policy link to the rest of the Agency, and personnel assignment policies which placed policy-oriented Foreign Service Career Reserve Officers in key posts in the media services. The delegation of authority to the assistant deputy director (media content) by Rowan also strengthened policy control. By 1965 the policy control hierarchy was crystal clear. Under Marks, central policy control was upgraded by assigning the top responsibility for worldwide media content to the deputy director of the Agency, but was in turn made more flexible by an increasing receptivity to the needs of individual field posts. Even in 1963, it was evident that newly appointed directors or deputy directors of the media services worked wholeheartedly to forward Agency policies. By 1967, there were few old-timers still directing media services. Differences today are more those of judgment or perspective than active opposition to the continuing Agency emphasis on policy-program relationships—both in Washington and at field posts.

As stated in *The Agency in Brief* of 1966, [1] "the Assistant Directors of the Agency for the six geographic areas are the Director's principal advisors on all programs in or directed to countries in these areas. They help to formulate information policies . . . " They "are responsible for the direction, coordination, and management of information programs for the countries of their geographic areas . . . They arrange with media services to provide media products to their areas." "The Assistant Directors in charge of the four Washington media services are responsible to the Director for the quality and persuasiveness of their output. They work with the Office of Policy [and Research] and the Assistant Directors for Areas to provide media products which will help advance United States foreign policies generally and specifically in each area." Although the differences in phrasing are small, the statement in 1966 is less assertive of area office dominance in policy control of programming than that in *The Agency in Brief* of 1963. By 1966, policy control was better established, more accepted, and required less emphasis.

The problem of policy guidance and control of the media services today is in large measure a question of organizational techniques and of refinement in relations, along with better evaluation of program effectiveness and impact, though personnel questions remain. How can Civil Service personnel with technical specializations, whose entire career may be served at headquarters, be made fully conscious of the wide variety of cultural and political differences both within and among countries overseas so that the media products they create will have the desired impact on target audiences? Availability of additional analytical and evaluative studies produced under the direction of Office of Policy and Research—and increasing recognition that "intuition" is not enough—will help. Assignment of additional Foreign Service Career

Reserve Officers for duty in the media services will help educate domestic employees on overseas conditions, as well as place personnel with such knowledge in positions where they can sensitize media products to overseas requirements. Additional in-service training and short-term visits overseas by Civil Service personnel are other possible steps. The problem does not lie wholly with Civil Service personnel, many of whom are well aware of the complexities, or with the media services. Foreign Service Career Reserve Officers kept too long in the field and brought back to area offices are not aware of the abilities and limitations of the Civil Service headquarters personnel in the media, do not understand their outlooks, and find it difficult to communicate area or country needs to them. Neither group is to blame for a situation which has already received much Agency attention and undergone substantial improvement—and which ought to be further helped if a measure like the Hays bill were to be approved by the Congress. There is an almost complete absence of blame-placing in USIA today, though human error, problems of communication, and honest differences of opinion can still heighten blood pressures momentarily on a day-to-day basis. There probably is some foot dragging on the post-1961 look in policy guidance and control by a few personnel in the media services, but there is much less in 1968 than might have been anticipated in 1961—when the Agency moved rapidly from emphasis on rather general objectives at the end of Allen's regime as Agency director to stressing short-term foreign policy support and more specific targeting under Murrow and Rowan.

Because of program differences and the distinctive nature of their communications tools and products, the organization of the media services is more difficult to summarize than that of the area offices, which was explained under four simple headings: directors, policy officers, program coordinators, and desk officers. Without taking into account individual variations, several important levels in the media policy, program, and production hierarchy can easily be identified. Heading each media service are an assistant Agency director and deputy director, or deputy directors in the case of the Press and Publications Service. A step lower on the policy and program planning ladder is likely to be a program manager, assisted by a policy applications officer or chief of a policy staff. The program manager may have responsibilities for program policy and for management generally; his policy relationship is more long range than that of his policy applications officer, and he is also involved in planning technical facilities to meet long-range situational trends abroad. Policy applications officers are primarily interested in the day-to-day policy nuances, though they must also work in a time perspective. Organizational variants increase at the next step down. Some media services have area divisions under the Office of the Program Manager to help relate worldwide policy to area and country needs. Others among the media services break their organization down by program or product, with area branches specializing in adjusting programs to particular areas and countries or servicing the needs of the individual posts in the areas they cover. Field services are separately organized in some of the media and then broken down by area. Such technical support services as operating, maintaining, and planning the construction of broadcasting facilities, of teletype equipment, and of printing plants are normally organized separately from programming, production, and field services units. The policy direction line within the media services is relatively clear, running from the director level through the policy-applications level to the production level, with each maintaining lateral relations within the Agency. While this oversimplification is subject to exceptions, it provides a rough springboard for jumping off into general analysis of the organization and performance of some of the more significant policy-related functions of the individual media services and for taking note of some among the wide variety of programs and products generated by each of the media services.

THE BROADCASTING SERVICE (IBS): VOICE OF AMERICA

Most glamorous of the media services of USIA and better known through the years than the Agency as a whole is the Broadcasting Service, popularly known as the Voice of America. Here work radio personalities whose voices are as familiar to listeners in foreign countries as those of Chet Huntley and David Brinkley are to Americans, and a host of "unknowns" who give policy guidance, write scripts, produce shows, or build and maintain the facilities that make broadcasts possible to most parts of the world. In 1968, as facility expansion begun in 1958 is completed, the Voice of America will blanket the world with its signal, speaking some thirty-eight languages and on the air approximately 824 hours a week, grinding out more air shows than ABC, CBS, and NBC put together. The VOA signal is now so strong that only intense jamming by a foreign government can prevent its being heard. In a world of nation-states, still groping for new relationships necessitated by technological revolutions or nuclear weapons, and by the end of colonialism or rising expectations, the ability to speak over the heads of governments to the people of other nations is a tremendous opportunity—and an awesome responsibility.

Certainly there are many limits on how influential, persuasive, or educational the Voice of America can be. Other governments are able to beam their views to the same listeners. The credibility of all government radio broadcasts, even those of the highly respected British Broadcasting Corporation, is subject to question. It is difficult to limit program listeners to a single nation; the whole Arab peninsula (at least the relatively elite listening public) hears what is said to the Israeli by short-wave radio and vice versa. By an electronic quirk, a listener in Spain may pick up a broadcast to Latin America. If an unexpected individual listener does not hear a broadcast, the Voice can be sure that government monitors of other interested nations do. Tailoring programs to be effective—or even of interest—in a particular nation thus may be viewed by non-target listeners as tantamount to "talking out of the other side of the mouth" and be counterproductive in the long run. On the other hand, even with the spread of transistor radios, not all potential listeners own sets. Those who do are not particularly panting to hear the full text of what President Johnson or other official American spokesmen say; they may work long hours when they cannot listen and then go to bed with the setting sun; they may listen and be drunk or too malnourished to care what they hear; they may live in countries where listening is forbidden. Among the people who present none of these obstacles, there are those for whom listening to the Voice of America would be akin to a member of Americans for Democratic Action tuning in Barry Goldwater or the officers of the Freedom Foundation gathering to listen to a speech by Fidel Castro. And even if they want to hear and are predisposed to accept the message, propagation conditions for broadcasting vary and may be worst at times of day when people can listen so that static or fadeout discourages all but the most hardy.

In spite of difficulties, the "world" does listen to the Voice of America, both officially and individually. What the Voice says in behalf of the United States is important and can sometimes backstop a particular diplomatic, military, or economic operation; or it can build an "image of America" which, hopefully, will make people more receptive to American initiatives or responses in world politics. Personnel of the Broadcasting Service point repeatedly to their "Charter" as the code for determining what the Voice will say to its listeners. They retreat to its protective phrases when pressured by policy makers elsewhere in the Agency or when members of Congress criticize Voice broadcasts. The 1960 directive which they quote was approved by George Allen when he was Agency director and reaffirmed by Murrow, Rowan, and Marks. It is disarmingly simple, essentially sound, and more likely to be seconded by American ambassadors in the field—who also listen to the Voice for information—than by those USIA policy makers in 1963 who advocated hammering home policy points whether anyone overseas wanted to listen or not. According to the "Charter,"

> The long-range interests of the United States are served by communicating directly with the peoples of the world by radio. To be effective, the Voice of America must win the attention and respect of listeners. These principles will govern VOA broadcasts:
>
> 1. VOA will establish itself as a consistently reliable and authoritative source of news. VOA news will be accurate, objective, and comprehensive.
>
> 2. VOA will represent America, not any single segment of American society. It will therefore present a balanced and comprehensive projection of significant American thought and institutions.
>
> 3. As an official radio, VOA will present the policies of the United States clearly and effectively. VOA will also present responsible discussion and opinion on these policies.

Although the Voice speaks from an American point of view, it cannot "tilt the table" or "stack the cards" too much if it desires respect; it cannot present one-sided political harangues if it wants attention. Its music and drama programs must be attractive, its news "on time" and with no significant omissions, its features demonstrative of freedom of discussion and the right to disagree in American society.

The tone of the Voice and its credibility may fluctuate over time, depending upon the nature of the policies of the United States government or the demands placed on the Voice as a policy tool. It was strident and harsh in its handling of Soviet Union and East European affairs before 1957, during the McCarthy era and the peak of the Cold War. It has since accepted and encouraged slow change within the Soviet Union and East Europe rather than revolution, becoming more positive and—since jamming ceased in the Soviet Union and certain other areas—conscious of the need for sophisticated, interesting programming. Because of domestic political pressures exerted by Cuban exiles through members of Congress, its Cuban broadcasts were probably less reasoned between 1963 and 1967 than its Soviet output (or that to Communist China). In a delayed policy shift after the partial failure of the "great leap forward" by the Mainland Chinese in 1958, the unexpected response to the invitation to "let a thousand flowers bloom," and the best intelligence insights available, USIA de-emphasized broadcasts to the overseas Chinese early in 1963 and directed the great bulk of its Chinese radio programs to Mainland China, shifting from Amoy and Cantonese to Mandarin. The Agency adopted a "reasonable tone" and built up content to make listening attractive.

Typical Voice programs run for half an hour, featuring fifteen minutes of news—much more comprehensive on political affairs than the American listener will receive in the United States except at election time—and fifteen minutes of music and commentary. To the chance listener to broadcasts in English to South Asia, the news seems to be presented as objectively as it would be to an American audience by private broadcasters. The real political "freight," of course, is carried in the so-called "back-half" of the program, in the commentary. Here, where the subject matter is topical, the comments can be related to Chinese-Indian border difficulties, with the "freight" obvious but the tone informative. Indians may be reminded that if defense of their territory against Chinese aggression becomes necessary, the United States has military equipment which it can make available for that defense which is particularly well adapted to the physical requirements of fighting in the mountain terrain of north India. In a sense, the Chinese are portrayed as potential aggressors, but this is not said directly and even if it were such a charge would jibe with the Indian government's position on the border problem. Specific mention of United States mortars and possible American assistance is probably intended to encourage the Indian will to resist by projecting one of the Agency's five themes—"the strength image of America." Such a broadcast is probably typical of broadcasts to a "neutral area" facing an outside politico-military threat. On November 7, 1966, John Chancellor, then director of the Voice of America, introduced "the new sound" on IBS worldwide English programs (representing one-quarter of VOA's broadcast time)—"a blend of world news, special news reports for particular parts of the world, music, weather reports, features, news analysis, and humor, "a breezy soft-spoken approach that is a far cry from the heavy-handed propaganda of the Cold War and more moderate than the tone of 1963 broadcasts. An English broadcast interview with Charles Gogolak, now a professional football star in the United States, would be considered poor propaganda in 1967 if it called attention to the fact that an immigrant boy could achieve success in America. That a comment on immigrant success might be broadcast is evidence that it is hard for older personnel at the Voice of America to adjust to the "new sound" and the "softer sell."[2]

The Broadcasting Service is the largest of the media services, with about 1,359 employees in the United States and another 1,013 abroad in 1967.[3] It dwarfs in size the Office of the Director, the Office of Policy and Research, or any of the area offices which provide it with policy guidance. Headed by an assistant director of USIA for broadcasting and his deputy, the Broadcasting Service is divided into two major operating elements—the Office of the Deputy Assistant Director (Program) and the Office of the Engineering Manager. The former is emphasized here, as this is the element which relates Voice of America programming to American foreign policy. The deputy director for program—with his assistant deputy—is responsible for the management, planning, and supervision of the Broadcasting Service. Key figures who assist in fulfilling these duties are the chief of a Policy Application Staff, the chief of the News and Current Affairs Staff, the chiefs of five area divisions, and the chief of the Worldwide English Division. Knowledge of the duties, relationships, and problems of these individuals, and the activities they direct, will help in understanding the Voice of America and its programs—how VOA translates information policy into radio programming, with the help of the Office of the Director, the Office of Policy and Research, and the area offices.

The Director of the Broadcasting Service

The director of a fast media like the Voice of America has considerable policy responsibility, for the Voice is under competitive pressure, similar to that of a private radio news room, to respond as rapidly as possible to unexpected events. Broadcasting a flood of information in thirty-seven foreign languages, which would have to be retranslated into English for policy review, the Voice often must speak before detailed formal policy guidance can travel the funnel from State and down the hierarchy in USIA. In times of real crisis, the Agency chiefs are so busy consulting and advising their superiors at State and the White House that they may have little time for giving detailed guidance to USIA personnel. In its quick reactions, the Voice not only reaches over the heads of foreign governments to speak to people abroad, it speaks to foreign governments, who monitor its broadcasts, over the heads of American ambassadors. In addition to his rather delicate policy responsibilities, the director of the Voice must be the top manager of a complex bureaucratic operation. Beyond his day-to-day focus, the director must be a farsighted planner, aware of the need to change policy emphases and targets, to obtain new facilities, to seek additional personnel with different language skills, and to shift budget priorities to meet emerging opportunities. A deputy director and an executive assistant relieve him of some of the more detailed aspects of his policy and administrative responsibilities.

Not the least of the duties of the assistant director of USIA for broadcasting in the period since 1961, when USIA sharpened the relationship of media programs to American foreign policy, has been that of protecting the credibility of the Voice of America. While it is recognized that government information agencies are limited in their coverage of news by the fact that they represent a government, a reputation for honest reporting is important if overseas audiences are to listen. Henry Loomis, director of the Broadcasting Service from July, 1958, to March, 1965, resigned after seven successful years of leadership of the Voice, apparently because of concern that VOA's credibility was being sacrificed for policy lines of the Johnson administration. News content of broadcasts was said to be diluted with propaganda. Director Rowan defended the administration, recognizing the importance of credibility in news reporting, but arguing that commentary by the Voice would naturally express administration policy.[4] Voice personnel noted with satisfaction that references to the importance of maintaining VOA's credibility made by Loomis in his final message to Voice employees was very similar to the first statement by John Chancellor when he officially assumed direction of the Voice in September, 1965. Chancellor worked hard during his period as director to have the Voice report the news "credibly, accurately, and comprehensively," to prove to the public that the VOA "is engaged in honest journalism."[5] James Reston could write near the close of Chancellor's service with the Voice, "With due respect for the commercial radio and television networks in the United States, this Government news service to the world must be the most detailed and accurate account of America and world news out of the United States today." He went on to say, "It is not peddling political propaganda. It is telling not only what the President and his associates say, but what the opposition says."[6] John Daly, Jr., after his selection by Director Marks as Chancellor's replacement was announced May 29, 1967, said that he planned to broadcast all the news in all of the Voice's languages, including "current dissent on the administration's conduct of the war in Vietnam."[7]

To make it convenient for the assistant director of USIA responsible for broadcasting to keep in close touch with the Office of the Director and the Office of Policy and Research—from which his most important policy guidance comes—Chancellor was provided a special office in the Executive Secretariat (near the office of the Agency director) from which he could operate during visits across town from Voice headquarters at the foot of Capitol Hill to USIA headquarters near the White House. Daly fell heir to the office and continues to come to the Agency for consultation, as necessary, with the director or the deputy director for policy and research. Relations were informal during Marks's leadership of USIA, in keeping with his more relaxed approach to exchange of views among the Agency's top leaders. As problems of policy control occurred during the Agency's transition from the somewhat cultural to more political approach under Murrow after 1961, Loomis was invited to attend the 10 o'clock Monday, Wednesday, and Friday meetings of the Agency director, deputy director, and deputy director for policy and plans. Here he was briefed on the secretary of state's staff meeting and that of the special assistant to the President for national security affairs. Not only did he learn what the latest thinking was "at the top," but also he could seek direct policy guidance on current problems. In this particular relationship, the director of the Voice was closer to the USIA "brass" than were the area office or media service directors who were not present at these sessions.

The Voice leadership actually considers that its policy guidance comes primarily from the Office of Policy and Research, and the director of VOA deals directly with the deputy agency director for policy and research or his associate deputy director. The relationship of the Voice director and the area office directors varies with the personalities of the individuals in the jobs and with the inclination of the top Agency leadership. The director of VOA is responsible for all radio programs of the Agency; the area director for Africa is responsible for all Agency programs in Africa. The balance in the division of power between these overlapping functional and regional interests swings back and forth, but the somewhat independent position of the director of VOA is protected by the sheer volume of material the Voice produces; the area office directors and their staffs cannot look in detail at all that the Voice does. Although an ambassador, an office director or desk man from State, and an area office director in USIA can make suggestions on how the Voice should respond to a particular event, only the Office of Policy and Research can "tell" the Voice what to do. If his aides at lower levels and the director of VOA himself disagree with guidance from the Office of Policy and Research, the director can call the Agency director or the deputy agency director direct. In fact, the disagreement would first be taken up with the deputy agency director for policy and research, who normally accepts the Voice position. Only rarely is a policy question carried to the Agency or deputy agency director. Typically, such intervention by the Voice director results from someone in the policy hierarchy insisting on adherence to a general policy guidance in facing a specific situation, which no one could reasonably have anticipated when the guidance was prepared. There is a tendency for those with broad responsibilities to think in generalizations and those with narrower tasks to think in terms of particulars. The role of the director of VOA is in part to be an honest broker in obtaining a proper mix. Spanish-speaking Latin America can understand broadcasts to Cuba, Bolivia, or Argentina. General guidelines are useful here; specialization or use of differing emphases would only be overheard and lead to trouble. On the other hand, few outside Turkey understand Turkish, and special adaptations of general guidances can be made and heard only by the Turks themselves.

The director of VOA has no continuing organizational device for identifying or discussing major emerging problems. When Soviet jamming of Voice broadcasts ceased on June 19, 1963, the question of how the Broadcasting Service should adjust to the cessation naturally came to the fore. Loomis, as director of VOA, started conversations with his program manager and with the chief of his European Division. Then the area office director for the Soviet Union and eastern Europe and his staff were drawn into discussions, and views were solicited from the American embassy in Moscow. There were differences of view. At the request of the Agency director, the deputy Agency director, the area director concerned, and his area policy officer, began reading all of the Russian output of the Voice and then commented on it. A meeting with Murrow, of those most interested, allowed differences of opinion to be aired, and a representative from the area office was sent to the field to consult the embassy. In the meantime, the chief of VOA's European Division, working with the program manager, was altering the format of Voice programs, increasing the number of voices used in a single program, trying to lighten up programs which by necessity had been hit and run—repeating their messages over and over to make certain the "word" got through. New listeners had to be attracted for longer periods. Time was available for a wider variety of ideas to be worked into programs. Discussions somewhat similar to those on Soviet broadcasts preceded the policy change on broadcasts to China. In addition to discussions within the Agency, the Bureau of Far Eastern Affairs at State was drawn in and the final decision signed off by the Agency director and the assistant secretary of state. On the question of broadcast balance between local vernacular and English to overseas areas, Loomis several times assigned a top-level USIA officer to head a special study group which consulted all levels in the Agency and visited the field. (The director of VOA may pay an occasional brief visit overseas in resolving a particular problem, but he is far more Washington-bound than area office directors.) The foreign language-English balance in broadcasts was a question which Loomis had to keep on his calendar, because former Agency Director Allen was still pressing for more broadcasts in English, arguing that language broadcasts pinpointing target areas lacked credibility because listeners knew that the broadcasts were especially prepared for them. On a number of other policy and administrative problems, Loomis invited several of his assistants to spend a weekend at his home, where questions were explored in an informal atmosphere.

Because of the sprawling nature of VOA, with its thirty-seven language broadcasting services, central determination of all details of policy and administration is impossible, and both Loomis and Chancellor relied on the chiefs of the individual language services for many decisions and program suggestions. Although the language services are given quite a bit of responsibility, the VOA director has a review mechanism presided over by his deputy director (program) which serves to keep the language services "honest" and conforming to shifts in tone and policy directives. Without warning, program material for several days already broadcast will be singled out, re-translated into English, and reviewed by Voice, area office, and embassy personnel. Then the language service chief is called before Voice policy directors to defend any deviations from policy guidances. Since the VOA director participates in some of these meetings, he is kept well aware of problems of adapting broad policy guidelines to radio programs beamed to individual countries.

If much of the director's time is devoted to policy-oriented duties, he must also be aware of manpower and money needs, congressional opinion, the politics of negotiating for overseas relay stations, research developments on antennas for the frequencies assigned the Voice, propagation differences in tropical and temperate zones, and construction problems related to expanding the relay network overseas. He is well aware that he heads a broadcasting operation and not a communications system, that he is firing a heavy naval gun that will blast through obstacles rather than a sporting rifle at a receptive target. The Voice, on the assumption that the United States could not predict the areas where its broadcasts would be important to American policy in future years, embarked upon a $100 million building program in 1958 to construct six new relay stations which would quadruple VOA's power by 1968 and allow it to lay down a short-wave signal everywhere in the world. Although State was responsible for the negotiations for relay station sites, Loomis as director had the over-all responsibility for the technical feasibility of sites for Voice use. Not technically trained himself, he was briefed on such matters by the experts, serving in the office of his engineering manager, who actually participated for VOA in the negotiations. Since the Voice may tread from time to time on the sensibilities of minorities in congressional districts, the Voice director must be aware of public relations with the Hill, yet keep this in balance with the policy requirements of the United States government. The director of VOA needs to be a man of broad interests and sharp insights, capable of inspiring initiatives and loyalty among subordinates, and of making balanced judgments with foresight on issues facing the Broadcasting Service.

The Deputy Assistant Director of VOA for Program

If the director of VOA is the "big leader" of the Voice, the deputy assistant director (program)—and his deputy—is its real secondary leader. The deputy assistant director (program) has responsibilities almost as broad as those of the director, though he is probably a bit less conscious of domestic politics, and conducts intra-agency relationships just a notch below those of the Voice director. While the director considers his program duties as coming first but spends an equal time on management questions, the program manager is even more aware of management problems but still deeply involved in policy and program considerations. His management duties involve oversight of personnel, budget, logistic support, purchase of hardware, obtaining creative talent from outside government on contract, knowing what is the best type of portable tape recorder, and determining how many studios the Voice will need in three years. Like the director's broad policy concerns, those of the deputy assistant director (program) are long term, providing direction in the compass sense. Looking ahead in 1963 to the period after 1970, in what directions should the Voice move when its 1958-68 building program was completed. He is also concerned with the general nature of the programs that broadcast divisions and language services will be putting on the air within the next three months. His is the broad outlook, seeking to view the total interrelationship of international events, technological aspects of media development, American foreign policy, information policy, and resources available to the Voice of America. His problem is how to bring these together in the immediate months ahead, and how to move effectively toward a less distinctly envisioned future.

While the director of VOA works with the Agency director, his executive assistant, or the deputy agency director for policy and research, the deputy assistant director for program's chief contact is the deputy agency director, who has responsibility for media content. Within the Voice, the deputy assistant director for program approves the quarterly program projections which must then be reviewed by the deputy director of USIA. The deputy assistant director for program is quite conscious of the Agency's policy themes, and of the need to emphasize or de-emphasize the themes as appropriate in Voice programs beamed to different parts of the world. Disarmament as a policy theme for programming was excellent for the Voice in Europe but utterly inappropriate in Southeast Asia, where the United States strength image was stressed. The Voice did not see much use in stressing the Berlin theme, which placed the blame for tensions there on the Soviet Union, unless events were going on in Berlin or elsewhere which made discussion of the theme relevant to Voice listeners. Otherwise, people in neutral lands were not interested and did not listen to Voice broadcasts. Although the deputy assistant director for program is aware of the themes as general policy guidance to VOA, he is more disturbed by situations where specific policies have yet to be formulated in times of crisis and the Voice is held in check by the Office of Policy and Research, sometimes prevented from discussing a question at all—an embarrassing position for a radio news room or even for those who prepare rapid political analyses for fast media dissemination. The deputy assistant director for program might argue that the Voice ought to be allowed to set events in perspective, trace developments leading up to a situation, even though interagency agreement had yet to be reached on what the specific United States reaction should be to a particular event. If the Voice waits three days for policy direction, "the commentary is often dead, the facts no longer newsworthy, and the Voice's credibility impaired." He is likely to feel that the Office of Policy and Research is too "sensitive" about broadcasting criticisms of administration policy. The Voice through the years has believed in an "honest interpretation" of the news, not because of any abstract devotion to truth, but because it considers this the best way to represent the facts of American politics. There are differences of opinion within America, and the audience must not be misled—whether it be our own people overseas or other listeners abroad. Bombings in Birmingham, sniping in Cincinnati, or rioting in Detroit must be reported. The deputy assistant director for program would not feel that the news program was the place to discuss a balancing favorable development—the establishment of a new biracial commission in another city. Should the Department of State and the Office of Policy and Research caution the Voice on handling a comment on possible economic inflation or recession in the United States, the Voice would report the speech and source without comment. Often the Voice is allowed to report events straight even when no United States government position has been formulated.

Although the deputy assistant director for program is drawn into questions of how to "play" the day to day, he is actually more concerned with major shifts in information policy and with contingency plans—what should the Voice do if there is revolution in Spain or Jordan? Long before the Soviet Union stopped jamming, it became apparent that changes within the Soviet Union made possible Voice program changes—to reach the uncommitted, the non-Marxists, members of the "new class," those who were not for us but who did not belong wholeheartedly to the Soviet regime either. The program manager of that time (predecessor of the deputy assistant director for program) was unable to get a new policy guideline from State. He asked his

assistant manager for policy application to bring together relevant government studies or memoranda from the embassy in Moscow, to state the facts,
and then draw up a statement of positive broadcast objectives. Such a statement, even though not "official," became a program policy paper—prepared by the Voice for its own use to be followed until an interagency policy
was developed after Soviet jamming of Voice broadcasts ended. In 1963, the
program manager did not feel that post-jamming changes in Voice programming represented any softening of United States policy toward the Soviet
Union. He did believe that good propaganda uses persuasion, and did not
consider himself to be a member of the "kicking in the rear school," so prev-
alent in USIA during the early 1950's. Even more in 1968 than 1963, the philosophy of the Voice is that of "one reasonable person talking to another,"
however imperfectly implemented. It is true that the Voice may "zig and
zag" as administration policy shifts, for the Voice must reflect the foreign
policy of the administration in power. Although the Voice carries statements
of varying tone by the President, it also indicates contrary policy currents in
Washington and America.

The policy of broadcasting to the Chinese mainland introduced in 1963
represented a major change in information policy. It did not indicate that the
administration was about to recognize Red China or that Sino-American
relations were improving. It did mean that different types of programs had to
be prepared and that native Chinese Voice personnel long used to talking to
the overseas Chinese found it difficult to adjust their thinking to address the
Communist Mainland effectively. How were post-revolutionary developments in China analogous to those which had already taken place in the
Soviet Union to be encouraged? Were such changes possible, and if so, could
they be speeded? What audience should USIA address? How could the
Agency find out more about the tastes of those who actually listen? What new
information was required to backstop programs to the mainland? What
increase in staffing was necessary to research the materials to be used in the
China broadcasts? What language or languages should be used in broadcasts? Mandarin was expected to reach the educated elite who were more
likely to own short-wave receivers than the uneducated masses. Could those
personnel displaced by the change who spoke Amoy and Cantonese be used
in other Voice assignments? If the Agency decided to concentrate on Mandarin, how many new reporters would have to be employed on contract? What
would be the impact of reporting development progress in Africa to Chinese
intellectuals who had long viewed Africa as a "savage area" lacking "culture"? What would be gained by straight factual news broadcasts of Soviet
charges against China to the mainland—or Chinese charges against the

Soviet Union to Russia? A number of the questions asked by the program manager in 1963 had yet to be answered for the deputy assistant director (program) in 1967, though attention was being given to such matters by the Research and Analysis Staff of the Office of Policy and Research.

The deputy assistant director for program's policy interests often phase over into his administrative responsibilities, demanding equal attention. A ten-thirty meeting with office directors and division chiefs, held regularly on Wednesday mornings in 1963 but more irregularly by 1967, offered an opportunity for policy discussion but dealt primarily with administrative matters. Some administrative questions are now discussed in the VOA director's daily 9:30 A.M. meeting with division chiefs. The Voice has a number of personnel problems, stemming from its need for some 1,359 permanent American employees and another 800 on contract or on "purchase order" arrangement (performing specific services, such as five scripts a month, on a part-time basis). Most of the 1,359 permanent employees are Civil Service personnel. Only about forty-five Voice employees are Foreign Service Career Reserve Officers, rotated to the Voice from the field for their Washington assignment. Most of these are division, branch, or language service chiefs, directing mixed Civil Service and contract staffs. Overseas employment for Voice personnel does exist; for example, at the Munich Program Center. In time, there may be between sixty and eighty broadcasting positions open at similar centers overseas. This would make possible rotation of civil servants to foreign lands to broaden perspectives. They would go overseas in a Foreign Service Career Reserve (Limited) category, normally a two-year appointment. Many of the top broadcast-related Civil Service positions in the Voice are held by individuals who have been with the Voice for two decades or more. This means that a typical younger civil servant may find his promotion possibilities cut off at GS-11 or GS-12 until those in the hierarchy above him retire or die. Service overseas may win selection for higher posts over those less venturesome when positions do open up, or allow young civil servants to broaden their knowledge and escape to the Foreign Service Career Reserve for duty elsewhere in the Agency and at other posts abroad. Some among the older personnel are European or Chinese refugees, with strong feelings against the regimes which forced them to flee from their mother countries—which sometimes makes it difficult for them to accept new trends in Voice programming toward the Soviet Union and Red China.

The new China broadcast policy in 1963 involved the program manager in technological considerations. The antennas of Project Bamboo, the relay stations being built in the Philippines to beam Voice programs to Mainland China had to be constructed and set up in a different way if the Agency was primarily intent on reaching China proper than if it also wished to broadcast to Tibet and Mongolia. Since the technological problem was related to political projection, the Voice went to Department of State and Policy Planning Council papers in order to project political conditions upon which to formulate assumptions concerning to whom the Voice would want to talk. To determine what languages should be given priorities in Voice broadcasts within five years, the program manager would encourage State to make a political projection, which could then be related to the developing technical capabilities of the Voice. Sitting down with Voice engineers to find out what is technologically feasible, the deputy assistant director (program) can decide to beam new transmitters at one primary target or to build in flexibility so that targets can be shifted quickly as conditions change. The deputy assistant director (program) is a forward-looking synthesizer and coordinator of policy, program, personnel, and technology, in the very practical terms of "money available." He is less involved in day-to-day affairs than the chief of the Policy Application Staff.

Chief of the Policy Application Staff

The world with which the chief of the Policy Application Staff deals is one of current events. He must provide fast policy guidance for rapid response by VOA. Although he is aware of and supports change of long-range voice policy toward the Soviet Union to "persuasion," his attention is riveted on today and tomorrow, the daily shifting nuances of information policy. Although he stores in his mind the long-term stance toward the Soviet Union—that the Voice no longer "rub in" the Soviet people's basic dissatisfactions or encourage them to oppose their government—his advice is how to play a particular story, the alteration of a single word. On the firing line, the chief of the Policy Application Staff is aware of pressures outside broad policy guidelines— congressional inquiries and constituent letters forwarded to USIA on specific broadcasts. The policy application post is normally held by an FSCR on three-year assignment in Washington from the field. The chief must find the "1,000 fingers in every pot" at the Voice quite different from the much simpler clearance and decision process at most American embassies overseas.

The chief's day at the Voice begins at 7:30 A.M., and by 8:15, after the CBS and NBC world news roundups, he is on the phone with policy guidance personnel in the Office of Policy and Research or with the associate deputy agency director for policy and research. He is assisted in the performance of his duties by five area policy officers, covering Africa, Europe, East Asia and the Pacific, Latin America, and the Near East and South Asia. By 9:15 the chief and his staff are meeting with members of the News and Current Affairs

Staff—the personnel in the VOA news room who write news and commentary—to explain how the day's events are to be handled. By then the chief and his assistants have prepared the "IBS Early Guidance," which will also be distributed at the Voice director's morning meeting at 9:30 A.M. In 1963, the chief's title was assistant manager for policy application, and he held a daily 9:30 A.M. staff meeting attended by heads of the news room and of central program services (combined in the News and Current Affairs Staff), broadcasting divisions, branches, and language services. "The IBS Early Guidance" was distributed, updating the more highly classified "IOP Meeting Notes," distributed at the IOP policy guidance 12:30 P.M. briefing of the day before. The IOP document has a much more restricted distribution within the Voice, reaching only the division chief level. These sessions often stimulated questioning and debate by participants because those attending were operators who would be acting specifically on the guidances during the day. The assistant manager led off by calling special attention to certain items in the "IBS Early Guidance," a document of about one page, with several lines of guidance on each of twelve to eighteen items. Each Thursday, the nine-thirty briefing also included a presentation from an outside speaker, from State or another element in USIA to present a broader picture of policy developments. By 1967, the broadly attended briefing by the assistant manager for policy application had been replaced by a smaller nine-thirty meeting of division chiefs in the director of VOA's office, attended by the chief of the Policy Application Staff. This session deals with non-policy as well as policy questions. When policy of the day is discussed, the chief of the Policy Application Staff plays a major role in the discussion. The old nine-thirty meeting was usually no longer than half an hour; the present session may run from fifteen minutes to an hour. By 10 or 10:30 A.M. the regional division chiefs are holding briefing and discussion sessions with the members of their staffs. In both 1963 and 1967, the area policy officers serving the manager for policy application or the chief of the Policy Application Staff attended the regional division briefings—to keep their bosses abreast of division discussions and decisions. The regional division meetings also aid the area policy officers in identifying problems which need to be raised with IOP by phone or brought up at the 12:30 P.M. IOP briefing at 1750 Pennsylvania Avenue when relevant. It is the chief of the Policy Application Staff's job to obtain the flow of policy guidance from State and the White House via the Office of Policy and Research and see that these directives are passed on to the chiefs of the Voice's operating divisions, to their branch chiefs, and to the language services.

The chief of the Policy Application Staff is encouraged by his immediate superiors and even the Agency director to "fight back" if the guidances passed down to the Voice are "unrealistic." Issues are appealed to the deputy agency director for policy and research or even to the Agency director himself. If the Agency is forbidden to do a commentary on a particularly sensitive issue, a draft may be done and walked through the policy guidance hierarchy to see if VOA can skirt the pitfalls sufficiently to broadcast it. This procedure may delay airtime, but it oftens enables the Voice to speak on controversial matters, avoiding an embarrassing silence. Presentation of the historical background in such situations has been accepted by the Agency director. The general background approach is also used sometimes in situations where American policy support for a nation or government is quiet or very low key. There has been a running battle within the Agency on the role of Voice commentary, with the Office of Policy and Research believing it should be devoted solely to clear explanations of American policy and the Voice believing it should also include discussion topics of interest to the audience where no direct policy objective of the United States government is involved. Voice personnel believe that if the VOA discusses all kinds of topics, overseas publics will listen to American policy presentations included in Voice programs and find them more credible.

The briefing notes and the daily briefing sessions set the framework for the day's work of the chief of the Policy Application Staff, but they actually take up only one-tenth of his time. The other nine-tenths of his day is spent talking with people, discussing how things should be said, or if they should be said at all. He has the general responsibility for review of centrally prepared scripts done by members of the News and Current Affairs Staff (news, features, or talks), is often in touch with the chiefs of these operations, as his area officers are with the regional specialists within them. The chief of the Policy Application Staff is a familiar figure in the "news room" or in "special services" (where commentary is drafted), often pausing to answer questions or to sit down and review copy before it is transmitted to the language services for airing.

The Chief of News and Current Affairs

By 1967, the chief of News and Current Affairs coordinated functions which in 1963 were serviced by two Voice divisions, the News Division and the Central Program Services Division. The News Division remains in 1968 much the same as it was in 1963, though its "house wires" have been reorganized, and it now has responsibility for guiding an Overseas Correspondents Staff and a Domestic Correspondents Staff. It is the basic source of news stories for the Voice, both English-language newscasts and those done by the language services. The Central Program Services Division was divided by

1967 into a Features and Special Services Division and a Talks Division. The latter consists of a Forum Branch, which prepares lectures for a forum series on science, art, the novel, or other topics; an English Teaching Branch, which gathers material to backstop the teaching of English by radio; and a Political Analysis Branch. If an event occurs that is related to a basic long-standing policy of the United States, the Political Analysis Branch provides a script recalling the policy, tracing the history of the situation, and discussing the arguments for and against the American stand—providing, it can be assumed, an "on balance" justification of the American position. Where the United States has finalized no clear-cut position, but in the long run may have a policy involvement, a background discussion would be written without taking sides. Very little original comment goes into either of these products, for much of what is said is based on "fact" and the United States position as stated in official speeches or policy documents. The Features and Central Services Division provides material for full musical programs or background music for dramatic productions, covers events of special interest taking place in the United States which may be of interest overseas, and assumes responsibility for providing much of the "backhalf" of Voice programs, which carry the "political freight," to the six broadcasting divisions and their thirty-seven language services (English being the thirty-eighth language and handled by one of the six divisions). Regional or more parochial subjects are handled by the broadcasting divisions on a regional basis or by the individual language services. Provision of a wide variety of material through a central source assists in assuring that the Voice speaks with one "voice," while allowing the servicing of special interests and broadcasts with differing nuances, emphases, and levels of sophistication. For policy purposes, the most important parts of News and Current Affairs are the news room of the News Division and the Features and Special Services Division, because it provides the policy-related commentary to current world developments being reported by the news room. Both divisions are headed by a chief.

The chief of the News Division is responsible for a somewhat hectic operation, guiding some fifty-two professional writers and editors who work long hours to process a volume of news unequaled in volume by any other radio news room in the world unless by the British Broadcasting Corporation. Understaffed like the Agency's area offices, the News Division's newsmen are overworked. They are underpaid in comparision with reporters for American newspapers. The central News Division of the Voice provides the only source of news for all of VOA's English broadcasts and is a basic source for news scripts written in, or translated into, thirty-seven other tongues by the language services. The News Division relies upon the standard press services for most of the information used in its stories, including Associated Press, Universal Press International, Reuters, Agence France Press, and the UPI sports wire. In addition, it receives information on United Nations events by direct wire from News and Current Affairs' New York Program Center and has access to FBIS reports based on foreign broadcasts. It has a small staff of USIA correspondents roaming the world to provide in-person and in-depth news coverage of major overseas events. House wires within USIA enable the News Division to forward news stories to the broadcasting divisions and to exchange material with the Office of Policy and Research to check materials before release and to forward material for use by the Press and Publications Service on its daily Wireless File. The Voice A wire serves as the main news wire for Europe, the Near East and South Asia, and East Asia and the Pacific. The Voice B wire moves most of the material from the news room to be used in broadcasts to Africa or Latin America. The Voice C wire keeps in touch with the Office of Policy and Research and services the Press and Publications Service. A News and Current Affairs (NCA) wire opened late in 1966 carries reports from USIA correspondents, news expansioners, features, backgrounders to spot news, editorial packages, and analyses—and is fed both by the News Division and by the Features and Special Services Division.

Excellent as the private news coverage is upon which USIA places great reliance, errors are made, and the Voice has on occasion been taken to task by the secretary of state for using material without checking it out thoroughly—leading to the decision that stories are not to be released unless the facts are carried by at least two of the news services. Otherwise, stories must be confirmed by USIS posts, by reports from American embassies, or by cross-checking with area offices in USIA. Often the time element precludes much additional research, and a telephone call is placed to an overseas USIS mission or to an American embassy to check the facts. Reuters and Agence France Presse, excellent news sources though they be, tend to give a British or French slant to the news, which the Voice must take into account. Associated Press or Universal Press International leads may be overly sensational, and the Voice must discount them. The chief of the News Division emphasizes speed next to accuracy in handling the news, because Voice broadcasts are often beamed to particular countries only once or twice a day. When a deadline is missed, BBC may scoop the Voice on American political news. Essentially, the news gathered by the News Division consists of facts about events, editorial opinion from American newspapers, editorial opinion from foreign newspapers, comments by columnists, stories on new personalities or obituaries on those passing from the scene, and excerpts from speeches, hearings, or press conferences involving leading government figures, either American or foreign.

News was not considered a particularly vital element in the program of the old Office of War Information, and even after World War II information broadcasts tended to continue with a psychological warfare motif. During this period, news was selected primarily to do a propaganda job, not for its newsworthiness. After the separation of USIA from State, in part because Dulles was not interested in operations and wished State to concentrate on policy, the Voice of America was able to upgrade its news effort and by the mid-1950's became more sensitive and objective in its handling of the news. The trend toward greater objectivity and broader coverage was reinforced by Edward R. Murrow's belief that "truth" was the Agency's greatest weapon and by his reaffirmation of the 1960 directive which VOA recognizes as its operating "Charter." Even those in the Agency who are not "Boy Scouts" have accepted the shift because it increases the Voice's credibility. From a Voice point of view, it is more important to be credible than truthful. The truth is often not believed. Nonetheless, if truth is on "our side" and if people overseas are informed, in the long run News Division personnel believe the United States gains by presenting facts. The audiences listening abroad—though they constitute a small proportion of their countries' total population—are influential and often sophisticated groups which appreciate presentation of views opposed to administration policy. This does not mean that American public opinion as expressed in the press will be carried overseas by the Voice in exactly the same balance for and against a policy or program; the distribution of quotations is quite likely to be shaded in favor of current administration policy. The opposition is likely to be quoted first, on the assumption that what the audience hears last will be remembered more favorably. If it is administration critic vs. the President, the President has the final word. In doing this, the Voice is probably far more objective in balancing the facts than are publications of either of the national political party committees in the United States, or any congressman who calls up Legislative Reference Service of the Library of Congress and asks that a speech be prepared justifying his position on a particular bill. Even within a political democracy, the contenders for influence are less objective than ivory-tower researchers, who find it difficult to separate themselves from their own value orientations. It would be too much to expect that USIA could be perfectly objective in the international political arena.

The chief of the News Division would say that Voice news coverage reflects United States government policy, reporting what is said and done at a variety of levels. If debate in Congress runs contrary to administration policy, the Voice is limited in what it can do to minimize its reporting of the opposition. It must let the moods of the various elements in the country come through. The Voice will carry material on the race crisis and on the scientific competition to get to the moon. The American people are discussing both these topics and sometimes disagreeing on what should be done. The Voice cannot go far beyond the policy decisions of the United States government. If the policy is palatable to the target audiences, the Voice has an easy job. But if the people in India are starving and Congress or the President hesitates in providing wheat and loans, there is little the Voice news reports can do to soften the blow—except to explain why the American political system works the way it does. The bread and butter of Voice news is foreign policy, but to understand how the American government acts and what its policy objectives really are, it is necessary to communicate much background material in news broadcasts about the American culture, the form of government, the pluralism of ideas, and "how we operate." When a Negro student was denied entrance to the University of Mississippi, the events still made a good story for the Voice because the federal government took action in support of admission. Most listeners overseas are sophisticated enough to understand that progress requires difficult social changes. If there are differences and struggle within America, it indicates that American life is progressing, not that it is failing. The Department of State is likely to worry when the American people's debate of an issue is carried by the Voice. News-room personnel believe that reports indicating conflicting views and American freedom of expression demonstrate the strength of American society. Southern congressmen may be less certain than the Voice of the rightness of such a broadcast policy. The American ambassador in Vietnam may understand the Voice of America's interest in credibility and reasonable objectivity, but he may question particular broadcasts. Most government policy people accept the Voice reporting policy until it involves their agency, country, or program. The news room knows that stories it does not broadcast will be carried by less friendly sources which will not take the trouble to set the facts in an American perspective. Letters from the field commenting upon Voice news coverage are answered by the chief of the News Division, his reply subject to normal clearance procedures within the Agency.

The policy guidances which reach the News Division from the chief of the Policy Application Staff, based on thinking in State and in the Office of Policy and Research, normally consist of little more than instructions to give a particular news item minimum treatment for credibility or to build up a particular item. There has been no total ban on Voice broadcasts concerning a piece of news in the public domain since a brief period of restraint during the

Cuban crisis in the fall of 1962; but controls were also tight during the crisis in Santo Domingo in the spring of 1965. Problems of following guidance in news coverage are quite often only a question of emphasis: How much backgrounding should be done? How much editorializing should be included? The Voice believes neither that it should comment, in its news coverage of Soviet cosmonauts, on recent American space achievements, nor that in reporting on civil-rights events it should point out civil-rights problems in the Soviet Union. It is felt that United States government radio news is not the most effective media for this type of counterpunch. Voice personnel would argue that policy makers should not "destroy a potent weapon for a single victory, that a sneak punch is not good if you get knocked out yourself." The questioning of Voice news policy may come from several sources within USIA and may point in different directions. When the news room changed the lead story in newscasts to the Far East from one on the Soviet cosmonauts then in space to reporting the settlement of the West Irian dispute, the director of the Broadcasting Service questioned the decision though he did not override it. On the other hand, USIA's Office of Policy and Research may have approved and wished additional news breaks would reduce the coverage of the Soviet feat. When American wheat sales to the Soviet Union were being discussed, this topic was the lead story for a time on the European wire from the news room. When it was relegated to second place by the Italian flood story, the Office of the Assistant Agency Director for the Soviet Union and Eastern Europe (IAS) objected to the shift. The news room argued that the American government was interested in human conditions, that reporting the flood and efforts being made to care for the persons involved was a true reflection of American concern for individuals. The Office of Policy and Research apparently thinks of stories in terms of: "Is this in the American interest? If it is, play it up. If not, play it down." Voice news personnel believe that if you do not talk about what is interesting to the listener, no matter how carefully material of interest to policy makers is relayed, the listener will switch the dial. They have no desire "to make policy" all by themselves but feel a need to talk about situations of vital interest to Voice listeners, whether the United States has a policy concern with the problem or not. Although the diplomat can use silence effectively, the radio man cannot. The Office of Policy and Research vs. News Division positions represents something of an anomaly, for the Office of Policy and Research, responsible for the Agency's long-range plans as well as daily guidance, often tends to be more interested in short-range impact. The Voice of America news room, which feeds off the grist of daily events, is more concerned with long-run credibility.

The chief of the Features and Special Services Division is far down the policy guidance funnel. Between the regional bureaus in the Department of State, often responsible for foreign policy formulation, and the Division is the Department of State policy guidance office, the USIA policy guidance personnel in IOP and the chief of the Policy Application Staff in one policy control line, not to mention the secretary of state, the director of USIA, the deputy Agency director for policy and research, the director of VOA, and the deputy assistant director (program) at a different level of control. Within the Voice, the Division chief's closest policy guide is the chief of the Policy Application Staff. The Division chief checks out any story with "domestic political implications" with the chief of the Policy Application Staff, but makes a high percentage of decisions "on his own" as he reviews scripts prepared in the various branches of the Features and Special Services Division. Just as he is too far buried in the policy structure to feel that he has any direct relationship with the Department of State, he is likely to feel that even though he has the opportunity to review the Agency's themes, controlled by the Office of Policy and Research, his suggestions weigh lightly on the policy scales. He is aware of larger USIA studies on what image of America should be conveyed overseas and of how the media might cooperate in preparing products so that they do not do the same work twice, but he feels far removed and untouched by the work of the Agency planning officers.

Just as the Office of Policy and Research is interested in "themes" or "emphases," the chief of the Features and Special Services Division stresses commentary or background materials which give the themes "meaning" to the listener, which may cause the deputy Agency director with responsibility for media content to ask, "What theme does this program support?" It is difficult to explain to Office of Policy and Research personnel why it is important to do a series of broadcasts to the Soviet Union on mass suburban living in America, based on the experiences of a representative family. The Voice, in the past, has told Soviet listeners about three-bedroom homes in the United States, since many Soviet workers live in mass housing developments, often with a single room for a whole family. The Soviet press has responded to the American broadcasts with "horror stories" about American families being in debt for twenty to thirty years. It seems useful to Division personnel to make it clear how our system works. A background piece on the United Nations may be questioned by the Office of Policy and Research, but the Features and Special Services Division would defend its presentation on the basis that an understanding of United Nations peace-keeping operations, and more broadly of collective security and disarmament (at one point an Agency theme), needs to be set in an informational context. The Office of

Policy and Research may want to reduce the time given to musical presentations, but the Division would argue that cultural programs of this nature hold listeners and provide a better understanding of American life. Popular music is beamed for twenty to forty-five minutes at least five times daily (about two hours of a total of eight each day) to the Soviet Union, with narration in Russian, featuring the entire range of American popular music: jazz, dance music, folk songs, spirituals, cowboy songs, stage and motion-picture musical hits, light musical orchestras, choirs, and brass bands. The daily program in Russian to the Soviet Union includes eight ten- to fifteen-minute newscasts. "Backhalf" type materials include "Current Comments," fifteen minutes of "VOA news analyses, U.S. and foreign editorials on events of the day"; "American Perspective," a forty-five minute "review of political, economic, social, scientific, cultural, educational and technical developments in the U.S. and abroad"; and "Events and Opinions," a forty-five minute "review of current events through news analyses, press reviews and correspondents' reports."[8]

The daily guidances from the Office of Policy and Research, with their "don't overemphasize this" or "play this carefully," leave many fine decisions to be made within the Features and Special Services Division. The Office of Area Director for the Soviet Union and Eastern Europe is also active in giving policy guidance, and the chief of the Features and Special Services Division, caught in an argument between the Office of Policy and Research and the area office, may have to wait to prepare broadcast material until the question has been settled at the top. USIA has had the problem of laying the psychological groundwork overseas to prepare foreign publics for the detonation of the first and later Chinese nuclear devices. In part, the problem has been how to support the "strength image" of the United States without "saber-rattling." When the President of the United States, addressing a domestic audience, emphasized that the United States was stronger than all the rest of the world together, the Division did not particularly want to stress this point but felt that since the President had said it the words should be carried overseas. The Soviet desk officer in the area office said, "Why rub it in?" Whatever the position taken by the Office of Policy and Research in this instance, the difference was carried to Director Murrow, who supported the Voice position. In another instance of Voice differences with the area offices, during discussions of the limited nuclear test ban treaty, what was then the Central Program Services Division recalled a historic fact favorable to the Soviet Union in a commentary—to which the area office objected. Again, the Agency director ruled with the Voice. These illustrations are not intended to indicate that the Voice is always right or always wins intra-agency arguments, or that the Voice necessarily represents a "balanced" view—but they illustrate the nature of policy differences.

The Features and Special Services Division does not seek to be objective but to be credible; "what is objective depends on the perception spectrum of the receiver, so in Voice work 'objective' means 'credible' or 'believable.'" The American who tells a Russian his family has five radio sets and four television sets in his home may be stating a fact, but such a fact would be useless to the Voice, because it would not be believable to Soviet listeners. The commentaries, analyses, and background pieces of the Division seek to counter distortion. In the process, they may use counter-distortion in order to influence the listener's perspective into a new balance more favorable to the United States position. During discussions of American wheat sales to the Soviet Union, the Soviet Union emphasized to its people that the balance-of-payments difficulties of the United States made America anxious to consummate such an agreement, downgrading their own need for wheat. In response, the Voice broadcasts emphasized agricultural shortages in the Soviet Union and pointed out that grain was being sought by Soviet leaders in many countries besides the United States. If both sides told the truth, neither emphasized the whole truth. Voice newscasts carried a similar message, but commentary could go ahead and explain why the United States had a bumper crop and was willing to sell. Although USIA newscasts on September 16, 1963, carried the Birmingham bombing of a Negro church (near the bottom of the news list and not as a lead story), reporting only the shock to Americans of briefly stated facts, commentary could note a favorable offsetting fact (there had been no lynchings in the south for several years) and indicate positive steps being taken by the United States government to overcome racial problems. Thus, the News Division and the Features and Special Services Divisions provide related but distinctly separate policy tools to the broadcasting divisions and language services of the Broadcasting Service.

The Chiefs of the Regional Divisions

The central elements in the whole broadcasting operation, the voices of the Voice of America, are the VOA's five regional divisions, covering Africa, Europe (mostly the Soviet Union and eastern Europe), East Asia and the Pacific, Latin America, and the Near East and South Asia—each headed by a division and deputy division chief. Divisions are subdivided into branches, each headed by a branch chief and deputy chief; the branches are based on language (there is a French Branch in the Africa Division), on geography (the Central European Branch speaking to the "satellites" and Albania in the

European Division), or on function (the Production Branch in the Africa Division is responsible for rehearsing and putting dramas or other broadcasts on the air, for interlocking people with script, music, and microphone). In the European Division there is a single Russian Branch, broadcasting to the Soviet Union in the Russian language, and a North and East European Branch, broadcasting six different languages to minority groups within the Soviet Union. The geographic branches are broken down by language services—the Voice broadcasting in thirty-seven foreign languages plus English, much of the latter under the auspices of its Worldwide English Division. The Africa Division, however, has a relatively new English to Africa Branch, which speaks in English primarily about African events. Typical of the language services are the Japanese Service and the Korean Service in the East Asia and Pacific Division. Each language service employs from seven to ten people. The language services, led by a chief and a deputy chief, include an editor (often the deputy chief), a foreign-language editor, and four to seven adapter-announcers. The chiefs and deputy chiefs of the divisions, geographic branches, and language services have both policy (or program) and administrative duties. Language service editors review material in English, rewriting or adapting materials coming to the services from the News Division or the Features and Special Services Division and handing out work assignments to subordinates. The foreign-language editors are responsible for the quality of the translation and for further adaptation to area use. The adapter-announcers translate from English into the language, announce, act, or do special events—having both script and voicing functions. The China Branch of the East Asia and Pacific Division, now really a large language service working in Mandarin, is divided into a Program Section, with eighteen people concentrating on "backhalf" materials, a News Section of five working on "news" programs, and a Production Section with five employees. A considerable amount of program writing must be done in some of the branches or language services because there is not always enough material produced for specialized area use by the Features and Special Services Division. The China Branch prepares some seventeen scripts a week on its own, commentaries or political analyses dealing with Mainland developments, relying upon material from Mainland newspapers or unclassified intelligence resources. Branch chiefs do no writing but keep abreast of events—reading political-economic reports, USIS post reports, and general popular and scholarly writing on their areas of concern—in order to suggest appropriate topics for treatment by language service personnel. Chiefs of divisions, branches, and language services are Americans and normally members of the Foreign Service Career Reserve or the Foreign Service

Career Reserve (Limited). Editors are normally Americans and sometimes Foreign Service Career Service Officers. Foreign-language editors and adapter-announcers are quite likely to be of foreign extraction, often naturalized but sometimes not American citizens. The largely Civil Service composition of the language services, with some foreign citizens serving on contract and not under Civil Service, and the specialized nature of the duties performed pose problems of promotion for younger personnel which make it difficult to attract new employees. However, because staffs are aging with many near retirement, promotions when they come are likely to be rapid. There are also problems of policy control, because the chiefs and deputy chiefs of the divisions, branches, and language services who pass through the Voice assignments on rotation work with personnel who "outlast" them in office. Naturalized civil servants, perhaps once refugees from a foreign land in revolution, find it difficult (even after ten, fifteen, or twenty years of Voice service) to pursue moderate policy lines toward the governments in their former homelands as USIA modifies its approach (for example, to the Soviet Union in 1957 and 1963 or to Mainland China in 1963). Few pragmatic Foreign Service Career Reserve Officers remain "psychological warriors" of the 1946-56 vintage. Policy control of so-called "purchase-order vendors," hired part time as announcers, translators, or script writers, is also a problem. They are not regular Agency employees and, therefore, are less well oriented on Agency policy.

Policy guidance to the regional divisions after 1957 was very rigid for several years, with the European Division restricted to broadcasting material emanating from the News Division and the old Central Program Services Division word for word to insure that it would not keep the old hard-line policy approach. With the coming of the Kennedy administration and the emphasis on more targeting in individual areas, and the lapse of time which allowed the European Division to adjust to the new policy trends, more autonomy was given to the language services, but they are still subject to careful policy direction and review. Revisions of News or Features and Special Services Division materials by the language services must be cleared, but this causes no real problems to the regional divisions. Their suggested changes are usually approved. At one time, the divisions had to determine what specific scripts they would need three months ahead, which cut down on timeliness, but in recent years quarterly projections require only general topics, which can be adapted to events. Thus, the deputy agency director, responsible for media content, is aware of general categories or types of broadcasts planned by the Voice for the next three months, but the Voice still has program flexibility. Day-to-day policy guidance comes from the chief of the

Policy Application Staff or his area policy officers to the division chiefs, and is relayed and discussed at daily ten o'clock staff meetings in the regional divisions. The division chiefs have attended the nine-thirty briefing and discussion in the VOA director's office. They then meet, along with the branch chiefs and the Policy Application Staff's area policy officers, with the chiefs of their language services. The materials received daily from the News Division and the Features and Special Services Division—with the changing patterns of their "must" stories or commentaries, those recommended, and those optional—constitute a different form of policy guidance to the regional divisions. The regional divisions rarely disagree with these priorities unless they have been set on the basis of an overriding policy decision imposed from outside USIA, with the regional divisions not privy to all the facts. Perhaps it is fortunate that division chiefs feel that not all policy is handed down. They believe that some of it is passed up in the form of suggestions or recommendations. One division chief envisions his policy relationships with the Office of Policy and Research, the area office paralleling his regional responsibility, and the chief of the Policy Application Staff as a box, the lines linking four policy-initiating points—any one of which can make a policy suggestion but has to clear it with each of the other three. He feels that the relationship is that of thinking together rather than fitting a master-servant pattern, though he recognizes that when he initiates a matter he goes "up" to discuss it with others. The division director may call the policy officer in the area office, who in turn contacts the deputy chief of policy guidance in the Office of Policy and Research, who gets in touch with the chief of the Policy Application Staff at the Voice—with whom the division director has already talked. Thus, there is a circulatory flow in policy making, the direction not always predictable.

Policy control cannot be complete, for no desk officer in an area office, no area officer on the IOP policy guidance staff, and no area officer on the VOA Policy Application Staff can read all the scripts broadcast by the Voice to his countries—and perform his other duties as well. A small monitoring service under the chief of the Policy Application Staff prepares brief summaries and comments on broadcasts. Adverse reports bring questions from the Policy Application Staff chief to the division chief which are relayed to the appropriate language service for explanation. An even more important device which helps assure policy conformity by the language services and stimulates them to do a "quality job" at all times is the Program Review Committee of the Broadcasting Service. At least once a year for each language service and sometimes more often the Program Review Committee plays the role of Caliban. Instead of selecting at random a crab to crush on the beach, the committee chooses a particular day's broadcast by a language service for thorough review. The original translators of the scripts retranslate the foreign language back into English (without the help of the original English scripts), and then forward the new English versions for careful review by the committee members. Among the members sitting at each hearing will be the deputy assistant director of the Voice for program, the chief of the Policy Application Staff, the chief of the appropriate regional division, the chiefs from the News and the Features and Special Program Services Divisions, and a representative of the area office, usually the desk officer for the country to which the language service broadcasts. The language service is formally notified about three weeks before the hearing. For example, on November 8, it might be told that the broadcasts of November 1 will be reviewed by the committee on November 30. Not even the division chief knows ahead of time what the spacing or timing of the sessions for his language services will be. The Program Review Committee hearing is hard nosed, looking for trouble, and the language services go up with some trepidation to attempt to justify any seeming policy aberrations or careless work. Division chiefs have usually already had mock hearings with the language service scheduled to be on the frying pan before the hapless language service personnel face the Program Review Committee. Obvious "fluffs" have been identified and the best possible explanations for the variances prepared. Language service personnel always feel that some special occurrence made this particular day's broadcasts atypical, and that almost any other day would have been better for review. "Cruel" as the inquisition appears to be, it is taken in good stead by all concerned and is considered a vital instrument of program management.

Division chiefs through the years have been well aware of the Agency's five themes and have had access to the Policy Guidelines or National Policy Papers on individual countries for their areas prepared under the aegis of State's Policy Planning Council. Country papers are relatively broad and leave considerable leeway for information policy and, more specifically, for radio programming. Country Plans and the new Country Plan Program Memoranda give more specific direction. The flexibility in use of Agency themes introduced in the new CPPM's helps resolve a long-time problem of the Voice division chiefs. The Berlin theme had little personal meaning to most Africans. Their thoughts were on their own national or continental problems. (A visit to Berlin by an elite group of Ghanaians suggested by a VOA division chief and conducted by the West Germans themselves had considerable impact, however.) In Africa, it has been possible to stress the United Nations theme, since it is apparent to most listeners that the United Nations does benefit small, new nations. Africans were interested in the disarmament theme; they believed and still do that if the United States and the

Soviet Union disarm more help will be forthcoming to them for moderniza-tion. A more specific guidance, like one in 1966 on the tenth anniversary of the Hungarian revolution, may have little meaning when a program based on it is beamed to Africa. Generally, before the slow growth of flexibility on use of themes over the past several years—given impetus by the new CPPM's— the division chiefs considered the themes "hard to live with." Most of the planning done by the division chiefs is closely related to the five-year projec-tions and justifications related to the budget process. They do look ahead at division needs for that period, help consider where relay stations might be built or overseas program centers established, project the number of broad-cast hours desirable in what languages, indicate the number of personnel required, and suggest ideas for types of programs. Planning at this level is mainly geared to priorities established by the area offices.

Regional divisions have day-to-day working relationships with the area offices and with other elements in the Agency. Not all Voice radio broadcasts go directly from the studios in the Health, Education, and Welfare Building via relay stations to individual listeners overseas. Seven to ten times as much program material is sent in tape form by air or sea pouch to field posts for distribution, usually for unattributed use on local radio stations. The servic-ing of field needs is primarily by the regional divisions, backed up by the News and the Features and Special Services Divisions, with additional USIA correspondents being assigned overseas and new overseas program centers expected to take over some of this load. Since area offices backstop field operations, regional divisions work closely with the area offices in ful-filling field requests. Regional divisions of the Voice hold joint interviews with prominent personalities in cooperation with the Press and Publications Service. Language assistance may be provided to the Motion Picture and Television Service. Press and Publications Service "stringers" in the United States may do radio tapes for the Broadcasting Service.

While planning and day-to-day operations are important, evaluation of programs is also of interest to Division chiefs. They believed that Research and Reference Service studies were becoming increasingly valid and will benefit from the policy-oriented studies of the Research and Analysis Staff. They also seek to verify results from reading audience mail and comments from field personnel. Although they find survey results useful, they under-stand the sensitivity of foreign governments to overt survey research for USIA purposes. They believed the old "transistor contests," in which listen-ers sent in their names to be drawn for a transistor radio prize, gave them some indication of the number and types of listeners to radio programs—but this program, which was considered of some importance in 1963, is little used in 1968. Division chiefs do not have to rely entirely on the reports of others. They make inspection visits to the field, perhaps two or three month-long trips a year, visiting ten posts per trip for one to four days each. Branch chiefs may also visit the field occasionally. The regional divisions are the Voice's primary means of speaking in their own languages to publics which do not speak English or which prefer to listen to their own tongue. They are the major Voice elements which individualize the Broadcasting Service's approach to regions and specific countries.

The Chief of the Worldwide English Division

The Worldwide English Division is the Voice's means of communicating with millions overseas for whom English is a second language—often the reasonably well educated who are likely to be members or potential members of influential elites—or who are trying to make English their second or even third language. The role of the chief of the Worldwide English Division is similar in many ways to that of the chiefs of the regional divisions. His Division feeds off the same raw material, the same policy guidance meetings and papers, the same news scripts or political analyses from the News and the Features and Special Services Divisions. Since his regional editors attend the daily regional division staff meetings, there is some coordination between the Worldwide English Division and the regional divisions, but the relationship otherwise is minimal. Relations within the Division are informal, with most information passed by word of mouth. Division meetings bringing together the branch and section chiefs are held on Tuesdays and Thursdays at 10 A.M., just after the daily 9:30 A.M. briefing of division chiefs in the office of the VOA director. The Division has no direct relationship with the area offices or the Office of Policy and Research, all problems being "buffered" by the Voice director, the deputy assistant director (program), or the Policy Application Staff chief.

The chief of the Worldwide English Division works with a total staff of about sixty-five persons, thirty-three in a Program Branch, eight in a Special Projects and Documentaries Branch, twenty-one in an Operations Branch, plus a secretary and the deputy chief. The Program Branch edits, writes, and prepares for broadcast all Worldwide English Division programs. Its Regional Features Section is most involved in producing the Voice's "new sound" introduced by VOA Director Chancellor in November, 1966, now carried five hours Monday through Friday each week, to be heard overseas in two two-hour and one one-hour blocks. The first hour of "The New VOA

Service" is general and is beamed to all areas, but the second hour is sometimes regionalized. Before the "new sound," the Section prepared half-hour special reports to various regions, an unregionalized "Opinion Roundup," and a half-hour topical program called "Dateline," often based on a speech by a figure like Dean Rusk or W.W. Rostow. The Breakfast Program Section continues to do the "Breakfast Show," a light two-and-one-half-hour program beamed to Europe and Africa, including music, features, and short newscasts—a program which appears to have been the progenitor of the "new sound" within USIA as television's "Morning Show" and radio's "Monitor" were outside the Agency. The General Features Section still prepares cultural programs, covering the arts and sciences, literature and music. The Special English Section works up five fifteen-minute newscasts and a half-hour special feature each day to be broadcast slowly, using the 1,000-word vocabulary. Special Projects and Documentaries Branch personnel go out to handle special events, such as space flights, presidential press conferences, or election broadcasts, occasionally preparing documentary broadcasts on particular issues. They also do several regular programs, one being "Press Conference USA," broadcast on Saturday. The Operations Branch is a typical production unit, responsible for announcing, producing, and putting shows on the air.

The Worldwide English Division has an advantage over the regional divisions and the language services, because it works in English, can easily find American experts to speak on any topic, and can take network shows off the line on standard continuing clearances, only clipping the commercials before overseas use. Educational broadcasts are also available, covering material from the most topical to the timeless. Perhaps the real justification for Voice broadcasting in English is that it is America's native tongue and is a leading world language at the present time. Listening to the Voice in English helps maintain this language facility for many people overseas. Since the special English broadcasts by the Division are produced using the 1,000-word vocabulary, spoken slowly, they aid learners in improving their English. George Allen, writing as a former Agency director, has argued that broadcasts in English—based on domestic programs—are very effective with people overseas because the programs are not thought of as specially prepared propaganda. A large portion of the Worldwide English Division's broadcasts, based on this type of material, are sent to all parts of the world without any regionalization. More special broadcasts in English are sent to Latin America than to other geographic regions. Elsewhere, the regionalization is normally less and the broadcasts are likely to be repeated several times a day, though in South Asian broadcasts the news is fresh each time. Only the

Africa Division and the Far East Division of the Voice do any English broad-casting; the Africa broadcasts are primarily on African topics instead of fol-lowing the Worldwide English Division's emphasis on projecting ideas and events of the United States and the outside world. Although Worldwide English Division programs beamed to various areas may vary in length and airtime, they are generally transmitted between six and eight o'clock in the morning and from six to twelve o'clock at night—when audiences are best and broadcast propagation conditions the worst.

The Engineering Manager of the Broadcasting Service

The engineering manager, through his own office and the Frequency and Technical Divisions operating under his direction, is responsible (1) for determining sites where relay stations are required in the United States or overseas; (2) for USIA technical representation in negotiations for relay sta-tion sites abroad and for frequencies to be used in USIA broadcasts; (3) for engineering designs and supervision of contractors during construction of relay stations or other Broadcast Service facilities; (4) for the technical oper-ation and maintenance of all Voice facilities in Washington and abroad and cooperation with other communications systems used in Voice transmis-sions; and (5) for monitoring broadcasts abroad to determine propagation conditions and adequacy of reception. The engineering manager requires a lead time of approximately five years between the beginning of planning and actually putting a signal into a new area. The McCarthy era in the United States, and some lack of understanding of the scope of the broadcast network required by the Voice if it were to lay down a worldwide signal on the part of early Agency leaders, postponed the go-ahead on expansion of Voice facili-ties from 1953 when the Agency was separated from State until 1958. The program initiated at that time will give the Voice worldwide short-wave broadcast capabilities if completed on schedule in 1968. Although the Department of State actually conducts the negotiations for sites, it is some-times direct contact with radio personnel in countries abroad by members of the Voice engineering staff that paves the way to acceptance of the request by the other foreign office. The engineering staff determines technically within a broad area where sites suitable for the type of facilities can be con-structed. Actual negotiations usually obtain one of the several possible sites. Negotiations for frequencies, also conducted by State at international con-ferences, are backstopped on a technical basis by members of the engineer-ing staff. Frequencies are becoming difficult to obtain as more new countries enter international broadcasting either to propagandize or inform their neighbors or to show off their national progress and status. It is important that members of the engineering staff work closely with contractors building relay stations or other facilities to insure that broadcasts can be laid down under almost any conditions to target areas which have been projected as being of importance by policy planners. Maintenance and operation of such a system requires persistence and technical agility, for in areas where jamming is still practiced changing frequencies must be employed and signals beamed in from relay stations at different locations to prevent blockage of signals. The United States is in a more difficult geographic location from a propagation viewpoint to broadcast throughout the world than is the Soviet Union. Voice broadcasts must be heaviest in the morning or early evening when people are home to listen, but it is at these times that reception is poorest. Periods of poor reception make the job of the engineering manager more demanding and difficult and increase the importance of his role to the Broadcasting Service. He relays each day to the VOA deputy assistant director (program) the nature of propagation conditions and the quality of reception on the preceding day so that the regional divisions and the Worldwide English Division can know how well their messages are getting through. The Voice of America's political and technological limitations must be minimized, its political and technological potentials maximized, and its political and technological planning synthesized if the Broadcasting Service is to make its full contribution in support of American foreign policy.

THE PRESS PUBLICATIONS SERVICE (IPS): NEWSMAN TO THE WORLD

Although the Broadcasting Service because of the Voice of America is sometimes considered the "most glamorous" of the media services, the Press and Publications Service (IPS) is certainly the "most colorful," its "newspaper-type" personnel writing and editing a variety of products unmatched by any other media service. IPS operates with 420 staff members in Washington (about 95 per cent of whom are Civil Service), assisted by 24 American and 326 local employees overseas (most assigned to the IPS Regional Service Centers).[9] Among its many products are the Wireless File, which pumps approximately 10,000 words daily of governmental news to 119 monitoring posts abroad; *America Illustrated*, the slick *Life*-like publication addressed to the Soviet Union; and *Problems of Communism*, a bimonthly periodical featuring reprints of scholarly articles on communism. Much of the material appearing in USIS post publications abroad also originates in IPS. Until

1960, the Press and Publications Service was headed by a director and deputy director, both policy-oriented, with administration and operations standing in the wings and often not closely related to policy and plans. Since the reorganization at that time, the director (as an assistant director of USIA) has two top assistants, a deputy director (editorial) and a deputy director (operations). Functioning under the deputy director (editorial) are the Policy and Columns Staff and three divisions: the Central Services Division, the Publications Division, and the Field Services Division. The Policy and Columns Staff maintains policy guidance relations with the Office of Policy and Research, relays policy guidance throughout IPS, and prepares signed columns to be carried by the Wireless File to the field, both as an indication of the "policy line" and also for distribution or publication. The Central Services Division, functioning through a News Branch, a Features Branch, and a Pictures Branch, prepares news material for the Wireless File, special features or commentary for air or sea-pouch transmission, takes or obtains pictures of personalities or events, and gathers cartoons on political or cultural topics. The Publications Division prepares *America Illustrated* and *America*, similar but separate magazines for the Soviet Union and Poland; writes or contracts for the writing of pamphlets and supports post periodicals; edits *El Hayat*, similar to *America Illustrated* but in Arabic for Near East sales and distribution; edits *Problems of Communism*; and prepares *Topic*, the French-English magazine addressed to Africa since 1966. It took over the preparation of flat paper exhibits, used by USIS posts, in 1967. The Field Services Division, with its area branches, paralleling the Agency's area offices, adapts Central Services Division materials to regional needs and also writes news and feature material in response to regional needs or individual post requests. Functioning under the deputy director (operations) are the Communications and Photo Services Division, the Printing Division, and the executive director of IPS who heads an administrative staff. The Communications and Photo Services Division is responsible for technical operation of the communications system serving the IPS Wireless File and for sending and receiving administrative and policy messages serving the Agency as a whole. It also produces picture reprints for all field requests or Agency needs; for example, it made 60,000 reprints of pictures of Cuban missile sites in 1962. The Printing Division contracts for printing of pamphlets or periodicals in the United States and operates three overseas Regional Service Centers, which print USIA publications with area or country distribution—often those prepared at USIS posts. Budget, personnel, and management responsibilities are coordinated by the executive officer of IPS and his staff.

The Press and Publications Service differs from the Voice of America in its coverage of news. If the Voice "must" speak on every important news event and put out a well-rounded broadcast, IPS covers only events of direct political value. It has the option of saying nothing, or of holding back until facts from the most reliable sources are in, though it is normally not silent for long. There are usually favorable aspects for the United States in almost any situation, though the total balance may be unfavorable. Like the Voice, IPS is concerned with credibility, takes pains to be factual and to quote all sides of policy arguments both domestic and international. The pseudonyms of some of its columnists or cartoonists whose work appears in foreign newspapers are as well known to readers as the voices of Broadcasting Service announcers and newscasters are to listeners. Because IPS is farther from the overseas scene and less sensitive to public-opinion pressures abroad, the Press and Publications Service, without policy guidance, would tend to pursue a somewhat harder policy line than the area offices (more closely linked to field posts) might wish. Field officers are usually anxious not to alienate those with whom they work directly. Although the Press and Publications Service might be too inflexible in approach, and the field too flexible, policy guidance from the Office of Policy and Research and the area offices to IPS and to the field tends to be a moderating influence which helps insure that products conform to current American foreign policy objectives and to broader long-term goals.

Direction of the Press and Publication Service

In many ways, the duties and activities of the director of the Press and Publications Service parallel those of the director of the Broadcasting Service, but the programs supervised by the former are visual rather than "audio" presentations. The deputy director (editoral) performs a policy function somewhat similar to that of the deputy assistant director (program) of the Broadcasting Service, and the deputy director (operations) oversees necessary technical services for IPS as the engineering manager does for the Voice of America. The director of the Press and Publications Service attends the Agency director's weekly staff meeting and reviews many proposed IPS projects after they have been checked in the area offices before they are forwarded to the media content officers in the Office of Policy and Research or to Deputy Agency Director Akers for final clearance. The director of IPS also travels overseas to visit IPS installations (Regional Service Centers) and USIS posts to get firsthand information about printing problems and the usefulness or shortcomings of Press and Publications Service products. Like the director of IBS, his view must be broad and his time perspective long range, though he will be consulted during resolution of the more difficult day-to-day problems. He is IPS's voice to the director or deputy director, to the deputy director (policy and research), to the area directors, to the other media directors, and to the assistant agency director for administration. In return, he is their voice to his colleagues in IPS. He chairs the weekly staff meeting of his media, held at 11 A.M. on Thursdays and running for an hour, attended by his deputies, the division chiefs, and the executive officer of IPS. Problems can be raised here which may be carried by the director to the top Agency leadership, to an area office director, or to one of his peers—the director of one of the other media services. During his absence on an overseas inspection tour, the deputy director (editorial) takes over his intra-agency policy relationships and the deputy director (operations), his administrative responsibilities.

The deputy director (editorial) is the IPS "policy expert," constantly consulted during the day by division and branch chiefs, or even by writers directly. It is also his job to be a judge and reviewer of IPS products after the fact, to talk over with staff members their policy deviations or their use of inadequate research sources or faulty logic. Less tied down on the daily firing line than his division chiefs, and somewhat more distant from their personnel, he can make objective suggestions which keep staff members "on their toes." He does chair the IPS daily editorial meeting, held for half an hour at 9:30 A.M. The briefing is done by a member of the Policy and Columns Staff with the "duty" for the day. The briefer of the day will come into USIA headquarters between 6:30 and 7 A.M., happily escaping the morning traffic but finding the building a lonely place. He checks the "house file" (all the material fed by ticker from the News Branch of the Central Services Division to the regional branches of the Field Services Division), carefully scans the early edition of the *New York Times*, and goes over more quickly the *Washington Post* and the *Baltimore Sun*. He may consult with the "cable editor" in the news room to see if important cables from posts or IPS correspondents have come in overnight. By this time, it is near eight o'clock, and he is likely to go up to the Office of Policy and Research to listen to the morning CBS news roundup and to get any suggestions the area policy guidance officers may have. He returns to his office about 8:30 A.M. to draft his notes for the nine-thirty IPS editorial meeting. At this session, about twenty-five persons are present, including members of the Policy and Columns Staff and division and branch chiefs of the Central Services and Field Services Divisions. The meeting is primarily for briefing, though there may be comments or policy questions after the briefer reads his notes. Any problems that cannot be settled immediately are checked out with the Office of Policy and Research after the meeting. The edited briefing notes for the meeting are then mimeographed and distributed widely (108 copies), not only within IPS, but also to area country desks in USIA, and to some country desks and to all public affairs advisors in the Department of State's regional bureaus. The fast guidance function supervised closely by the deputy director (editorial) has been stressed, even though it consumes a reasonably small portion of his time. IPS is particularly concerned with fast guidance, because it is responsible for the production of major elements in the Wireless File, which actually serves to provide field posts with a thorough daily policy briefing. If much of the deputy director's time is taken up in relations meeting the daily needs of the Policy and Columns Staff, the Central Services Division, and the Field Services Division, he still is interested in the slower-moving products of these divisions and those of the Publications Division.

The deputy director (operations) is the IPS technical services and administrative expert, immersed in problems of communications or photo reproduction, personnel, and budget. Like the director of IPS, he may travel to the field, where he inspects the communications system or the printing facilities of the Regional Service Centers. He works closely with the executive officer of IPS who is specifically engaged in facing budget, personnel, and management problems. The deputy director (operations) and his administrative staff have many dealings with program coordinators and area office directors, for IPS receives and negotiates approximately $3.6 million each year from the area budgets for products and services requested by the field, approved by the area office directors, and assented to by the Agency Program Review Committee. Although IPS would prefer to carry these items in its own budget for the sake of convenience and economy of time, the deputy director (operations) realizes that what appears to be a lot of lost motion between the area offices and the media services in determining what services will be provided yields a better decision than could be obtained through direct field relations by the individual media. IPS does receive copies of field requests addressed to the area offices and on the basis of these costs-out what the budget requirements will be. It is these figures which are discussed and modified as the budget is firmed up by the area offices. Important as was the installation of the new IPS teletype system for the Wireless File, which upped transmission from thirty-five to sixty words a minute, this item had to be sold by IPS to the area directors because the costs of installing the new system were carried in the area office budgets. The area offices apparently were slow to accept the change, though they recognized its importance, because they feared it would mean cutbacks in their regular programs. In connection with the work of the Program Review Committee, which passes on the Press and Publications Service budget as well as that of other Agency elements, some concern was expressed in IPS about the fact that committee membership is drawn from top Agency personnel who because of many other responsibilities are often not able to attend the session when a particular media budget is being considered, thus leaving major decisions—vital to a media service—to "subordinate" staff members. Because of the specialized nature of jobs in the Press and Publications Service, it is a haven for Civil Service employees and still provides negligible opportunities for using Foreign Service Career Reserves in Washington for headquarters duty. In 1963, it had only six FSCR "slots," and one FSCR serving on detail above the approved IPS complement. By 1967, FSCR's numbered twenty-five. Civil Service IPS personnel believe that continuity is important for most IPS jobs and that FSCR's often lack the necessary writing experience. The general attitude among IPS civil servants is that members of the USIA foreign service are "jacks of all trades" and that "specialists" rather than "generalists" are required to meet IPS personnel needs. Some feel that too many Civil Service personnel must give up their specialty and assume administrative duties if they want promotions in IPS, thus sacrificing their writing abilities; this is coupled with the belief that satisfactory careers with promotion opportunities should be available in "specialties." Chances for promotion may be more limited within the Agency for civil servants than for members of the foreign service. While training programs of short duration are available for IPS Civil Service personnel, opportunities for longer periods of training are not considered equal to those for Foreign Service Officers or Foreign Service Career Reserves. There is a belief that wider use of Civil Service personnel as deputy directors of area offices, media services, and other Agency elements would help provide a better career ladder for civil servants than is now available in USIA. Although technical operation developments in IPS have a less obvious relationship to policy than those affecting the Broadcasting Service, the deputy director (operations) parallels the engineering manager of the Broadcasting Service in his interest in technical and organizational changes to improve the conduct of Agency programs. Speedier transmission by the new teleprinters, the building of modern regional printing plants in Manila, Beirut, and Mexico City, and the availability of cheap plastic printing plates which can be widely distributed overseas do have an impact on Agency activities supporting American foreign policy.

The Chief of the Policy and Columns Staff of IPS

The chief of the Policy and Columns Staff of IPS is the main policy link of IPS with the Office of Policy and Research, paralleling in this respect the chief of the Policy Application Staff in the Broadcasting Service. His staff, however, is organized by functional interest (which by chance may lead to some area specialization). The age and experience of his colleagues makes him first among five rather senior "equals," whereas the Policy Application Staff of IBS, clearly organized by area responsibility, is more junior in rank. The difference in rank and experience stems from the "columns" responsibility of the IPS staff, which requires experienced writers, experts in subject-matter fields and related policy. These men write political editorials under bylines known on five continents but not in the United States. They are Civil Service personnel. The members of the Policy Application Staff in IBS are young Foreign Service Career Reserves, with experience in their regions of responsibility. They provide policy liaison but draft no product.

Members of the Policy and Columns Staff follow fast guidance activities of USIA closely, taking a leading role in the IPS daily editorial meeting as already indicated. In addition, they attend the noon (12:30 P.M.) briefing by IOP's deputy chief of policy guidance *en masse*, making IPS and the Office of Policy and Research the only two elements of the Agency with multiple representation at this session. On the basis of this briefing, and with the help of the classified "IOP Meeting Notes," a Policy and Columns Staff member then prepares the "IPS Noon Notes," which carry the title "Periscope" and are written for IPS alone and distributed only within IPS and to the Agency director, executive assistant, deputy director, and deputy director for policy and research. Group attendance by the Policy and Columns Staff at the IOP noon briefing is an expression of its collegial organization and a mark of its importance in contributing daily policy guidance to the field in columns prepared by its members for the IPS Wireless File. When President John F. Kennedy made his now famous "Family of Man" speech at the University of Maine, the Wireless File carried the speech in full, followed by a 550-word editorial, written by a member of the Policy and Columns Staff, approving of the speech and clarifying the points made by the President. The editorial, useful to personnel at USIS posts and other members of the embassy staff, was distributed with other Wireless File material to private members of the American community abroad and given to foreign correspondents at the United Nations and newsmen in cities abroad to be used as background in their stories. It was also made readily available to foreign newspaper editors with the thought that they would use it as background for their comment or use it in its original form in their own editorial columns. Most verbatim use of such "columns" is by smaller foreign newspapers outside the metropolitan centers, just as understaffed village weekly papers in America make use of unattributed "boilerplate" copy from assorted sources.

Three regular columns are prepared by members of the Policy and Columns Staff for the Wireless File, leaving several days free for special columns like the coverage of the "Family of Man" speech. In addition, two regular columns go overseas by air pouch each weekend. One or two times a week, the Wireless File carries "Behind the Curtain," 600 words or so of comment on Soviet Union affairs, perhaps dealing with some aspect of the Sino-Soviet split. Somewhat irregularly, the "file" carries "An Economic Letter from the United States," for a number of years concerned only with private and commercial economics but more recently also treating government economic developments. The same staff member drafts "Economic Developments," a weekend air-pouch column, which has always emphasized government economic matters. Thursday the Wireless File sends "The Week in the United States," which covers domestic political developments, possibly treating the problem of reapportionment in state legislatures or civil rights. The Friday "file" has "The World Today," based on policy points in speeches or news conferences by high government officials during the week, sometimes stressing an Agency theme, like disarmament or the United Nations. A second column of "The World Today" may fill in one of the free days during particularly eventful weeks. A column of "Americana" (more cultural and less policy directed) written by a member of the Policy and Columns Staff is forwarded abroad by air pouch once a week. Columns are not just based on events seen as important from the United States, but represent topics which field posts feel need to be dealt with in their countries, often determined by discussions of USIS "local" employees with foreign editors or other opinion molders.

All the columns are statements of American policy, without saying so in so many words. The Policy and Columns Staff members are well informed on relevant policy matters, receiving the essential flow of information of both USIA and the Department of State. They have ready access to materials and information from other government agencies through the special advisors in the Office of Policy and Research. On day-to-day matters, handling *ad hoc* queries from the Central Services Division or the Field Services Division, the chief or one of the staff members checks out matters with IOP or sometimes calls State direct, but would inform IOP of such a contact. Members of the Policy and Columns Staff have not been overseas, at least not on Agency business. Occasional short-term visits to posts would probably be helpful. Others in IPS do travel abroad and help communicate to the field the broad use which can be made of the columns and bring back suggested topics to be treated. The members of the Policy and Columns Staff feel that their analyses have uses beyond policy statements or handouts to the press, that they should be more widely distributed to leaders, study groups, and schools abroad. Although service on the staff would be a valuable experience for

Foreign Service Career Reserve Officers, it might be difficult to find very many officers with writing and research ability, well oriented in Washington affairs, and interested in such an assignment.

The Chief of the Central Services Division of IPS

In a very real sense, the Central Services Division of IPS stands in the same relationship to the regional branches of the Field Services Divisions as the News and Current Affairs Staff of the Broadcasting Service does to VOA's regional divisions. The chief of the Central Services Division guides a News Branch (handling news, background stories, and speech texts for the daily Wireless File), a Features Branch (dealing with less timely features, byline articles, and analyses sent mostly by air pouch though sometimes by wireless), and a Pictures Branch (which produces photographs and political cartoons, reproduced after clearance from domestic or foreign commercial press sources).

News and features are handled by branches at IPS rather than by divisions as at the Voice. This is indicative of the difference in size of the two media services, VOA having almost three times as many domestic employees as IPS. The Central Services Division of the Press and Publications Service produces news stories, features, and photos intended for worldwide or multi-region distribution through the regional branches of the Field Services Division. In fact, almost every news or feature story is used by at least one of the regional branches; half, by two or three of the branches; and one quarter by all five. The regional branches of the Field Services Division produce specialized materials for their own regions, initiating approximately 40 per cent of the news stories and a somewhat smaller percentage of features. Until July, 1963, the regional branches produced most of their own pictures; since that time photographs have been centralized in the Pictures Branch of the Central Services Division. On a normal weekday, the Central Services Division prepares materials, the regional branches of the Field Services Division determine which stories will go on the individual regional Wireless Files or by pouch to their respective areas (and how much rewriting is required for area adaptation), and members of USIS field staffs with press responsibilities in turn determine how and to whom the stories will be distributed. During the week, News Branch personnel do not see what happens to their copy in the Field Services Division before it is sent to the field. The finished products go direct to the "wire room" to be teletyped overseas. On Sundays a single "joint file" is prepared by the News Branch, with the aid of some Field Services Division personnel, and goes direct to all USIS posts. There is no Saturday file unless there is a major international crisis. In 1963, a "joint file" was made both Saturday and Sunday. Wireless material moves in English and is translated in the field for use.

The News Branch, normally known as the "news room," produces information for a purpose, stories which can stand on their own as political news, which must be credible but also be propaganda. This requires selectivity and emphasis, a choice of subjects and consideration of what to stress. Even news can show opinion by the topics it covers. Features Branch commentary is similar to newspaper editorials. News Branch personnel often react instinctively to developments without daily reference to policy papers, sometimes before any specific government-wide policy has been formulated in a particular situation. Their products go by "house ticker" both to the regional branches of the Field Services Division and to the news room of the Voice of America. A large portion of news stories and commentary, after review by the Office of Policy and Research, also go to the Foreign Correspondents Center of USIA in New York City, operated by the Office of Policy and Research for the convenience of foreign newsmen, many of whom cover the United Nations. The IPS news room has a central desk and a Washington desk. The central desk edits materials fed to it by the Washington desk before news room material goes on teletype. The central desk handles materials from the private wire services, from IPS reporters in New York and Paris, from "stringers" across America and throughout the world, and from the field posts—USIS Geneva and USIS Saigon being the most important among the posts as IPS reporters. The Washington desk has two reporters at the White House; one each covering the Department of State, the Department of Defense, and Congress; and three subject-matter specialists, one dealing with science, another with economic affairs, and a third with civil-rights developments. Since the Broadcasting Service has no Washington reporters, all of its stories are teletyped to the Voice of America.

The Features Branch, as its name indicates, prepares feature stories. It also gathers materials which have appeared in American periodicals, obtaining copyright clearance before making them available to the field. Personnel of the Features Branch often write about communist affairs, dealing with events behind the Iron Curtain, the tone based more on past experience on the job than on policy guidances. In addition, they prepare general features on a wide range of topics, including science, cultural matters, labor affairs, and women's activities. While the articles dealing with communism are among the most hard hitting of the Agency's products, the features on the other topics are at the other extreme, sometimes not appearing to be policy related. The branch prepares a weekly cultural column, a weekly science column, and a monthly labor packet. These may include articles or speeches by government officials. Certain of the features selected from periodicals or prepared especially for the Features Branch are considered "musts" for the regional branches of the Field Services Division. During the Johnson administration, a piece by John Roche, as a top White House aide, or by Orville Freeman, as secretary of agriculture, may be solicited and distributed. Many feature stories are illustrated by photographs secured through the Pictures Branch. Features discussing fashions or sports, and special calendars, produced at an earlier time, were taboo by 1963. Viewed as having peripheral policy impact, they lacked sufficient priority for survival when funds were low. Feature stories on the Los Angeles Airport, the domed stadium in Houston, the New York Thruway, or the old Waldorf-Astoria, though of interest to readers overseas, are less likely to be approved for use in 1968 than they would have been in the Agency's "full and fair picture of America" days under Allen. Nonetheless, after the old Metropolitan Opera House was torn down, to be replaced by the Lincoln Center in September, 1966, *America Illustrated* featured "the old Met" on its front cover and carried a special feature "on that beloved institution . . . to capture in words and pictures the glittering productions, dramatic moments and soaring voices that fuse together truly great opera."[10]

The Pictures Branch of the Central Services Division now employs about sixty-five people, three of whom are Foreign Service Career Reserves. It prepares major picture stories occasionally and shorter picture sequences weekly, plus taking many individual photographs and getting permissions to reprint political cartoons. Three quarters of a million prints of its pictures went to overseas posts in 1963. The number was reduced by 1967 since prints are no longer broadcast so widely. Instead, a monthly *Photo Bulletin* is prepared, with a photo story laid out in it as a prototype for field use. It also includes random shots, perhaps on American science or on the war in Vietnam. Posts can order prints they want by number and title. Photos of foreign leaders or students visiting the United States are sent to appropriate countries. The Fast Media Section of the Pictures Branch covers presidential trips abroad or speeches in the United States. It also takes shots of visiting foreign dignitaries. A Slow Media Section prepares pictures, stories, and sequences good for use at any time. Some of these may be human-interest pictures of the President with members of his family or facets of the American scene. The Post Servicing Section processes post requests for special picture coverage. For example, the USIA post in Japan might ask for pictures and a story concerning a Japanese student at George Washington University. Until the pictures function was centralized, acquisitions were sought by the individual regional branches of the Field Services Division. This is now handled through the Research and Acquisitions Section of the Pictures Branch. It also begs, buys, or borrows pictures at the request of USIS regional publications overseas, like *Spain* in India or *Free World* in Asia. *Life* and *Look* often allow USIA to use pictures overseas. There is no central acquisition of still picture rights in USIA as a whole; the Motion Picture and Television Service and the Information Center Service acquire photos for their own use. Until January, 1967, there was a Graphic Section of the Pictures Branch which produced cartoon series; for example, "Little Moe," "Visit to America," "True Tales," "Sports U.S.A.," and "It's a Fact." It also did special cartoon books. One on space activities was done at the request of the area office director for Africa and funded by the National Aeronautics and Space Administration.

Policy guidance problems may vary for the different components and programs of the Central Services Division. News moves fast. Policy guidance sometimes is slow; the government may not have made up its mind, or a problem may not be ripe for decision. There is the unexpected event that could not have been foreseen. Following President Kennedy's Friday assassination, the private wire services carried comments on Lee Harvey Oswald's past relationships with Communists. The news room made a conscious decision to omit this from its releases, with the concurrence of what was then the Office of Policy (now Policy and Research), until it could get reports from official government sources. By Monday it began to report such discussions in carefully attributed fashion. Participation in the daily editorial meeting of IPS usually provides all the guidance needed by the news room during the day. The news room considers a presidential speech good policy guidance; even though the speech may be directed toward a domestic audience, the President's advisers are aware that his words will be heard round the world. Occasionally the news room is caught in an interagency discrepancy or policy difference, with elements of State and Defense releasing statements on a situation which are or appear to be in conflict. Directors of area offices may get involved in questions concerning news coverage. This is because they are sensitive to "area dislikes"; they may worry that USIS will be tossed out of a country—as it was for a time in Indonesia. Sometimes policy guidance serves as a useful buffer between a field officer and his clientele or the Central Services Division and the field. A field post may request, because of personal interest or pressure from one of its contacts in the country, a story of information that would be costly in time and has low policy priority. The Policy and Columns Staff or the Office of Policy and Research can say "No"; the "heat" is taken off the USIS officer, and the Central Services Division has done the best it can. There may be a difference between what the policy people want done by the Central Services Division and what seems likely to be useful overseas. Indonesians could not be interested in the Hungarian revolution of 1956. The Features Branch can make better use of the five themes than the News Branch, but it is always hard to write theme-supporting materials that can really be used worldwide. It is not even easy to prepare a feature for use in an entire region. The Pictures Branch can emphasize pictures on topics supporting Agency themes or policies. Photos also indicate policy by "tone" — whether favorable or unfavorable. They are important to communicate policy to illiterates and sometimes have a great psychological impact even on those who can read. Facetiously, it has been said that 90 per cent of the time no policy advice is required from outside the Division for a particular story or picture; 5 per cent of the time, policy guidance is sought and not obtained; 5 per cent of the time, policy guidance is given though not wanted. The chief who supervises the varied policy-oriented activities of the Central Services Division is likely to be one of the small number of Foreign Service Career Reserve Officers on the Division personnel complement. He would probably believe that more Press and Publications Service personnel need field experience and that more Foreign Career Reserve Officers need Washington tours in IPS. Perhaps, since present "bodies" are hard to "change," the Agency could move to develop over a period of time new types of personnel with a better understanding of both headquarters and field requirements—as it probably can if a measure like the Hays bill (in limbo by late 1967) is ever passed.

The Chief of the Publications Division of IPS

If putting out the Wireless File makes the Press and Publications Service a "fast media," tied closely to day-to-day variations in policy guidance, the varied products of the Publications Division perform "slow media" functions—pursuing stable though distinct "policy lines." The chief of the Publications Division provides policy and administrative guidance for a periodical and pamphlet program ranging from subtle soft-sell to blunt hard-sell techniques, from stressing what is right with America to emphasizing what is wrong with communism. The America Illustrated Branch of the Division prepares and edits monthly the Polish *America* and Russian *America Illustrated*—the latter next to the Voice of America USIA's best-known information instrument. The Arabic Magazine Staff is responsible for the publication of *Al Hayat fi America*, similar to *America Illustrated* in many ways, but bimonthly and addressed to people living in the Arabic Peninsula; the Africa Magazine Staff is responsible for *Topic*, prepared for

African readers. An executive editor is responsible for *Problems of Communism*, scholarly in appearance but hard hitting in its approach to communism; a Pamphlets Staff prepares a host of brief publications, with topics ranging from the philosophic and cultural to those forthrightly political. Each issue of *America* or *America Illustrated* takes three months to publish; some pamphlets first printed ten years ago are still requested by field posts, and are relatively timeless. The pace of the Publications Division is quite different from that of the news room. Although its instruments might qualify it as a "mass media," its audience is small, consisting mostly of intellectuals, writers, teachers, artists, and young people. It is not the size of the target audience but the present or potential influence of its members which makes Publications Division products important to USIA.

America Illustrated is the only Western publication, except for the British quarterly *Anglia,* which the Soviet government allows to be sold on Russian newsstands. *America Illustrated* provides for its readers their only American written information on the United States. Under terms of the agreement providing for the exchange of *Soviet Life* and *America Illustrated* (both "beautifully done"), the periodicals must be nonpolitical and free of polemics. Neither would discuss the U-2 incident, Cuban missiles, or the temporary detention by the Soviet Union of Professor Frederick C. Barghoorn of Yale, a one-time USIA employee. Each operates on the thesis that you cannot convince people by insulting them. As a result, *America Illustrated* or *America*— whether in the Russian or Polish—may stress the freedom of American artists, without commenting negatively on Soviet or Polish institutions. The emphasis on policy-oriented products by the Kennedy administration had little impact on *America Illustrated* or *America* editorial policy. They continued scholarly articles on the American political system, on the role of the President, the Congress, the courts, capitalism, and the American concept of freedom. In an issue of that period,[11] J. Robert Oppenheimer contributed the article "Science and the Freedom of Inquiry"; another author wrote about freedom in America, from colonial days to the present. Indicating new opportunities for Negroes in America, color photos from *Life* were used in an article "Designed to Dazzle," in which Gordon Parks's camera captured "the chiseled features and slim elegance of his wife, Liz Campbell, high-fashion mannequin for New York's top model agency." "Registered Nurse," a series of articles on American workers, stressed the same theme. Articles on a Soviet basketball team touring America, the space travels of an

American astronaut, the process of creating a television star, vaccine for trachoma, contemporary American painting, young American designers, and rural American literature were among the twenty picture features in a representative issue. The front cover was a colorful shot of the "rides" at the Indiana State Fair; the back, a shot of the Soviet and American women's basketball teams in action.

Articles tend to portray America at its best, often dealing with situations which pose problems for Soviet or Polish leaders. If wheat is in short supply in the Soviet Union, an article on American agricultural abundance is likely to appear in *America Illustrated*. If Polish leaders resist production of consumer goods, *America* indicates the wide range of items available at low prices to American consumers. Since 1956, issues of *America Illustrated* (or *America*) have not been cleared by the Soviet (or Polish) government before publication. This lenience in allowing the United States to stress its positive accomplishments in what are their problem areas is indicative of the slow changes in Soviet and Polish society and government which give hope for better future relations. Soviet insistence on reciprocity of sales, and return of copies of *America Illustrated* when *Soviet Life* does not sell well in the United States, indicates present limits on American-Soviet relations. Poland does not insist on such reciprocity. Returned copies are mailed free to persons on a mailing list nurtured by the American embassy, some receiving copies regularly and others only when articles of particular interest to them appear. The editor of *America Illustrated*, the branch chief, learns what topics to emphasize or what will be of interest to readers by traveling in the Soviet Union and Poland. Much is also learned from the embassies in Moscow and Warsaw. The questions asked of American guides accompanying touring exhibits prepared by the Exhibits Division of the Information Center Service provide valuable guidelines. The area office in USIA may also make useful suggestions. These sources really constitute the policy guidances to *America Illustrated*, very little of the day-to-day fast guidance of the Office of Policy and Research being relevant. The staff of *America Illustrated* generally believes that "the most purposeful propaganda may be the most purposeless," that "to strike a blow for freedom" is not likely to accomplish Agency objectives. This understanding within USIA also provides hope for better relations with the Soviet Union and Poland in the future.

Al Hayat fi America follows the same type of policy line as *America Illustrated*. *Al Hayat* is addressed to an audience a little more neutral in the Cold War; it deals in general themes and ideas, supporting the United Nations and discussing problems of unity in American history, hoping that the relevance will be clear to Arabic readers. No "Berlin Wall" type material is used. *America Illustrated* has more opportunity to feature visits of American personalities to eastern Europe, but *Al Hayat* does the same for the Arab world, though the flow of traffic each way is far less. Just as *America Illustrated* provides reviews of American books, which include a summary of major ideas, so does *Al Hayat* for its Arabic audience. Both aim to create a hunger for American books which might lead to the establishment of book-exchange programs. *America Illustrated* for the Soviet Union was initiated in September, 1956, as the breakup of bipolarity in the Cold War first became evident. *America* in Poland and *Al Hayat* were not started until 1959. Many of the articles for all three magazines are staff-written, though some are done on contract by well-known academic or literary figures, and a lesser number are reprints from private American publications.

Problems of Communism, with its 21,000 copies in English and 7,100 in Spanish, is aimed worldwide at a small intellectual elite. An additional 5,000 copies are sold in the United States—only to American citizens. It is clearly anticommunist, though often academic in tone. In introducing articles on "The Persistence of Stalinism" and "Notes on a Somber Journey," written by a German journalist and a refugee from East Germany, the editor writes: "Mired in economic difficulties and its people apathetic and despondent under the oppression of one of the most reactionary of the East European regimes, the 'German Democratic Republic' presents perhaps the sorriest spectacle in all the Communist world." An essay-review of Ilya Ehrenburg's autobiography by the chairman of the Department of Slavic Languages and Literatures at Yale University is more scholarly in approach, and perhaps more typical. A three-book review by the managing editor of the *Slavic Review*, a professor of Russian history at the University of Washington, covers books dealing with "dilemmas of progress in Tsarist Russia," "social democracy and the St. Petersburg labor movement, 1885-1897," and "the rise of democracy in pre-Revolutionary Russia." Under the heading "Chinese Communism, Past and Present," another professor reviews four books on Chinese foreign and cultural policy or another on the Russo-Chinese borderland—"zone of peaceful contact or potential conflict?"[12] One special supplement of *Problems of Communism* is an article on "The Regime and the Intellectuals: A Window on Party Politics," well footnoted.[13] *Problems of Communism*, like *America Illus-*

trated, America, and *Al Hayat,* is reviewed by the Office of Policy and Research before publication.

Pamphlets on a wide variety of subjects are also turned out by the Pamphlets Staff of the Publications Division. Some are reprints of articles appearing in the Division's other publications. Others are original pieces. Pamphlets are more "durable" than news copy. They emphasize the Agency themes more than in the period before 1961, liaison being maintained between the staff and the media content officers in the Office of Policy and Research. Pamphlets were political and polemical with cultural topics reduced severely in the Kennedy administration, the period of Agency policy leadership by Murrow and Sorensen. Articles by Clinton Rossiter which first appeared in *America Illustrated* a number of years ago are still in demand, though they have no direct connection with any current Agency theme. While cultural pamphlets were not pushed overseas for a time, the posts kept a stock of them on hand and met requests for them as they arose. Such pamphlets have been used more under Director Marks than they were under Murrow. Local governments often prohibit the distribution of anti-Soviet material. Such "anti" pamphlets may have wide distribution in Iran, but few are used in neighboring Afghanistan. No pamphlets are distributed in the Soviet Union; there is no USIS post there. Sample "pilot model" copies of pamphlets are sent to posts in English. They can be adapted or translated by the post, with omission of some discussions or pictures. For example, no photos of cows being slaughtered appear in agricultural pamphlets distributed in India. Pamphlets are usually printed locally by the posts or in one of the three IPS Regional Service Centers overseas. A pamphlet which went well in Indonesia and other countries visited by Robert Kennedy, when he was attorney general, dealt with fallacies in foreign views of the United States. Where he had visited, the demand was large. Elsewhere, the usage was relatively small.

The Chief of the Field Services Division of IPS

The chief of the Field Services Division is responsible for directing five area branches (corresponding to the Agency's area offices and the Broadcasting Service's regional divisions) which adapt materials prepared by the Central Services Division of IPS to make such products more effective in their regions or even in individual countries. The chief of the Division participates in the daily IPS editorial meeting and holds a Division staff meeting weekly on Wednesday afternoon. He works closely with his branch chiefs in communicating policy guidance and considering suggestions for area adaptation of guidances. Personnel in the Field Services Division edit fast news for the regional wireless files and initiate feature stories requested by the field or get others to write them. They are "adapters" of Central Service Division news and features. They are "servants" of the field on requests for individualized news or features, photo or pamphlet coverage; and for back-up material for post publications. Of the work done by the Central Services Division, 30 to 40 per cent is used on the regional files or transmitted by pouch word for word, while 20 per cent is edited a little, a word changed here and there, a sentence deleted or added. Between 40 and 50 per cent of the material forwarded by the Division's area branches represents major change or modification of the original product, perhaps an entirely new story. Five days a week the area branches feed news stories, commentary, and "backgrounders" to the pneumatic tubes leading to the "wireless room," from which they are teletyped overseas. To Europe go about 8,000 words every weekday during a three-hour transmission; to Latin America, the Near East and South Asia, and the Far East 10,000 words each, with a four-hour transmission; to Africa, 15,000 in six hours, almost equally divided between English and French. A special two-hour file goes to eastern Europe; a separate file by land-line to Ottawa, and a third is broadcast in English to Rio de Janeiro and picked up by five other Latin American posts. Each file has a weekly amount of transmission time allotted; if the time allocation is exceeded one day, an effort is made to cut back the next; in normal times, the area branches must conform. During a crisis, an overage can be covered through special transfer of funds. On weekends or holidays, transmission of the "limited joint file" is the responsibility of the Central Services Division; it is usually 5,000 words or less per day and often can be transmitted in an hour. Requests to the Field Services Division from the field are channeled through the Department of State's communications system, linked directly with USIA headquarters. Products sent out to meet such requests would normally be sent air or sea pouch.

Presidential speeches or a statement by the secretary of state would be sent to the field complete, without change, by all the regional wireless files. A story on African delegates to the United Nations would probably be carried only on the African file, because it would mean little to a Latin American or other area audience. The Near East and South Asia Branch, on the other hand, has sent material on Chinese attacks along the Indian border to the other area branches for filing, in order to build support for the American policy in defense of India.

News and feature stories can be tailored to individual regions by changing the voice quoted, by the examples used, and by taking into account local attitudes. If a feature story supports development and modernization, the Latin American Branch would relate it to the Alliance for Progress. This would not be appropriate elsewhere. On the same theme, the Africa Branch would stress education, which is the present stage and emphasis in African development. In the Latin American Branch, the policy line might be self-help and industrialization. In Africa Branch news stories or features, the point can be made that the United States does not want the Cold War to spread to Africa, that it believes in self-determination for the people of Africa. Here American hopes and African desires are parallel. If Africans are convinced of American sincerity on this matter in Africa, the Africa Branch may have a better chance through news and feature stories to make American policies toward Cuba and in Vietnam more palatable to Africans.

The Field Services Division and the Wireless File are not alone in telling the American story overseas. The Field Services Division does not seek to duplicate the work of Associated Press, United Press International, Reuters, or Agence France Presse. The private press services cannot afford to carry, or are not interested in transmitting, to Europe the full texts of a 5,000-word speech by Secretary of Defense McNamara, which can be placed in papers with a circulation of twelve million readers. In some instances, USIA will provide full texts to AP or UPI overseas for release by their representatives. Advance copies of speeches can be sent to the posts for placement, and may be in the foreign press within an hour after a major speech is delivered. Even if the full texts are not printed, they are still useful. One Indian editor reads and files all such texts for ready reference, drawing upon them for his editorials concerning American foreign policy. Many others must do the same. Reuters and Agence France Presse do not represent an American point of view overseas. It is important that USIA provide foreign editors its own material "to place events in an American perspective." Frankly, USIA "refines what the conventional press services do, putting American policies and actions in a more favorable light." In assessing or improving the effectiveness of Central Services Division or Field Services Division products, the field posts and area offices have access to results of polls taken or studies prepared for the Research and Analysis Staff. A study in Brazil of radio, press, cartoons, motion pictures, and other Agency products, asking Brazilians facts about the United States or American policy and where they learned them, can be helpful. Reaction overseas to a widely publicized civil-rights event may be studied. USIA prepares and distributes materials that it believes will have a favorable impact. Later, if there appears to be no net reduction in opposition or less gain than anticipated, "some rethinking can be done" to improve the Agency approach the next time. Studies to determine whether overseas attitudes agree or differ with American policy can be used to adapt the tone of Central Services Division and Field Services Division products. Such studies are particularly valuable, because most employees of the Division are Civil Service personnel with little experience abroad. All of the branch chiefs of the Field Services Division have served overseas, but several are not members of the Foreign Service Career Reserve. They do make visits to the field. In the Field Services Division as elsewhere in the Press and Publications Service, there is a recognition of the problem of providing personnel with technical skills required in the media services and the field experience essential to better understanding of field post operations and foreign audiences.

Communications, Photo Services, and Printing

Communications, photo reproduction, and printing are essential to the conduct of Press and Publications Service functions. The Wireless File must be speeded to the field; the work of the Pictures Branch, multicopied to fill Central Services Division or Field Services Division requests; the orders for pamphlets and periodicals from the field must be filled; the overseas Regional Service Centers, supervised. The chief of the Communications and Photo Services Division and the chief of the Printing Division divide these tasks. The chief of the Communications Branch heads not only the teletype operation for the wireless files carrying unclassified material but also directs the handling of the Agency's administrative and policy traffic which is fed into or received through the Department of State's communications system. Liaison for air or sea-pouch communication of the Agency through State channels, however, is maintained by the Communications and Records Branch of the Agency's Office of Administration. The Broadcasting Service, as noted, also maintains separate communications facilities for its broadcasts. The Press and Publications Service assumes responsibility for Agency operational and policy communications because it has the "horses," the electrical equipment, to do the job. During the Office of War Information days in World War II, transmission of psychological messages was made through the Navy Department communications system to American embassies. When the war ended and the information function was transferred to State, a thirty-five-word-per-minute Morse code transmitter was installed to service information officers at about sixty posts, with qualified Morse operators at both ends of the line. About 1957, the Agency began converting to a sixty-word-per-minute teletypewriter system. By January, 1967, the wireless files to Europe and the Far East had been converted to one-hundred-word-per-minute transmissions as the Agency continued to take advantage of technical developments. The present method of transmission is an "open" system, does not use code, and carries no classified material. The Agency welcomes any outside "listeners" to the Wireless File; field communications staffs are normally made up mostly of foreign locals; sometimes contracts with foreign government communications systems are made for the pickup of Wireless File transmissions to USIS posts. Press material sometimes is moved by the diplomatic channel through State. This is a single-line channel which may have to be pre-empted for important State messages to or from the field. It can automatically stop a USIA transmission in mid-passage, hold it until the urgent State message is carried, and then resume transmission of USIA's story or operational message. Press materials are also sent through the multichannel Department of Defense system. Reception of file material at posts is assured, in spite of mechanical breakdown, by the installation of duplicate emergency equipment at each terminal.

Photo services since January, 1963, have been centralized for the entire Agency, with all developing and reproduction of photographs handled in a "photo lab" in the United States Auditor's Building. Although a picture file is maintained in the Central Services Division, the negative file is kept in the photo laboratory. It can reproduce pictures or cartoons in sizes matching postage stamps or up to forty by sixty inches. It reproduces "copy negatives," and it can print five hundred 5-inch-by-7-inch or 8-inch-by-10-inch prints from each negative. It turned out twenty thousand copy negatives and sixty thousand picture prints a month in 1963, mostly for field use. By 1967, use of the *Photo Bulletin* sharply reduced the number of prints shipped to the field, as copies of photos were forwarded primarily at post request. All of the USIA media services are on a quota basis for pictures, each having an assigned number of work units per month (a work unit figured at ten cents per man minute). Each type of work performed can be measured in these terms. Individual posts also have picture quotas.

The Printing Division is responsible for the operations of the Regional Service Centers in Beirut, Manila, and Mexico City, which are staffed primarily by local employees working under American supervisors. By these operations overseas, the Division saves the Agency salary costs, cuts shipping charges, and speeds service to the individual USIS posts. In November, 1963, the Office of Administration took over from the Printing Division liaison with the Government Printing Office and the responsibility for IPS contract printing. The Printing Division now gives technical guidance to individual post printing plants and purchases all printing and photographic equipment used at posts. Agency pamphlets and periodicals printed in the United States are stored by the Printing Division and orders for shipment overseas filled by it. Within the Press and Publications Service, there is someone responsible for each part of the IPS operation, from initiating an idea or receiving a policy guidance from top Agency officials to packing the finished product off to the field.

THE MOTION PICTURE AND TELEVISION SERVICE (IMV):

Background   MEDIA MARRIAGE

Although motion pictures have been a major element in the United States information program from the start, television is the "baby" of the information media. Television programs were conceived in 1952 as a "guy and gal" operation within the Voice of America, then located in New York City. The infant followed its mother to Washington, arriving in January, 1955, after the Voice had transferred operations from New York to the District of Columbia in the fall of 1954. The television staff had grown by this time to three "executives" and three secretaries. Television then existed only in the United States, West Germany, and England. The British did not need USIA television broadcasts, and West Germany was just emerging from occupation. The television item in the annual Voice budget was $120,000. During the next two years, television stations developed rapidly in Latin America. Japan acquired stations in the Far East; and in Europe, West Germany was joined by France and Italy. In two more years, by 1958, there were stations in Bangkok, Istanbul, Beirut, Baghdad, and Cairo—but none in the rest of Africa. Behind the Iron Curtain, the Soviet Union had television, and some of its peripheral stations were reaching viewers across the border, hampered by technical differences in western and eastern European television. Although there were still few receiving sets abroad, the television function was separated from the Broadcasting Service in fiscal year 1958, a Television Service (ITV) being created with a staff of over forty and a budget of $3 million. Cut to the bone in fiscal year 1959, the Television Service re-grew from a staff of thirty-two and a budget of less than $1 million to 115 personnel and a budget of $3 million by 1963, with hopes for continued rapid growth in the years ahead. Some of Ed Murrow's glamor as an eminent television personality had rubbed off on the Television Service, but the technical breakthrough which made it seem apparent that ITV's dreams would come true was the possibility of live broadcasting programs worldwide, foreseen with the launching of "syncom" and the development of "ComSat."

While ITV to 1963 had been primarily a contracting and packaging operation rather than a live producer of shows, it looked forward to increasing its live productions. Moved from cramped offices at 1776 Pennsylvania Avenue, it was housed in its own quarters—the Old Post Office Building at 12th Street and Pennsylvania Avenue, N.W., designed by Louis Sullivan, teacher of Frank Lloyd Wright, and completed in 1897. Something of an "old-fashioned monstrosity," the building had its gloomy interior rebuilt to provide television studios with the most modern equipment.

Back in 1776 Pennsylvania Avenue, the Motion Picture Service (IMS), under the direction of George Stevens, Jr. (who left the USIA on June 15, 1967) after February 1, 1962, continued to produce on contract USIA motion pictures which won increasing acclaim for their artistic excellence in international film competition. The Agency won its first American "Oscar" in April, 1965, when *Vine from Little Rock* won the Academy Award as the best documentary motion picture of 1964. The film illustrated civil-rights progress in America by showing the achievements after graduation of the original nine students integrated into Little Rock High School in 1957. IMS films were "purpose without popcorn," and there were few cowboys to be seen. Among films released by the Motion Picture Service during a representative six-month period, only *Agriculture: U.S.A.*, telling the "story of Agriculture in the U.S. from the time of the early settler . . . to the present time," gave any promise of showing the old West. Obviously, IMS was not spending much time portraying western life as every American five-year old knows it from "ancient" movies on television or as their parents enjoy it during their weekly television visit to Adam Cartwright's Ponderosa Ranch. Like the young Television Service, the more mature Motion Picture Service was concerned with USIA themes, with programs related to civil rights, to development and modernization; interested in living conditions under communism; in speeches by American political figures; in nuclear progress, education, medicine, land reform, conservation, self-help, or American astronauts—and even performances by the Juilliard String Quartet or the Boston Symphony Orchestra.

Although ITV was limited primarily to placement of its products with foreign television stations, IMS still had the motion-picture theater in the less-developed areas, and these theaters were hungry for ten-minute newsreels or twenty-to-thirty-minute features. While ITV's opportunities for placement were rapidly expanding, with the growth of new television stations and the emergence of "ComSat," opportunities for showing Motion Picture Service products in European or Japanese theaters—more highly developed areas with their own motion-picture industries—fell sharply. ITV's shows reached mainly city and peripheral areas, unless shown by one of the Motion Picture Service's "mobile units." IMS through mobile motion-picture units could project pictures wherever hardy USIS personnel could travel by motorcar—which in most areas served meant wider coverage during dry periods than in rainy seasons. The Motion Picture Service distributed for movie use the Television Service's civil-rights march pictures of August 28, 1963, to twenty-eight countries lacking television. Over time IMS distributed many other ITV-produced shows, and most IMS films were also cleared for television and many were used by ITV.

Although the Television and Motion Picture Services sometimes performed their functions in different ways, had organizational variations, and had their own individual staffing problems, they also had much in common. It would be tempting to say that use of 16-millimeter film by ITV and 35-millimeter by IMS was the one clear-cut distinguishing feature between the two, for good projection on motion-picture screens requires larger film than is demanded by the television monitor. But even here, the distinction was not complete, because both used some of each size film. Whatever their similarities, they had developed separately; though increased effort for cooperation between the two media services was made after 1961, the two services had not always worked closely in the past. Organizationally, each was headed by a director and deputy director; the Motion Picture Service had moved more rapidly than the Television Service to appoint a policy applications officer as Agency leaders asserted closer policy control over the media after 1961, but this step did not stem from any difference in type of product. The Motion Picture Service lacked the "program manager" level of organization that functioned in both the Broadcasting Service and the Television Service, but the ITV program manager's function was apparently shared in IMS by the director, deputy director, and a policy applications officer. IMS's production manager was responsible for tasks similar to those of ITV's production division chief, but all Motion Picture Service "production" was by contract, whether done for its Documentary and Topical Production Division by American film makers for worldwide distribution or for its Foreign Production Division, mainly through foreign producers, for use in specific regions or individual countries. An Overseas Operations Division in IMS performed many of the same tasks carried out by an Operations Division in ITV, but in addition took care of "acquisition" of privately produced films (a function performed in the office of the production manager in ITV). The Overseas Operations Division provided the language prints of films, the exhibition and distribution equipment, and the technical facilities for conducting film programs by each USIS mission in a foreign country where

USIA films were shown. IMS had ITV and separate New York offices for liaison with the motion-picture and television industries. Both had an executive officer with administrative responsibilities. The IMS staff was almost one and a half times the size of ITV's; its budget, more than two times that of ITV; it also led ITV in funds expended by USIA area offices for its services. In 1963, ITV's director, a Foreign Service Career Reserve Officer, introduced a system of policy control over ITV products that appeared to be stronger than that then existing in IMS. ITV's deputy director at that time had come direct from the television industry for a period of service with USIA. The director of the Motion Picture Service had been brought to the Agency by Murrow early in 1962 from the motion-picture industry. The deputy director of IMS was a civil servant and, with many years of experience in the Motion Picture Service, an effective administrator.

And Then There Was One

In December, 1965, a little more than three months after Leonard Marks assumed direction of the United States Information Agency, the young bride (ITV) was wed to the more mature groom (IMS), the new family christened the Motion Picture and Television Service (IMV). If the husband retained direction of the family, with both the IMS director and deputy director continuing in those positions in IMV, the husband moved in with the wife shortly after the marriage to reside at 12th and Pennsylvania in the 1897 "castle," more reminiscent of "Beverly of Graustark" than of the "ComSat" era. The marriage was a product of normal evolution, of growing policy relationships, and apparently has cemented close ties which already existed. If husband and wife continue to go about their separate tasks, using different equipment, they are much more likely to know what each is doing, and, indeed, like some couples, may grow to look more and more like each other over time. Current organization features of IMV include an executive officer and an International Communications Media Staff, attached as service units to the director and deputy director. The major activities of IMV are carried out by three offices—headed by a program manager, a production manager, and an operations manager. Functioning under the program manager are five three-man or four-man area staffs, each headed by an FSCR 2 or 3, to guide and service the programs of individual regions and posts; an Acquisition Staff, which seeks clearance of useful privately produced products for IMV use; and an Assessment Staff, providing a check on audience results and conditions under which IMV products are shown. Combined, the staffs serving under the program manager assist in providing policy guidance to the other elements of IMV, particularly to personnel serving in the Office of the Production Manager. The production manager is responsible for a Documentary Production Division, which guides contract production of motion pictures and television shows in the United States and abroad; a News and Special Events Division, which specializes in newsreels or news magazines made on contract here or with post help overseas; and a Staff Production Division, which handles Washington "in house" production—continuing a function which had been conducted in the Television Service and working to develop some "in house" capacity for motion-picture production. Under the operations manager are a Washington Facilities Division with representatives in New York, responsible for the operation and servicing of IMV equipment anywhere; a Laboratory Services Division, with approximately sixteen men in Washington and thirty-five in New York, which renders developing, printing, and language services; and a Special Services Division operating both in Washington and New York, which maintains film libraries, handles distribution of films to posts, and supplies motion-picture and television equipment needed by USIS posts overseas.

Direction of the Motion Picture and Television Service

Although the director of the Television Service after 1963 was very conscious of relating policy to television products and spent some time in helping devise a system for tight control of production by policy officers, the director and deputy director of the Motion Picture Service accepted the need for a policy relationship, but tended to emphasize the need to protect creative producers from undue intervention by policy offices. In the marriage of the two services, IMV retained the director and deputy directors of IMS and took over in considerable degree the program manager and policy-control system developed in ITV. The result was a tighter control of policy than had existed in IMS, with more direct right of appeal to the director and deputy director of IMV when program and production differed than existed between production and the director of ITV. The program manager of ITV was above the Production Division; in IMV, the program manager and the production manager head offices of equal status. Although television may be a slightly faster media than motion pictures, neither operates at the policy speed of the area offices, the Broadcasting Service, or the Press and Publications Service. Although either the director or deputy director of IMV may sometimes be absent from Washington on inspection trips to the field, perhaps to Europe or Latin America, their participations in IMV decisions is often "joint," bringing their diverse backgrounds to bear on IMV problems. The slower pace of IMV allows more group discussions, consideration of a wider number of points of view. The director and deputy director are usually closely associated with major products from their inception as an idea, through the complicated budget and appropriation process to production, review, placement, and even evaluation. A small five-man International Communications Media Staff assists them in fulfilling their responsibility for the selection of films to represent the United States government in international film festivals in cooperation with the private motion-picture and television industries. This staff also certifies in their behalf over 10,000 films a year as falling under the provisions of the Beirut Agreement for the exchange of educational or cultural audio-visual materials without censorship or duties. Although this type of operation would be too much detail for the director and deputy director to handle in addition to their other duties, they do know what motion-picture and television films IMV has overseas in post film libraries, what projection facilities are available for IMV products around the world, and "where the holes are." Awareness of major policy changes, like that upgrading United States relations with Latin America by initiation of the Alliance for Progress, would lead the director or deputy director of IMV to discuss directly and through representatives with the appropriate area office a new emphasis—in that case, on development-related films—to support the new program. Not only are the director and the deputy director conscious of the over-all Agency themes, which IMV worldwide products project, but they are aware of regional objectives, for which other films are especially prepared—either because of difference of topical interest, in level of audience sophistication, or the need to adapt to distinct cultural patterns. Much of their work is review of suggestions by area staff program officers in the Office of the Program Manager, discussing proposals by production supervisors or producers in the Documentary Production or News and Special Events Divisions, preparing to discuss IMV proposals with the Agency deputy director or with area office directors, studying the balance in television and motion-picture production and use, attending screenings of IMV products, or ironing out lower-level differences between IMV and the area offices on films being produced locally overseas. Although the deputy agency director makes the final decisions on worldwide IMV products, it is in fact the director of an area office who normally authorizes IMV work done for a region or specific post. Filmwork for individual countries or regions is budgeted partly in the IMV budget and partly in the mission budgets, with money transferred to IMV by the area offices to carry out approved projects. IMV has its own budget funds for cameras, film supplies, and other equipment needed to produce or exhibit shows. The USIS missions and the area offices control the funds for writing and producing the shows. IMV budgets film reproduction costs and can question field orders if the number requested seems too high— as it may be, since it is not the field that pays for this. The budget interrelationship helps force and insure cooperation between the Motion Picture and Television Service and the area offices.

The Motion Picture and Television Service, like the other media services, has an obligation to relate programs to policy objectives. IMV leadership is well aware that films cannot be directed so completely to policy concerns that the audience turns off television sets or changes stations, or that broadcast stations are unwilling to put the shows on the air. In turn, they know that placement of motion pictures in commercial channels places limits on the policy orientation of movies. If films concentrate only on the Vietnam situation, the reorganization of NATO, or communist aggression, they are not likely to be very successful tools of American policy in many parts of the world. On the other hand, bits of "Americana"—shots of the Golden Gate Bridge in San Francisco or of the Tennessee Valley Authority dams—by themselves may not have significant policy impact, even though they are samples of American engineering or symbols of improved transportation and power facilities required by the less-developed for modernization. Race relations has been an important subject for IMV programs, because the question affects emotions abroad even though it is not directly related to foreign policy. How can Americans profess democracy and be undemocratic in racial matters? When a mass civil-rights march to the Lincoln Memorial Monument took place during the summer of 1963, USIA edited materials provided by the network pool down to a thirty-minute show, added commentary, and rushed it overseas for USIS placement; but usage was spotty and much lower than the Agency leadership had anticipated, even in Africa. Many stereotypes about America held abroad are quite inaccurate and probably need to be corrected, but certain stereotypes are assigned higher priority than others by USIA, because they are viewed as being politically significant. If people overseas view the American economic system as a Marxist would interpret it, they may lean toward communism. It is essential for films to attempt to undo this type of stereotype. The United States is not totally capitalistic but has a mixed economy; to emphasize that part of "Americana" becomes important. How can a better understanding of the American form of government be used to encourage peaceful change overseas, where student and other groups seeking a better life often use violence in an effort to achieve their goals? A successful democracy has a high level of citizen participation in community life, where its people live and work.

Government must be responsive to the needs of people and pressure groups. To tell this type of story, instead of focusing on conventions, campaigns, and election returns as in the past, a maturing USIA followed the election activities of six young Republicans and six young Democrats—all nonprofessional political workers—who when the election was over went back to their jobs and closed national ranks. The emphasis was on how the average person can participate; it could be a demonstration of an orderly change of leadership from one party to another. IMV can stress free choice as a theme, because American policy recognizes that there is no "one right way" for every country, neither our own system nor communism. IMV can indicate alternative paths to development, but it leaves its audiences with the understanding that each of their countries must tap its own unique genius to evolve a pattern of progress satisfactory to its people. This is the spirit of the new era in IMV. How is policy transferred into a tangible product?

The Office of the Program Manager

For the Broadcasting Service and the Press and Publication Service, the lifeline of policy is the Agency's daily fast guidance mechanism, culminating in the 12:30 P.M. briefing by the deputy chief of policy guidance in the Office of Policy and Research. Although IMV is represented at these sessions, the briefings are usually of little immediate use, serving more as cumulative input for understanding policy trends. The area program officers serving under the IMV program manager can get an idea from guidance given for a particular event. A television or motion-picture newsreel may be produced to show that an American Quaker group responded with hurricane relief to the Cuban people (though the United States did not have diplomatic relations with the Cuban government), emphasizing American humanistic as opposed to materialistic values. While the "IOP Noon Notes" are distributed in summary form within IMV, there is no need for IMV to jump into action with each policy guidance on the latest coup. With the Agency's policy emphasis, field posts report their or television motion-picture activities as related to themes or objectives; like other media services, IMV reports on all of its products to Agency Deputy Director Akers.

Through his area program officers, the program manager maintains close contact both with the area offices and the Office of Policy and Research, playing a major role in working out a balance between regionally directed materials and those with a broader distribution. He does this in consultation with representatives serving the production manager to see if what he wants is technically feasible. After the IMV budget is approved and funds appropriated, the program manager's office prepares documents for Agency Deputy Director Akers specifying what shows or series should be produced. After he approves, copies of the documents are forwarded to the program and production managers of IMV. This "go-ahead," drafted by the program manager's staff, approved by the Agency deputy director, and forwarded to the production manager, is a program paper, of one to four pages in length, which (1) lists the name of the motion picture, television program or series; (2) states the general concept of the television program or motion picture in a paragraph or two; (3) states why the program or picture needs to be done and its specific objective; (4) lists the policy points to be emphasized by stating which of the major Agency themes or emphases it supports and by spelling out the particular problem (possibly civil rights) with which it will deal; and (5) concludes with a budget figure for the picture, program, or series. Attached are any relevant research materials gathered by the program manager's staff from within or outside the Agency and/or a bibliography for use of the production supervisor selected by the production manager. When this document is received by the production manager or by the chiefs of the News and Special Events or Documentary Production Divisions, "production" becomes the "executer," responsible for maintaining technical excellence, quality of pictures, style of camera work, staging, and creative artistry—the field of its expertise. The program manager has no part in production except at specific check points to allow firm policy control of the final product.

Not all IMV products are prepared *de novo*. Out of the welter of motion pictures and television programs produced by commercial and educational motion-picture or television companies, or even by private business corporations, there are many films which may serve the policy purposes of the Motion Picture and Television Service. There was increasing collaboration between ITV and IMS in the acquisition of picture rights after 1963, and with the creation of IMV an Acquisition Staff was attached to the Office of the Program Manager. The acquisition program, still expanding, by 1967 had an eight-member staff. Films that the Acquisition Staff believes are suitable will be screened by the program officers of the area staffs and by appropriate area offices "uptown." Anyone, from an area director down through the policy officer or program coordinator to the country desk officers, is likely to attend such screenings. If the area decides to use the film, "orders" are placed with the program officers. Negotiations are then started by the Acquisition Staff with the owner of the television show or motion picture. The program may be acquired free, or the Agency may have to pay up to $5,000 for negative materials and rights. There are many rights and subrights. If the show itself is cleared but the music rights are held up, it is possible for IMV to produce its own music track. If a television station will release a program free but insists on pay for the station announcer who served as commentator, IMV can cut the local announcer and provide its own announcer for the narrative. With the acquisition finalized, the area staff program officers are informed that the film is available. Screenings are held for Agency review, and a decision is made on the languages into which the film is to be translated. Then an English test print is forwarded to USIS posts, which order the number of prints they want in particular languages. Overly large orders of films funded through IMV may be questioned by the area staff program officers. The Operations Manager's Laboratory Services Division is notified of what is ordered. Finished films are finally forwarded overseas by the Special Services Division. The area staff program officers serving the program manager notify the field posts that the film is on its way, probably by sea pouch, informing them what the film is and specifying any legal limitations on its use.

The area staff program officers of IMV number twenty-six, nine of whom backstop film production at USIS posts overseas. They serve under chiefs for Latin American, Near East, East Asian and Pacific, European, and African area offices, getting and giving information and helping develop country programs. They read policy directives concerning their areas of responsibility, though the flow of policy paper they receive is much less than that of an area office country desk officer "uptown." Within IMV, they are involved in providing policy guidance to IMV's production manager, both to his News and Special Events and Documentary Production divisions. In addition, they maintain liaison with the field posts in their areas to help meet their motion-picture and television needs and to monitor post usage reports of materials sent overseas. They are aware that "hard-line materials" are difficult to place at many posts overseas, and that IMV depends upon energetic and effective placement efforts by USIS officers or foreign locals if its function is to be performed successfully. Area staff program officers are not dissatisfied when they get a 50 per cent usage of films sent to the field, and they appreciate the need of field posts to edit pictures in order to tailor them more explicitly to local needs. Manila has exceptionally fine facilities for adapting film materials and often services post needs in its regional area.

An Assessment Staff helps IMV do a better policy-related job, thus protecting it from undue interference in the field of its expertise. Working with the area staff program officers, members of the Assesment Staff study the films produced and the use made of them overseas, seeking to determine whether the films themselves are at fault. Poor results may not be due to shortcommings in the films, however: They may have been shown to the wrong audience, or to the right audience but under poor circumstances. Before the establishment of the Assessment Staff, IMV had no means of checking judgments made by area officer or the Office of Policy and Research concerning the effectiveness of films; now it is in a position to make its own assessments to counter views which it considers to be unobjective or unfounded in fact. More positively, the Assessment Staff can help determine why certain films shown to certain audiences, under the right circumstances, have been effective—and make it possible to get favorable results from a higher percentage of films and audiences.

Office of the Production Manager

The production manager and his deputy preside over what appears to be a neatly divided producing world. The three major elements in production are: (1) a Documentary Production Division, which largely through contractors produces motion pictures or television programs of a documentary nature to meet worldwide, area, and country policy objectives; (2) a News and Special Events Division, which supervises the production by staff or contract in the United States and overseas of worldwide and area newsreels, and of news magazines covering special events in the United States or elsewhere; and (3) a Staff Production Division, responsible for "in house" production by IMV (primarily of television programs), either for worldwide or regional distribution, sometimes facilitative in nature (assisting foreign correspondents stationed in Washington to produce shows reporting on American developments). Prior to the joining of ITV with IMS, only the Television Service had an "in house" capability, but IMV has taken steps to establish limited but similar production of motion pictures. To get the "feel of the audience" that IMV films reach, the production manager may spend up to four months in the field each year talking with officers concerned with motion-picture and television distribution, and to other post personnel. Private discussions sometimes provide information which would not be forwarded in formal reports. Most of the worldwide films produced domestically now go to Africa, Latin America, and the Far East. Fewer are distributed in Europe, though European operations are being strengthened once again, in spite of placement difficulties and lack of understanding by some Senate and House members of why it is important for USIA to send films to longtime "friends." Not every motion picture or television film produced by IMV supports policy directly. In very special instances, they may deal with subjects of particular interest to influential people in foreign governments and may be used "to open the door" for other USIA products. Not all USIA films are produced in the United States; some USIS posts have the ability to produce films locally. Films produced overseas will receive some general policy supervision from the program manager's area staff program officers. Films produced overseas for use in a specific country are likely to be funded by area office budgets, with the area offices in Washington playing a strong policy-review role. Films produced from Washington for worldwide use are likely to be funded by IMV, with the deputy Agency director, now responsible for media content, playing a major review role, though the area offices are also participants in the policy-review process.

When an IMV worldwide project, domestically produced in the United States, is approved by the deputy agency director, the chief of the Documentary Division assigns it to one of his production supervisors. Films produced overseas at local USIS posts are reviewed carefully by the area offices whose budgets cover the films. On weekly newsreels of the News and Special Events Division, the policy-control process has to be simplified to preserve timeliness; essentially the same elements in the Agency have to be consulted. Whether the Documentary Production Division or the News and Special Events Division is involved, its production supervisor has the responsibility for hiring a suitable outside film-production company and writer, either together or separate, to do the proposed motion picture or television show. For a documentary television program series, the production supervisor may call in a professional writer or secure the services of a well-known television drama writer, depending upon the level of writing required for the particular program. From that point on, it is the production supervisor's job to get the best dramatic and artistic performance possible, while handling or avoiding policy points as prescribed in the program paper approved by the program manager. The production supervisor is IMV's liaison and guide to the "creative people." Upon receiving the program paper, the writer may do a "treatment," an expanded narrative, with examples of certain scenes he wants to include. This is discussed with the production supervisor and after revision goes to the area staff program officers under the program manager for review. Appropriate country desk officers or policy officers in the area offices also are likely to "have a look." Deputy Agency Director Akers may be drawn in if problems arise. Often on major products, the director and deputy director of IMV are involved in the review. The same reviewers are likely to see the writer's "shooting script" and have a chance to suggest revisions before filming. They also see the film in "rough cut"—longer than the final film will be, but presented in sequence though with no sound. At this point, an IMV area staff program officer or a country desk officer, or their superiors, might recommend cutting a scene showing teenage boys and girls alone in the evening without adult supervision or a shot of a woman in a bathing suit—both objectionable in certain foreign countries. Later, IMV policy reviewers see an "inter-lock," the finally edited film with the final script read in accompaniment, but not yet wed. Again, changes can be made, and then the film and sound are blended. The director and deputy director of IMV and other IMV staff members look at the final product and have a chance to reject or approve it. When the finished picture is made available by the contractor, it is screened by the area office or offices interested, and orders are placed or not for copies to be sent to their field posts. Some films are actually pretested in the field before the final revisions are approved by IMV. Although no large changes can be made after IMV approval and the placement of orders, it is still possible to make minor changes in the various language versions, and a directive may be sent to the field to cut a section of the film in a particular country. The film is finally printed in language versions by the Laboratory Services Division and sent overseas by the Special Services Division. When the film arrives at the post, it is previewed before being taken to possible outlets for placement. The field has autonomy on deciding whether it wants to use the show. Because of an unforeseen local event, its arrival may be ill timed. If the USIS officer in charge of placement does not like the film, he may not press it too hard—unless it has gone to the field with an "urgently request placement" appeal from headquarters. Placement appeals can be turned down by the field, but the decision to disregard such a directive will probably not be made without consulting the country public affairs officer. The degree of policy control is almost "complete"; there are likely to be few "grand mistakes." It is no wonder that the Office of Policy and Research was highly enthusiastic about this policy-production process when it was initiated by the Television Service and happy to see it form the basis for IMV production after integration.

Policy and production personnel are likely to approach the film media with somewhat differing viewpoints. On a film covering a speech made by a dynamic figure like President Kennedy in a Latin American country, area office policy personnel often wanted the President on camera throughout most of the speech. Because of the need to overlay the voice in English with a Spanish or other translation, IMV personnel preferred him on camera for as little as two of twenty-five minutes, showing other background shots to strengthen and support his message. In a film to a sophisticated European audience, policy people may shudder at the use of the latest and most modern motion-picture techniques, but IMV would be likely to support the contract producer who was up to date on motion-picture artistry. Many of the policy people place great value on the written word. Motion-picture and television productions convey ideas with pictures and the least possible narration. While motion pictures can convey more complex ideas than television, they must still be kept relatively simple because a movie is normally seen once and cannot be reread.

Most worldwide productions are tied closely to one of the Agency's five themes; even regional and country-directed productions may support one of the themes. IMV production personnel believed that audiences in less-developed areas lacked the background knowledge to be able to understand a film like "The Wall," which dealt with divided Berlin but was intended for worldwide viewing. "An audience in Thailand lacks interest in the Berlin Wall." It is difficult to project a "strength image" of the United States to India or to show a film indicating the danger of Communist China in Southeast Asia. The Indians may draw the conclusion from the film that the United States is a "warmonger," and the people of Southeast Asia may "learn" that China is too strong to resist and make less effort than before to counter Chinese attempts at gaining influence.

To help reduce the consequences of differences of belief between policy and production personnel, IMV production personnel are encouraged to approach problems from a media technique viewpoint: "We can't do it that way, but we can do it this way. What do you think?" If staff members serving IMV's program manager become "too sympathetic" to pressures resulting from policy considerations, the production manager's producers can carry their case to the director and deputy director of IMV, both of whom stress the artistic requirements of film production and are intent on turning out films competitive in quality with those produced by the best private motion-picture producers in the United States.

Illustrative of the worldwide products which have been produced by IMV are films like "Cuba Waits," a twenty-minute motion-picture documentary showing what befalls a nation that embraces the tactics of communism in preference to pursuing progress through democratic principles—and the success of the United States initiatives during the Cuban missile crisis of 1962. "Cuba Waits" was distributed in 700 16-millimeter prints to 103 countries, with 315 35-millimeter prints going to 73 countries. It was translated into twenty-eight foreign languages. Because it was considered to be of great importance by the Office of Policy (now Policy and Research), it was not "tested" in the field but sent direct. Country public affairs officers were not asked how it could be better adapted to their needs or asked to place orders. "Escape to Freedom," another worldwide motion-picture product, told about living conditions under communism and documented personal experiences of a native of East Germany which caused him to make the decision for his wife and himself to escape to freedom in the West. Like most USIA films, this one was "tested"—in seventy-six countries. In this instance, USIS posts suggested adaptations and placed orders if they wanted it shown in their countries—the cost for prints distributed borne by the Media Service rather than by area offices. Other representative worldwide products of IMV include "A Philosopher's Journey," covering a visit to the United States by the President of India; "World Peace," the highlights of President Kennedy's commencement address in June, 1963, at American University; and "The Valley Revisited," showing changes made in the Tennessee Valley by TVA over a thirty-year period. Among worldwide television productions are the programs in "The Continuing Revolution Series." "Integration" was a thirty-minute program showing the progress of the American Negro, participants being white and Negro university students actively participating in the civil-rights struggle, indicating that the majority of Americans of all ages favor desegregation. In the same series, a thirty-minute "American Economy" program showed that the American economic system does not conform to the traditional Marxist-Leninist concept of the laissez-faire system, that it is evolving toward serving the best interests of all the people. "Science Report," a monthly thirty-minute coverage of the latest significant advances in the field of science and technology in the United States, represents another type of worldwide television program. The "Let's Speak English Series" for television was so successful that it now includes three sets of sixty-five 15-minute programs of graduated language difficulty. The programs demonstrate aspects of American life as part of the language-teaching process.

The Motion Picture and Television Service does little work or backstopping for the larger USIS posts, which have film officers and can produce their own shows overseas. It has almost nothing to do for South Vietnam, where there is a good production team, with adequate facilities at the post for preparing films to support its specific objectives. IMV is more likely to be involved in film productions with wide regional distribution or those supporting small posts with little film expertise (where technical facilities and skilled local personnel are not available), and in handling newsreel-type productions. A motion picture such as "Hunger—The Present Enemy" (a twenty-minute documentary based on a school-lunch program supported by the Food for Peace Program), which was produced and photographed by USIS Lima, receives general supervision by IMV, with laboratory work, editing, and translation into Spanish the responsibility of IMV's Laboratory Services Division. This would also be true of films such as "Turbulent Waters," done by USIS Dacca. Released in Pakistan in English, Bengali, and Urdu, this motion-picture documented the building, completion, and inauguration ceremonies of the Karnafuli Multipurpose Project, the largest United States-aided project in Pakistan. Stress was laid on how, with Pakistani-American cooperation, this hydroelectric dam would serve as the key to agricultural, industrial, and economic development of East Pakistan. Representative of films produced overseas by IMV are three which supported the Alliance for Progress: "Evil Wind Out," dealing with the problems confronting a new doctor in gaining the confidence of the people in a rural village; "Letter from Colombia," telling how the landless become landowners through a land-reform program; and "School at Rincon Santo," describing the first schoolhouse ever to be built in a remote Andean community. These three particular films were distributed far beyond the Latin area, in more than one hundred countries and in ten to fourteen languages. Also supporting the Alliance for Progress was the television series "Nuestro Barrio," twenty-six related thirty-minute dramatic episodes, portraying events in an anonymous Latin American community, its successes and problems—a la American soap opera (more elegantly known as "continuing daytime drama"). Often using local photographers, IMV has produced films in more than seventy-five countries.

Two regional newsreels done on contract by private companies, paid for by area office funds, and produced in New York City, are under the general supervision of the News and Special Events Division. "Today" (Allegro) is a twenty-minute African newsreel issued monthly, produced in 35-millimeter for theatrical release and 16-millimeter for nontheater use in Africa. Besides supporting basic Agency themes, country objectives, and special programs such as United Nations operations in the Middle East, Cyprus, or the Congo, this news magazine carries stories related to the formation of new independent African states, regional cooperation, local government or local private efforts to improve living standards, student activities, and official meetings of significance to the whole area. One representative issue included such topics as "A Working Holiday in Africa" (American students), "U.S. Welcomes Prime Minister of Somali Republic," and "African Students in American Homes." Similar in nature is "Horizons" (Hearst Metrotone News, Inc.), also a twenty-minute monthly film, released in both 35- and 16-millimeter in Latin America. In addition to supporting the Agency's themes, country objectives, and special programs such as the Alliance for Progress, the newsreel carries stories related to hemispheric solidarity; government or local private efforts to improve standards of living (roads, communications, health, agriculture, education); student activities; and official conferences of significance to Latin America. One of the primary goals of "Horizons" is to acquaint peoples of Latin America more intimately with their neighbors—not only concerning government or official policies, but also their daily lives, aspirations, and mutual problems. Among regionally oriented television programs for many years was "Panorama Panamericano," a weekly fifteen-minute program widely used at prime times in Latin America, focusing on developments throughout the Western Hemisphere that were relevant to United States policy objectives.

Probably destined for expansion are the operations of the Staff Production Division under the production manager of IMV. The Motion Picture Service did no production "in house"; its work was done on contract or by USIS post personnel. The Television Service, on the other hand, maintained a small production staff, both for panel-moderator shows in its own studios and for co-producing "facilitative programs" with foreign correspondents. Additional stages for motion-picture use were constructed at "12th and Pennsylvania" after the merger of the two media services. Two large studios are now maintained. "In house" productions are done under the direction of a producer-director, a member of the Staff Production Division, assisted by a unit manager for business and administrative matters, who gets the talent and the props; by a production aide, who helps in research and in preparing material to be used on the program; and by a stage manager or assistant director, who helps line up the cameras and keeps the continuity going during the actual filming. For television shows, the action is recorded on video tape. To backstop a discussion between American and African students on topics of special interest to Africa, the producer of the show would hire an outside film company to provide six minutes of background film on the topic, which would be blended into the finished product. If the subject were "farm modernization," the photos might be of United States farming methods and implements. In facilitative programming by IMV, the producer and his staff may work in cooperation with a Swedish or other foreign television reporter stationed in the United States who comments regularly on current events or scientific developments here. In the cooperative venture, the correspondent provides some of his own props and script, but an IMV producer-director puts the show together, using IMV's production unit, studio, engineers, and cameras—working collaboratively with the reporter. "Facilities and friendship" of this type are not likely to be abused. Valuable services are provided to the correspondent, and the film is developed and subject to informal review by USIA personnel. Among the old Television Service's "in house" productions was a thirteen-program series called "The Experts Answer," in which American specialists in various academic and professional fields were questioned by two Latin American students and two Latin American journalists. The show was in Spanish, with simultaneous translation used when the American expert of the week did not speak Spanish.

Office of the Operations Manager

The operations manager of IMV is responsible for the studios where "in-house" programs are produced and for screening rooms where IMV films are reviewed, directing the technical personnel who operate and maintain the equipment through a Washington Facilities Division. Contracting for test prints of films, maintaining a stable of contract personnel to make language versions of films, and providing contractors to make up the number of prints finally ordered of each film are Laboratory Services Division functions. Servicing film libraries maintained in 226 USIS film centers overseas in some 106 countries is a Library Branch in the Special Services Division, also under the operations manager. A Services Control Branch physically fills orders, preparing shipments of films and other equipment for overseas. A Supply and Equipment Branch backstops the procurement and maintenance of the Agency's 7,541 projectors and 293 mobile units. Sometimes test prints are ordered through the Laboratory Services Division and sent to public affairs officers at posts overseas. In all instances, background information on a picture is forwarded to USIS posts to help them determine what films or prints they would like to receive. Orders must be returned to the Laboratory Services Division by a set date. An order from the field may ask for the film in six languages, one 35-millimeter and two 16-millimeter prints of each, and indicate how many prints in what size and language should go to specific USIS film centers in a particular country. Since the cost of prints is carried in the IMV budget, outsized orders from the field may be reviewed by the area staff program officers and reduced.

The Laboratory Services Division has developed a large list of qualified narrators and translators in New York City for making language versions of films; all of the narrators and translators are carefully cleared for security; language checkers are hired to see that translations and voicings are accurate; the contractor producers of the language versions hire the personnel IMV tells them to use in preparing the language adaptations. All language versions are checked at the receiving post overseas, by the public affairs officer or by a local employee under his supervision to make certain the language is up to date and does not include colloquial usages which will be embarrassing or reduce the effectiveness of the film.

The Executive Officer

Budget, personnel, and management problems of the Motion Picture and Television Service are the responsibility of its executive officer, an experienced civil servant who has been associated with the motion-picture program since 1952. The history of the motion-picture operation can be traced back to the Office of War Information during World War II. At the time USIA was separated from the Department of State in 1953, motion pictures required almost three hundred employees and a budget of nearly $9 million. With the Agency under fire from Senator McCarthy during the early days of the Eisenhower administration, the Motion Picture Service was cut to 141 employees and a budget of less than $3 million in fiscal year 1954. After that, there was a slow regrowth of funds, a lesser restoration of personnel, up to a personnel ceiling of 162 and $6.3 million in fiscal year 1964. While other parts of the Agency worked on budget cuts or small increases, the Television Service—after its first shakedown year—grew steadily. In budgeting for the Motion Picture and Television Service, it is considered somewhat difficult to project accurately what future requirements will actually be. Because situations change, money appropriated may be spent in a different way than originally authorized by the Congress. This often requires an explanation or defense before the subcommittee of the House Appropriations Committee handling the IMV and USIA budget. IMV can budget to cover visits of foreign heads of state, but it cannot be certain how many will arrive in a given year. Topical films like the launch of John Glenn and later astronauts on their historic missions in space depend on news events and scientific progress that cannot always be predicted. In longer-range documentaries, where the Agency attempts to relate subject matter to basic themes, there may be a 50 per cent change in topic of films made under an annual budget, though 90 per cent are likely to stay under themes projected.

Costs of USIA films which must compete for placement overseas are likely to be higher than Department of Defense training films shown to a captive audience. Production costs on the motion picture covering Jacqueline Kennedy's visits to India and Pakistan ran to $83,802, with an additional $92,103 for prints and $63,234 for language versions, as reported by the *Washington Daily News* of November 14, 1963. This was a five-reel, fifty-minute production in 35-millimeter color. An artistic and creatively done picture, it was first released through United Artists for showing in the United States on the basis of a Senate resolution with which the House had not concurred—arousing congressional ire. USIA was accused, according to the *Daily News*, of "making a 'concerted effort' to spread its propaganda at home as well as abroad." Normally, production costs on USIA films are likely to be under $1,000 a minute. Films are a larger portion of the USIA budget than of Defense, National Aeronautics and Space Agency, or Atomic Energy Commission budgets and receive correspondingly a closer scrutiny from Congress. This explains the importance of the Assessment Staff in the Office of the Program Manager in assisting the executive officer to prove the effectiveness of films. Reports received through the area staffs as well as particular Research and Analysis Staff studies are also considered helpful in evaluating films. Polls taken before use of a television series or motion picture overseas and later polls made after showing which indicate a significant shift in opinion still do not make it possible to prove to the Congress that IMV products are a major factor in the change. Other USIS activities, major events in the news, or fluctuating political situations may compete for recognition as causal factors. A Gallup poll in the United Kingdom after the flight of the Soviet Sputnik in 1957 indicated that on balance the people there believed the Soviet Union led the United States in scientific progress. With ups and downs, but a slow upward trend, the United States finally edged into the lead after the successful double Gemini flight in December, 1965. It seems likely that the Soviet Luna 9 flight in February, 1966, which made it possible for the "moon to speak Russian," once again restored the Soviet Union to "the lead." This in turn was countered by the American "soft landing" on the moon and pictures and probings of the moon's surface. Soviet "space spectaculars" in connection with the 50th anniversary of communism in 1967 may have turned the tables again. In these instances as in many others, the supplemental impact of any television show or motion picture would have to be accorded less public opinion significance than the actual scientific progress demonstrated by the accomplishments reported. But it is clear that the events must be reported because evaluations of Soviet versus American progress are being made by the peoples of the world.

The Motion Picture and Television Service shares some personnel problems in common with other media services, but perhaps more than others it has difficulty in competing with salaries paid by private employers. Television and motion-picture producers in private industry are paid far more than government civil servants. Some producers may be obtained who wish to gain a new type of experience. Others may be blocked in promotion in their present jobs and may turn to government work for a short-term experience before returning to private employment. A few may even be patriotic. The personnel turnover is high among producers, however; this may explain in part why so many IMV programs are done on contract. Because of the technical nature of the work done in IMV, it is difficult for older Foreign Service Career Reserve Officers or young Foreign Service Officers to be assigned to duties in the Motion Picture and Television Service. Television and motion-picture officers at USIS posts overseas as members of the foreign service often hold relatively low-ranking operational posts, and often they must give up their specialties and widen their fields of competency if they are to hope to move toward the top ranks in the foreign service. Most of them would be unable to staff the technical facilities or be unwilling to provide the mundane services provided by the Office of the Operations Manager. They could learn a good deal from training experience in the Office of the Production Manager, but most FSCR's or FSO's do not have the background to become producers. They might make poor unit managers, because they would lack production skills and not like the "grubby little tasks" associated with the job. Work at administrative assignments in IMV would be helpful to FSCR's or FSO's, and but few of them have an interest in such tasks. In the field, FSCR's and FSO's perform operational duties, and they tend to dislike paperwork. USIS has one "administrative officer" type position at each overseas mission, but these are usually filled by Civil Service retreads who have become FSCR's. Thus, though the Motion Picture and Television Service would be willing to take more Foreign Service Career Reserves or Foreign Service Officers for training even in some types of authorized positions, the chance of significantly increased opportunities for FSCR's or FSO's in IMV is not bright.

THE INFORMATION CENTER SERVICE (ICS): AGENCY COMPASS THROUGH STORMY SEAS

Although the Broadcasting Service resembles a fast racing craft, trimming its sails and changing course to take advantage of each shifting wind, the Information Center Service is more like a freighter following a compass course toward its destination. Other media services are populated by broadcasters and newspapermen or by television and motion-picture producers, but there is room in the Information Center Service for "Marian the Librarian" or for former professors who have forsaken the college campus. Least "propagandistic" of any of the media services and most "cultural" in approach, the Information Center Service in its own "slow" way supports American foreign policy. Even more than American embassies, the information centers and binational centers it services overseas are exposed to mass reactions in a variable international climate—may be at one moment cultural centers for learning, discussion, and folk dancing and in the next the target of stone-throwing mobs and arsonists. People overseas who are interested in America or admire its achievements, who hope to learn how to improve conditions in their own countries by understanding the American epic, walk into the centers as friends. Organized political groups, contending against American influence or institutions, march against the centers as they would go into battle against an arch enemy. The impact of the post-1961 emphasis on relating USIA programs to policy had somewhat less effect on programs substained by the Information Center Service overseas than on programs of the other media services. Nonetheless, there were more political discussions sponsored in the centers and less square dancing; but the book burnings in Indonesia or elsewhere were probably not the result of these modest shifts in the USIA cultural program. It is rather that in a period of turbulence in less-developed areas, in the framework of a not so "cold" war in the Far East, information centers or binational centers overseas stand as symbols of America—to friend and foe alike. The Broadcasting Service may be USIA's sharpest policy ax, but it is unseen and unreachable. The information Center Service is USIA's broad cultural tool, by nature somewhat more sincere and credible; but the centers it services are physically present, located where the crowds are likely to be the largest and usually having the biggest plate-glass windows in town (though this is no longer true in all countries).

Essentially the six divisions of the Information Center Service support four types of program abroad: (1) libraries or cultural centers for the study of American political, economic, and cultural affairs, history or science, and technology; (2) a commerical book program intended to place more American-written books in English and translation in bookstores and classrooms; (3) the teaching of English overseas among the influential and potentially so (students) to increase their ability to read American publications or listen to English broadcasts; and (4) exhibits, of different sizes, demonstrating American achievements and know-how in such varied fields as medicine and public health, transportation and industry, or the graphic arts. Overseas, these programs are the responsibility of information officers or cultural affairs officers, who also operate exchange programs for the Bureau of Educational and Cultural Affairs in the Department of State. Cultural affairs officers are USIA personnel, usually members of the Foreign Service Career Reserve, assigned to USIS posts with the approval of the director of the Information Center Service. The director and deputy director of ICS—assistant and deputy assistant directors of USIA—preside over their six operating divisions with the help of an assistant director for operations (performing the executive officer function), a special assistant, and several coordinators (who keep an eye on interagency or priority activities). The deputy director of ICS, an FSCR and former college teacher with Peace Corps service, has an overall view and policy interest similar to that of the program manager of the Broadcasting Service. Performing the day-to-day policy-guidance function for the Information Center Service, of far less importance to ICS than to the Broadcasting Service or the Press and Publications Service, is the chief of the Bibliographic Division. The Bibliographic Division and the Cultural Operations Division provide support services for the information or binational centers. The Bibliographic Division is concerned with the selection of books for use in center libraries or for presentation to foreign leaders and scholars. The Cultural Operations Division, broken down into area and functional branches, meets the Centers' requests for library and cultural services from the field (much as area staffs in the Motion Picture and Television Service serve field needs), and backstops their American studies programs, provides lectures on cultural-political affairs for use by USIS personnel in the field, and meets field needs for musical scores, recordings, and readings. The Publications Division still supports, and the old Informational Media Guaranty Division did support, book publication both in America and abroad for overseas commerical distribution. The Publications Division provides some financial assistance for writing or publication of books in English or foreign languages, including novels and texts. The Informational Media Guaranty Division, which assured American booksellers shipping books to "soft currency" countries that they would be paid in American dollars, thus broadening the markets into which United States publishing firms could afford to enter, became the Informational Media Guaranty Liquidation Staff by mid-1967 as congressional attacks on the program resulted in its demise. The English Teaching Division services programs for the teaching of English, especially in binational centers and at USIS posts; it also provides personnel to guide the "Let's Learn English" programs of IBS and IMV. The Exhibits Division used to have the responsibility for providing many small exhibits which were set up in the binational centers or in other locations arranged by USIS post officers; now it primarily produces major exhibits for tours of eastern Europe and the Soviet Union and prepares and administers American exhibits at international trade fairs.

If most of the products of the other media services make a one-time impact on foreign audiences (heard or seen once, read and thrown away), most products of the Information Center Service are of a more permanent and personal nature, available for study or purchase, for repeated listening or more leisurely reading. If the number of people who can be reached is thus reduced, because it takes time to attend lectures at centers, time to read books, time to learn the English language, the impact made in the long run may be deeper; the understandings developed, greater; whether this also makes the ICS audience more receptive to specific American day-to-day foreign policy actions in Vietnam can be argued either way. Advocates of the cultural approach would say that an understanding of American life and institutions, even when American short-range policy interests may be partially in conflict with those of another nation, tends to reduce opposition and sometimes makes acceptance of American initiatives possible even though active policy support cannot be given. The stress in USIA after 1961 on program-policy relationships, on immediate policy impact in day-to-day affairs, created a vague uneasiness within the Information Center Service, greater than among personnel of the other media services. Not only did they doubt that hammering the policy line would be 100 per cent effective in achieving audience response, they also feared that it meant downgrading Information Center Service programs and the long-range cultural approach of USIA emphasized under the leadership of Agency Director George Allen. They were uncertain how the new approach would affect USIA's credibility or that of ICS programs overseas. They were not sure whether the hare in fact could beat the tortoise in running the foreign policy race for America.

A thoughtful member of the Information Center Service staff unofficially diagramed the possible levels of USIA informational or psychological involvement in relations with foreign countries, noting a five-step range: (1) the free exchange of ideas, (2) developing mutual understanding, (3) political communications, (4) counterinsurgency measures, and (5) psychological warfare. The free exchange of ideas is an unguided and unstructured flow of information without artificial blockage; the development of mutual understanding is communicating the facts both good and bad to develop rationality; political communication is for the purpose of stating or justifying policy to convince others to follow or not to oppose actively; counterinsurgency programs are for the purpose of supporting stable regimes of a neutral or friendly nature in foreign countries; and psychological warfare is complete tactical and strategic involvement in an attempt to control public and government actions in a foreign country. His "barometer," prepared in 1963, looked something like this:

PRESENT BAROMETER OF AGENCY ACTIVITIES

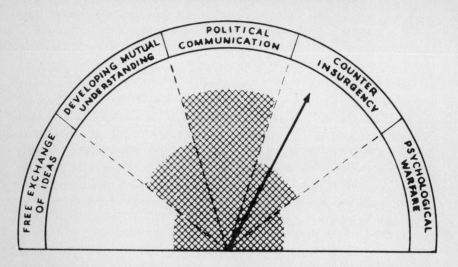

NOTE: The shaded areas have been added later, indicating an outsider's rough assessment of the relative emphasis within the Agency upon the five types of activity. U.S. programs in Vietnam in 1967 probably approximate Psychological Warfare; those once taken in support of Adoula in the Congo represented Counter-Insurgency. Professor Lucien Pye of the Massachusetts Institute of Technology has suggested the importance of communicating and supporting United States policy (Political Communication). Mutual Understanding and international cooperation are strengthened by informational and educational activities carried out under Public Law 402. Cultural exchange, non-political, involving music and the arts, is perhaps representative of Free Exchange of Ideas.

Direction of the Information Center Service

Director of the Information Center Service under Carl Rowan and under Leonard Marks until early 1967 was Reed Harris, formerly Edward R. Murrow's executive assistant, who a decade earlier had been deputy administrator of the old International Information Administration, before USIA was separated from State and became an independent Agency. In 1967, as Harris joined the Office of Policy and Research as assistant director for policy and plans, his acting replacement was Herbert Fredman, who had served

as assistant director of USIA for research and analysis after the breakup of
the Research and Reference Service and the creation of a Research and
Analysis Staff in the Office of Policy and Research. The deputy director of
ICS for several years under Harris had previously served as policy officer for
the Agency's European Area Office. His replacement, who continues to
serve, is an FSCR and former college teacher with Peace Corps service. The
appointments to leadership of ICS indicate a continued emphasis in USIA
upon encouraging receptivity of the media services to policy direction and
control. Either the director or the deputy director of ICS attends the Agency
director's weekly staff meeting. A special assistant to the ICS director is
responsible for monthly reports—one page on each ICS project—to the
Agency deputy director, who is responsible for media content. Formal coordination and passing on of the policy line is achieved within ICS by a 9:30
A.M. Friday staff meeting, chaired by the director of ICS, with the deputy
director, the special assistant, and the ICS division chiefs attending. Also
present, providing coordination with other elements of USIA, are the cultural advisor from the Office of Policy and Research and one representative
each from the legal staff of the Office of the General Counsel and from the
Office of Public Information. The deputy agency director and the director of
ICS, as well as the Publications Division chief are likely to be present at meetings of the Government Advisory Committee on International Book Programs—whose members are private book publishers—when questions are
discussed that concern USIA. The executive secretary of the Advisory
Committee is on the staff of State's Bureau of Educational and Cultural
Affairs. There is an ICS Senior Book Committee, usually chaired by the
director or deputy director of ICS, including the special assistant to the director; and the chiefs of the Bibliographic, Cultural Operations, and Publications Divisions. The Senior Book Committee usually meets on Fridays after
the director's staff meeting to consider suggestions from the Bibliographic
Division of books to be recommended for purchase by USIS posts for use in
information centers, binational centers, or USIS libraries. It also considers
recommendations from the Publications Division of books which should be
financially supported by the Agency or which should be translated into foreign languages. Book appraisals prepared in the Bibliographic Division
provide help in making these determinations. Participation and leadership in
policy coordination at the director and deputy director level in ICS is interagency, intra-agency, and intra-Service. Although the two top leaders of ICS
travel less abroad than the directors of the area offices or the other media
services, they do attend regional conferences of public affairs officers and
cultural affairs officers set up by State's Bureau of Educational and Cultural

Affairs. These meetings are sometimes held in conjunction with regional conferences of American ambassadors, often attended by the Agency director. Actually, post visits to inspect the operations supported by the Information Center Service overseas are usually made by ICS division chiefs. One of USIA's most-traveled individuals is the chief of ICS's Exhibits Division.

The Chief of the Bibliographic Division

The selection of books is central to the work of the Information Center Service. The nature of the books chosen will determine the ideas communicated by overseas programs supported by ICS activities. Because of these facts, the chief of the Bibliographic Division has "doubled" for many years as ICS's informal policy officer—even before the Agency push to have policy applications officers in the media services. Because his administrative duties are light, his staff primarily consisting of six book reviewers, the chief of the Bibliographic Division can give sufficient time to policy matters to be an effective policy officer. In performing his policy duties, he is kept abreast of shifting Agency themes and daily policy guidances. He attends the noon briefings given by the deputy chief for policy guidance of the Office of Policy and Research. He drafts for the benefit of the director, deputy director, and division chiefs of the Information Center Service the "ICS Noon Notes." In performing his bibliographic duties, he uses his knowledge of themes and daily policy, of changing Agency emphases, to guide the work of the Bibliographic Division. Currently, some twenty to twenty-five thousand books a year are being published in the United States. The Bibliographic Division sees seven to eight thousand of these each year, and its staff members prepare written reviews on three thousand of these. Another six hundred more technical books are reviewed on contract by experts for professional evaluation of content.

Reviewers are likely to judge books on the basis of four criteria. How closely does the book support policy? What might be "domestic" or congressional reaction to the use of this book? Is the book comprehensible to a foreign audience? Is it acceptable to readers with a different cultural background? The reviewers were well aware of the shift of emphasis after 1961 in the book programs and exhibits of USIA from Steichen's "The Family of Man" type of artistic response to the atom bomb to favoring books making more specific points in support of American policy—for example, spelling out blueprints for disarmament. During the Murrow period, a higher proportion of books selected were chosen for quick impact; fewer were aimed at a more diffuse or long-range result. There is a better balance in 1967. If a particularly lurid book arouses controversy when it is placed on sale in American cities or placed on the shelves of small-town libraries, USIA can be certain that an enterprising reporter will check USIA's book lists to see if the Agency has placed it in its libraries overseas or supported its publication abroad. Even if such a book had favorable policy overtones, the review staff would probably respond negatively to it. There may be some difficulty in having a Civil Service staff (even though some of its members have had overseas experience) judge the comprehensibility or cultural connotations of a book when read by a foreign audience. Some members of the Senior Book Committee and a number of personnel in the Publications Division (as well as USIS officers overseas) do have Foreign Service Career Reserve background which may be useful in judging these factors. The books to be reviewed are selected by a careful check of advance publication notices from publishers, and by a similar check of works actually published each year. Books reviewed are classified by Agency theme and the sub-policy topics they support, as well as by general subject matter, such as journalism, political science, or economics. The Bibliographic Division now has more than thirty-five thousand book reviews on hand, and believes it can assist the field in meeting requests for books of almost any type and fulfilling a wide variety of policy needs.

In evaluating and recommending the possible utility of books to USIA, the reviewers "note" books in four categories: (1) Maximum Promotion, (2) Normal Use, (3) Conditional Use, and (4) Not Suitable. Receiving a Maximum Promotion rating might be a book that treated a political subject just as USIA might itself, perhaps dealing with one of the five themes or with communist tactics of subversion. A very small percentage of all books reviewed would fit this category, probably not more than 1 per cent. Most books reviewed actually fall in the Normal Use category, which indicates they have some policy relevance and concur with or are not directly opposed to United States foreign policy. Conditional Use books may be those requiring special knowledge for understanding or interpretation, perhaps suitable for teachers but not judged satisfactory for general public use. Not Suitable would be books dealing critically with contemporary American political leaders or strongly advocating a policy line contrary to American foreign policy. If a post suggests use of one of these books or has a request from an important member of its local clientele for such a book, ICS might send the book after clearance by the director of ICS or by one of the Agency's top four leaders. Such a book, if properly justified by the post, is supplied by ICS to protect USIA's "credibility" and reputation for responsiveness. Although the Agency has shifted in emphasis, somewhat toward politically oriented books, cultural materials on sports or identifying the United States with the humanistic tradition are still included among books recommended for Normal Use. Novels and books of adventure are provided to arouse reader interest and to acquaint them with some of the best American fiction. Although readers who frequent USIA library facilities overseas are hardly average individuals and usually are interested in political affairs, even they might find USIA offerings unattractive or find it embarrassing to make use of USIA facilities if the stacks were not leavened with nonpolitical work.

The Chief of the Cultural Operations Division

The Cultural Operations Division exists primarily to service "field" requirements, especially those of USIA's 223 libraries and reading rooms in eighty-four countries and its 130 binational centers in twenty-nine countries. These centers and libraries require books, periodicals, equipment and supplies, sheet music and recordings, films and slides, lecture materials, and even buildings. Although the chief of the Cultural Operations Division does not have the responsibility for staffing the centers or libraries, he is aware of the need for well-trained personnel in them, and the Cultural Operations Division cooperates in orientation programs before new librarians or other personnel go to the field. While the information centers sponsor political lectures from time to time, and books found in the reading rooms deal with political or international topics, much of the work of the Cultural Operations Division supports "purely cultural programs," which may have political overtones but are definitely "soft sell." Many of the books, plays, or music sent to the field emphasize freedom of expression, stress the progressive rather than the traditional, and point out that Americans are not just "materialistic." Foreign intellectuals are shown that the United States is not a government-controlled society. A considerable number of the novels and plays recommended by USIA for field use deal with facts of American life which their writers consider objectionable—for example, the living conditions of the Puerto Ricans in New York City as portrayed in "West Side Story." Recordings of American "Jazz" demonstrated the break from the traditional music, indicating that the United States is still in "revolution" and far from status quo oriented. That Americans are interested in humanistic values might be pointed out by supplying books on medicine and art.

The Cultural Operations Division functions under a chief and deputy chief, assisted by a manager for center operations, who guides five libraries and centers branches—one each for Africa, Europe, Latin America, the

Near East and South Asia, and East Asia and the Pacific. The area libraries and centers branches perform services rather similar to those of the area staffs in the Motion Picture and Television Service. A Cultural Services Branch supervises the preparation of lectures for use by USIS personnel overseas and the preparation of materials to further American studies by foreign students. A Music Branch selects music running from jazz to the classical for use at USIS posts and in centers, and obtains right for the performance of American-written plays or the showing of films about American composers in centers or by private groups abroad. A Program Services Branch actually makes purchases or places orders for things needed by the centers; it also procures government documents and obtains free or inexpensive materials for use at USIS posts or in centers, like college catalogs or the house organs of industrial corporations. USIS Tokyo placed one order for eleven thousand copies of American college catalogs for use in advising interested students about schools in the United States. The chief of the Cultural Operations Division and his branch chiefs have numerous contacts with the Agency's area offices, dealing most often with the program coordinators and less often with country desk officers. The chief sits in discussions with area office program coordinators on direct support budget items for information and binational centers or USIS reading rooms, backstopping ICS budget personnel. While budget people look at programs as amounts of money, he looks at budget as support of specific programs and knows how much financial support is needed. During an overseas inspection trip of several months, he may take a close look at the work of selected centers and libraries. Among the thirty officer-level personnel in the Division, which has a total of fifty-four employees, ten are Foreign Service Career Reserves and twenty members of the Civil Service. This is a far higher ratio of FSCR to Civil Service than is normal in the media services as a whole. Each of the area libraries and centers branches has at least one FSCR. The Division is in a position to make suggestions about field needs based on experience and knowledge, as well as preserving continuity and expertise in its stateside operations.

Directly on the firing line in providing field services and in maintaining day-to-day relations with the area officers are the chiefs of the area libraries and centers branches. They deal directly with the program coordinators, never with policy officers, because they are operating with policy that is already an established fact. The content in the centers or libraries they support may vary over time, by area, and by type of facility. After World War II, USIS librarians in Japan responded to an interest in scientific technical materials. Now the Japanese are able to buy this type of book for themselves, and USIS services in this field of knowledge have been reduced in Japan. Although American studies materials, dealing with American history, literature, economics, the social and other sciences, make up a portion of the materials in all USIS facilities, information centers are more likely to emphasize politics, the social sciences, and international affairs. There may be relatively little material of interest to an English teacher in an information center, especially if it is located close to a binational center; binational centers tend to emphasize the teaching of English and place a greater emphasis in their libraries upon American literature and history. In areas lacking information centers, binational center libraries may include political materials but seldom with the degree of emphasis found in information centers. Besides servicing library facilities, the area branches support "book presentation programs" to particular individuals abroad or to groups. They also monitor book orders from the posts, and may check with country desk officers if "too many" books are requested. The area office director is ultimately responsible for any operation affecting the budget of the center or USIS reading rooms. Area branch chiefs make suggestions to the USIS posts on books to be purchased for use in centers and reading rooms. Posts also have ideas on books they wish to use, and they make requests through the area branch chiefs. If these are not on ICS lists, they will be reviewed and approved by the chief of the Cultural Operations Divisions, or at a higher level if sufficiently controversial. The area branches are small, with staffs of five, two of whom are secretaries. Area branch chiefs participate in orientation programs for personnel leaving for centers or reading rooms. They also may brief foreign nationals employed in centers or reading rooms, some of whom are occasionally brought to Washington for training courses.

Responsible for stimulating American studies is the chief of the Cultural Services Branch of the Cultural Operations Division. From 1959 on, separate American studies reading lists on the humanities and the social sciences were made available to USIS posts, to centers, and reading rooms. The program developed into a special certificate program in American studies, run for USIA by the University of Pennsylvania. *The United States of America: A Syllabus of American Studies*, a two-volume book edited by Arthur Dudden, was prepared in 1963. It provided topics for study, summaries indicating subject matter of readings, and reading lists in literature, language and the arts, and in history and the social sciences. Included in special "lecture program packets," developed by the American Studies Section of the Cultural Services Branch and sent to 215 USIS installations overseas to promote the American studies program, were sample certificates, a program handbook for post use, a copy of the syllabus, slides of the University of Pennsylvania and historic Philadelphia, and an order list for the post to use in requesting sets of the syllabus for presentation. The American studies course can be given as an advanced English class, taught in a foreign university, or offered in the centers of reading rooms as a reading course. Questions in the syllabus are pitched at the college freshman level, more difficult than are actually required to pass the certificate examination prepared and graded by the University of Pennsylvania. Posts are encouraged to suggest the value of the course to foreign teachers, to students planning to come to the United States, to students planning to enter their country's foreign service, to businessmen, writers, and journalists, and to local employees of USIS posts or embasies. In a first response to the improved certificate program in American studies, the posts requested two thousand sets of the Dudden book for presentation. Most of its suggested readings can be found in the libraries of the information centers and binational centers or in USIS reading rooms. The program serves a twofold purpose. It stimulates reading about the United States and the use of USIS library facilities overseas.

The Chiefs of the Publications Division and the Informational Media Guaranty Liquidation Staff

Although the Information Center Service is interested in stimulating the use of USIS centers and reading rooms, it also supports publication of books in English and in translation—many of a technical nature—which it puts on the library shelves in its facilities and which it hopes additional people will buy through commercial channels overseas. For many years, to stimulate the publication and sale of USIA-approved books in dollar-short countries, it arranged with publishers to change the "soft currencies" obtained for their overseas book sales into American dollars. Guiding these programs for a number of years were the chiefs of the Publications Division and the Informational Media Guaranty Division of ICS. Financially supported by USIS for publication in English or translation from fiscal year 1950 through fiscal year 1966 were a total of 13,632 books in 123,969,405 copies. Of these, 13,157 books with 111,239,819 copies were printed abroad. All of the 12,180 books printed in translation were published overseas. Only 475 books printed in 12,729,586 copies were published in the United States. In fiscal year 1966, books in translation numbered 1,270, printed in 9,068,744 copies. Even 287 of 343 books in English were printed overseas, 1,599,605 out of 3,198,621 printed in English.[14] USIA support for publication normally consists of an agreement to buy 5 to 20 per cent of the edition—which will be used in its centers or reading rooms or be distributed through its "book presentation program" to foreign leaders and scholars. The Publication Division arranges the printing of approximately fifty low-priced books each year by American publishers in paperback or simplified English editions. These may cost overseas buyers the equivalent of fifteen to twenty-five cents. Simplified editions are published in a graduated series (so-called "Ladder Editions"), employing one, two, three, four, and five thousand English words, with glossaries to define words contained in the book but not in the basic word lists. The ladder books are often used in the teaching of English overseas. Books to be supported are suggested by the Publications Division, making use of materials supplied by the Bibliographic Division and considering field suggestions, and approved by the Senior Book Committee. About thirty of the fifty low-priced books published each year deal with American literature and culture, with science, or with economics, history, or government. The others discuss international relations or consider ideological problems. The commercial book program cannot be a blatant propaganda tool. The books are not attributed to USIA. They are representative of the best books published in America. Sold through commercial channels abroad, they have to be books that readers will want to buy. Although USIA hesitates to push books by United States government officials, occasionally one may become a "best seller" overseas—at least it sells out a 25,000-copy edition and is reprinted. For many years, the Publications Division has had a "book development program." Under this program, when no present book seemed to deal adequately with a topic and USIS was interested in producing a book to fill the gap, it sought out an author and contracted for a book or had a publisher approach an author to write such a book. If the finished product was satisfactory to ICS, USIA would purchase the number of books for it contracted. The book was then in existence and available for translation or for use in the low-priced book program. Always a modest program, it came under congressional fire and review in 1967, with the possibility that it would not be continued. About half of the books printed with USIA assistance in paperback are also produced in simplified English. This required editing and clearance of the simplified version by the original author. The Publications Division also works with American publishers to encourage them to donate and send books for display at trade fairs or other book shows abroad. In areas where publishers have no distributors or ready market, USIA may purchase books itself in order to display representative American products. Book displays prepared for use in the United States are sometimes contributed to USIA for exhibit overseas. The *Washington Post* Children's Book Fair in

Washington was sent to Pakistan and India one year and to Nigeria, Ghana, Sierra Leone, and Liberia another. USIS posts overseas handle publicity, and often find opportunities to show books during a "national library week" or at meetings of national professional associations.

The Publications Division is guided by Bibliographic Division recommendations and by those of the Senior Book Committee in suggesting to the field books which might be useful in translation. A Current Books Recommended list goes to the field every two weeks, with some books on the list identified as suitable for translation. Among topics recommended are space activities, Vietnam, regional alliances, and the dangers or problems of communism (with fewer of these than ten years ago). At least 50 per cent of the books translated are those first suggested by the USIS posts themselves. All publication of books in translation is done overseas, because of lack of suitable translators in America, the cost of publication in the United States, and the cost of shipping books overseas. In addition, USIA is interested in promoting growth of indigenous book publishers and distributors abroad. Books in translation can often be published and sold overseas at a cost equivalent to about twenty-five to thirty cents a copy. When USIA decides it wants a book published, a USIS book officer will go to a foreign publisher and offer to assist him to get publication rights on the book if necessary (perhaps in an exotic language). In some instances USIA will agree to buy up to 20 per cent of a 3,000- to 25,000-copy edition. This assistance may help the overseas publisher see a chance to make a profit; American book publishers and authors have been cooperative in making language rights available for token payments. The largest translation programs are in the Near East and South Asia, especially India. The Far East is also an active area, primarily because of Japan. Since 1963 there has been a major expansion of the program in Latin America. Texts in translation may be published with the assistance of Public Law 480 funds, using up foreign currencies acquired by the United States. Textbooks are published under USIA sponsorship in all of India's twenty-two major languages. Books are placed in the information centers, binational centers, and USIS reading rooms, and distributed in the "book presentation program," but 75 per cent or more are put on sale by commercial booksellers. Field posts check on sales; a percentage remain unsold. Books translated into Bengali in India during a representative year dealt with such familiar figures as Benjamin Franklin, Henry Ford, William Faulkner, Abraham Lincoln, Robert Fulton, Thomas Jefferson, John Kennedy, and George Westinghouse; covered topics like electricity, science, liberty, democracy, atomic energy, and communism. Books in the same language published in Pakistan included a greater emphasis on literature, featuring short stories by Dorothy Canfield, F. Scott Fitzgerald, Sherwood Anderson, Stephen Vincent Benet, Ambrose Bierce, Bret Harte, Jack London, Edgar Allen Poe, and James Thurber. What is the effect of such publications? Measurement is difficult, but personnel in the Publications Division with field experience and cultural affairs officer backgrounds feel that the longer-range programs of USIA, like book publications and exchange programs staffed by USIS personnel overseas, have a more lasting impact than the programs of USIA's other media services.

By January, 1967, the Informational Media Guaranty Division had become the Informational Media Guaranty Liquidation Staff, its chief heading what was left of a program which enabled American publishers to enter overseas markets in some "soft currency" countries they might otherwise have avoided. The chief was liquidating the program while the Agency sought new legislation from the Congress which would restore Agency support for such publication and re-create the Informational Media Guaranty Division. The guaranty program was initiated because American book publishers have little use for foreign currencies, and many foreign book distributors are forbidden to use dollars to pay for books published in the United States. Under agreements with publishers, books approved by the old Informational Media Guaranty Division were paid for by the United States Treasury in dollars in return for foreign currencies if sold to dollarless foreign distributors. Before 1962, books under this program were approved by ICS and the Division so long as they did not reflect in a strongly unfavorable way upon American policies or institutions. After congressional hearings (held in part because of a fear that American publishers were using the program to ship "lurid" books overseas, which was not the case since USIA was understandably opposed to this), only books which reflect favorably on American life, institutions, and policies received dollar support. This disturbed some American booksellers, but USIA's answer to the charge of "censorship" is simply that USIA did not prevent the sale of books anywhere. It just did not help in the sale of certain books by providing American dollars. ICS personnel feel that books sold under the Informational Media Guaranty program were especially beneficial to the United States. They were ordered by foreign book distributors, usually small orders, for serious individuals. An interested reader was waiting to receive the book. More than three-quarters of the books were nonfiction. By October, 1967, the Informational Media Guaranty Liquidation Staff had disappeared from Agency organization charts. Apparently the Agency had failed to convince Congress of the program's usefulness.

The Chief of the English Teaching Division

The chief of the English Teaching Division is responsible for USIA's worldwide English teaching programs, coordinating all Agency activities in this field, including the clearance of messages to the field. His Division develops some teaching materials directly and produces others on contract. It also supplies technical advice or guidance to USIS and other English teachers overseas, to the Broadcasting Service, and to the Motion Picture and Television Service in Washington. Until early in 1961, the present Division was a small four-man English Teaching Branch in the Cultural Operations Division. By 1963, it had a staff of fifteen, including secretaries; five of its eight officer-level personnel were Foreign Service Career Reserves. Two officers program ICS English teaching activities, working with the area offices. Three work on developing teaching materials, one of these almost full time for television programs of IMV. Three others serve as consultants in developing seminar programs overseas for national associations of teachers of English in foreign countries. They spend much of their time abroad, living out of suitcases for three to six months at a time. The chief of the Division has participated in government-wide discussions during the development of English teaching "policy" which were coordinated by the Bureau of Educational and Cultural Affairs in State. The cultural advisor in the Office of Policy and Research, a former English-teaching specialist, is the Division's major IOP contact. Within an Agency led primarily by people with fast media backgrounds, personnel in the English Teaching Division at one time believed the "top brass" viewed its "long pull cultural programs" with "enlightened tolerance." By 1967, the Agency leadership had become ardent supporters of the English-teaching program. There is more to English teaching than just teaching a language; though it is primarily American life and culture which are communicated through English-teaching materials, American foreign policy objectives are also sometimes supported by the materials studied.

English teaching has been in the program of USIA and its predecessor agencies since World War II days, when binational centers were introduced in Latin America, with English teaching as one element among their activities. During the war, English teaching spread to other areas, to North Africa and to Asia. The growth of this teaching is part of a general "language explosion"; since World War II there has been a greater interest almost everywhere in learning a second language. English is the number-one "second language" in the world today. Although the British have an early lead in English-teaching activities, the United States is now seriously trying to build up its own program, working in close collaboration with the British Council. At the present time, the British are likely to have more elite student personnel than USIA in many countries, but the Agency considers this condition as "unlikely to last forever." The United States may still feel the need to produce a Broadcasting Service program showing how similar "American" English is to "British" English. The United States has yet to learn one English-teaching device used by the British. Many students at British centers attend year after year—never "graduating." Students learn English in American programs, receive their certificates, and move on. If the British use English teaching as a means of maintaining friendly relations over time, it would be hoped that the American "graduation" approach is followed by some means of keeping foreign students interested in the United States (perhaps the "book presentation program" or IBS's special English broadcasts).

In the post-World War II period, the methods of language teaching have been revolutionized. "Speaking" has replaced "reading" as the initial teaching emphasis. In the long run, the English Teaching Division's programs increase the opportunities for all kinds of USIA materials in English to reach people abroad. The new nations of Africa and the less-developed nations everywhere are eager to establish contacts abroad and access to scientific and technical materials. Learning English will help. At the third annual two-and-a-half-month seminar for Mali's teachers of English, President Modibo Keita addressed the graduation ceremony held in Bamako, requesting intensive English courses in Mali's schools and approving the rapid development in the English-teaching ability of teachers at the seminar. He pointed out that Africans speak two languages, English and French, and that French-speaking Mali is now obliged to learn English in order to make contact with other parts of Africa. He emphasized the importance of training Malian youth in English so that they could make contact with English Africa and the outside world.

While the English Teaching Division helps organize such national seminars, most of its overseas effort is directed through the USIS posts, the information centers, and binational centers. Courses in English are offered in some universities. USIS personnel may teach government officials in their offices; in one or two instances, when the national Congress adjourns for the day, a USIS teacher comes into the chamber and gives English lessons to its members. USIS personnel even teach classes in their own homes, in spite of housing difficulties in many areas of the world. Some of the teaching is informal, without pay and in addition to regular jobs, or done by USIS wives. Most of it is done with pay, often on contract, budgeted by the area office responsible for the post where the teaching is done. This involves the English Teaching Division in the annual negotiations with the area offices, and in ongoing relations with area office program coordinators.

Much of USIA's English teaching abroad is now done with the aid of a six-volume series, for junior through senior high school level, produced on contract for the English Teaching Division by the National Council of Teachers of English. Special material has also been prepared for adults. *Let's Learn English*, now used as the basis for the IMV's "Let's Learn English" television series, was written privately in 1956 by the American head of a binational center who felt there was no suitable English-teaching material then available. In the *English Teaching Materials Catalogue* for fiscal year 1966, a wide variety of materials are listed, each evaluated and recommended for specific types of use. Generally speaking, as students progress in English, they can be exposed to more complex subject matter; by midpoint in the six-volume series, the reader learns about the United Nations. Though outright political material is eschewed, Americana is woven throughout the series volumes.

Other American agencies besides USIA, of course, teach English overseas or to personnel from abroad in America. Even the Peace Corps now does English teaching, both in the classroom and informally. The Agency for International Development trains English teachers in regular schools or in special institutes in foreign countries, but USIA teaches English on contract to persons scheduled to come on AID programs for training in the United States. American professors going abroad, with Fulbright grants from the government, may get involved in direct teaching or in training English teachers. The Department of Health, Education, and Welfare finds and processes many of the teachers going abroad on State programs, and helps in the orientation of foreign English teachers who come to the United States to study. The Department of Defense brings thousands of military personnel from abroad to the United States each year, and English is part of the visiting trainees' programs. Abroad, Defense representatives help foreign organizations set up English-training programs, and may provide English-teaching laboratories and tapes.

The Chief of the Exhibits Division

Although USIA's exhibits participation in trade fairs sometimes was supervised or operated by the Department of Commerce up to July, 1966, and watched over by an ICS Coordinator of Inter-Agency International Exhibits Activities, the Information Center Service and the chief of the Exhibits Division are now responsible for the Agency's participation in trade fairs, and for a special exhibits program authorized under a section of the Soviet-American cultural agreement, which also provides for the magazine and cultural presentation exchanges. Until July, 1966, the Exhibits Division was responsible for post exhibits, receiving about $2 million for this purpose in fiscal year 1955. By fiscal year 1964, the figure was down to less than one-sixth that amount. It was even lower by fiscal year 1966. In July, 1966, the function was transferred to the Press and Publications Service—since post exhibits consist mostly of pictures and posters, so-called "flat" or printed exhibits. By fiscal year 1964, the bulk of the Exhibits Division effort was directed toward creating and operating large-scale exhibits to tour eastern Europe and the Soviet Union at an annual cost of approximately $1.7 million. USIA's new trade-fair program and the exhibits in eastern Europe combined were a $3,287,000 item in the budget of fiscal year 1966, but fell to $2,334,800 in 1967. Of the Division's approximately thirty-five personnel in Washington, fourteen service the eastern Europe and Soviet Union programs directly—planning and building exhibits and recruiting the personnel who will accompany the exhibits on tour (from ten to fifty-five people may be abroad with these exhibits at any given time). Policy guidance is provided to the Exhibits Division by the chief's attendance at the ICS director's Friday morning staff meeting, or through the ICS "policy officer," the chief of the Bibliographic Division. The chief of the Exhibits Division does not serve on the ICS Senior Book Committee, as do other ICS Division chiefs. He is assisted in formulating exhibits policy by a deputy chief (policy and programs), who was formerly the ICS coordinator of interagency international exhibits activities. The Division relates most of its products to policy through its Development and Production Branch, which also plans and contracts for the building of exhibits. An Operations Branch, the Division's housekeeper, is responsible for circulating exhibits. The Development and Production Branch maintains contact with policy officers and country desk officers in the Agency's area offices—though the contact was somewhat reduced after post "flat" exhibits were turned over to the Press and Publications Service.

Prior to the Kennedy administration, the Exhibits Division had as many as 300 exhibits circulating in the field. By 1963, the figure was down to 160. Exhibits were being "retired" faster than they were being built. Most of these were flat paper or printed exhibits for post use. The exhibits for eastern Europe and the Soviet Union are three dimensional, displaying objects as well as pictures. Funding post exhibits was always a problem for the Exhibits

Division because funds were budgeted through the area offices on the basis of "sales" made by the Information Center Service and the Exhibits Division. When the Agency budget was tight, post exhibits could always be cut, because such a reduction did not require closing an installation or firing overseas personnel. Travel, salaries, and rental costs have gone up slowly, while the Agency budget has not risen greatly. Television activities within the Agency were strengthened. It was the exhibits budget, aside from support for trade fairs or the East-West cultural agreement, that absorbed a portion of the losses required elsewhere. Why was it post exhibits? Why are exhibits still considered valuable in eastern Europe and the Soviet Union but less so elsewhere?

Normally exhibits are not closely related to current political events. There are a few political exhibits (for example, dealing with nuclear arms control or Vietnam), but it takes time to produce exhibits and get them to the field. It is difficult for the Exhibits Division to treat the day-to-day or the ephemeral; exhibits are relatively costly and must last for awhile. Paper exhibits for the posts can be gotten together in two or three weeks, but the exhibits for eastern Europe and the Soviet Union or for trade fairs may take six months to produce. Because of the National Aeronautics and Space Agency's need for relay and observation stations overseas to support its space program (and a concurrent need for some overseas public relations), NASA for several years spent $100,000 annually on exhibits that were circulated by the Exhibits Division of USIA. A color photography exhibit of John Glenn's first American orbital flight around the world was prepared ahead of time, and went on display abroad when he had completed his mission. Although it was possible for some Exhibits Division products to be used in this way at posts, the area offices emphasize different aspects of American policy, and few exhibits are desired worldwide. Exhibits that can be used around the world are less costly per participating area office; as exhibits become more specialized or adapted to a single area, even if of some use in a second area, they may not be shown because the price is higher than if all area offices ordered them in quantity. Personnel in the Exhibits Division believe that the Agency's emphasis on a closer relationship of media products to day-to-day short-term policy objectives after 1961 reduced the Division's share of the area office budgets; they also believe the new policy orientation of the Foreign Service Career Reserves, with increased representational and observation duties, coupled with an aspiration for promotion from specialized information activities to assignment as ambassadors or chiefs of mission, makes FSCR's less appreciative of quality media products and less willing to make arrangements for displaying exhibits—a time-consuming task. Added to this, shipping costs of three-dimensional exhibits were, and remain, high, tending to inhibit post use.

Although the area offices now make considerably less use than in the past of specialized country or area exhibits, the eastern European and Soviet Union program is still considered a success. A hand-tools exhibit was scheduled for Rumania in April, 1967. In Rumania, during the showing of a "transportation exhibit" while Kennedy was President, 600,000 people visited the display during a four-week period. They took away with them 200,000 copies of a 56-page, larger than *Life*-sized pamphlet, done in black-and-white and color. It showed all forms of modern American transportation and their historic progenitors—covering automobiles (passenger cars, house trailers, and trucks); trains (sleek streamliners and freights carrying fourteen automobiles per three-deck freight car); ships (featuring the St. Lawrence Seaway, liners, and tankers); pipe lines; taxis, busses, subways, and mammoth parking garages in New York City; passenger and cargo planes and airports; and vehicles used in American space programs. Six major exhibits in as many years have displayed services provided to American consumers, from transportation, to medicine, to the graphic arts (which through advertising art demonstrates the wide range of commodities available to the American public). The area behind the Iron Curtain has been a fertile ground for the large three-dimensional exhibits. Through talking with tour guides, the people in East Europe and the Soviet Union gain knowledge and are encouraged to ask for additional information, creating a pressure for relaxation on restrictions on the flow of information between East and West. By observing what is available to the American consumer, Soviet and eastern European citizens can wonder if their money has not gone more for strategic services than for consumer goods. American homes and supermarkets displayed have "bowled the people over." During a three-city run in the Soviet Union in 1965, "Architecture—USA" was seen by nearly 240,000 in Moscow, 223,000 in Leningrad, and 250,000 in Minsk—in spite of what USIA believed was "harassment and intensive advance efforts to indoctrinate citizens against the exhibit." Through such exhibits, the United States hopes to encourage evolutionary change, so that the people in the East will want better living conditions and seek to reduce amounts spent on armaments.

With a "medical exhibit" which toured the Soviet Union went eight doctors, six nurses, plus several X-ray technicians and dentists, on a twenty "man" tour-guide staff. A staff of ten accompanied the "medical exhibit" to Yugoslavia. The American Medical Association had cooperated in preparing the display, arranging for the lending of $300,000 worth of equipment; the equipment proved fascinating to foreign doctors as well as to the lay public.

Those accompanying the tours are usually able to speak the language of the country visited. Language specialists accompanying the exhibit, who might not be technical experts on exhibit subject matter, are given six to twelve weeks of training (on medicine or art, etc.) so that they can understand enough to explain the exhibit thoroughly to members of the general public. A "graphic arts exhibit" carried a staff of twenty-one to the Soviet Union, sixteen of whom could speak Russian. Even the nonexperts on the staff go well briefed, with USIA answers provided for 95 per cent of the questions which will be asked. Touring libraries of five hundred to a thousand books on relevant subject matter sometimes accompany the exhibits and are open for use by specialists in the countries visited.

It is said that American government agencies now spend about $12 million annually on exhibits abroad, and there is some cooperation among USIA, Agriculture, Commerce, Defense, the Atomic Energy Commission, and the National Aeronautics and Space Agency. USIA is not always consulted about exhibits which reach foreign publics. Exhibits Division personnel in 1963 believed this indicated a lack of coordination of United States government exhibit activities overseas. Today, ICS leaders believe coordination has become closer as the exhibits programs of government agencies have matured. From USIA's point of view, relations with the Department of Commerce have been particularly improved since the reallocation of responsibility on trade fairs. It is believed that USIA could do a great deal more exhibit work to support the Agency for International Development programs overseas, to help create a climate to encourage self-help and modernization. Only on Alliance for Progress projects for Latin America does the Exhibits Division actively support AID programs. Here it is only "a little involved." The future growth or reduction of exhibit activities overseas may well depend on the results of cost-effectiveness analyses produced under the Planning-Programming-Budgeting System.

VII

Public Relations and Policy:
Dealing with the Agency's Publics—
Domestic and Foreign

USIA's Publics

All of the activities of the director and deputy director of USIA, the Office of Policy and Reasearch, the area offices, and the media services would be relatively useless or at least considerably less effective in a truncated United States Information Agency, lacking policy-related units working with the Agency's varied publics, at home and abroad. Because the Congress of the United States holds the power to feed or starve Agency programs, the understanding of USIA which can be generated among members of the Senate and House by the general counsel of the Agency and his assistants lays the groundwork for feast or famine—for programs with impact or ineffectual holding operations. Because American public opinion may overreact to Agency successes or "failures," question the use of propaganda overseas, or fear its use domestically, the Office of Public Information helps smooth over the peaks and valleys so that USIA is neither damned into nonexistence nor touted as the single tool which can resolve all America's international problems. Because Americans believe that they and people overseas should engage in community activities, practice self-help, and cooperate as individuals or groups in resolving national problems by unleashing private initiative to backstop government efforts, the relations of the Office of Private Cooperation (which by October, 1967, had ceased to exist as an organizational entity) to American citizens, cities, and other groups (business, labor, or professional) were expected to add momentum to USIA's regularly budgeted programs. Because government agencies are largely made up of bureaucrats (long-time members of the Civil Service or Foreign Service, specialists in the work of a single agency, who are not always trusted by the public or Congress to state their own case or to make a fair analysis of their internal problems), the private members of the United States Advisory Commission on Information—distinguished representatives of American

276

information media and communications professions—can be helpful in providing independent insights for USIA's guidance and private support for recognized Agency needs. Although policy could be made in Washington and the Broadcasting Service could relay its signal to peoples throughout the world without USIS field posts, operations by field personnel carry other programs overseas to reach additional audiences that USIA seeks to influence, provide local insights and policy and program suggestions which allow sensitive adaption of USIA programs impossible without on-the-spot observation, and build relationships with communications and educational leaders which make placement of headquarters policy-related products in local media not only possible but probable. Understanding the work of the Office of the General Counsel, the Office of Public Information, the Office of Private Cooperation, the United States Advisory Commission on Information, and USIS Field Posts will help place the tasks performed by the director, Office of Policy and Research, area offices, and media services in a broader perspective.

THE OFFICE OF THE GENERAL COUNSEL (IGC): TARGET — CAPITOL HILL

For all of its farflung operations in influencing opinion overseas, USIA runs a remarkably small program to explain itself to members of the Congress of the United States. This stems not from any desire to withhold information, but from the fact that members of the House and Senate are sensitive to being the target audience of a propaganda agency. Most Executive Branch agencies employ discretion and moderation in their dealings with Capitol Hill, but USIA must play the role of Caesar's wife. As a result, congressional relations of the Agency are conducted by a subordinate unit attached to the Office of the General Counsel, the majority of whose ten nonsecretarial employees worry about the Agency's legal affairs or securing clearances for music or other copyrighted materials for Agency use. No longer do any of the cabinet-level departments of the United States government combine their legal and congressional relations function in a single organizational unit. However small the USIA operation, congressional relations are tremendously important to an Agency fighting for recognition and acceptance as the fourth dimension of overt foreign policy. In fact, since the Agency operates overseas and has been discouraged from providing much public information to the mass American public about the job it does, the members of Congress are USIA's major domestic constituency. Only in times of crisis abroad, when the war in Southeast Asia becomes increasingly important to average Americans, would Barry Zorthian, USIS mission director in South Vietnam, or Agency Director Leonard Marks appear on NBC-TV's "Morning Show" to talk about aspects of USIA's role abroad—perhaps discussing the functions of the public information and press officer in Saigon or the Agency's "psychological warfare" activities in support of military operations.

USIA services its congressional constituency with care and without ostentation. While the Agency is interested in building a favorable image with congressmen in general, its key "constituent," as for the Department of State, is Congressman John J. Rooney, chairman of the House Appropriations Committee subcommittee responsible for the State and the USIA budgets. Mr. Rooney is not one to be swayed by doting or undue efforts at persuasion. He is a man of independent mind, with many questions—a high percentage of them shrewd and penetrating, focused more on operational detail than broader policy matters—who has studied "his agencies and departments" for years and sometimes knows more about them than they know about themselves. Preparation of USIA personnel for appearances before his subcommittee or other congressional committees is done as carefully as time and staff available permit. It would be impossible to be too carefully prepared. Leadership in maintaining the Agency's routine relations with the Congress and in providing insights on members of Congress for hearings or other dealings rests with the Office of the General Counsel. The general counsel himself plays a major role in deploying the Agency director and deputy Agency director, or the deputy Agency director for policy and research, to speak before congressional groups, to attend private luncheons, and to appear at hearings. Two congressional liaison officers, with the help of three secretaries, maintain important if more routine relations—providing numerous services to members of the Congress. The general counsel's legal responsibilities are carried out primarily by the deputy general counsel and five assistant general counsels, who give advice on Agency contracts or handle legal actions in which the Agency has an interest. The Rights Clearance Division handles many copyright clearances for USIA, though some of this work is also done by the individual media services.

The General Counsel of USIA

The general counsel is the Agency's general overseer of congressional relations. Working closely with the Agency director, he is "in at the take-offs as well as the crash-landings" in Agency affairs. By philosophy and experience, he believes that a good job by the Agency is the best relations it can have with the Congress. The legacy of the McCarthy era and the Agency's adolescent years left many negative feelings among members of the Congress—

some based on fact, others a bit distorted—which a more mature USIA is now patiently trying to correct and live down. Whatever reservations observers on the Hill may feel toward the closer relationship of USIA programs to policy objectives, under the leadership of Edward Murrow the Agency completed turning the corner leading to respectability and began to be viewed by congressmen as "better than before" and "a good outfit now." Shy as Murrow was in fact, he came through in discussions with members of the Congress as "a straight from the shoulder guy"—whether his words were accepted or not. Rightly or wrongly, Murrow also acquired a reputation with other congressmen of "running around end"; for example, the release by USIA for public showing in the United States of the color films of Jacqueline Kennedy's visit to India and Pakistan—on the basis of passage of a Senate resolution with which the House of Representatives did not concur. Under Marks, Agency behavior has purposely been more circumspect, though it is not yet clearly evident that congressmen have become more trusting. Important for the Agency in improving its congressional relations is an increasing understanding by the members of the relevance of positive "ideas" to foreign policy, for even in a plural world where the old Cold War has been dampened down some members of Congress still prefer to view USIA as participating in a "war" of ideas. A few members of Congress from the South have been critical of USIA for its coverage of the administration's civil-rights efforts in its overseas programs; the Agency takes great pains to straighten out in direct contacts what it does say overseas about integration, preferring to be "hit on the facts and not on rumors," making the point that it is both accurate reporter of events and administrative policy representative in speaking to the world. Fortunately, the bread-and-butter issues which get most American congressmen re-elected have less to do with United States information programs overseas.

The general counsel has a number of useful tools in his kit for strengthening USIA's ties with the Congress. When a Seattle or New York World's Fair is held, USIA is likely to give overseas coverage in Voice of America shows or with pictures and stories in *America Illustrated*. It may be a story on the Mayo Clinic. The senators or congressmen most interested are informed of the use of materials about their cities or institutions. Sometimes members of Congress have participated in opening ceremonies at a world's fair and may actually be pictured or heard in the Agency product. Congressmen are often quoted in Voice broadcasts as representing responsible American opinion and may be asked to appear in person to participate in a discussion program. By law, USIA is required to provide Congress with reports on its operations every six months. Letters accompany the reports mailed to individual members, calling their attention to pages in the report which they will find of special interests. Although these routine services appear to lack glamor, most congressmen are flattered to be quoted or to participate in an overseas broadcast. During the Murrow days, the Agency director was willing to appear with members of the Congress on the television or radio shows they prepared for use in their local districts. His status as a celebrity added luster and held viewers or listeners to the program. The Agency director, his executive assistant, and the deputy Agency director make a number of appearances at breakfasts of congressional groups—of which there are almost limitless numbers, from the Burros Club or the Bull Elephants, composed of administrative assistants of House Democrats or House Republicans, to the 88th Club or the 83rd Club, made up of members of the House elected for the first time for the session which gives the organization its name. The general counsel and the "speaker" of the early morning arrive for breakfast by 8 A.M.—some congressmen must never breakfast at home with their wives. The director (or deputy director) makes some informal remarks and then answers questions. Other luncheon or office meetings place the Agency leaders in personal contact with most if not all members of the Appropriations Committees of the House and Senate. These are "meat" meetings at which the director, executive assistant, or deputy director can explain what USIA needs and why. Congressmen often request jobs for constituents with USIA: the people recommended do get to see the right people quickly and get fair treatment, but are hired only if "they have the stuff"; congressmen expect no more. If someone is appointed, the congressman is informed before the person is notified so that he can concurrently congratulate the new appointee. Individual luncheons with congressmen who were to have new Voice of America relay stations in their communities to explain the new operation encouraged a number of members of Congress to have an interest in the installations and collaterally in USIA.

The general counsel has the over-all responsibility for Agency testimony or presentations before congressional committees, except on appropriations matters, though he must use the substantive elements of the Agency in the preparation of the basic materials. "Briefing Books" are prepared for the use of the director, the executive assistant, or the deputy director when they are scheduled to appear at a congressional hearing. For example, the deputy director appeared before the Latin American Subcommittee of the House Foreign Affairs Committee to talk about USIA's information activities connected with the Cuban missile crisis in 1962. The original draft of the statement to be made by the deputy director was drafted in the Area Office for Latin America. The general counsel reviewed the first draft, made suggestions, and asked for additional information; after further work a second draft was submitted. Then the general counsel met with the deputy director for a discussion of the paper and additional changes were incorporated. At the same time, a representative of the general counsel was attending hearings of the Subcommittee to learn what was on the minds of the members, to see the line of questioning. The background of members of the Subcommittee was checked in the file maintained on members of the House and Senate which indicates their relationships with the Agency and their particular interests. Twenty or so possible questions were identified. In a dry run, the deputy director was "tested" and corrected, provided with current information about the congressmen who would attend so that he could talk with them about some of their personal and timely interests. Most statements are drafted by Agency area or media specialists working on "the front line," but some work may be done by the special assistants of the Agency director or deputy director. Of all the hearings, those in support of appropriations are probably the most vital to the Agency's effectiveness—at least from USIA's view. The assistant director of USIA for administration has the primary responsibility for the Agency's appropriations bill, "the gut work," but the general counsel sits on the Program Review Committee which considers the budget before it goes to Capitol Hill and is involved in the rehearsals before appearances of the director, deputy director, or the executive assistant at congressional hearings. A "Book of Horrors," containing all the thorny questions which may come up, and answers, will be prepared before any budget hearings. Of thirty items prepared, eight may come up at the hearing. Marks is said by his associates to make good use of the "Briefing Books" prepared by Agency elements, to have an excellent memory which enables him to answer most congressional questions without reference to notes. When questions got too rough for the USIA specialist from the area office or media service who was on the stand, Murrow sometimes stepped in and answered the questions. He once sat through an entire appropriations hearing, intervening whenever it seemed useful. Specialists know about area and media affairs, but the director is more knowledgeable of congressional interests and may better understand what lies behind an explicit question. Too much intervention by Murrow, of course, may sometimes have backfired and irritated committee members who felt he was shielding the area or media experts from questioning. Marks has resolved this problem by taking over leadership of the Agency testimony himself, assisted by his executive assistant and the assistant director of USIA for administration. Anyone who has read a number of congressional hearings is aware that some members of Congress take pleasure in "heckling" middle-level bureaucrats. No one appearing before a congressional committee is "equal" to its members, but an Agency director is less unequal than subordinates who are area or functional rather than political experts.

The Agency has few legislative bills of its own. The Office of the General Counsel is responsible for Agency comment on legislative proposals of other Executive Branch agencies. One of the assistant general counsels handles these, consulting the substantive experts in the Agency, with the reply to the Bureau of the Budget signed by the general counsel. The general counsel keeps as much of the burden of congressional relations away from the Agency director and deputy director as possible, but on public matters which may "explode" or that have political overtones, they would be drawn in and consulted before Agency responses were given to congressional inquiries. Mark's general counsel spends about one-quarter of his time on the Hill when Congress is in session. A former staff member of a congressional committee, he often works through congressional staffs—with whom he can be influential because of his Agency rank. A member of Congress may be less impressed, and sometimes requires attention from the Agency director. The Agency director maintains a close watch over the reaction of southern congressmen to Broadcasting Service or Motion Picture and Television Service handling of civil-rights matters.

As the Agency approaches maturity and gains additional recognition as a foreign policy tool, the congressional relations task of the general counsel will become heavier, and some modest increase may have to be made to support his activities and those of the Agency leaders. Up to a point, such an increase should be welcomed by Mr. Rooney and his House Appropriations Subcommittee—for once he has reviewed the budget and made selective cuts, the program is his own; he defends it before the full House with skill and ingenuity. In part, he gains support for "his bill" from whatever effective continuing liaison on matters other than budget that USIA is able to maintain with members of the Congress through the Office of the General Counsel.

The Congressional Liaison Officers

USIA's two congressional liaison officers, both members of the Civil Service with past staff experience on Capitol Hill, handle the more routine relations with members of Congress, concentrating on congressional staffs, providing the daily services requested of the Agency, following the legislative action through the *Congressional Record*, and maintaining files on voting records and relationships of members of the House and Senate with the

Agency. In many ways, their work is quite similar to that of the legislative officers serving under the assistant secretary for congressional relations in the Department of State. There are only two of them instead of seven; their interests are centered more directly on the House Foreign Affairs Committee and the Senate Foreign Relations Committee than their State counterparts. They may spend a higher portion of their time on the Hill—the senior liaison officer half of his working day, and the junior, at least a quarter of her time. The general counsel under whom they serve is somewhat less often on the Hill, but it is not unusual for him to be there with the Agency director or deputy director in tow. State's assistant secretary for congressional relations may spend most of his working day in the corridors and offices in the Capitol or Senate and House office buildings. Because USIA is less well known to congressional staffers than State, the liaison officers answer many queries by personal visits, to broaden contacts and talk about Agency programs and problems. When foreign nationals employed by USIS posts overseas are in Washington for headquarters training courses, liaison officers may take them to visit Capitol Hill, calling a member of the Senate of House off the floor to meet and talk with visitors. This provides an opportunity for the "locals" to see the ease of access to public leaders in the United States, and allows the members of the House or Senate to ask questions about USIS work overseas. The problem of bringing members of Congress in contact with USIA products and programs in a positive way is one which is much on the minds of the liaison officers. They were quite pleased when Agency Director Murrow held six private screenings of USIA films for members of the House and Senate, representatives of the press, and other Executive Branch departments' but they believe more of this needs to be done. Congressmen can understand the need to spend money for power projects or defense, but the purpose of sending books overseas is less apparent to them. Liaison officers feel circumscribed by congressional legislation which restricts USIA information in the United States and "forces it to start at the water's edge." With members of the House and Senate knowing too little about USIA, the liaison officers fear that congressmen on overseas trips go primarily to view diplomatic or military operations. Even if the public affairs officers are informed of the visits, tight schedules make it difficult to work in a look at USIS libraries or binational centers—which liaison officers think would be helpful, whether the visitor is friendly or unfriendly to USIA programs.

A typical day at 1750 Pennsylvania Avenue brings thirty to forty phone calls from Capitol Hill to the liaison officers or their three secretaries, and twenty to twenty-five letters. Some of the phone calls can be answered directly; others must be checked out in the Agency and a return call made to the Hill. A House member requests the Agency to send a copy of "Religion Under Communism" to an Indiana constituent. Another member of the House requests the Agency to show the films of Mrs. Kennedy's visits to India and Pakistan at the Sulgrave Club in Washington. A House office requests special tours of the Voice of America for visiting constituents. A Senate office asks for Agency assistance in getting an interview for a constituent with the Italian diplomatic mission to the United Nations—for a constituent who had wanted to work for USIA in Italy. (This had been an impossibility for the Agency, because its overseas employees are primarily FSCR's or members of the Foreign Service Staff Corps, subject to assignment anywhere.) A congressman from Kansas calls to ask if a USIA motion picture, "Symphony Across the Land," which included a shot of the Wichita community orchestra, can be borrowed and shown to support that organization's current fund-raising campaign. The liaison officer raises the question with the general counsel. Taking a strict inforcement viewpoint of congressional directives to the Agency not to show its products within the United States, the general counsel says, "No." A record is kept of all calls; and a typed summary indicates the Agency's action. Letters may demand more detailed responses. A member of the House is interested in the facts about the cutback in Soviet jamming of Voice of America broadcasts. (So many inquiries arrived on this that the Public Information Office prepared a standard discussion of jamming, indicating past actions and the present situation.) A member of the House inquires in a critical letter, "How many copies of an *American Dictionary of Slang* have been sent overseas?" The Agency replies that seventy-nine copies are overseas, each sent in answer to a field request. A senator forwards a thoughtful letter from a constituent suggesting that Americans donate books to USIA for shipment overseas. The Agency notes (on the basis of experience) that only 10 to 20 per cent of the books collected would be useful for overseas use, and that the operation would require too much staffing. (A program of this type has been carried on with much of the work being done by Foreign Service wives under the general aegis of the Office of Private Cooperation.) A lady constituent of a New York senator, now living in Thailand, was offended by a Buddhist religious ceremony at the opening of a new USIA Information Center in that country. She had also written to the Department of State. The Agency's reply (drafted in the appropriate area office, its substance cleared with the Thai Desk Officer in State, and reviewed by a liaison officer in USIA) noted that the ceremony was a customary traditional event on such an occasion in Thailand. Drafts of letters written by the area offices or media services must often be modified by the liaison officers, because the experts may not always know whether the receiver of the letter is a supporter or opponent of Agency programs. To save time, the liaison officer may handcarry the letter to the drafter and explain background facts to save a later rewrite. All congressional mail is logged in and date stamped when it arrives and is similarly logged at each stage of its journey through USIA. Known as "Green Hornets," because they are accompanied as they move about within USIA by a memorandum on a green sheet of paper, congressional letters are given priority handling at every level.

Copies of the *Congressional Record* are provided for all USIA elements; to guide busy readers, a special "Daily Summary of the Congressional Record" highlights eight to thirty topics each day in one to three pages. This also goes to most offices in the Agency. Although the Agency's comments on legislation proposed by other Executive Branch agencies are prepared under the guidance of an assistant general counsel, the liaison officers have an opportunity to review such comments. They maintain the file on House and Senate members for the use of Agency personnel talking with congressmen on the Hill, but they have nothing directly to do with the preparation of "Briefing Books" for appearances at congressional hearings. State's legislative officers have the over-all supervision of gathering the materials for "Briefing Books" in their areas of specialization—a function performed by the general counsel for USIA. USIA and State Congressional Relations are in contact from time to time, particularly to check correspondence that may overlap or to exchange letters that are better answered in the other agency. Any request for information from State by USIA's liaison officers is channeled through State's legislative officers.

Tied down by routine telephone requests and "bird-dogging" written replies to congressional mail, the liaison officers spend less time on the Hill than might be useful. With Foreign Service Career Officers sometimes not able to be placed within area officer or media service complements, it is possible that some might be available for "detail" to help with USIA's congressional relations. This was not considered in the Agency as a very likely source for relieving the workload of the liaison officers in 1963. Most FSCR's have served many years overseas, with little opportunity to learn to know the Executive Branch, let alone the Hill. It was believed that the learning process would be time consuming. The present small staff has little time to provide the orientation which might be necessary, especially since the man might find a spot within the approved personnel complement of another element at any time and be lost just as he was beginning to become useful; but, by 1967, the general counsel was receptive to the idea of assigning FSCR's or young FSO's to temporary duty as congressional liaison aides for two- or three-month periods. This might be of more benefit to the foreign service officers assigned than to the general counsel. Within complement, on a slight.y larger staff, use of foreign service officers with their knowledge of field operations might also add a valuable tool to the liaison program.

The Assistant General Counsels

The general counsel is involved in the work of all elements of his office, but most of his time is spent on legislative matters or congressional relations. The deputy general counsel is sometimes involved in congressional work but spends more of his time on the legal affairs of the office. There is also an associate general counsel (contracts). He was responsible for all construction contract work of the United States government at Montreal's Expo 67 and will deal similarly with preparation for the Osaka Fair in 1970. One of the assistant general counsels is responsible for USIA comments (in response to Bureau of the Budget queries) on legislative proposals by other Executive Branch agencies, but most work done by the assistant general counsels centers on review of Agency contracts, on advice to the Domestic Service Personnel Division about Civil Service regulations, and on representing the Agency when it has an interest in a legal action. The five assistant general counsels are organized so that each is responsible for legal advice to an area office (one has both of the separate halves of Europe), each has one media service, and several have other USIA elements and handle special functional problems—serving as the Agency's equal employment officer or contract compliance officer. One assistant general counsel is now responsible for legal aspects of rights clearance. Most of the work done by the assistant general counsels relates to the media services, which have large Civil Service staffs and which produce many products on contract. The work done by the assistant general counsels is almost completely separated from the tasks performed by the legislative liaison officers. They hold biweekly staff meetings with the general counsel and the deputy general counsel; the liaison officers meet informally with the general counsel as necessary. Most problems raised by the area offices with an assistant general counsel involve a particular media product. When this is clear, the assistant general counsel turns over the case to his counterpart with responsibility for the particular media service involved. The assistant general counsel for Africa and the Press and Publications Service is doubly responsible for legal considerations involved in negotiations for construction of a printing plant in Nigeria. If the plant were being planned for Japan, the question would probably have gone first to another assistant general counsel and would then have been forwarded to him as a representative of Press and Publications Service legal interests to insure that any agreement reached would conform to statues, mostly American federal law. Proposals of operating elements are reviewed and opinions furnished, often after discussion and informal consultation among the assistant general counsels or with the advice of the deputy general counsel.

While the Contract and Procurement Division of the the Office of Administration is responsible for most contract work of the Agency, its drafts are sent to an assistant general counsel for review and clearance. If the General Accounting Office takes exception to a *per diem* payment for travel or to a housing allowance granted by the Office of Administration's Finance and Data Management Division, the assistant general counsel would talk informally with General Accounting Office lawyers and help the Division draft an answer to the GAO. All leases or land purchases made by the Agency either in the United States or abroad must be reviewed and cleared by an assistant general counsel. Their work may require visits to USIA installations in the United States or overseas, particularly when they are concerned with a question that requires a study of Agency records. When the America Houses in West Germany were converted into binational centers, limiting United States contributions and increasing contributions by the Germans themselves, contractual arrangements had to be worked out on the spot with individual German cities, and bylaws were drawn for the operations of the centers that would protect United States interests. In Washington, the Office of the General Counsel tries to act in concert with State on questions of employment or severance of local nationals overseas, cooperating with the office of State's legal adviser. Assistant general counsels are likely to maintain working contacts with the Civil Service Commission and with the Office of the Legal Counsel or the Civil Division of the Department of Justice.

When Civil Service personnel are dismissed for cause by the Domestic Service Personnel Division of USIA's Office of Personnel and Training, an assistant general counsel would represent USIA at an administrative hearing if the employee had employed legal counsel. The media service or area office concerned would long since have sought the advice of the assistant general counsel before taking the action up with the "Personnel." After the administrative hearing, if the employee wishes, he may file suit in the Court of Claims. At this point, the assistant general counsel would assemble all relevant material on the case for the Department of Justice which would conduct the court defense for the government. The general counsel serves as USIA employment policy officer, and one of the assistant general counsels is his deputy. An employee who believes that he or she has been denied equal employment opportunities because of race, religion, or national origin can complain informally, and an assistant general counsel will investigate and attempt to remedy the situation if there appears to be substance to the claim. Only three formal complaints were lodged in a recent two-year period. If th∷ employee wishes, there can be an Agency hearing, presided over by a senior USIA officer, possibly the general counsel. On the basis of this hearing, the Agency director can make a "determination." Either without an Agency hearing or after the "determination," the employee can take the question before the President's Committee on Equal Employment Opportunity, normally chaired by the Vice President. It can investigate and make a finding and can refer the matter back to the Agency for reconsideration if it disagrees with the original "determination." It is left to the Agency director to make a final decision; but if the Agency's original position is seriously questioned, the director would be likely to make some adjustment toward the views of the President's Committee.

Rights Clearance

Even a United States government agency, operated in the interests of all the American people, must respect the rights and property of creative individuals. USIA is a mass consumer of all varieties of music, plays, books, and television and radio shows "off the line"—all owned by an author or subject to restrictions on performance. Every one of the media services uses copyrighted materials. Every USIS post overseas places copyright materials on radio and television stations, in motion-picture theaters, and in foreign press and periodicals or authorizes publication of books in translation. It would not take long with this variety of activities for USIA to run up a $50 million bill for rights if it had to pay for full and final clearance for each item used throughout the world.

Rights clearance at one time was handled by the individual media services. Most of the clearance work done in the Office of the General Counsel is still done in behalf of the Broadcasting Service. The "expert" for the Broadcasting Service was attached to the staff of the general counsel in 1962, her work expanded to include the Motion Picture and Television Services. She had been the Voice of America's rights clearance specialist since 1941, when broadcasts started to Latin America, with Nelson Rockefeller as coordinator of inter-American affairs. Although she was not an attorney, she developed a hard-to-equal expertise in copyright law. She is still the best-known beggar or wheedler in government to the American Federation of Musicians, the American Federation of Radio and Television Artists, the American Guild of Musical Artists, and the International Alliance of Technical Stage Hands and Electricians. Most of her clearances are obtained free, they cost USIA nothing but her salary and that of a small clerical staff plus travel expenses for attendance at national conventions of appropriate associations to keep up contacts. No one has ever sued for the improper use of any materials she has procured; this is because any limitations on performance are carefully conveyed to the operating elements of USIA making use of the materials obtained.

Not all the work of rights clearance has been centralized in the Agency, though in 1967 USIA was seriously studying the advantages and disadvantages of centralization. To strengthen the role of the Office of the General Counsel within the Agency in rights clearance, there is now an assistant general counsel for rights clearance. The Office of the General Counsel has already taken over some of the rights clearance work formerly done within the Press and Publications Service. Most of the materials used by the Information Center Service and much needed by IPS are still cleared for Agency use through these media services. Many of the clearances for ICS and IPS must be paid for, usually by token payments. Those for IBS and IMV have long been obtained free because of the tradition developed in the early days of the Broadcasting Service.

Individuals protecting the rights of composers or performers often view clearance for USIA use as "in the public interest," but the question can be raised: "If you pay General Motors for tanks, why not pay us for our music, our plays, our performances?" It is a good question, but USIA could not hire enough individuals to write the music it uses; it could ill afford to pay great actors and actresses or singers for their costly talents. Congress can understand the need to pay for tanks. Would it understand the need to pay full price for music? Of course, many of the books translated for overseas use and much of the music played on the air by the Voice or used by the other media services would not reach overseas audiences by private means. Authors and artists may figure they are really not losing anything. Their work has already been done, so why not become an internationally known author or performing artist. On the other hand, tanks are not made for other than government use; they are not already produced, ready to be re-used at no cost to the producer. This may be the crucial difference, but a singer or writer lives by his work just as a munitions maker does. To raise the issue is not to resolve it. USIA is thankful for rights given to it without cost by individual American citizens to be used in the national interest.

THE OFFICE OF PUBLIC INFORMATION (I/R): TARGET—MAIN STREET, U.S.A.

Although the overseas information program of USIA is figuratively of blockbuster size and nuclear powered (so far as government overseas information programs go), the domestic information program of the Agency can be equated with a peashooter or slingshot. The Office of Public Information, though competent enough and well organized, is not the most active element in USIA. Congress is reasonably permissive in its view of domestic public information by the Department of State (which has to inform the American people about foreign policy), but its attitude toward dissemination of information about USIA is more an enjoinder to refrain from any positive program to explain the work of the Agency to the American people. The Congress does not want any "tyranny over the minds of men" in the United States; on the other hand, it probably would not mind if USIA were even more persuasive overseas than it already is. Perhaps the congressional fear is legitimate; if the Voice were beamed inward, is it not possible that a party in power could use government facilities to convince the voters of its virtues? USIA chafes little under the restrictions on public information. It maintains a modest program, mainly answering questions when asked, taking only a limited initiative in telling USIA's story in America as it concentrates on telling America's story to the world. Although Edward R. Murrow led the Agency toward a more positive public information policy (arranging for distribution of the films of Jacqueline Kennedy's visits to India and Pakistan in the United States through United Artists), there was no basic change in operations of the Office of Public Information. Under Marks, its staff was even further reduced in size.

Four reasons can be given to justify some level of public information operation by USIA. Not the least important is the maintenance of staff morale. USIS personnel serve in 106 countries, some in faraway places, well buried in the "boondocks." They need some reassurance that Americans remain aware of them and what they are doing. Unlike trained guerrilla fighters in uniforms blending with the terrain, they are uncamouflaged targets for overseas groups opposing American policies. While there are certain esoteric advantages to living overseas, life abroad is often a far cry from the comfortable coke-and-hot-dog existence of average Americans. From a practical point of view, USIA must compete for new recruits to carry information about the United States and its policies to every corner of the world—to unpleasant climates as well as temperate ones, to unhealthful areas as well as to those where cholera is under control. USIA needs 100 to 150 new employees a year, 50 to 75 young men and women for its junior officer trainees program. More qualified individuals are attracted if they and their friends and families have heard about the organization they plan to join. Any government agency needs some support among the American people so that pressures can be brought on Congress for support of agency programs. If Americans do not know about the information tool and its relationship to American foreign policy, members of Congress are likely to make their biggest cuts where it affects their constituents' knowledge the least—USIA. If they know about the Agency's programs, their congressmen can vote an adequate budget for USIA without fear. In a democracy, government agencies have a responsibility to report to the people what they are doing. USIA particularly must make an effort to do this because most of its products are invisible to Americans and the results intangible to the lay observer.

Although USIA can report to the American people, Congress makes it clear that appropriated money cannot be used to "propagandize" Americans. The Office of Public Information is small, with some fifteen employees, almost half secretaries. It is headed by a director and deputy director. Two of its public information officers service the press; another works with radio and television. One supervises the preparation of the Agency's semiannual *Report to Congress* and may write speeches for delivery by Agency personnel invited to make public appearances. Another answers public mail. The eighth is stationed at the Voice of America, serving as its information channel across town to the rest of the Agency and holding responsibility for the operation of USIA's exhibit there—seen each year by some twenty thousand Americans and foreign visitors to Washington—housed with the Voice in the Health, Education, and Welfare Building. In January, 1967, the Office of Public Information "gained" several employees as publication of the *USIA Correspondent*—the Agency's house organ for its personnel in Washington and abroad—was shifted from the Press and Publications Service to I/R.

DIRECTION OF THE OFFICE OF INFORMATION

Like the directors and deputy directors of other USIA offices, the leaders of the Office of Public Information have access to the Agency director and deputy director, attending the director's weekly staff meeting. They may contact one of the Agency's "top four" twice a day on an average. They are in a position to make a "public-relations" input into Agency thinking on policy and programs. They have no relations with the Department of State's public information operation: "State is not USIA's adviser on its domestic public relations." They work informally with the area offices and media services, clearing public responses to the press with them, checking both facts and wording. Unlike State's Office on News, they have no press conferences by the agency head to worry about, though Ed Murrow did have one press conference. USIA Agency directors have preferred to talk informally with individual representatives of the press. No facilities for reporters are provided in USIA, and most of the news on USIA is covered by reporters stationed in State—who often prefer to call by phone rather than to take the time or pay the taxi fare to confer directly with USIA personnel. The substance of most telephone calls or visits and the answers given is reported to the Office of Public Information informally. In the competitive news jungle of Washington, USIA has a low priority. At times, this may be an advantage. The director and deputy director of I/R do participate in the editing and review of "all" speeches or manuscripts given or prepared by USIA personnel, including speeches or articles by the director of the Agency. The Office of Public Information does not insist on full texts of speeches to be made by old hands at USIA. They review answers to public letters if there are unusual problems or if a new type question arises—approving form replies if many queries focus on a single issue. The director or deputy director can give permission for members of the press to see USIA films or other products upon request, or even screen a typical product for visiting high school or college groups—sometimes giving a briefing on USIA to the visitors and answering their questions.

The Office of Public Information, like public information offices throughout government, maintains a mailing list. Included among the ten thousand addresses are those of editors, teachers, schools of journalism, libraries, foundations, etc. All receive the semiannual *Report to Congress*. This necessitates an obvious overprinting of the Agency's *Report*, to which the Congress has not taken execption. Some fifty press releases a year are sent to the editors of specialized trade publications on new films or exhibits. Another twenty-four general press releases go to one thousand on the mailing list, including many newspaper editors. Texts of one or two speeches given by the Agency director are distributed by the Office of Public Information in two to three hundred copies to the news media—press, radio, and television—and to the members of the Executive Reserve (men or women who might be called into government service with USIA in case of national catastrophe, if USIA leaders were wiped out before they could be removed from Washington to special underground emergency quarters). Occasionally, tapes are made available to radio and television stations or networks. In servicing speaking requests, the Office of Public Information arranges between 170 and 200 appearances by Agency personnel each year. Ed Murrow received six thousand requests to speak during his tenure as Agency director. He actually gave about sixty talks, making the chance of getting him as a speaker one in a hundred. Marks makes fewer appearances and is highly selective of his audiences. The Office of Information fills some requests for the Agency director with other Agency personnel, perhaps the director of the Voice of America or the Agency deputy director for policy and research. About half of the speaking engagements of Agency personnel are in Washington; half, out of town. The Agency has no funds to cover speaking costs, so groups requesting speakers must cover the cost of travel and accommodations. The Office of Public Information answers 7,200 letters a year from members of the American public. Many letters ask the same questions, and form letters are drafted and cleared for general use. Many are requests for samples of Agency output. Some may be answered with printed pamphlets which give the general information about some aspect of the Agency often requested. About thirty groups, either composed of adults interested in foreign affairs or colleges and high school students, come to USIA each year, may be shown a film, given a briefing, perhaps escorted on a tour of the Voice of America. Relatively few Americans are reached by all these public information services, but American citizens are said to be better off in this respect than French and British citizens. They are almost totally unaware of the major overseas propaganda efforts of their governments. There is no inclination in USIA to alter the level of domestic public relations; the equilibrium is considered satisfactory if not optimal.

THE SEMIANNUAL REPORT TO CONGRESS

Required semiannually by Section 1008 of Public Law 402 (80th Congress), USIA's *First Report to Congress* covered the five-month period from August 1 to December 31, 1953. The United States Information Agency had been created under the President's Reorganization Plan No. 8, effective August 1, 1953. Format, type size, number of pages, and even tone changed over a ten-year period. The *First Report*, in large type, was thirty-two pages long and contained four pictures. By the *21st Report*, type size had diminished, but pages had grown to forty-eight, including more detailed figures on operations, capsule comments on successes in the field, and sixty-four pictures. The *First Report* covered ten topics: the *21st Report* took only three, emphasizing the assassination of President Kennedy and the succession of President Johnson, overseas book programs, and the graphic-arts exhibit in Russia. Typical reports through the years have covered seven or eight topics. The *Reports* changed quickly from an administrative tone to one of moderate public relations, obviously prepared in the Office of Public Information. They are excellent sources of facts and figures but may be more optimistic in evaluation of program achievement than would be likely in survey research reports of the Research and Analysis Staff.

Subjects to be covered in the semiannual *Report* are often determined by events. The *19th Report to Congress*, for the period July 1 to December 31, 1962, featured "Cuba: Challenge and Recoil" and "Race Relations at Home." Under "Personal Contact Abroad" it discussed USIA coverage of Jacqueline Kennedy's visits to India and Pakistan and Vice President Johnson's visit to the Near East. Under "Communications Techniques," it discussed Telstar—always citing the USIA products and programs turned out in connection with the particular events or developments discussed. Topics are also determined by a feeling of need to tell about USIA programs that are new or not well known. A section on USIA handling of United States scientific developments is prepared to offset earlier press reports that foreign publics believe the Soviet Union leads the United States in science. USIS posts with science information programs are requested to report activities and accomplishments. With the help of dispatches from the field and materials from media services, a science section can be prepared for the *Report* by a special assistant to the director of the Office of Public Information. To call attention to the relatively new junior officer trainees program, the special assistant may participate in orientation programs with junior officer trainees for a week, gather information from the Training Division of the Office of Personnel and Training, have photographs taken in Washington and overseas, and talk with recruiters and with a member of the Joint Board of Examiners. The result is an excellent section in the *Report*, conveying to members of Congress and to others on the mailing list a better understanding of a program which helps get young recruits off to a good start when they enter the Foreign Service to serve USIA. Nothing critical of the program is included, of course. This is a public-relations report and not an administrative or research document. The JOT program story would be cleared with the director of the Office of Public Information and with the Office of Personnel and Training. Before a *Report* is published, it will be thoroughly read by the executive assistant to the Agency director, and any questions the assistant may have will be brought to the attention of the director. The *Report* is released to Congress under a covering letter addressed to the President of the Senate and the Speaker of the House and signed by the director.

The Voice of America Information Officer

In a sense, the Voice of America information officer—now a part of the Office of Public Information—is a vestigial organ, a carryover from the pre-1955 days when the Voice was in New York and the rest of USIA in Washington. In part, he is a necessary convenience to service the public information needs of the Agency's largest and best-known single element, located across town from the main headquarters at 1750 and 1776 Pennsylvania Avenue, N.W. Anything of major public information importance must still be cleared through the Office of Public Information; the Voice of America information unit is "not on its own." A long-time civil servant of the Voice now services rvice Career Reserve officer and secretary on complement, assisted by a second FSCR on "detail." The regular public information officer concentrates attention on stories dealing essentially with the Voice. He prepared the background statement on "jamming" which is distributed by the Office of Public Information. He wrote press releases on the purchase of giant transmitters for the new Voice relay station in the Philippines or elsewhere, which dwarf the power of American domestic stations (but which make little impact on a blase American press and public). In connection with the Agency's takeover of staffing and operation of domestic relay stations, he did a host of home-town stories for the Agency's new employees. Each employee may have had a half-dozen home towns during his lifetime and may have attended several colleges. The Office of Public Information across town has done some of this successfully in past years on returning Foreign Service Career Reserve officers. No one of these stories reaches many people, but over a time they can be an effective means of reminding millions of readers about USIA and its programs. He answers most of the mail coming to the Agency which concerns the Voice of America. Of the Agency's 7,200 letters per year, he is likely to answer 2,000. He services requests from ham broadcasters who have picked up Voice short-wave broadcasts and sent reception reports for so-called QSL cards, verifying their reception of VOA programs. These would be helpful to the Agency in determining who was listening to broadcasts if they came from less-developed areas, but most come from the United States and Europe. He may assist writers from periodical or news staffs who are gathering information for feature articles on the Voice of America, including journalists from *Newsweek*, *True*, *Look*, and the *New York Times*. He may have Voice script material reproduced for distribution at the National Press Club or through the Office of News in the Department of State. A foreign policy discussion by Senator Wayne Morse with invited journalists on a Voice broadcast would certainly be newsworthy. A comment on Voice policy and programs made by the President at a press conference may bring a dozen reporters to the Health, Education, and Welfare Building for follow-up information. This happened when the sale of wheat to the Soviet Union became a public issue. On hot issues, the public information officer does not volunteer information but responds to journalists' specific requests. To provide information quickly, he has gathered information from within the Voice on size and location of audiences, content of broadcasts, types of equipment used, and distribution of receivers capable of picking up the Voice and has comparative figures on what Red China and the Soviet Union do in radio broadcasting. He relies upon the division chiefs of the Voice as his major information source. Attendance at Office of Public Information staff meetings each Monday keeps him updated on domestic information policy of the Agency. He leaves to the FSCR on "detail" the general supervision of the USIA exhibit, or the task of accompanying special visitors on a tour of VOA. The exhibit is a series of displays in a corridor of the Health, Education, and Welfare Building—within the section occupied by the Broadcasting Service. In about fifteen minutes, it is possible to see a Voice broadcast, to learn generally about the organization of the Agency and the function it serves, to view models of relay stations, and to see many examples of USIA products used overseas.

OFFICE   OF PRIVATE COOPERATION (OIC):
RECALCITRANT POTENTIAL

The Office of Private Cooperation, partially replaced by a Private Resources Division in the Information Center Service by October, 1967, actually performed a twofold duty. It attempted to channel private interests in foreign affairs into activites which would serve the policy and program needs of the United States Information Agency—seeking to get from private sources equipment or materials which the Agency felt it needed but had not been able to get through the budget. Historically, and in a diminishing amount, it served as a public-relations device, bringing private groups into contact with USIA and helping them learn about its policies and programs. The Office dates back to the late 1940's, at one time operated branch offices in major cities like San Francisco, Chicago, and New Orleans. These were closed when it became clear that the local offices were serving as ambassadors of the localities to the information service rather than as information program envoys to the cities. At the height of the "people-to-people" programs of the Eisenhower administration, the Office of Private Cooperation was working cooperatively with some forty private people-to-people groups. When the people-to-people programs failed to raise the millions they sought privately to sustain their operations, gathering less than $100,000, USIA stepped in to assist in financing some of the more promising organizations, hoping in time to turn the groups back into independent organizations. The

Office of Private Cooperation largely accomplished this purpose, though it still did some staffwork for people-to-people groups—which have provided at best minor assistance to USIS programs overseas.

Shortly after Ed Murrow became Agency director, the Office of Private Cooperation was slated for abandonment. It was in "limbo" from February to May, 1961, without a director. A special study done by a Foreign Service Career Reserve officer indicated that there was a role for the Office to play but that its potential had never been realized. The function of providing posts with things they needed but lacked money for, or which could not be purchased with money; and the need for a central office to channel the interests of people in foreign affairs was spelled out. A third function, added later to the aims of the revived Office of Private Cooperation, was encouragement of American business to improve its public-relations activities abroad—to make the presence of 35,000 American businessmen overseas a positive advantage to the United States. The "new" Office of Private Cooperation quickly endeared itself to the Congress by reducing its staff from forty-two to thirty-two and cutting its budget 20 per cent—ceasing grants-in-aid to people-to-people groups.

Organization and Direction of IOC

In view of the policy emphasis in USIA after 1961, the Office of Private Cooperation reorganized its nineteen remaining officer-level employees into two groups, program advisors and area officers, serving under a director and deputy director. The idea of having area officers was new; four of them, all FSCR's, worked closely with USIA's area offices, keeping in touch for policy guidance and learning post needs which could not be satisfied within area office budgets. One covered western Europe as well as eastern Europe and the Soviet Union; another, Latin America and Africa; a third, the Near East and South Asia; and the fourth, the Far East. Program advisors were organized by program or function; for example, working primarily on book programs or the "Sister Cities Program," or maintaining relations with business, fraternal, or service organizations. By January, 1967, with the Agency's policy emphasis in better balance with its cultural efforts, the area officers had disappeared. The program advisors still worked closely with business organizations with overseas interests, while other OIC personnel maintained relations with national business and labor organizations, served business or labor publications, or were responsible for special programs—such as donated books. Business and labor liaison was apparently maintained after October

1967, following OIC's demise, by advisors and liaison officers on the Policy and Plans Staff of the Office of Policy and Research.

The role of the OIC leaders was primarily one of maintaining liaison with the Agency leadership and their peers in the area offices or media services, and of establishing useful relationships with private groups. A great deal of enthusiasm for the task was required, for attempting to mesh private interests and activities with Agency objectives required far more imagination than would be needed if the Office of Private Cooperation were only a public-relations function. If this were so, the director and deputy director could have offered encouragement and support for almost any activity, providing it did not positively endanger United States interests overseas. With the post-1961 functions of OIC, the director and deputy director—without any funds to use as bait—attempted to stimulate private organizations to establish or make revision of programs which would support United States foreign policy interests.

OIC Programs

What were some of the major program activities of the Office of Private Cooperation involving liaison of its staff members with private organizations? Although all program activities were conducted in pursuit of Agency objectivies, they were quite varied in nature, dealing with many types of groups and utilizing different media techniques. OIC leaders believed that business men in America and overseas needed information on foreign policy, so OIC mailed pamphlets covering such topics as Vietnam, the Middle East, or nuclear proliferation to them each month, some 8,000 copies through 450 business firms. Some were government pamphlets; others, privately produced and circulated by permission. Two program advisers backstopped this program. Through it, they made many contacts and have consulted with corporations about their overseas public relations operations. In 1965, a project in cooperation with American business organizations led to donations and delivery of nearly $2 million worth of free gifts to the people of South Vietnam—ranging from medicine to candy.[1] Although the Office of Private Cooperation took the leadership in getting several American ambassadors to cooperate overseas with business firms to help them establish joint public-relations programs, the project worked in only one of four countries where it was tried. As a result, IOC receded into the background and a major private corporation has become the bellwether among the businesses in stimulating better public-relations programs overseas. IOC representatives later participated in a private study group on how businesses can help the United States and themselves in Latin America through better public relations.

Most of USIA's book programs are the responsibility of the Information Center Service, but the Office of Private Cooperation had its own book acquisitions and distribution programs. OIC had tried used book drives some years ago, and these were singularly unsuccessful. Most of the books obtained were outdated or on the wrong subjects. The emphasis in recent years was on securing donations of publishers' returns (books returned to publishers from customers) and acquiring books collected at dead-letter centers of the Post Office Department. USIA wives, some seventy of them, worked half a day each week as volunteers on these programs, sorting and cataloging. The Agency in 1963 was obtaining fifty to sixty thousand books a year from these sources—but field requests based on notices of books available ran over one million a year. The Post Office contributions were particularly valuable, representing a cross-section of current books being sold in America. They have included such finds as a nine-volume series on the Life of Abraham Lincoln and a beautifully done book on art worth up to fifty dollars. Wives also sorted back copies of American medical journals for use overseas, more than 37,000 copies. When new editions of books were announced in *Publishers' Weekly*, the Office of Private Cooperation would ask if the publishers would make a gift to USIA of the copies remaining on their shelves from the old edition. In addition to this type of "scrounging" effort, in 1963, the Office of Private Cooperation started a "Books,USA Program," in which each of six paperback publishers was encouraged to prepare packets of ten books to sell to the public at low prices as "intellectual care packages." Only 1,500 of the packets were sold in the first push. Then, the Office of Private Cooperation turned over the venture to Books, USA, Inc., a private organization with foundation assistance. Although the book donation program started small, by 1965 it was obtaining 1,500,000 volumes annually—including books from publishers. [2]

In answer to a post request, a private manufacturer contributed 10,000 pencils to be given away at the opening of a new marketplace in Laos. Each pencil was inscribed in Laotian with a statement of the lasting friendship of America and Laos. Parker Pen gave 2,000 ballpoint pens worth two dollars each, similarly inscribed, to be given away at a foreign trade fair. Why are pencils and pens considered excellent USIA giveaways in less-developed areas? They are a symbol of education, and they last for some time. Most Laotions who received the pencils were almost completely illiterate and could not write. Other types of gifts from private sources have sometimes caused problems. A television salesman contributed fifty to sixty second-hand-trade-in sets, which were sent to Guatemala at post request. A good proportion of the sets were finally made usable, but many had to have repair before they could be distributed. Fortunately, shipping costs were seldom borne by USIA on items such as this. With USIS providing publicity in the recipient country and identifying the company transporting the gift, carriers were willing to carry such cargoes free of charge.

Although OIC's Town Affiliation Program was privately run, the Office of Private Cooperation provided advice and guidance, helped arrange new "sister city" projects when requested by USIS posts, and worked with participating American cities upon post request to meet needs best serviced by the program. In such projects some 250 American cities established close bilateral relationships with foreign cities in fifty countries. In addition to numerous exchanges of visits by community leaders, a city like Pensacola, Florida, raised $50,000 to build a community recreation center for its affiliated city in Peru or provided $10,000 worth of drugs for a medical clinic. New York and Tokyo are affiliated cities; the New York City program is run on a $50,000 annual budget with no financial assistance from USIA. The affiliation program is one of the few successful remains of the people-to-people days in the Agency; no more than two or three of the programs "folded" and new relationships continued to be established. Middle-sized American cities, with a high percentage of retired residents, are particularly interested in such arrangements. Overseas, many parts of the world do not have the feeling of "community" found in an American city; for example, much of Latin America and Italy. Japan on the other hand is a particularly fruitful country for the affiliation program. OIC personnel were not certain that USIS posts fully realized the potential of the program.

An interesting youth program sponsored by the Office of Private Cooperation, after Congress had refused funds for sports equipment to be given by USIS posts to foreign youth organizations, attempted to raise money through private giving for "Sports Kits." These included gloves, bats, hoops, and balls for boxing, baseball, basketball, or football. The Agency's viewpoint was that a political pamphlet is not the best way for USIA to introduce itself to youth groups. A colorful boxing personality served as chairman of a private committee which attempted to raise funds. Lions and Kiwanis clubs among others pitched in to help. The Sports Kit Program was plugged at college and professional football games and other sports events. It quickly raised $6,000, enough to purchase 250 kits. Post requests for kits by this time totaled 12,500. Like some other OIC programs, based on interesting ideas which might be quite useful to USIA, "Sports Kit" fund raising was difficult, insufficient to meet post requests. The Agency was more successful in obtaining private publications for overseas distribution. When posts requested 10,000 copies of a speech delivered by the head of the Columbia Broadcasting System at Dartmouth University, the network provided them free. The house organs of many business organizations are contributed free for use in USIS information centers and branch libraries. Some include an article regularly on some aspect of USIA in each issue—98 per cent of which go to readers in the United States but 2 per cent of which are read abroad. American magazine publishers, through their national association, now give all returns from newsstands overseas to USIS posts for distribution—about 1,200,000 copies a year. Another 500,000 copies a year are made available to USIA from returns in the New York City area.

ADVISORY COMMISSION ON INFORMATION: OBJECTIVE DUALITY

No group of citizens contributes more to maintaining effective American information programs overseas and an efficient USIA than the members and staff of the United States Advisory Commission on Informations. Its members outstanding personalities and leaders in the communications and informaton media fields, and its staff director a scholar trained at the University of Chicago, the Advisory Commission is highly qualified to observe and assess USIA operations at home and abroad. Representative members in recent years have been Edwin Canham, editor, *The Christian Science Monitor;* Sigurd Larmon, chairman of the board, Young and Rubicam, Inc.; Professor Mark A. May, director, Institute of Human Relations, Yale University; J. Leonard Reinsch, executive director of station WSB, Atlanta, Georgia; and John L. Seigenthaler, editor, *The Nashville Tennessean.* In 1966, current members included Chairman Frank Stanton, president, Columbia Broadcasting System, New York City; Sigurd Larmon, Chrysler Building, New York City; Palmer Hoyt, editor and publisher, *The Denver Post,* Denver, Colorado; and M.S. Novik, public service radio-TV consultant, New York City. The Advisory Commission's annual *Report to the Congress of the United States*—reviewed by no one in USIA before publication—is the best single public source for understanding USIA's problems and for finding enlightened suggestions for resolving them. Functioning half in and half outside USIA, it is a neutral bridge between the Agency and Congress. A creation of Congress, budgeted by Congress through the USIA appropriations process, the Advisory Commission has its headquarters and small staff located in USIA. At one point, more than a decade ago, the Advisory Commission, having gotten the new Agency started, felt that it had outlived its usefulness and discussions were conducted with members of Congress looking toward its demise. Typical of the congressional response was the comment, "It's worth $65,000 a year for me to know that people in USIA know someone is looking over their shoulders." The Advisory Commission remained in existence. From the Agency's point of view, it has no better avenue for conveying objective needs to the Congress and no stauncher supporter for the continuation of an independent USIA—subject, of course, to policy guidance from the Department of State.

The Advisory Commission's products include the formal annual *Report,* made semiannually before 1956, and quarterly informal reports to the director of USIA. While either may examine Agency programs and policies critically, both also are likely to include positive suggestions for meeting any deficiencies noted. The tone is objective, the recommendations moderate and practical, but with a forward perspective. The Commission members may follow up reports by discussions with the Agency director, with members of the Congress, or with the President of the United States. They are presidential appointees. Other more specialized public advisory groups to USIA have become somewhat inactive, except for the Voice of America Science Advisory Group. An appointment to the United States Advisory Commission on Information is no perfunctory honor, however, but an invitation to responsibility and hard work. Traditionally, the Advisory Commission has assembled six times a year for meetings (either in Washington or New York) that begin at 9:30 A.M. and often run until 4 or 5 P.M. By 1963, the frequency of meetings was almost doubled. Sessions normally include presentations by and discussions with one of the Agency's top officers or one of its program specialists. Occasionally, a senator or representative just back from an overseas trip will meet with the Commission. Members themselves may report on overseas visits at an Advisory Commission meeting. These may be based on a five-week study of Agency operations in Japan by one of the members, or it may be a six-week survey of USIS posts in twelve African countries—or a report based on several weeks of observation in Vietnam.

The staff director is responsible for calling attention of the members of the Advisory Commission to significant developments affecting USIA policies and programs. When an Agency study is made upgrading the Agency's emphasis in one field or foreign area and downgrading others, this is reported to members of the Advisory Commission. Since the staff director appears at congressional appropriation hearing in behalf of the Advisory Commission, he also reports on the response to the Commission's budgetary request and discusses congressional reception of the Agency's budget proposals. He may brief the Commission on new developments in Chinese Communist propaganda operations. He has access to all Agency information, reports, and documents—and those relevant from other government agencies. From his reading of these, from keeping up with congressional affairs, and from personal contacts, he must use his judgment in informing members of the Advisory Commission on things they need to know about the Agency in order to function effectively. He also attends many meetings of USIA working groups—probably being viewed both as a friendly spy and constructive critic. Personnel from within the Agency may come to the staff director to discuss their own problems or those of the Agency as a court of last resort. If there is a real problem, it may be taken up with the Commission at one of its working sessions.

The members of the Advisory Commission devote a good portion of their time at meetings to preparation of the Commission's annual *Report*. Working under general guidelines from the Commission, the staff director prepares a first draft on the annual *Report* and sends it to the members for review. The *Report* varies in size from thirty-five to sixty pages. The members come to the next meeting and pick at the draft or decimate it. After discussion at the Advisory Commission session, another draft may be prepared. Three drafts are sometimes necessary before the Advisory Commission accepts the document with amendments. The members have made it thoroughly their own by this time, giving to the Agency the benefit of fresh minds, unstifled by a bureaucratic milieu. They may deliver a copy of their *Report* to the President in person, accompanied by the Agency director and the staff director, and discuss their findings with him for almost an hour. Functioning with five members, a staff of one professional and one clerical employee, and a current annual budget of approximately $50,000, the Advisory Commission is well worth its salt to Congress, USIA, the President, and the American taxpayer. Overseas—from USIS Bamako in Mali to the reading room in Luang Prabang, Laos; from USIS Tehran in Iran to the binational center in Koblenz, West Germany; from USIS La Paz in Bolivia to the radio monitor station in Belgrade, Yugoslavia—employees of the United States Information Agency support United States foreign policy objectives more effectively than they would if there had been no Advisory Commission, if it were not an effective force for improvement of USIA policies, programs, and operations.

USIS POSTS ABROAD: FIELD OPERATIONS[3]

USIA without United States Information Service posts overseas would be a public speaker without a voice, a professor without eyes, a boxer without arms. Lacking field operations, USIA would play a much more modest role among the United States government foreign affairs agencies. If there were no USIA, USIS posts might become special pleaders for foreign populations rather than attempting to persuade them toward acceptance of American policies, be staffed by a rootless group of Americans-in-exile incapable of representing the interests of the United States government to the peoples of the world. USIS posts need USIA as much as USIA needs its field posts. The efforts of either without the other would be rather fruitless. Together they make a whole and can hope to blend their labors, balancing an understanding of American aims and interests with the needs and aspirations of the great majority of mankind. The field is the life's blood of USIA's foreign service officers, even when they serve at headquarters in Washington. The greater part of their working lives is spent in the field; to most FSCR's and FSO's, Washington is only an interim assignment, a good place to be when the children are in school or because of illness, stimulating because the work is so different, a pleasant opportunity for reorientation on American life and culture in a temperate climate (though Washington's muggy summers and raw winters may seem less salubrious than service at USIS Addis Ababa or USIS Mexico City).

USIS post operations drive home the point to USIA policy and program makers that most of the world is non-American in history, culture, and physical environment. More positively, they help USIA understand the basic hopes and fears of individual national groups and even of important but diverse subgroups within specific nations. If USIS posts are primarily considered purveyors of Washington's ideas, they also contribute a great deal to the formulation of information policy. Their initiative in planning country programs, drafting Country Plans or Country Plan Program Memoranda, and their reports are as essential as their contacts with local leadership groups in the conduct of operations. Their firsthand coordination of information activities within the "country team" under the leadership of the American ambassador minimizes problems of interagency coordination in Washington, though field disputes may be forwarded there to be worked out if agreement cannot be reached overseas. Although administrative duties are less complex abroad—or sometimes seem to be taken less seriously than Washington bureaucrats might like—even field operators recognize the necessity of tidying up procedures as the American overseas commitment becomes less temporary in nature and is accepted as a normal function of the government.

The individual USIS posts conduct programs adapted to local needs—backstopped by USIA's area offices, the products of the media services, and the research analyses of the Research and Analysis Staff—but also use worldwide products and (in greater or lesser degree) promote the Agency's "five themes." If the mix in each country program is different, many of the same program elements and products are still employed. Individual USIS posts do adapt their organization and operations realistically to varying programs and projects. Posts vary in size; their American and local employees speak different languages. Some deal with relatively broad and highly sophisticated audiences; others, in less-developed countries, may tend to work through leadership groups, or operate mass programs at an unsophisticated "cartoon book" level. Some work in countries whose policies are incompatible with those of the United States; others find friendly cooperation. Nonetheless, the over-all structure of USIS posts is much the same everywhere; staffing patterns vary more in size than type of position. There is a country public affairs officer at USIS Ouagadougou in Upper Volta as well as one at USIS Bonn in West Germany. There is a country information officer at USIS Accra in Ghana as well as USIS Tehran in Iran. There are cultural affairs officers at both USIS Karachi in Pakistan and USIS Madrid in Spain. There are branch public affairs officers at Chiengmai in Thailand, responsible to USIS Bangkok, and at Kaduna and Ibadan in Nigeria, responsible to USIS Lagos. There are binational center directors at Vientane in Laos, at Marburg in West Germany, and in Uberaba in Brazil. There are radio relay stations in Colombo, Ceylon, and in Thessaloniki, Greece. There are local employees operating reading rooms in Bilbao, Spain, and at Can Tho in South Vietnam. An understanding of the organization of a hypothetical but typical middle-sized USIS headquarters post within an American mission abroad and of the relationships and responsibilities of a synthetic country public affairs officer should help complete the picture of how the Agency translates American foreign policy into information policies, programs, and operations.

The USIS Post

How is a USIS post organized, and what is its relationship within the "country team" working under the direction of the American ambassador? Heading the USIS post is the country public affairs officer, the CPAO. He is very near the peak of the career ladder, normally an FSCR 1 or FSCR 2— often a former director or deputy director of one of the USIA area offices or media services. When he completes his overseas tour and returns to Washington, it is likely to be to one of these positions or as a policy officer. He may be assigned to training at the National War College, the Senior Officer Course at the Foreign Service Institute, or serve as a special assistant to the

Agency director or deputy Agency director. He may head the Office of Policy and Research or be put to work on a special Agency study. As CPAO, he is Mr. USIS in his country. He is responsible for all USIS operations, completely responsible for employment of all local personnel, and is consulted by Washington on the appointment of American personnel who will serve under him. At a larger USIS post, he would have a deputy CPAO and an executive officer assisting him; but he has neither at medium-sized posts, staffed by five to nine American employees and perhaps fifteen local nationals. As a personal aide, the CPAO has a public affairs assistant or an American secretary, normally serving on Foreign Service Staff appointments. He is also assisted as necessary by local clerk-stenographers and possibly a receptionist. When he is absent on leave or for official travel, he is likely to designate the country information officer or the country cultural affairs officer to take over his general supervisory responsibilities.

The country information officer (IO) is the CPAO's top assistant for press and periodicals, radio, television, and motion-picture operations. The CPAO often serves as the American mission's press attaché; his IO may be the assistant press attaché. When the CPAO is counselor of mission, as he sometimes is, the IO may be the press attaché. The country information officer administers a broad segment of the total USIS operation, perhaps aided in a larger country by American press, radio, film, motion-picture, or television assistants. At the medium-sized post, his staff is more likely to be made up entirely of local personnel. They do much of the placement work of media service products or operate the mobile motion-picture units, translate materials into the local language, and edit materials prepared and printed locally, maintaining distribution lists for Agency materials. The IO position is viewed as excellent preparation for later service as a branch public affairs officer—heading USIS operations in a major city other than the capital—or for service as a country public affairs officer.

The country cultural affairs officer, the CPAO's top assistant for cultural and educational affairs, may serve as the embassy's cultural and educational attaché. The CPAO sometimes is designated as the mission's cultural and educational attaché, in which case the CAO is likely to be an assistant attaché. In addition to supervision of USIS libraries or more indirectly of binational centers in the country, with their related activities (lectures, concerts, discussion groups, seminar's, English teaching, American studies, and exhibits), he is responsible for any private cooperation projects, and for all exchange programs. In this latter capacity, he is servicing the Bureau of Educational and Cultural Affairs in the Department of State rather than USIA—this portion of his work funded from the State Department budget.

The CAO works closely with the Fulbright Commission in many countries abroad, normally headed by an American director, but with many local nationals as members. He is responsible for working with educational institutions, with musicians and artists, and does much of the advance and follow-up work on special international presentations (also under State's aegis) when American performers appear in his country—whether it be a symphony orchestra or jazz band, a play cast, or a folk singer.

The branch public affairs officer or PAO is the little CPAO for the city and surrounding area in which he operates, performing both information and cultural duties, sometimes supervising a neighboring binational center and outlying reading rooms, though the book ordering and cataloging of his operations are likely to be conducted by an American librarian. There are nine PAO's in Brazil, six or seven in Thailand, West Germany, or Italy; four in Iran, India, or Japan; one in Venezuela, Bolivia, Cameroon, or Ethiopia. The librarian is in charge of maintaining USIA book collections for reading and reference, including mobile units, and also maintains a record library; helps in promoting books related to Agency programs, and assists in answering reference inquiries, assisted by a small local staff. Binational center directors, responsive to joint boards of local nationals and Americans residing in the country but serving under the direction of the CPAO and the CAO, arrange lectures and concerts at the centers, promote and supervise English-teaching programs, and maintain specialized libraries in support of binational center activities. They may sometimes be assisted by contract employees from the United States in teaching or in planning activities for labor or youth groups. The CPAO may also have responsibility for special regional officers, serving an entire geographic region—such as the regional research officers or regional book officers, the latter responsible for promotion of the Agency's book programs.

A thumbnail sketch of the organization of a USIS mission cannot convey a real sense of the host of personal contacts maintained by American personnel or the importance of the local nationals, who often test products before showing or distribution, and who actually build contacts and relationships within the countries which it would be impossible for Americans to acquire or maintain. Their importance is demonstrated by USIA's increased interest in bringing "local" employees to the United States for training experiences, and in the feeling held by some headquarters personnel that the Agency should assume a greater role in directing the hiring or personnel practices governing the employment of locals in the field. Country public affairs officers try to make local employees feel an integral part of the Agency team, knowing that without their support, enthusiasm, and dedication, USIS programs cannot be successful. Members of the American staff in USIS overseas posts may hold meetings without local employees in attendance, but there are also combined staff meetings attended by all employees. Although local staffs are not entrusted with all classified information possessed by USIA, they are certainly aware in general of all the Agency's programs and objectives.

Nothing better indicates the scope of the country public affairs officer's duties than the documents which the Agency requests him to discuss with his successor when turning over his job before moving on to another USIS post or returning to the United States. In addition to introducing the new CPAO to USIS and embassy personnel and to important USIS contacts in the country, he reviews with the newcomer the Country Plan and recent Assessment Reports on the relative success of Agency programs in the country (or the Country Plan Program Memorandum), the Country Budget, the Exchange Program Plan, the USIS Reports Calendar, the Inventory of Equipment, the post's Organization Chart, Staffing Patterns, Performance Rating Reports on personnel, Contact Cards on relations maintained with members of target groups, any Audit Report on post activities (made by visiting USIA inspectors from the Office of Administration) and the Administrative Support Agreement with the Department of State (since State provides office space, handles pay checks, procures basic equipment and supplies, etc.).

The Country Team

Meshing of the individualized country programs of USIS posts with over-all United States operations is achieved through the concept of the "country team," headed by the American ambassador. While the special responsibilities, objectives, and interests of each of the elements in the American mission are recognized (the diplomatic function, defense assistance, economic assistance, and the informational-cultural program), the ambassador has a responsibility to work toward over-all United States objectives, which can only be furthered effectively to the degree that all American activities in a given country are complementary and mutually supporting. Coordination is achieved both in the planning and operational phases through direction by the ambassador and by his adjudication of differences. USIA's country public affairs officer has a dual obligation—to the ambassador and to the Agency. While the CPAO must support the ambassador, he is legally entitled to a direct line of communication to the director of USIA through his area office director on any question pertaining to USIS programs or personnel. Nonetheless, on important decisions, it is expected that the CPAO will obtain concurrence from the ambassador before proceeding. If he dissents from an ambassadorial decision that affects USIS operations, he informs the ambassador of his dissent; he informally discusses the matter with his area office director, after which he may or may not prepare a formal dissent for the director of USIA, a copy of which would be communicated to the ambassador. In working with the ambassador, the CPAO informs him of the psychological climate of the country and the possible effect of any current developments upon this climate (either resulting from statements to be issued from Washington or contemplated diplomatic, military, or economic initiatives by other elements of the Country team). Certainly the CPAO must keep the ambassador abreast of developments related to USIS responsibilities, new program activities or changes in emphasis. He normally drafts for the ambassador the psychological-informational-cultural section of the "Weeka" report prepared by the embassy for the Department of State and the other foreign affairs agencies. He is also responsible in behalf of the ambassador for visits by prominent Americans interested in USIS programs and operations. In addition, he calls to the ambassador's attention opportunities for speeches or public statements which may benefit American policy, manages the American mission's press relations, and keeps the ambassador informed of visiting American correspondents, briefing them on the local situation or offering them assistance in making local contacts. In return, the CPAO requests the ambassador's cooperation in preparing the USIS Country Plan or Country Plan Program Memorandum, in observing American holidays in a way furthering USIS objectives, by inviting USIS contacts and USIS personnel to embassy receptions, appearing at USIS programs or ceremonies, and sharing contact lists prepared by other elements in the American mission.

USIA's relations with the Agency for International Development in Washington seem far fewer than would be normal, since by law USIS is responsible for providing information in support of AID's local program operations overseas and also disseminates materials (in cooperation with the host country) on the worldwide AID program or projects in other countries relevant to the local program. Instructions to CPAO's in the field call for anticipation of support to the AID Mission (USAID), note that the CPAO should include in the Country Plan or Country Plan Program Memorandum USAID information objectives and activities, and state that the CPAO should consult USAID in preparation of the Country Plan. Theoretically at least, the CPAO is drawn into USAID projects at the selection and planning stage. He works with raw data provided by USAID in preparing USIS publicity in behalf of USAID. Working arrangements are sometimes formalized in a joint written statement, approved by the chief of mission and submitted to the Department of State, AID, and USIA. However satisfactory the relationship is considered in the field, there is little evidence at headquarters of a similar level of cooperation between AID and USIA. Close relationships between the agencies would be desirable, because USIA cannot adequately direct the field which should strive to create an appropriate "climate" for development unless it is privy to AID's short-, medium-, and long-range plans. It seems highly unlikely that at the rather operational field level there can be a sophisticated perception of the psychological prerequisites for modernization. Without a wholesome interplay between the agencies in Washington, it seems unlikely that USIA would give development of a modernization climate a sufficiently high priority to plan truly effective informational-cultural programs. In the field, the CPAO and the USIS staff are also responsible for insuring an adequate local understanding of the work of any United States Military Assistance Group in the host country, working in cooperation with the military, naval, and air attachés of the American embassy. Although the Department of Defense carries the public relations assignment for armed forces attached to its overseas Commands, the CPAO is expected to work with the military in developing effective troop-community relations programs, cooperating with the Commands in planning and support of public activities of the military, and orienting the Commands on local problems and sensitivities.

Relationships in the Host Country

Among the CPAO's most important relationships with the country where he is stationed are those with influential local citizens. He is expected to accept as many invitations as possible and to do reciprocal entertaining and to encourage his staff to do likewise. CPAO's are expected to call on important Agency contacts to introduce themselves as soon as possible after their arrival, to travel extensively to learn about the people, their customs and culture; to accept speaking engagements, and to join local groups—avoiding alignment with any one of several rival organizations. With staff assistance, the CPAO usually attempts to establish contacts with youth groups and political organizations of many types, including those who may produce tomorrow's leaders. Formal contact and mailing lists are necessary at each post, for FSCR personnel serve no more than two two-year tours at hardship posts or two three-year tours at less difficult posts, and new officers would have difficulty in building contacts from scratch. Among lists maintained in card files at an average post are a CPAO contact and social list, similar lists prepared by individual American officers, a library membership list, a presentation list, a mailing list, a binational center list, a list of returned exchange grantees, and a motion-picture borrower's list. Pruning of lists is as important as adding new names. Cards are helpful to USIS personnel and to others in the embassy, identifying each individual by target group. They provide information on the contact's job, address, and language ability; on his wife, sons and daughters (and their activities); on visits abroad, writings, political party, specific political feelings, religion, and memberships in professional and social organizations; and on USIS materials sent to the contact, participation in events sponsored by the embassy or the United States government, and any cooperative actions helpful to USIS or the embassy. Local employees have free use of such card-file lists in carrying out their assignments. Among persons listed are host government officials, leaders of political, professional, cultural or commercial organizations, and returnees from exchange programs.

In addition to maintaining or establishing relationships with foreign nationals of the host country, the CPAO and his staff are expected to work closely with American private citizens, media representatives, business firms, religious groups, and foundations active in the country—though warned not to allow themselves and their time to be swallowed up by the American community. USIS wives are encouraged to play an active role in supporting their husbands' work, to participate informally in community service work and other activities, but they are discouraged from accepting routine employment in the Embassy. Besides working with American nationals in the host country, the USIS staff is asked to know their counterparts in other foreign missions, to be in contact with representatives of the United Nations or its specialized agencies as well as with employees of regional associations, such as the Organization of American States or the Southeast Asia Treaty Organization.

Relations With USIA In Washington

The country public affairs officer's point of contact in Washington is the area office director, with the area desk officer backstopping the director's relationship to the USIS post. All cables and Field Messages from the CPAO to the Agency are assigned upon arrival to the appropriate USIA element for action, with information copies sent automatically to the area office. Operations Memoranda are forwarded to the area office if requested, but these usually concern media matters and may or may not be of importance to the area office. Field Messages involve requests from more than one media service, or evaluation and substantive reporting, and are widely distributed within the Agency. Official-Informal letters are not action documents, normally reserved for amplifying or explaining personal views. As already noted, the field is often visited by headquarters personnel, representatives of the area offices, the media services, or auditors and others from the Office of Administration.

In return, USIS posts direct about eighty different reports to headquarters, some prepared weekly, monthly or annually; others, "if and when." The country public affairs officer and a top aide, the CIO or the CAO, may attend USIS area conferences about once a year—a gathering of CPAO's of a particular geographic region, attended by the area office director, perhaps by a policy officer or program coordinator, often with a media service director and either the Agency director or deputy agency director thrown in for good measure. This helps maintain Washington-field contacts and also allows lateral relations of field representatives for the discussion of common problems. On a written basis, headquarters encourages an interchange of ideas by publishing and circulating the so-called TIE reports, a cross-file of suggestions explaining useful operating techniques or projects submitted by individual posts. CPAO's and other USIS personnel may correspond or occasionally exchange visits if there is need for discussion of a shared problem or for a general exchange of views. Before a CPAO returns to headquarters at the completion of his tour, with the help of his staff he prepares for Washington debriefing sessions, drawing up a list of problems and questions demanding Agency attention.

The Country Plan And Research: Operational Guides

The annual Country Plan (or Country Plan Program Memorandum) is the USIS post's most important document; it provides the rationale for the post's activities, serves as the basis for the post's budget; and is the yardstick against which the post judges its progress in the annual Assessment Report. It is particularly important because it forces operational personnel who are used to "doing," often caught up in a whirlwind of daily events, to take the time once a year to rethink what they are doing and where they are going. CPAO's sometimes organize three-day retreats to do joint thinking with their American staffs on the Country Plan. Among the new CPAO's first duties upon arriving in a country is a careful review of the Country Plan to see if in his view parts of it need immediate adjustment, whether he can work with present plans until time to prepare new ones. The Country Plan or Country

Plan Program Memorandum relates United States foreign policy objectives to informational-psychological considerations, is concerned with the particular attitudes and images held by the people of the host country. It sets up target audiences and realistic objectives, assigning priorities to various target groups for each specific objective. It attempts to spell out limited goals related to particular aspirations, hopes, national interests, misconceptions, and antipathies of influential groups in the host country. Several posts have experimented with assigning primary responsibility for achievement of each major objective to a different "control" officer, adding to the normal media specialization of each American officer oversight of the Country Plan objective entrusted to him. At many posts, programs, projects, and media products are related to specific target audiences and to USIS objectives in monthly reports, which review what has been done and look ahead to what will be done. By such means, CPAO's have a checklist which insures a current knowledge of where the USIS post stands in accomplishing objectives at any time during the year. The purpose of such reporting is not just "for the record," but to make thinking tangible. Over-all program trends can then be summarized, giving the staff a fixed point of departure for the next month or three-month period ahead.

Nothing can be of more help in planning and operations to the country public affairs officer and the USIS staff than research studies dealing with their country done under the auspices or with the assistance of the Research and Analysis Staff. Unfortunately, posts often operate on a pragmatic, *ad hoc* basis, with a "feeling" or "sense" of the situation, rather than recognizing the need for a more scientific analysis of psychological conditions in their country. The CPAO may hesitate to use staff time for research which must be "stolen" from operations. CPAO's are urged to make use of research officers, occasionally assigned at larger posts, or the regional research officers which can be obtained on request "to discuss research needs or problems and to offer advice on criteria and methods for solving them." They are reminded of the existence of Communication Fact Books; also, informed of media habits and preference, target audience, and USIS media studies (the latter comparing the efficiency of USIS media or surveying a situation for special guidance), public opinion, attitude and value studies, other special background studies, and reaction reports—all available on request until limited personnel resources are overloaded or the budget runs out. CPAO's are encouraged by the Agency to stimulate research efforts and use of improved research techniques by local governments, universities, industries, or newspapers to widen the sources available to guide post operations. In many less-developed regions, locally gathered facts and figures on most topics are at best "guesstimates" at the present time.

The USIS Post's Media Resources

Each of the programs or products prepared or backstopped by the Agency's media services is a channel to audience groups, reaching particular targets or having greater impact on certain groups. The good country public affairs officer has at least thirty-five keys on his program instrument which he presses down with proper timing and coordination if his country program is to be in tune with Country Plan or CPPM objectives. Using the medium of radio, he can place Voice of America packaged programs on local radio stations, use programs produced by Regional Service Centers or by other posts, produce radio programs at the post, make use of direct broadcasts from the Voice of America, or employ special or regular feeds off the commercial broadcast line to listeners in the host country. Using the medium of television, he can place Agency packaged programs on local television stations or produce programs at the post. Through the press medium, he can place background news stories, features or photographs in local newspapers, magazines, or on radio and television stations; adapt or produce articles for periodical publication; distribute pamphlets, or cartoon books, and arrange photographic displays. Via the motion-picture medium, he can use documentary films, newsreels, and "news magazines," either Agency produced in the United States or overseas, or Agency acquired, or post produced. These can be shown in USIS centers and through mobile units, lent to organizations, or placed in commercial theaters. Aided by the Agency's Information Center Service, he can maintain libraries with books, magazines, and records, and USIS-supervised outlying reading rooms; through bookmobiles, operate circulating book collections; in USIS Information Centers, hold lectures, concerts, dramatic performances, or organize discussion groups and seminars; in addition, he can stimulate English teaching and book translations or sponsor local authors, plan presentations of books, strengthen American studies in local universities or by private groups, set up exhibits or displays, and cooperate in programming binational centers. He also guides the exchange programs of leaders, specialists, students, and teachers, assisted by the Bureau of Educational and Cultural Affairs in State, and the Special International Program involving artistic performances and participation in trade fairs. He can draw on the resources of private cooperation people-to-people, provide some technical assistance and training to develop media personnel of the host country, talk with people in person in their offices or on social occasions, and make speeches. He can conduct tours of United States facilities or participate in community events commemorating historic cooperative relationships of the United States and the host country. Program assistance may sometimes come from other posts whose materials can be adapted to his needs. It is much easier to provide a listing of his resources than to provide a recipe for the proper blending of them. No matter how computerized government operations may someday become, the work of the CPAO will retain much that is art rather than science, common sense rather than theory—but the present-day balance may be more favorable than necessary to art and common sense, give too little recognition to science and theory. The suggested criteria for the CPAO's decision on relative use of the different communication media include: "(1) Extent of the media resources in the country—number of radio sets, newspapers, theaters, organizations, universities, etc.; (2) the resource as a potential channel to priority groups (which people read what or attend what); (3) the capacity of the medium to carry certain types of messages; and (4) USIS's opportunity to gain access to the desired channel." CPAO's should perhaps not be blamed when they overuse channels to which there is easy access, or those in which they have an expertise based on past specialization and experience—but their activities may be less effective than if more carefully structured. For use of country public affairs officers, the Agency has carefully spelled out the uses and problems of the various media programs and products in a special *Handbook*—from which much of the present material on post operations is drawn. Helpful as the *Handbook* undoubtedly is for experienced Foreign Service Career Reserve officers, it probably would be little more practical operationally for a person without USIA and USIS experience than a book on golf by Arnold Palmer to the individual who has never swung a golf club. There are so many things to be done concurrently; the job itself cannot be divided into neat chapters.

Guidance of Exchange and Special Programs

The country public affairs officer, under the ambassador's guidance, is responsible for the administration of the educational and cultural-exchange programs of the Department of State's Bureau of Educational and Cultural Affairs. Operational guidance on the exchange process is provided by the *International Educational Exchange Manual* issued by the Department of State. Normally the operational tasks of the exchange programs are delegated by the CPAO to his cultural affairs officer. In countries with exchanges sponsored by the Agency for International Development, either the country public affairs officer or the cultural affairs officer will serve on the embassy's coordinating committee for USAID programs. The CPAO and the CAO serve on the embassy committee to consider and nominate candidates for leader grants to the Department of State. In countries where there is a Fulbright exchange program, the CPAO or the CAO serves on the Board of Directors of the Fulbright Commission (sometimes called "Foundation"), which generally is composed of an equal number of resident Americans and local citizens. The CPAO also serves on the Committee on Study and Training in the United States, a binational body established in most countries that participate in educational exchange programs. This committee attempts to consolidate information on opportunities for study and training in the United States and assists in screening candidates for government or non-government grants as requested by private organizations. To play an effective role in exchange programs, the country public affairs officer and the cultural affairs officer must maintain close contact with government officials and leading figures in educational and cultural activities. They play an active role in the "alumni" association and other activities which bring together returned grantees. The CPAO and CAO must also keep informed on the exchange programs of private organizations. Although exchange activities are time consuming, they also help the CPAO and CAO make many contacts useful in furthering other USIS projects. Reports are made to the Department of State on Bureau of Educational and Cultural Affairs exchange programs.

The CPAO and the USIS post are also involved in activities of the President's Special International Program, funds for which are shared between the Departments of Commerce, Labor, and State for trade fairs, trade and labor missions, and for assisting cultural and athletic groups to make foreign tours. As previously noted, the funds, though treated as a separate appropriation, are included in the USIA budget. The CPAO includes such events in his Country Plan, and programs will not be scheduled without prior approval by the USIS post. The CPAO makes program suggestions which are forwarded to the Bureau of Educational and Cultural Affairs. Ultimate selections also take into consideration recommendations by the American National Theatre Academy. At a small post, handling a cultural or sports attraction may mean shutting down almost all other operations for a short period; the gains must be weighed against the losses. Although much of the field work involved in promoting trade fairs or the visits of trade or labor missions is done by Commerce or Labor field staffs, the CPAO and the USIS post are responsible for publicity on such events. Since the primary purpose of many American exhibits and related activities abroad is political and psychological, the CPAO is often a key man in the country team in field planning of theme and content of trade-fair exhibits. Cultural and athletic presentations are often handled through a local impresario on a commercial basis or by cosponsorship with local groups, with USIS making up any financial losses and contributing staff time, resources, and publicity.

Program Assessment at Field Posts

Although personnel back in Washington, particularly on the Research and Analysis Staff, are interested in a double check on assessments made of field operations by USIS posts themselves, the country public affairs officer and his staff are clearly instructed by the Agency to give assessment of effectiveness continuing attention, to make assessments objective, and to adapt operations to the findings made. The Country Assessment Reports of USIS posts are due in the Agency by February 1 each year, but CPAO's are also urged to make periodic over-all appraisals, utilizing staff meetings, on the basis of which special or highlight reports can be forwarded to area offices. The CPAO knows the area office directors want the weaknesses of programs as well as their strengths pointed out. To insure objectivity, if there are differences of judgment within the staff of a USIS post on the level of achievement, such differences are supposed to be reported. Such differences might lead to survey research studies in the country concerned to ascertain the facts. Essentially, the Assessment Report calls for measurement of programs in terms of impact on local audiences, and an evaluation of appropriateness and usefulness of various media techniques for transmitting ideas or reaching audiences. In addition, it asks for a statement of the problems faced at the post, the means used to resolve them, and what opposition has been encountered—either from sources within the country or hostile propaganda directed from other nations. Assessments must be based on facts to be useful. Members of the American staff are expected to monitor their media in the host countries. Motion-picture specialists should know what films are playing throughout the country commercially, what is being shown by individual organizations, and what films are produced locally. Radio personnel listen to both local and international broadcasts. Television staff members keep a close watch on relevant television programs. The cultural affairs officer knows what the intellectual literature and academic journals are saying, and should know the general pattern of thinking in the universities and among cultural groups. Press personnel follow editorial shifts, news trends, and expressions of opinion in newspapers and periodicals, both city and provincial. Librarians check book popularity, what is being published, what texts are being used in eduational institutions. In order for the CPAO to judge this flow of information, he must do some monitoring himself, of newspapers, other publications, and broadcasts—watching labor, business, or commercial group opinion, groups with which USIS staff may not deal on a daily basis since they are largely observed by labor or commerical attachés. Collection of evidence of program success is important, but it is not assessment. It provides the support for development of an over-all picture and current trends which can give Washington policy makers a "true" perspective, probably in shades of gray rather than in black and white. Human-interest stories about program activities and audience reaction are useful for USIS public-information activities—to be used in the director's speeches or in press releases—but CPAO's are well aware that these are not "assessments" of the type desired by their area office directors. As important as watching the use made and the impact of American products may be, it is just as essential to see what other nations are accomplishing. Only in this way can American information policies meet new challenges or act to offset an unfavorable impact in a balanced fashion—enough to reduce their effectiveness substantially without stirring up an unnecessary hornet's nest. Knowing what friendly countries are saying, the USIA program can complement their output and build on it.

Administration in the Field

At larger USIS posts, country public affairs officers are assisted by an executive officer, responsible for budget, finance, personnel, and organizational problems. At the medium-sized post, the CPAO has these duties in addition to all his other tasks. The Country Budget, for which the CPAO is responsible, is not only the heart of the Agency's budget process but also the meat on which his Country Plan will feed. Apparently the Agency's budget and its programs have traditionally been written in highly different forms which make it difficult to coordinate Country Plans with USIS post budgets, and this circumstance led to the development of the Country Plan Program Memorandum. Among the many interests which demand the attention of field personnel, none can be more important than funds to operate programs and personnel policies which provide effective operators, but in the welter of activities by relatively specialized personnel it is likely that administrative matters do not have the highest priority or receive the most attention in the field. The CPAO's Country Budget is due in the Agency by August 1 in response to the June Budget Call. He must provide an itemized statement, covering relatively fixed cost operating requirements, media support needs, and personnel. A "Guidance" from the Agency Budget Division in late June follows the Budget Call and tells the CPAO the total amount into which his requests must be compressed. When congressional appropriations have been made, some time after the start of the new fiscal year in July and usually before December, the Agency takes responsibility for adjusting the country-proposed budget to the level of the congressional authorization. In working out the quarterly Financial Plans, which serve as the basis for apportioning funds to the USIS post during the year, the CPAO can request help from the Administrative Section of the American embassy, under the Administrative Support Agreement between State and USIA. CPAO's are responsible for carefully checking out administrative support costs in their countries before signing administrative support estimates used in interagency negotiations. The most helpful single administrative document available to the CPAO and USIS staffs is the Agency's *Manual of Operations*, updated by Agency circulars. Most communications services for the USIS posts are handled by the embassy's Administrative Section and charged to USIA under the Administrative Support Agreement. Contracts and purchase orders are also handled through the Administrative Section. The CPAO is responsible for the morale of his local employees, but the working relationship of the employee on personnel questions is direct with the Administrative Section of the embassy. Thus, the CPAO and USIA are freed of much administrative detail which would require a duplication of staff if the services were not provided by State Department personnel in the embassy's Administrative Section. The CPAO is responsible for making performance ratings on those members of the American staff who are members of the Agency's foreign service. In the long run, this is one of his most important tasks, for a successful Agency future is dependent upon developing an increasingly able foreign service. Objective judgments of work done and the qualifications of personnel for advancement are the foundation of an adequate personnel system. His interest in on-the-job training for American personnel, either in language, communications theory, or the culture of the host country, can have a visible impact upon post efficiency.

VIII

The State of the Art:

Growing Maturity and Need for New Purpose

What useful grist emerges from the mill of facts and comments on the organization, policies, programs, and operations of the United States Information Agency? In a turbulent world, what has happened to the infant almost killed by the wrong kind of attention during the McCarthy era? An assessment of the facts seems to indicate that USIA, while still a young and vigorous agency, has survived its growth pains and has grown in maturity and effectiveness, making an increasingly positive contribution to the formulation and conduct of American foreign policy. Although its organization is complex, its pattern has been adapted over time in an attempt to meet realistic needs. Its information policies and programs have become more sophisticated, depending less on the bludgeon and more on ingenuity and persuasion. If there is room for personnel improvement in any government or private organization, USIA stands up reasonably well to comparison in the late 1960's, even with the Department of State. There has been great progress between 1953 and the present. Just as Agency programs point with pride to American accomplishments and attempt to show what the United States is doing to resolve its current problems, American citizens can now take pride in USIA, and give objective consideration to making it an even better organization. The Agency no longer needs to be hypersensitive to suggestions, as it was during earlier, more trying times, for it has now built for itself a recognized role among the foreign affairs agencies. However the work of the government may be organized and coordinated to support American foreign relations, the functions of USIA will be performed by an integrated information organization, working closely with the other elements in the over-all American foreign relations mechanism. The information machine has passed through its Model-T days to emerge as a front runner in the race for influencing world opinion—though real limits on its influence are recognized. Its operators have had sufficient experience, much of it in the school of hard knocks, to provide a surer sense of direction in information policy or operations than at any time in the past. To point to progress is not to confuse radical improvement with the attainment of perfection. USIA is a very human mechanism. Like all machinery of government (or private organizations), it undoubtedly has made, is making, and will make many mistakes. But carefully surveyed, the Agency seems to have incorporated within its organization some of the factors required for further improvement and for critical self-judgment; these factors give promise of a more effective future. No matter how objective the outside observer attempts to be, he brings along his own intellectual baggage and perspectives which color his perception of Agency "reality." Any suggestions for adjustment of Agency organization need to be considered against counteralternatives marshaled by other "objective" men, from within or without the Agency, perhaps with backgrounds in media operations or communications theory. To recognize the pitfalls and realistic limits of this assessment is not to feel relieved of a responsibility to make tentative judgments. The Agency is well worth careful thought, and it is capable of digesting and applying relevant insights. In a real sense, the recommendations made here represent a summation of views already expressed in the earlier discussions of the USIA elements. They are at best selective, and no effort is made here to cover every aspect of USIA organization or operations. Hopefully, these remarks cover those problems areas most relevant to the formulation and conduct of information policy and to its transmission within the Agency (including the field) and to other foreign affairs agencies.

THE STAFFING OF THE AREA OFFICES

If trends were charted in USIA of increases and decreases in policy influence by various Agency elements since 1953, the media services would be shown as starting strong and falling off, the USIS posts as increasing in influence through the 1950's during the foreign affairs agencies' "the field knows best" era, with the Office of Policy (now Policy and Research) asserting itself more strongly after 1961 on worldwide matters. The area offices emerged with some degree of influence after 1957, but their staffs have remained small while their duties have been expanded. Many of the Agency's operational problems stem from overworking and understaffing the area offices. The area office director and his deputy are often in the field on inspection tours. This destroys the continuity of their relationships with other foreign affairs agencies, where they are instructed to provide informational insights during the formation of diplomatic, economic, or military policy. It reduces their thinking time, when they can work with the Research and Analysis Staff to plan studies which will give them a better check on field conditions and achievements, a deeper understanding of communications theory, or cooperate in Agency planning operations.

The area office desk officers also perform at a hectic pace, serving field requests, monitoring media products, reading policy messages, maintaining interagency contacts, making an occasional field inspection, projecting a sense of guidance to the field by drafting field instructions or portions of Agency policy papers and reports. They normally cover from two to five countries, doubling up on the job when an outgoing officer is detached before a new one reports in, receiving little if any formal orientation when taking over the desk though they may have been eight to twelve years in the field and many have had no previous Washington experience. From the start, they are too busy to take time to get an over-all sense of Agency direction which they can project, to fulfil their interagency advisory relations person to person (the most effective way), to be attentive to research findings or to participate in planning activities and communicate such information to the media and the field, to take the time to put Agency actions and thoughts on paper to preserve or create an Agency memory, and to monitor the media more effectively and knowledgeably (for policy and impact). Often lacking Washington experience when they arrive, they are thrown into their jobs with neither time nor formal training to learn the ways of the bureaucracy.

To resolve such problems, serious consideration should be given to increasing the number of country desk officers (by more than one or two per area office—to provide the time for a more creative participation in the policy process) and to upgrading the FSCR rank assigned to desk officers "in charge" of information affairs for particular countries. As FSO's who entered Agency service as junior officer trainees return to Washington in increasing numbers, slots in the area offices are likely to be the most desirable assignments for them in the Agency. The Agency has a real need to provide actual jobs in Washington complement for more of its officers, to rid itself of a situation in which seventy to one hundred FSCR's serve on "temporary detail"—many feeling unwanted and few throwing themselves wholly into their assigned tasks. The balance between field and Washington service for area office personnel during career needs to be shifted toward more time in Washington—so that the area offices can actually play the intra-agency and interagency policy influence role now envisioned for them.

Agency personnel marshal many arguments against a build-up of area office staffs, even though it would be possible to increase their complements sizably by modest reduction of field staffs. (There are only 6 area offices and approximately 104 USIS posts.)

> USIA is an operating agency; keep the field strong.

> The Congress wants us to operate, not sit in offices.

> I'd rather have a lean and hard Agency, with people working overtime and not sitting around.

> If you have more personnel, Parkinson's Law comes into operation—there is more work but no more gets done.

> USIA has enjoyed the informality made possible by the fact that it is a small organization; this would be lost if the Agency grows.

> We are understaffed in the field.

> You can't really plan information policy anyway. The Agency depends on State for policy. All USIA needs is people to react.

> Research is still too imprecise to be worth staffing-up to pay careful attention to it.

There may be some validity to these arguments, but they are far outweighed by Agency needs.

The more serious charge which can be leveled at strengthening the desk level in area offices is that tactics might be strengthened at the expense of strategy, short-range policy valued over the medium and long-range view, country policies upgraded at the expense of a worldwide view, day-to-day public relations practiced instead of developing an over-all program to change the psychological climate. These tend to be the present biases of the area offices. This will not necessarily occur. If the Washington experience is repeated more often during the officers' careers and becomes a vital part of their work experience, they will cease to be "operators only" and develop perspectives of a broader nature. If Agency planning and research functions are further strengthened so that more worthwhile products are available and explained to the area offices, they will be used. If officers scheduled to serve in area offices receive additional training at mid-career, they will be more receptive to long-range views and to the concepts of communications theory. If the area director and his deputy spend more time in Washington and less in the field, they will be similarly influenced. The area office would still provide an area point of view, but one which was more in balance with over-all Agency requirements, better able to adapt the Washington or worldwide outlook to the needs of individual countries. It is perhaps difficult for individual USIS posts to adapt to worldwide needs; just as it is somewhat difficult for the media to adapt their products to the needs of the individual areas. The area office must have its foot planted firmly in both doors—the Agency and the field—and provide enlightened guidance to each.

PLANNING AND RESEARCH APPLICATIONS

Even if the area offices over time are better staffed, they will need the assistance of planning, research, and research applications personnel to help them look ahead, to provide sophisticated analyses of problems, and to relate research findings to operational problems. The staffing pattern for planning and research applications was thin in 1963. The old Research and Reference Service functioned as a somewhat separate and not fully appreciated or used research element of USIA, distant from the area offices and media services whose officers were too busy to make full use of its research findings. Assignment of a single planning officer and later of a research applications officer to the Officer of Policy was a step—but quite a limited one—toward recognizing the relevance of planning and research to policy. Recurring temporary assignment of these officers to other duties indicated some lack of understanding of the importance of their functions. In the past, USIS posts and USIA personnel have operated too much on intuition and feelings, sometimes limiting their opportunities for achievement of long-range objectives by focusing on conflicting day-to-day activities which foreclosed future success. The reorganization of the research function, and its location in the Office of Policy and Research is indicative of an Agency interest in making better use of research in policy. The use of Program Action Memoranda and the emphasis of the Research and Analysis Staff on policy-oriented research studies are steps intended to upgrade the use of research in the area offices and media services. Continued reorganization of the new staff in late 1966 and during 1967 raise questions concerning whether the changes are living up to expectations. Research must be related to planning as well as operations. The number of planners assigned to the Office of Policy and Research remains at approximately the same level as in 1963, and it is not clearly obvious that broader and longer-range aspects of planning even now are receiving adequate attention. It appears that much of the planning in the Office of Policy and Research is—as it should be—for relatively short-term operational purposes. Although outside consultants are used from time to time, the small planning operation remains primarily an inbred program, staffed by USIA Civil Service employees or Foreign Service Career Reserve Officers.

Long-range forward planning related to new insights provided by relatively basic research is as important to USIA's future programs as short-term planning of programs and operational research. To achieve a better balance in both planning and research, additional personnel with more varied backgrounds are probably required. Some increase in staff size is necessary to allow a productive interaction of minds, freed from day-to-day operational thinking. Personnel selected for periods of service from outside government, with different academic preparation and professional backgrounds, would assists such a staff to inject varying perspectives into its projections or assessments. A staggered system of rotating membership might assure both continuity and fresh ideas. Civil servants or FSCR's slated to serve on such a staff could make good use of periods of academic study and reflection before assignment. They should not be pulled away from their planning and research applications duties once assigned to put out "brush fires," which are better handled by properly staffed operational offices. The staff should be mature but vigorous, selected from personnel recognized and respected for their abilities as civil servants or FSCR's within government or for their professional contribution outside. Periods of assignment might normally be from two to four years. There could be from three to nine members, perhaps with a five-to-seven range being both preferable as a minimum and practical as a maximum. The reduction in field staff required would be negligible. The field is important, but not all important. A man with a better mind and one arm may accomplish more than a less shrewd one with two. The Agency appears to be active enough in its production of materials and in its overseas operations. There may be room for further improvement in effectiveness—by a further emphasis on and upgrading of planning and research—in spite of steps already taken. PPBS cost-effectiveness analyses may help Agency policy-makers, but they cannot reduce the need for an increasingly effective application of the solid and behavioral sciences to Agency planning and research.

INTERAGENCY FORWARD PLANNING

It is impossible to be sure of many things, but though there has been some interagency planning which relates USIA to programs of the Departments of State, Commerce, and Defense—in the administrative area on support services overseas, on trade fairs, and on the impact of nuclear developments—

there seems to have been less of it that involves the Agency for International Development. The economic and AID post for a special adviser on the staff of the Office of Policy and Research in USIA—though filled in 1967—has remained unfilled for prolonged periods. While there is cooperation on information aspects of the Alliance for Progress, this may be because AID personnel serve back to back with State desk officers in what appears to have been a successful attempt at coordinating political-economic affairs, with a spill-over to the information field. Apparently there is some cooperation between AID and USIA in the teaching of English overseas and in book programs. In the field, the public relations of USAID is the responsibility of USIS posts. Whatever relations presently exist, USIA personnel apparently feel that they are minimal in Washington. Whether there are organizational problems so that a structure for communication is lacking, personnel problems so that USIA lacks the knowledge to communicate development information, fears by AID that USIS efforts will politicize economic programs, or a lack of understanding of the importance of psychological readiness and public education for successful modernization programs—the level of interaction reported by USIA personnel is far lower than necessary for successful cooperation. Perhaps it is up to the Department of State to stimulate relationships of this nature, because of the secretary of state's role as principal advisor to the President in the foreign affairs field. By and large, while USIA personnel noted the relative absence of any important coordinating relationships with AID in Washington, they appreciated the need for common endeavor. In past years, AID has had planning and evaluation staffs, whatever their title. It would seem that the relationship between USIA and AID for forward planning would be furthered if USIA did develop an adequate planning and research applications staff—and if AID were to clearly identify a complementary planning unit and indicate that the two staffs should collaborate to the degree necessary to help achieve psychological climates overseas conducive to the phase of development currently possible, looking ahead to the next step, and attempting to create realistic aspirations for the future.

UNITY AND OPPORTUNITY FOR AGENCY PERSONNEL

USIA, like the Department of State, has the problem of two distinct personnel systems (civil service and FSCR), and the problem of providing equitable promotion opportunities to specialists in its foreign service. Of some 4,500 American citizens employed by USIA at home and abroad, about 800 are Foreign Service Career Reserves and 500 Foreign Service

Reserves (Limited)—serving temporary appointments, often with "retreat rights" to Civil Service status when tours are completed. USIA's problems are compounded by the fact that its top-notch younger recruits now go into the Foreign Service of the United States—a third personnel system. During the late 1950's there were no more than 200 foreign service slots in Washington, the rest of the 2,500 to 3,000 positions being of a Civil Service nature. This posed and still poses real problems for USIA, necessitating carrying many FSCR personnel on temporary detail in Washington rather than assigning them to full-fledged jobs. The problem is not easily overcome. Field specialists find that Washington positions require quite different abilities than overseas operations. On the other hand, Foreign Service Career Reserve officers serving in Washington sometimes feel that they have more trouble working with the "natives" here than they do with "locals" overseas. Increasing the number of policy positions in the Agency for FSCR's and FSO's has some but limited possibilities. The problem of getting the Civil Service employees to the field is as difficult as getting FSCR's or FSO's to Washington. Travel funds for Civil Service visits to the field are minimal. While some Civil Service personnel have accepted temporary assignment abroad for two-or three-year tours, this is the exception rather than the rule. There is no really unhealthy state of feeling between FSCR's, FSO's, and Civil Service personnel in USIA, but neither is there a real sense of sharing the same interests or problems, no feeling of oneness. Certainly Civil Service personnel who entered Agency service with the understanding that they would not be asked to serve abroad should not now be swallowed up by the foreign service and sent overseas. Much remains to be done even after Chairman John Macy's distinguished service with the Civil Service Commission to make overseas duty within the Civil Service comparable to Foreign Service personnel conditions—though progress is being made. Without any degree of assurance of a proper answer, it would seem that consideration may well be given to creating a single information service preferably within the Foreign Service of the United States, containing different career ladders, with many personnel subject to normal periods of assignment overseas, others to somewhat shorters periods, with some still Washington-centered. This may be achieved if the Hays bill which passed the House in 1965 and was before the Senate in 1966 was ever enacted and implemented—which in 1967 seems unlikely. Whether a separate career service for USIA could provide the necessary flexibility of assignment remains to be seen, but clearly, such a step would be a great improvement in many ways over the present personnel system.

The Department of State has sometimes had difficulty in providing adequate promotional opportunities for its cultural affairs specialists within the Foreign Service. In USIA, there is some question whether its FSCR's who have come up the cultural affairs officer ladder have equitable opportunities for promotion or assignment with those who have come up the information officer ladder. This is the old problem of the political officer vs. the cultural officer; the fast-media expert vs. the cultural-media specialist with slower impact. Today, of course, exchange programs can have rapid impact on participants. The Foreign Leader Program of the Department of State, serviced by USIS posts in the field, can point to dramatic changes in views and actions after such study visits to America. Educational development is tremendously important now in Africa; the work of binational centers contributes strongly to USIS programs in Latin America. There must be a number of countries or even entire geographic regions where a career within the cultural affairs rather than the information ladder might be the more relevant for supervision of USIS country programs. Certainly USIA should attempt to provide its cultural affairs officers with a breadth of experience which will make them capable (if they desire) to assume top Agency positions. Many of them are more thoroughly grounded in academic subject matter than information personnel, and some are operators as well as "thinkers." State has on occasion been more kind in its appointments and made better use of a culturally oriented FSCR in the Bureau of Educational and Cultural Affairs than USIA has done on assignments within the Agency. On the other hand, there is a relative equilibrium maintained in appointments to area office director positions between men with information and cultural affairs backgrounds. The Agency is aware of the problem and is consciously trying to offset the natural built-in bias. The shift in Agency emphasis between 1963 and 1968 has already favorably affected the importance of cultural activities. As the Agency's program continues to grow in success and mature over time, the need for fast political action in crisis is likely to become less crucial, and programs of a more cultural nature will come into their own—in an equitable balance which will tend to resolve this particular type of personnel problem. The issue of extending career ladders for narrower media experts and specialists also deserves Agency attention and may not be resolved by lapse of time and changed conditions. Little Agency study has been devoted to personnel practices governing selection and promotion of its national employees at USIS posts, though it has recognized the need to bring some of them to Washington for training and to visit the United States. USIA has been able to upgrade training opportunities within the Agency for FSCR's, FSO's and Civil Service employees, but the program is still smaller and less sophisticated than an academic observer might desire.

AGENCY AND NATIONAL PURPOSE

The "barometer" of Agency purpose swung after 1961 from "mutual understanding" toward "political communication" and "counterinsurgency." Has the increase in payload or political freight caused many people to find USIA products less credible? There is no clear-cut answer. It would seem that the impact depends upon the judicious use of political communication, relating the freight to a specific act that is visible to foreign publics. USIA in connection with the Cuban missile crisis in the fall of 1962 was quite forthright in its communication of the facts of the situation and in seeking support for American policy. Latin Americans found the message credible, and the United States received widespread public support there. On the other hand, as English teaching and cultural activities were diminished in binational centers after 1961, sensibilities of local members of the Board of Directors required some of them to resign, and others who had made use of the centers stayed away. Perhaps this means that primarily cultural programs carry political freight less well than press releases or VOA broadcasts. Certainly this problem requires careful Agency study.

What benefits come from trying to create a broad educational exchange of ideas for mutual understanding? Is USIA the proper agency to operate programs with such a long-range goal? Few if any of USIA's current activities seek random unstructured educational exchanges for this purpose. There is no proof that such activities would bring a foreign public to give outright support for present American foreign policies in all circumstances or even in most instances. On the other hand, there is reason to believe that such programs might prevent active opposition, preserve neutrality, or even lead to adaptation of United States policy to respect the legitimate needs of others—which would be useful to American policy makers.

Does the United States gain real benefits from a free exchange of knowledge and cultural performances, primarily for nonpolitical purposes? Some would argue that the exchange of performing artists for the sake of culture alone is a waste of public funds. In a world in which the United States has often been tabbed as materialist and lacking in culture, our notable educational achievements and cultural and educational activities can take on a political connotation and increase American prestige or influence in former colonial areas. In dealings with bloc nations, exchanges of this type are particularly useful and healthy. With the countries of eastern Europe and the

Soviet Union, these types of exchange have provided contacts when most others were severed. In a shrinking world, where failure to communicate or to achieve some degree of mutual understanding can lead to nuclear catastrophe, preservation of the most tenuous communications at cultural or educational levels during trying times may be better than complete elimination of contacts. The mere fact of such exchanges tends to reduce tension between the people who view the performances or participate in the discussions, to normalize their attitudes toward other peoples, to reduce the possibility that either side in contention can rely on the "devil" theory.

What about information programs of a counterinsurgency nature—the support of an Adoula in the Congo or a Diem in South Vietnam? In these particular instances, the work may have been largely for naught. Neither is now in power. But there may be many other areas where American support of leaders has helped or is helping national leaders to do the things which must be done for development and modernization in spite of the sacrifices which foreign publics must undergo in the process of moving forward. Counterinsurgency efforts, if once "oversold," should not now be written off as useless.

Finally, can a democratic government in peacetime engage in all-out psychological warfare—the total coordination of diplomatic, economic, military, and psychological programs in support of national policies? The answer must of course be a categorical "no," but more needs to be said. Certainly in Vietnam psychological warfare has been a necessary part of the USIS program. Although the completeness of informational intervention in nonwar situations must necessarily be less than attempted in time of conflict —and the nature of the message carried substantially different—the importance of coordinating national policies for effectiveness in peacetime is no less a requirement for national survival or world progress. Perhaps the only rational conclusion is that an emphasis on any one of the Agency purposes on the "barometer" spectrum may be in the national and even world interest at the proper time and place, that the United States Information Agency must be organized and staffed so that it can serve these varied purposes (either alone or with the help of other agencies) in a selective mix as appropriate to widely varied and emergent conditions throughout the world.

Beyond the present spectrum of purpose, consistent with the Agency's "Pursuit of Peace" theme, but perhaps implying a new dimension of effort, is the concept of psychological or educational "peacefare." A realistic, full-scale search for peace with security, recognizing the needs of other peoples and nations in balance with the United States national interest, requires not just better coordination of the foreign affairs agencies and their present programs. It would also require an increasing exchange of ideas, a creative reintegration of belief and action, and more sophisticated policies than the United States or the other great powers have yet organized themselves to formulate or implement. Of course, USIA cannot rush ahead in this direction alone or on its own. As educated and experienced an observer of foreign affairs as Senator William Fulbright, in a verbal exchange with Director Marks before the Senate Foreign Relations Committee on August 17, 1966, seemed adamant in demanding that USIA remains a "propaganda" agency and not become involved in "educational" activities. This represents an inflexible Cold War view of USIA's function, most unfortunate in the type of world which Senator Fulbright himself sees in the process of development. In the long run, so-called propaganda programs are likely to be able to afford and benefit from a heavier educational output. They have the communications tools beamed overseas to conduct positive as well as negative programs, and can train enlightened personnel to help educate—or propagandize, if you will—the world toward increasing acceptance of the facts of interdependence and the necessity of community. Even propaganda need not be conceived by governments only or even primarily in terms of serving narrow national purposes—in an era when cooperation among and more objective understanding between the peoples and governments of the world may be necessary if mankind is to remain on his own planet, let alone reach others in the solar system.

Psychological-informational-cultural-educational tools can be (and in some instances already are being) put to use for very broad goals, respecting differences and beneficial to the emerging needs of all men. If they are not, in increasing balance, put to such use by the United States government through USIA and other existing or yet to be founded government agencies during the final decades of the twentieth century, America will have thrown away an opportunity to help channel mankind toward the growing community of interest of which men have always dreamed, which may already be or could become a stark necessity for survival.

To achieve or even to approach a more fruitful web of human relationships and a realistic reassessment of the national interest in a changing world will require additional attention to communications theory; to understanding and being sensitive to ideological, cultural, and semantic differences; a greater willingness to "listen" to what others are trying to say; a more serious study of audiences and media available for communications; and inspired leadership by the President of the United States. It will also require a close examination of national social problems by increasing numbers of American citizens, and a new sense of dedication to making America a truly Great Society among other great societies in a more helpful, cooperative, and dynamic world.

NOTES

PREFACE

1. Major published studies of USIA since 1953 include Oren Stephens, *Facts to a Candid World* (Stanford, Calif.: Stanford University Press, 1955); and Wilson Dizard, *The Strategy of Truth* (Washington, D.C.: Public Affairs Press, 1961). Stephens' study, developed from research done during an assignment at the National War College, focuses on relatively broad issues and is not intended to be particularly descriptive. Dizard's study, written primarily from the perspective of the Agency's overseas United States Information Service, emphasizes field activities and relations, though indicating the nature of Agency programs and the products of the Agency's media services. Major unpublished studies of USIA include John E. Harr, "Key Administrative Problems of the United States Information Agency" (M.A. thesis, University of Chicago, 1961). The Harr study discussed four major Agency problems: objectives, organization, research and evaluation, and personnel. Slightly more specialized but of equal value for understanding USIA is Ben Posner, "Major Budgetary and Programming Problems of the United States Information Agency in its Operation of Overseas Missions" (Ph.D. thesis, American University, 1962). In addition to an introduction, conclusions, and recommendations, Mr. Posner includes chapters describing the United States Information Agency, the process of budgeting within the federal government, the process of budgeting within the Agency, an evaluation of the country as a principal unit of planning-programming-budgeting, and an evaluation of the mechanism for setting and adjusting priorities. When Posner prepared the thesis he was deputy assistant director of USIA (administration). He is now assistant director of USIA (administration). Also unpublished, and still classified, is a 900-page report made by Lee Bogart of the McCann-Erickson advertising agency which was based on 142 interviews with "top operators" of USIA conducted during the winter and spring of 1953-54. Some conclusions drawn from the study appear in Lee Bogart, "A Study of the Operating Assumptions of the U.S. Information Agency," *Public Opinion Quarterly*, Vol. XIX (Fall, 1955), 369-79. He indicated some problems of applying communications research to the work of propagandists, citing a lack of knowledge within USIA of what was being said by the Agency to foreign audiences, of who was in these audiences, and of what impact USIA programs were having. He called for the use of broader studies by representatives of the various social sciences to assist the Agency. He also suggested a fresh look at the Agency's official operating premises.

CHAPTER I

1. Management Division, USIA, *The Agency in Brief* (1966). These figures are based on the estimates for FY 1967, pp. 26-27.
2. Stephens, *Facts*, 66-68.
3. Voice of America (VOA), USIA, *Fact Sheet* (January, 1967). By comparison, in December, 1966, Soviet Union international short-wave broadcasts averaged 1,555 hours weekly; Communist China, 1,109; the United Arab Republic, 910; the United Kingdom, 731; and West Germany, 721.
4. USIA *26th Review of Operations* (January-June, 1966), 5, 16-17.
5. Replaced by John Daley in September, 1967.
6. See *Time* (December 9, 1966), 31. Also note Warren Rogers, "America's Voice 'swings a Little,' " *Look* (November 15, 1966). Also see VOA Program Schedules for November, 1966, through January, 1967, for Europe, Latin America, and Africa.

7.   The Wireless File consists of seven separate transmissions to different areas of the world, which during the 1963-66 period have averaged 10,000 to 12,000 words each.

8.   *America Illustrated* appeared an additional five years, from 1947 to 1953, as *America*. At that time it was subject to precensorship by the Soviet government. *America Illustrated* was instituted in 1956 and has no prior censorship.

9.   Most figures of this type may be found by consulting issues of USIA's *Report to Congress*, made semiannually. Its twenty-sixth semiannual report was retitled *Review of Operations* and covered the period January-June, 1966.

10.   Figures from USIA's *Books Published in Translation and in English* (as reported July 1, 1965-June 30, 1966).

11.   The figures given are for FY 1967. For comparison with earlier years, see USIA, *The Agency in Brief* (1966). Since 1963, the number of foreign locals has fallen slightly, the difference made up by an additional number of Americans overseas. Total positions, FY 1963, 11,880; FY 1967, 12,051.

12.   Biographical information from USIA, *The Agency in Brief* (1965).

13.   *Ibid.* (1966).

14.   Members of USIA's foreign service would become members of the Foreign Service of the United States if the U.S. Senate would confirm the nominations of 760 FSCR's for lateral entry into the Foreign Service, but this now seems unlikely to occur.

15.   Much of the description and functioning of the USIS post is taken from USIA, *Country Public Affairs Officer Handbook (March, 1962)*.

16.   Lucien Pye, *Communication and Political Development* (Princeton, N.J.: Princeton University Press, 1963).

17.   Wilson Dizard, *Television: A World View* (Syracuse, N.Y.: Syracuse University Press, 1966).

18.   George Kennan, *American Diplomacy 1900-1950* (Chicago, Ill.: University of Chicago Press, 1951).

19.   USIA, *25th Report to Congress* (July-December, 1965), 5-6.

20.   Bureau of the Budget, "Planning-Programming-Budgeting," *Bulletin No. 66-3* (October 12, 1965).

CHAPTER II

1.   For a discussion of problems in foreign policy arising from the development of nuclear weapons systems, see Henry A. Kissinger, *Nuclear Weapons and Foreign Policy* (New York: Doubleday & Co., Anchor, 1958); Louis Henkin, ed., *Arms Control: Issues for the Public* (Englewood Cliffs, N.J.: Prentice-Hall, Spectrum, 1961); Seymour Melman, ed., *Disarmament: Its Politics and Economics* (Boston, Mass.: The American Academy of Arts and Sciences, 1962); Frederick H. Gareau, ed., *The Balance of Power and Nuclear Deterrence* (Boston, Mass.: Houghton Mifflin Co., 1962); Ernest Lefever, ed., *Arms and Arms Control* (New York: Frederick A. Praeger, 1962); Robert Goldwin, ed., *America Armed: Essays on United States Military Policy* (Chicago, Ill.: Rand McNally & Co., 1963); Alastair Buchan, ed., *A World of Nuclear Powers* (Englewood Cliffs, N.J.: Prentice-Hall, 1966); David W. Tarr, *American Strategy in the Nuclear Age* (New York: Macmillan Co., 1966).

2.   For a discussion of problems in foreign policy arising from the economic, social, and political revolution in the new developing nations, see Gunnar Myrdal, *Rich Lands and Poor* (New York: Harper & Bros., 1957); Warren Hunsberger, ed., *New Era in the Non-Western World* (Ithaca, N.Y.: Cornell University Press, 1957); Council on Foreign Relations, *Social Change in Latin America Today* (New York: Harper & Bros., 1960); Eugene Staley, *The*

Future of Underdeveloped Countries: Political Implications of Economic Development (New York: Frederick A. Praeger, 1961); Center for International Studies, MIT, "Economic, Social, and Political Change in the Underdeveloped Countries and Its Implications for United States Policy," Study No. 12, in the U.S., Congress, Senate, Committee on Foreign Relations, *United States Foreign Policy*, 87 Cong., 1st sess., March 15, 1961, pp. 1165-1268; Robert A. Goldwin, ed., *Why Foreign Aid?* (Chicago, Ill.: Rand McNally & Co., 1963); J. Roland Pennock, ed., *Self-government in Modernizing Nations* (Englewood Cliffs, N.J.: Prentice-Hall, 1963); Bruce Russett, *Trends in World Politics* (New York: Macmillan Co., 1965), 106-56; John D. Montgomery, *Foreign Aid in International Politics* (Englewood Cliffs, N.J.: Prentice-Hall, 1967).

3.   For an indication of changes within the Soviet Union which may affect its foreign policy and that of the United States, see Erich Fromm, *May Man Prevail* (Garden City, N.Y.: Doubleday & Co., Anchor, 1961); Zbigniew Brzezinski, *Ideology and Power in Soviet Politics* (New York: Frederick A. Praeger, 1962); Arnold Wolfers, ed., *Changing East-West Relations and the Unity of the West* (Baltimore: The Johns Hopkins Press, 1964); Charles O. Lerche, Jr., *The Cold War . . . and After* (Englewood Cliffs, N.J.: Prentice-Hall, Spectrum, 1965); David S. McClellan, *The Cold War in Transition* (New York: Macmillan Co., 1966).

4.   For a discussion of the changing world environment to which foreign and information policy makers must adapt, see Harrison Brown, "Science, Technology and International Relations," in the 1956 Brookings Lectures, *The Changing Environment of International Relations: A Major Problem of American Foreign Policy* (Washington, D.C.: The Brookings Institution, 1956); Harrison Brown, "The Prospective Environment for Policymaking and Administration," in The Brookings Institution, "The Formulation and Administration of United States Foreign Policy," Study No. 9, in U.S. Congress, Senate, Committee on Foreign Relations, *United States Foreign Policy*, 87 Cong., 1 sess., March 15, 1961, pp. 937-59; Charles Lerche and Abdul Said, *Concepts of International Politics* (Englewood Cliffs, N.J.: Prentice-Hall, 1963), 119-41; Bruce Russett, *Trends in World Politics* (New York: Macmillan Co., 1965), 1-17.

5.   For a spectrum of views of the United Nations and American foreign policy toward the United Nations, see Lincoln Bloomfield, *The United Nations and U.S. Foreign Policy* (Boston: Little, Brown & Co., 1960); Francis O. Wilcox and H. Field Haviland, Jr., eds., *The United States and the United Nations* (Baltimore: The Johns Hopkins Press, 1961); Andrew Boyd, *United Nations: Piety, Myth, and Truth* (Baltimore, Md.: Penguin Books, Pelican, 1964); Inis Claude, Jr., *Swords into Plowshares* (New York: Random House, 1964); Franz B. Gross, *The United States and the United Nations* (Norman, Okla.: University of Oklahoma Press, 1964). For a discussion of western European integration or development of a broader Atlantic Community, see Francis O. Wilcox and H. Field Haviland, Jr., eds., *The Atlantic Community* (New York: Frederick A. Praeger, 1963); Lawrence B. Krause, ed., *The Common Market* (Englewood Cliffs, N.J.: Prentice-Hall, 1964); Michael Curtis, *Western European Integration* (New York: Harper and Row, 1965). For a discussion of an increasing need for personnel trained in multilateral diplomacy, see M.H. Cardozo, *Diplomats in International Cooperation* (Ithaca, N.Y.: Cornell University Press, 1962).

6.   For conflicting views of Soviet-American relations since World War II, see Norman A. Graebner, *Cold War Diplomacy 1945-1960* (Princeton, N.J.: D. Van Nostrand Co., Anvil, 1962); Robert Strausz-Hupé, William Kintner, James Dougherty, and Alvin Cottrell, *Protracted Conflict* (New York: Harper and Row, Colophon, 1963).

7.   For a discussion of problems in foreign policy arising from the emergence of Communist China as a major power in Asia, see A. Doak Barnett, *Communist China and Asia: Challenge to American Policy* (New York: Harper & Bros., 1960); statements by A. Doak Barnett and Robert Scalapino in U.S. Congress, Senate, Committee on Foreign Relations, *U.S. Policy with Respect to Mainland China*, 89 Cong., 2 sess., March, 1966, pp. 3-16, 561-75; John A. Fairbank, "The People's Middle Kingdom," *Foreign Affairs* (July, 1966), 574-86.

8.   The point of view expressed in the historical review and analysis of traditional American responses to international affairs is the result of a careful and appreciative reading of George F. Kennan, *American Diplomacy 1900-1950* (Chicago, Ill.: University of Chicago Press, 1951); Edmund Stillman and William Pfaff, *The New Politics: America and the End of the Postwar World* (New York: Coward McCann, 1961); and Norman A. Graebner, *Cold War Diplomacy, 1945-1960* (Princeton, N.J.: D. Van Nostrand Co., Anvil, 1962). Additional useful factual information on the post-World War II period was found in Gordon Connell-Smith, *Pattern of the Post-War World* (Baltimore, Md.: Penguin Books, 1957); W.W. Rostow, *The United States in the World Arena* (New York: Harper and Row, 1960); and Hugh Seton-Watson, *Neither War nor Peace: The Struggle for Power in the Postwar World* (New York: Frederick A. Praeger, 1962).

9.   For a provocative collection of foreign commentaries on American life and foreign policy, see Alan F. Westin *et al.*, eds., *Views of America* (New York: Harcourt, Brace, and World, 1966).

10.   Martin Merson, *The Private Diary of a Public Servant* (New York: Macmillan Co., 1955).

11.   For a discussion of the arguments for and against establishing a career foreign service for information officers about two years after the establishment of the USIA as an independent agency, see Robert E. Elder, "A Career Service for USIA?" *Foreign Service Journal* (February, 1956), 26-27, 40, 42, 44.

12.   Material on the history of information programs and on the history of USIA is primarily drawn from the following sources: Charles A.H. Thomson, *Overseas Information Service of the United States Government* (Washington, D.C.: The Brookings Institution, 1948); H. Rowland Ludden, "Development of Informational Activities," in Stephen D. Kertesz, ed., *American Diplomacy in a New Era* (Notre Dame, Ind.: University of Notre Dame Press, 1961), 492-524; Wilson P. Dizard, *The Strategy of Truth* (Washington, D.C.: Public Affairs Press, 1961), 29-47. Additional information was obtained from John E. Harr, "Key Administrative Problems of the United States Information Agency" (M.A. thesis, University of Chicago, 1961); Brookings Institution, "The Formulation and Administration of United States Foreign Policy," Study No. 9, in U.S. Congress, Senate, Committee on Foreign Relations, *United States Foreign Policy*, 87 Cong., 1 sess., March 15, 1961, pp. 870-77; USIA, *The Agency in Brief* (1963, 1965, 1966). Information on the various directors of USIA was obtained by interview and from information printed in the USIA's house organ, *USIA Correspondent*.

13.   Information on the government-wide foreign affairs mechanism was drawn from Robert E. Elder, *The Policy Machine: The Department of State and American Foreign Policy* (Syracuse, N.Y.: Syracuse University Press, 1960); Brookings Institution, "The Formulation and Administration of United States Foreign Policy," Study No. 9, in U.S. Congress, Senate, Committee on Foreign Relations, *United States Foreign Policy*, 87 Cong., 1 sess., March 15, 1961, pp. 799-987; American Assembly, Don K. Price, ed., *The Secretary of State* (Englewood Cliffs, N.J.: Prentice-Hall, Spectrum, 1960); Senator Henry M. Jackson, ed., *The Secretary of State and the Ambassador: Jackson Subcommittee Papers on the Conduct of American Foreign Policy* (New York: Frederick A. Praeger, 1964); Robert E. Elder, *Overseas Representation and Services for Federal Domestic Agencies* (New York: Carnegie Endowment for International Peace, 1965); Burton M. Sapin, *The Making of United States Foreign Policy* (Washington, D.C.: The Brookings Institution, 1966). See also Allan S. Nanes in U.S. Congress, House, Subcommittee on International Organizations and Movements, Committee on Foreign Affairs, *The U.S. Ideological Effort: Government Agencies and Programs*, January 3, 1964, pp. 1-66.

14.   The Office of Emergency Planning in the Executive Office of the President assists and advises the President in coordinating and determining policy for all emergency preparedness

activities of the U.S. government. This includes plans for emergency use of manpower, materials, industrial capacity, transportation, and civil defense; it also concerns itself with continuity in government in an emergency.

CHAPTER III

1.   The figures given on Agency telegraphic flow are based on a six-month average for July-December of FY 1967. The outgoing figures, of course, do not include the words sent overseas in the Wireless File of the Press and Publications Service. USIA telegrams in FY 1964 numbered approximately 1,900 outgoing a month and 1,400 incoming. About 117,000 words went out a month, and about 195,000 words were received by the Agency a month during FY 1964.

2.   Present with Marks are the executive assistant and the deputy director, plus the inspector general, the deputy director of policy and research and the associate deputy director, the general counsel, the assistant director for research and analysis, the assistant director of policy and research (policy and plans), the six assistant directors of USIA who head area offices, the four assistant directors of USIA in charge of media services, the assistant director of USIA for administration, the assistant director of USIA for personnel, several liaison or policy officers from the Office of Policy and Research, and perhaps the director and deputy director's special assistants.

3.   USIA, *The Agency in Brief* (1966), 21.

4.   On August 17, 1966, Director Marks appeared before the Committee on Foreign Relations of the U.S. Senate to open hearings by the committee on new policies in Vietnam. The hearing had been triggered by a story in the *Washington Post* of August 11 concerning USIA activities in sponsoring visits by foreign newsmen to Vietnam. It was the director's first appearance before the committee. The following excerpt from the first ten minutes of the hearing indicates the hazards of such appearances, as two committee members attempt to place the director on the defensive:

MR. MARKS: I appreciate this invitation to appear before this committee to discuss USIA's program designed to assist selected foreign correspondents to report on the Vietnam scene from firsthand knowledge. It is an excellent program.

This program was started in the fall of 1965. We in USIA are charged with the responsibility of trying to see that full and objective information regarding the Vietnam situation is available to newspapers, radio, and television outlets abroad. The question is not whether such media favor or oppose the policies of the U.S. government, but whether they have the facts upon which to form intelligent opinions.

I have said time and time again that a man's opinion is no better than the facts upon which his opinion is based, and unless he has the facts, his opinion isn't worth anything.

We have found that in some instances reporting has been based on lack of information or on misinformation. The best way to correct this situation is to enable reporters to go to the scene of the story, ask questions, and see for themselves what is happening.

I have talked to foreign journalists and invariably they say to me, "I would like to go there and see what is happening through my eyes. I would like to report it through the eyes of a Latin American, or an African, or an Asian, and not through the eyes of an American."

The technique of providing transportation to correspondents so they can see for themselves and get a firsthand acquaintance with the facts is not new in the field of foreign affairs or anywhere else. It is a time-honored practice and a respected one and a good one.

To a great extent—

SENATOR GORE: Why would you say "time honored?"

MR. MARKS: It has been going on for a long time, sir; and the major correspondents of the world—

SENATOR GORE: That is a better description.

MR. MARKS: Yes. It has been going on for a long time and there is no discredit to a newsman, to an educator, or a scholar, to a scientist, to be a guest of the U.S. government, or of a business organization, to be transported to a scene so that he can observe for himself.

SENATOR GORE: The only purpose of my interjection was for clarity. Lots of things have been going on for a long time that are not "time honored."

MR. MARKS: This has been going on a long time, and I approve of it. I think every major correspondent in this room, if asked, would tell you that at one time or another he has been pleased to be on the scene of an event, and that the transportation has been furnished through the courtesy of a government or a business organization. I would like to point out that when a new hotel opens in the United States, it is customary to have a flight of newspapermen. I would like to point out that when a new play opens at the National Theater, the newsmen are given tickets so they can report the play. Baseball games take place every day and there are newsmen in the press boxes as guests of the management, so there is nothing new about this, and nothing wrong about it.

SENATOR GORE: So, in consequence, you take them to Vietnam?

MR. MARKS: That is right.

CHAIRMAN FULBRIGHT: Do you mean to equate the significance of these events with the significance of the war in Vietnam?

MR. MARKS: No, sir. But I want to point out, Senator, that we have been under the educational exchange program, bringing people to the United States for more than 20 years so that they can see for themselves what is going on; they can study in this country; they can talk to their counterparts; they can find out firsthand, what the practices are in their industry, or in their field of learning.

CHAIRMAN FULBRIGHT: I hope you won't get too far afield. Do you mean to equate the exchange program with the USIA's program?

MR. MARKS: The same theory applies, sir.

CHAIRMAN FULBRIGHT: Does it? I don't wish to let that stand. We had a great battle over this very matter about 15 years ago, whether the USIA should take over the cultural exchange program, and it was very thoroughly discussed and considered. We decided, and I think quite rightly, that the cultural exchange program was not a proper part of our propaganda activities. I would not want anybody to think either the purpose of that program or its administration is the the same purpose as USIA.

MR. MARKS: They are different programs, Senator.

CHAIRMAN FULBRIGHT: Quite different. But you seem to leave the impression that they are just about the same, or are the same.

MR. MARKS: No, Senator. What I have tried to say is that we invite foreigners to be our guests, to come to the United States, whether they are educational leaders or scientists, so that they can see firsthand what is happening. In the program we are going to discuss this morning, the U.S. government, through the USIA, transported foreign journalists to the scene in Vietnam so that they could see firsthand what is happening.

CHAIRMAN FULBRIGHT: That is all right. Leave it at that. Do not try to take in too much territory and bring in the exchange programs. These are very broad programs and have implications far beyond what we are concerned with this morning. I did not want the record to stand that I accepted the idea that they were comparable activities.

MR. MARKS: We are in agreement, Senator.

CHAIRMAN FULBRIGHT: All right.

See U.S. Congress, Senate, Committee on Foreign Relations, *News Policies in Vietnam*, 89 Cong., 2 sess., August 17 and 31, 1966, pp. 2-4.

CHAPTER IV

1. A country paper on "Guidelines for Policy and Operations in Ruritania" would be organized under four headings: I. Basic Approach, II. Background, III. Objectives, IV. Lines of Action.

Under "I. Basic Approach," the paper might state that the United States should work with Ruritania as a respected nation which with us seeks independence and well-being for all nations —noting that Ruritania is suspicious of U.S. motives and quite conscious of racial matters in the United States. Although American aid is accepted, the regime plays down the United States' role in development. The United States needs Ruritania's help in both military and scientific arrangements. Communist domination of Ruritania or infiltration of her police or military would be dangerous to American interests. The United States must therefore make it possible for the regime to deal with us without having to confront directly the popular prejudices in Ruritania against involvement with Western powers.

In "II. Background," such a paper might point out Ruritania's past experience with classic colonial exploitation; the country's one-crop economy; and its lack of a popular school system, of a trained civil service, of locally owned businesses, and of political democracy. Ruritania has taken considerable aid from Communist countries. It recognizes Communist China, North Vietnam, and North Korea, as well as the eastern European "satellite" countries. It claims to be a non-aligned power, often voting against Western-sponsored United Nations resolutions, but it also votes against Communist moves where the rights of smaller nations are involved, as in Hungary and Tibet. Though not joining military pacts, Ruritania has let it be known that it feels one pact of which the United States is a member is favorable to its continued independence. Because of its border with a Communist state, Ruritania fears that a United States MAAG program would create difficulties. Communication is limited in the country. About 90 per cent of the population engage in one-crop agriculture, living in small villages under a headman. A provincial policeman visits a village once a month, representing the ruling family of Ruritania. The policeman is hated and courted, as he is the "government" to the villagers. Although there is talk of democracy, since local opinion supports the party in power, there are clandestine student and labor organizations. These groups are "leftist," and an embarrassment to Moscow's friendly relations with Ruritania. In practice, the Ruritanian regime is autocratic, controlling business, government, finance, and military posts. Those who suggest greater popular participation in politics are under surveillance. Communist propaganda in Ruritania includes magazines, films, scholarships to Ruritanian students, training in Moscow for Ruritanian scientists, short-wave broadcasts in the local language, and yearly trade fair exhibits. There is talk of starting television in Ruritania but no action yet. Although an armed insurgency problem is possible, because of the border with a Communist country, the present regime is friendly enough to the Communists to make a change of regimes a dubious risk for them. American businessmen are often harassed, American motives villified, and the United States portrayed as having racial discrimination and growing poverty. Negotiations with the government for the renewal of a base agreement on our small naval station, with additional facilities for a satellite tracking station on the same premises, have not progressed in recent months.

Under "III. Objectives," the guidelines paper might list United States aims of depriving the Communist bloc of military and economic resources in Ruritania; furthering Ruritanian support of Western programs for disarmament, a nuclear test ban, and a strong United Nations; securing the enlarged base agreement to permit a tracking facility to be set up; securing investment and tax arrangements which would encourage American and free world investment in Ruritania; and interesting Ruritania in supporting a regional organization which it has not heretofore joined.

Under "IV. Lines of Action," it might be suggested that the United States attempt to persuade the Ruritanian government to undertake realistic economic reforms, to broaden educational opportunities, to lessen dependence upon Communist aid while increasing the size of the small United States AID mission; to seek approval of the new base tracking station agreement; to convince Ruritania of the danger of accepting further Soviet military aid, while opposing proposed Communist assistance to the national police; to conduct information and cultural programs to support United States policy objectives and to offset Communist propaganda; and to encourage Ruritania to broaden popular participation in government as public attitudes and education permit in order to reduce Ruritania's vulnerability to revolution.

2. Under the "pursuit of peace" theme, it was declared that "the United States has no more urgent task than the pursuit of peace. In the words of President Johnson, 'We will be unceasing in the search for peace; resourceful in our pursuit of areas of agreement even with those with whom we differ.' We believe this search for an attainable and honorable peace should be based on a gradual evolution in human institutions and on a series of concrete actions and effective agreements (such as the limited nuclear test ban) leading to general and complete disarmament. The United States will continue to encourage the settlement of international issues by peaceful means rather than force." The "strength and reliability" theme meant that "the United States, matured and tested under the responsibilities of free world leadership, will maintain its strength in all fields to protect its own freedom and to aid in the defense of other free nations against threats to their independence and institutions. The United States can and will keep its commitments to its allies and to other countries." Under "free choice," it was said "the United States believes in a peaceful world community of free and independent states, free to choose their own future, free to build and change their own systems so long as they do not threaten the freedom of others. We believe in the dignity of the individual, and will continue to help other nations in their efforts to modernize their societies, to resist coercion, and to construct and maintain free institutions." Under the "rule of law" theme, which probably came into being both as a result of the assassination of President Kennedy and the continuing civil rights struggle in the United States, it was pointed out that "the fundamental commitment of the United States is to the freedom of the individual, of the community, and of the nation under law. This commitment is the hallmark which distinguishes societies of free men from societies where rule is based on privilege or force. Historically, the rule of law was a commitment of the people of the United States to themselves; today it is the cornerstone of both our domestic and international policies. We will continue to work toward perfecting the rule of law at home and encourage its extension to and among all nations." Finally, on the "United Nations" theme, it was noted that "the United States will continue its full support of the United Nations, seeking in concert with other countries to strengthen the UN's peacekeeping machinery. It will also continue to support UN functions which assist all free nations, large and small, to maintain their independence and to move toward political, economic and social justice."

3. A phrase used discussing American military policy in Maxwell D. Taylor, *The Uncertain Trumpet* (New York: Harper & Bros., 1960).

4. Although no single advisor or liaison officer can be considered typical, since they are highly individualistic in temperament and approach, a closer look at the work of the policy liaison officer may clarify the role the advisors and liaison officers play. A GS-15, exceptionally well organized and capable, who has served in the Office of Policy and Research since 1955, his title and duties have changed as policy emphases have been altered through the years. Coming to IOP as Atoms for Peace Officer from USIA's Press and Publications Service, after studying law and joining the Office of Strategic Services during World War II, his subject matter responsibilities were expanded to include test ban and atomic testing problems by 1956. Working as atomic energy and disarmament advisor after 1957, he handled broader questions of disarmament and atomic testing. By 1961, as USIA moved to counter the widespread belief overseas in a

United States "missile lag," he became national security affairs advisor. Today, he serves as policy liaison officer, working on drafts of papers for the use of the Agency's director, executive assistant, or deputy director in interagency policy discussions. He may prepare memoranda for their use or brief them orally. As national security affairs adviser, 60 per cent of his effort dealt with matters affecting the "strength image" of the United States; some 25 per cent, with disarmament; and most of the remainder of his time was spent in maintaining liaison with the Atomic Energy Commission. Today as in 1961 he is less an expert on military and atomic science than on the impact of military and atomic developments on policy. In his relations with the media and areas, he reviews materials which help prepare Far Eastern and South Asian opinion for upcoming Chinese Communist nuclear explosions. His relations with the media and areas are often "lateral" in nature, informal, without dependence upon the authority of his "bosses"—either Harris or Ryan, "just working together" to reach mutual agreement through discussion and persuasion. All information material that flows through the government dealing with his special interests, except for a very "closely held" event, would pass across his desk, routed to him by USIA's communications unit in the Office of Administration. Although he reads weekly intelligence summaries from the Central Intelligence Agency and the Department of State, most of this information has already reached him though the daily flow of telegrams and dispatches— the main substance from which he works. Reports of military attachés also reach him, often more detailed than his needs require. In addition, he reads books, newspapers, and periodicals; he particularly enjoyed Herman Kahn's *On Thermonuclear War;* benefits from the *New York Times,* and reads such journals as the *Bulletin of the Atomic Scientists,* the *Journal of Arms Control, Foreign Affairs,* and *Orbis.* He reads presidential speeches with great care and follows public opinion studies—such as the Gallup poll or USIA overseas polls—related to his interests. Using all of this information to assist him in the formulation of his opinions, which may become Agency decisions, he likes to bounce his ideas off colleagues in other agencies who share his interests before setting his ideas down on paper. He will consult anyone who may be able to contribute an idea or criticize his tentative conclusions, whether the individual is in or out of the government, at RAND or at the Institute for Defense Analysis. His memoranda are always brief, never over three pages if they carry a recommendation and often only a short paragraph if he is just conveying information. On a typical day, he is on the telephone a third of the time, taking queries from the media or doing business with other agencies, engaging in thirty to forty short telephone conversations a day. Another third of his time goes into reading the "government paper flow" and relevant privately published material. The rest of his time is spent putting ideas to paper. The telephone calls break up the day and constantly force him to shift his planned priorities, dropping project A to do B, which is interrupted to work on C, so that A is not finished until tomorrow. Most of his advice goes to the media and is fairly detailed, a question of fact, how to say this, or should this commentary be done. The advisor or liaison officer is a servant to the media, taking their calls as they come, unless he is drafting a paper of overriding importance.

5.   Oren Stephens, *Facts to a Candid World: America's Overseas Information Program* (Stanford, Calif.: Stanford University Press, 1955).

6.   The USIA Librarian now functions from within the new Information Resources Division of the Office of Administration to service headquarters and field needs—including those of the Research and Analysis Staff. It is anticipated that much of the factual reference work performed by the Regional Divisions in the old Research and Reference Service will be taken over by Agency Library personnel. The Agency Library, now with a staff of about forty-eight (no more than two or three of whom are FSCR's), is essentially a documents collection of between two and three million separate documents filed by subject under 80,000 topics. It includes in its collection reports and studies by the federal and state government agencies in the United States, by foreign governments, by the United Nations or specialized international agencies, by labor unions, and by foundations. The Library's book collection, serving mainly as

a reference service, is only 25,000 volumes—about one quarter of which are in Russian or deal with the Soviet Union in languages other than English. The Library also has foreign newspapers and magazines, either microfilmed or bound. It subscribes to approximately 375 periodicals and as many newspapers—foreign and domestic. It houses a propaganda collection of 10,000 examples of magazines, books, newspapers, pamphlets, and posters produced by other governments. Each month the Library responds to over 4,000 inquiries for information from the media services, the area offices, or the field posts. Field requests for information come direct to the Library for action, with information copies to appropriate area officers.

The Agency Library produces few regular reports. A daily 2-page digest of magazine articles, calling attention to the general content of some twenty items, is done for the use of program officers in the media services. Each month a 50-page report provides selected statements of the President of the United States on a variety of policy topics, for use in the Agency and by the field. Quarterly, the Library publishes a "Selected Guide to Scholarly Literature," listing university press books, doctoral dissertations, and articles in scholarly journals. As a service to the Voice of America, questions asked by letters from abroad to the Voice are answered for use in broadcasts at the rate of about twelve a week—covering a wide range of Americana (from sanitary engineering and economics to life on a farm in Iowa). The Agency Library procures books ordered for post or overseas library use, with funds carried in post allotments, filling some 7,500 purchase orders a year. To send materials to the Voice of America, located across town in the Health, Education, and Welfare Building, the Library employs a Western Union Inter-Fax machine to copy pages from books or magazines at the rate of six minutes a page. Following the Kennedy assassination in 1963, the machine ran twelve hours a day transmitting background material on President Kennedy and on President Johnson for use by the Voice.

7.   For example, featured in the Foreign Media Reaction Report of Wednesday afternoon, January 11, 1967, was reaction to President Lyndon Johnson's State of the Union message of Tuesday evening. As additional material came in, reaction to the President's message was also a major element in reports on Friday, January 13, and on Monday, January 16. President Johnson's attendance at the Manila Conference and his Asian tour in October and November, 1966, were covered by the Media Reaction Unit with sixteen pre-Conference analyses, three daily analyses during the Conference, and an additional seven during the President's post-Conference tour.

8.   Nonetheless, there is a continuing interest by the Research and Analysis Staff in defining and measuring the values and aspirations of people in the less-developed areas, their needs and desires, so that the United States can develop and communicate sound policies relevant to their interests. It is still engaged in the study of reactions of foreign audiences to developments in the field of international affairs to improve the quality of political weather forecasting by doing barometer surveys to study the storms and turbulences in international relations. There is a need for repeated testing to determine trends; even though individual studies may be subject to undiscovered error, studies with a "constant" bias tend to validate trends. USIA has been and still is interested in the image of America or of American leaders held by people overseas, not because of any preoccupation with wanting foreign people to "like" Americans or American Presidents but because popularity serves a useful purpose. Generalized popularity gives access to audiences: If the American President is liked, people listen and may be converted to the policies he expounds. If the American people are disliked, if the climate is unfavorable, listeners are inattentive, practicing selective reception and perception to reinforce their already negative feelings. Although USIA has been accused in the past of conducting polls for "prestige purposes," it has never done this. It is interested only in how better to communicate political ideas and not in useless popularity contests. Seen through the eyes of professional communications experts, USIA contributes a fourth dimension to diplomacy—added to the traditional political, economic, and military dimensions. If the traditional tools deals with the realities of policy, the

information program deals with how policy is perceived and interpreted. Fact and intention are not enough; policies must be understood—at least by foreign leaders—if they are to be effective. Knowing foreign reactions in the past and present, it is possible to deduce what can be done or what ought to be done in the future. People overseas cannot be asked what the American government should do, but they can be asked what satisfies or dissatisfies them. From these answers, likely reactions to policies and programs can be projected. Although USIA is interested in the response of the general population—mass reactions—overseas, survey research and other studies are often focused on target audiences, specially selected priority groups, leadership elements, elites, decision-makers and opinion-makers—not only the present leadership but also the reservoir of emerging leaders.

To reach special groups requires a thorough understanding of the channels of communication in foreign countries—television stations and television receivers, or newspapers and subscribers, for example—and the listening or reading habits of the various target audiences. Will a particular group be persuaded to accept the American position by discussing the pros and cons of a situation or by presenting the American stand and leaving other conflicting arguments untouched? The answer may depend upon the composition of the target audience and its background. With a sophisticated group, the two-sided approach is more likely to be effective—admit some of the cons in advance. But if the message is reaching simple people, who will not be exposed to an opposing point of view, a two-sided presentation may gain little or nothing. If not all the evidence is in on such questions, the Research and Analysis Staff—like IRS before it—must try to test these and other ideas in order to increase media effectiveness. The study of program or product impact is crucial to evaluation of USIA's effectiveness. It fulfils a need which mere reaction reports to American policy initiatives or summaries of Communist propaganda do not adequately meet. Studies are occasionally done on the effect of a presidential visit to a foreign country—a before-and-after look at attitudes of the population toward America. Studies have been done before and after people have seen major American exhibits. Studies could be done on the effect of visits by leaders of competing states, and plans made to offset any resulting American "losses." Historically, very little time and Agency effort was actually devoted to an accurate measuring of accomplishments or misfires of American programs and products. Empirical measurement of Soviet and Chinese Communist propaganda efforts remains in its infancy. This is critically important. If we overestimate the impact of their propaganda, we overstate our case in defense, unnecessarily making it more difficult for the United States to work with individual target country and the Soviet Union or the Mainland Chinese, further exacerbating problems of maintaining a tenuous improvement in relations with the Soviet Union or holding the level of tension with the Chinese below the threshold of open conflict.

CHAPTER V

1. USIA, *The Agency in Brief* (1966), 13-14, 31-49.
2. *Ibid.*, 13-14, 27.
3. *Ibid.*, 35-36, 49.
4. The Hays bill, passed by the House of Representatives in 1965, did not pass the Senate. It was an attempt to move toward ending this separation. In a letter of May 6, 1965, President Lyndon Johnson noted to House Speaker John W. McCormack that the amendments to the Foreign Service Act sought to establish ". . . a single foreign affairs personnel system, broad enough to accommodate the personnel needs—domestic as well as overseas—of the Department of State, the Agency for International Development, and the U.S. Information Agency. . . . " If the bill had been passed, it would have provided "a new category of professional career officers who would serve in the Foreign Service without time limitation, primarily

for service in this country. This category should be called Foreign Affairs Officers." For the letter, see U.S. Congress, House, Special Subcommittee on State Department Organization and Foreign Operations, Committee on Foreign Affairs, *Foreign Service Act Amendments of 1965*, May 19, 20, and 25; July 13 and 14, 1965, pp. 2-4. Also see U.S. Congress, Senate, Special Subcommittee, Committee on Foreign Relations, *Establishment of a Single Foreign Affairs Personnel System and Nominations of USIA Officers as Foreign Service Officers*, 89 Cong., 2 sess., April, 1966, 1-326.

CHAPTER VI

1. USIA, *The Agency in Brief* (1966), 7. In 1963, *The Agency in Brief* noted that the six area directors, "acting for the Director of the Agency" with the assistance of their small staffs, "administer and direct the Agency's worldwide overseas operations . . . and are responsible for the information programs in their respective areas." They "decide on the content of the information programs in their areas and evaluate the effectiveness of the programs and the methods used to carry them out." Media directors were said to participate in Agency programming and to be "responsible for planning the media program to be executed in support of world wide Agency and country operating plans, after appropriate consultation with and the concurrence of . . . "the area/directors, the Office of Policy, and the Office of Administration." The media directors and services "develop and supervise the broadcasting, cultural, information, press and publications, motion picture, and television programs in support of Agency and country objectives." See *The Agency in Brief* (1963), C-4, C-5. Also see *ibid*. (1965).

2. See *Voice of America Program Schedule* for Europe (November and December, 1966, and January, 1967), 1-2. See also Jack Gould, "Voice of America Speaking Softer," *New York Times*, November 13, 1966.

3. According to *The Agency in Brief* (1966), 13, VOA has 1,384 domestic positions, 164 overseas American positions, and 788 local employee positions abroad.

4. *New York Times*, June 6, 1965, 21; June 11, 1965, 30.

5. *Ibid.*, May 30, 1967, 1, 14.

6. *Ibid.*, September 2, 1966, 30.

7. *Ibid.*, May 30, 1967, 14.

8. *Voice of America Program Schedule* for Europe (November and December, 1966, to January, 1967), 12.

9. USIA, *The Agency in Brief* (1966), 14.

10. USIA, *America Illustrated*, No. 124 (February, 1967), 2-8.

11. *Ibid.*, No. 84 (October, 1963).

12. USIA *Problems of Communism* (July-August, 1963).

13. *Ibid.*, Special Supplement (Winter, 1962-Summer, 1963), 1-27.

14. USIA, *Books Published in Translation and English* (as reported July 1, 1965—June 30, 1966), 1-2. *Ibid.*, July 1, 1962—June 30, 1963, indicated that USIS had financially supported for publication in English or translation from FY 1950 through FY 1963 a total of 8,695 books in 85,575,603 copies. Of these, 8,376 books with 77,460,025 copies were printed abroad. All of the 8,060 books printed in translation were published overseas. Only 319 books printed in 8,115,578 copies were published in the United States. In FY 1963, books in translation numbered 1,013, printed in 7,057,005 copies. Even 133 of 189 books in English were published overseas, 2,340,865 copies out of 3,796,836 printed in English.

CHAPTER VII

1.   USIA, *25th Report to Congress* (July 1 - December 31, 1965), 14.

2.   *Ibid.*

3.   The material in this section draws heavily upon USIA, *Country Public Affairs Officer Handbook* (Washington: USIA, March, 1962). The *Handbook* was written by a task force of five CPAO's representing five geographic areas and was based upon suggestions from thirty-six CPAO's in the field. It was reviewed by over one hundred other Agency personnel with CPAO experience. Interviews with Agency personnel who had overseas experience at a variety of levels were also useful in preparing this section.

4.   See Note 4, Chap. III.

INDEX